Born in 1922 in Avon, South Dakota, Senator McGovern began his political career in the House in 1957. He was elected to the Senate in 1962, and ran as the Democratic nominee in the presidential election of 1972.

GRASSROOTS

McGOVERN, George Stanley. Grassroots: the autobiography of George McGovern. Random House, 1978 (c1977). 307p index 77-5999. 12.50 ISBN 0-394-41941-3. C.I.P.

CHOICE   JUNE '78
History, Geography &
Travel
   North America

The 1972 Democratic presidential nominee has written his memoirs and, in certain ways, they are interesting. The reader is bound to learn more of George McGovern by what he has omitted than by what he has included. One wishes that he were more expansive on his childhood and his formative years. It is likely that we would have a better understanding of him than by reading the several chapters dealing with myriad details of the "Eagleton affair." According to McGovern, he possibly could have won if Tom Eagleton had told all to McGovern's aides. This will come as a surprise to many pollsters, election analysts, etc. In many ways, this is a fascinating book, but it is frustrating as McGovern seems willing to let you inside but then as you approach the threshold, he closes the door. There are some amusing and enlightening anecdotes. A good academic and public library purchase.

The Autobiography of
GEORGE McGOVERN

GRASSROOTS

RANDOM HOUSE NEW YORK

Library of Congress Cataloging in Publication Data

McGovern, George Stanley, 1922-
Grassroots.

Includes index.
1. McGovern, George Stanley, 1922-
2. Legislators—United States—Biography.
3. United States. Congress. Senate—Biography.
4. United States—Politics and government—
1945-   I. Title.
E840.M29   973.924′092′4 [B]   77-5999
ISBN 0-394-41941-3

Manufactured in the United States of America

2 4 6 8 9 7 5 3

FIRST EDITION

*Dedicated to the people of South Dakota,
who have honored me as their Senator,
and to those Americans
who stood with me in 1972*

Preface

The late Adlai Stevenson noted in 1952 that "a wise man does not try to hurry history." Since—Stevenson notwithstanding—some of my public life has been an effort to hurry historical change, I seriously considered titling this book *Hurrying History*. But while I have sometimes advanced public proposals that were said to be "ahead of the times," my views are grounded in the old values of the Judeo-Christian ethic and the founding ideals of the American Republic. Thus I found it natural to plead in 1972: "Come home, America."

I wanted nothing more for my country than to see it come home to the old-fashioned values of dignity and compassion which we associate with Jefferson and Lincoln, Norris and Roosevelt.

Beyond this as a product of the Dakota prairies, my physical and spiritual heritage is in the land and among ordinary Americans of all walks of life. My years of building a two-party government in South Dakota were referred to from the beginning as "grassroots organizing." My campaigns for the Congress, the Senate and the presidency have constantly been designated "grassroots campaigns." So this informal memoir is called *Grassroots*.

Since I have written this volume at the age of fifty-four, I hope it is only a *partial* autobiography! Written largely during the pre-dawn hours of the last two years, it makes no pretense of being definitive history. It is simply a partial account of those events in my life that

I can recall which I trust are not too tiresome or shameful to relate. Perhaps this informal account of victories and defeats, hopes and disappointments, will help to lift some other soul along the way.

I am indebted to several persons who have read the manuscript critically and given me the benefit of their suggestions: Robert Shrum, Allan Lichtman, John Douglas and Jacqueline Kennedy Onassis. Pat Donovan, my matchless secretary, typed the entire manuscript repeatedly, correcting errors in spelling, grammar and style as she has done for many years.

Robert Loomis of Random House, a superb editor, has placed me heavily in his debt, as has the president of that publishing firm, my long-time friend Robert Bernstein.

As always, my wife, Eleanor, was my most perceptive, patient and forthright critic.

GEORGE McGOVERN

Washington, D.C., July 1977

Contents

GRASSROOTS

1
THE
MITCHELL YEARS
1922-1940

I was born July 19, 1922, in the Wesleyan Methodist parsonage at Avon, South Dakota—a community that then had about 600 inhabitants, and still does.

My father, Joseph McGovern, ministered to a congregation of fifteen or twenty Avon families before arranging a transfer to Calgary, Alberta, so that my mother could be near her ailing mother. We lived in Calgary for two years before moving to Mitchell, South Dakota, where my father assumed a Wesleyan Methodist pastorate. Mitchell has been my permanent home address ever since.

When he was very young, Joe McGovern was a "breaker boy" whose job was to follow the older miners through the underground work areas and pick up pieces of coal missed by the shovels and the machines. It was not unusual for boys to enter the mines at daybreak and come home with their fathers or older brothers after dark.

My father, the oldest child in the Thomas McGovern family, was thirteen when his mother died. The family then moved to Iowa, where Joe assumed major responsibilities for the rearing of four younger brothers and sisters. As a small boy I remember hearing stories about my grandfather's heavy drinking and the financial hardship this imposed on the motherless young McGovern family. In later years I had reason to question these stories when I understood that "heavy drinking," by the lights of my elders, was anything that took pennies away from a low-income family.

Grandfather McGovern was a nominal Catholic, but his deceased wife had been a dedicated Scotch-Irish Presbyterian and her children were brought up accordingly. It was, however, his conversion to a fundamentalist Christian faith that brought my dad into the ministry as interpreted by John Wesley.

He managed to save a few dollars, partly by playing professional baseball, and enrolled at the Wesleyan Methodist College in Houghton, New York. The years at Houghton nourished a love for study and meditation in my father that was an important element throughout his life. In one corner of his bedroom he always maintained a desk and several shelves of books that he referred to as his "study."

Growing up in a deeply religious home was a source of both strength and anxiety for me. I never doubted the essential integrity and sincerity of my parents—a priceless parental gift to a child. They gave me a thorough knowledge of the Bible and the Christian faith. Indeed, every morning after breakfast my father assembled the family for a brief period of Bible reading and prayer. After the reading of one or two chapters, we all knelt in our living room while my father prayed. Sometimes, to my embarrassment, neighborhood pals would peer at these rituals through the big bay window in our living room.

There was never any question that Sunday was devoted to the church. The day began with Sunday School at nine-thirty, followed by the morning worship service at eleven, which was conducted by my father. At four o'clock in the afternoon we returned for YMWB (Young Missionary Workers Band), or for the Young People's meeting at seven. Then came the evening worship service at eight, when my father preached again in more evangelical style.

At least once every winter there would be a visiting evangelist who conducted special nightly services for a two-week period. These were the times when, after fervent sermons, altar calls were made to the mournful strains of "Almost Persuaded" or "Just As I Am." I remember trembling with fear and guilt as I listened to the earnest pleas of evangelists describing the awfulness of unforgiven sin and the eternal agonies of the damned in the hereafter.

Usually I resisted the pressure to go forward to the altar to be "saved" and I never did reach the second stage of "sanctification." But sometimes as others sank tearfully to their knees at the altar, I would join them. I never really knew whether I was "saved" or simply relieved that I had responded. But I went through this experience several times at the winter evangelistic crusades or in the summer tabernacle with its straw-covered floor at the Holiness Campground near Mitchell.

On one occasion at the campground, the visiting evangelists were a family of four converted former vaudeville entertainers—a man with a booming voice and a turgid oratorical style, and his three vastly overweight sisters. The sisters had lost whatever musical grace they might have had at an earlier day, but they compensated for declining quality by the sheer volume that poured out of their mighty bosoms as they sang and banged their banjos. When their brother completed his sermon at a fever pitch, the altar call would begin and the three big sisters would swoop down the aisles of the tabernacle to bring the sinners forward. One night I was standing with "Big Bob" Millage and several other boys in the back row of the tabernacle. Bob was the only friend I had who was more bashful about public display than I was. His neck and face literally turned crimson when one of the aggressive sisters urged him to come forward. Mistaking his embarrassment for a clear sign that the Holy Spirit was gripping his soul, the sister called in reinforcements. When Bob still failed to move, two hefty sisters attempted to help him overpower the devil within by pulling him forward. Although he was a large, man-sized boy, Bob lost his footing in the straw and skidded a foot or two toward salvation. But he then gripped the back of the bench ahead of him, planted his feet and stood there like a mighty oak. I was troubled that none of us had broken free of our sin, but I was also proud that we had resisted uninvited pressure, and I was especially proud of "Big Bob" for standing his ground—assisted only by an invisible devil against two highly visible female giants. I was further cheered later that night to discover that two girls who had been saved nevertheless responded with undiminished enthusiasm to the advances of two boys still caught in the web of carnal sin.

Even though religion was a vital factor in my life, I came to resent the excessive emotionalism of some evangelists. Indeed, to this day I tend to recoil from speakers—religious, political or otherwise—who are heavy on emotion and light on reason. My own inhibited style of speech delivery may be partially explained by the discomfort experienced in listening to flamboyant evangelists at an earlier age.

On the other hand, my father was a man who preached with dignity and restraint. He always prepared his sermons—usually typing out his major points on an old Woodstock typewriter. He quietly broke with those preachers who became too emotional when they delivered their sermons. And there were other preachers, such as the Reverends Reisdorf, Kindschi, Harris, Simpson, Brannan and Jeffers, who were thoughtful, kindly, dedicated men. In later years the sincerity of these Wesleyan Methodists, their commitment to spiritual values, their concern for others, their capacity to quote Scripture—all of this enriched my life and deepened my confidence in the worthiness of a calling beyond self-serving materialism.

George McGovern, my father's younger brother and the man for whom I was named, was an infant when his mother died, and his father arranged his adoption by the King family in Des Moines. George King became an ambitious, determined young man who developed a profitable lightning-rod factory. He died of diabetes and perhaps overwork in 1913 at the age of thirty-three. His picture hung in my father's bedroom—in a handsome oval mahogany frame—throughout all the years I can remember. My father never forgot the sadness of giving up his brother for adoption and the experience of his premature death. But one had to sense such concerns in Joe McGovern; he seldom spoke of his own personal feelings or his experiences.

Indeed, I was twelve or thirteen years old before I knew that my dad had been a professional baseball player. On several occasions he had deliberately discouraged me from becoming involved in sports. This puzzled me at the time because it did not seem to square with Dad's favorite pastime—listening to radio broadcasts of big-league baseball. Then one day when we were outside our family tent at the Mitchell Holiness Campground, my dad took on a new heroic dimension. A field mouse had surfaced from under the temporary board flooring of our tent and was crouched just outside. "Let me see that ball," my dad whispered to one of my friends who had been pegging a baseball into the mitt of another boy, and with the unmistakable coordination and skill of a practiced professional, he scored a dead hit on the mouse from twenty-five or thirty feet. Word of this feat spread to every kid at the campground. "How did you do it, Dad?"

He told me with some hesitation that he had once played professional baseball with Des Moines. His next step would have taken him to the St. Louis Cardinals. He had enjoyed playing second base, but he came to believe that professional baseball was not a safe livelihood. He had seen too many gamblers, prostitutes and "drinkers" associated with traveling baseball teams. He did not want his sons to fall before such temptations. It was better, he said, to concentrate on other school activities such as speech, literature, music, and getting high marks in the classroom.

Dad's fear of professional sports did not extend to discouraging an active life of play and adventure. Even the annual two-week summer revivalistic camp meetings, which were designed to save souls, became for me a time of romance and discovery. H. L. Mencken once observed that there were "more souls made than saved" at these emotion-charged evangelical camps. He may have been right—although the romantic ventures of which I have knowledge seldom proceeded to *that* stage. But there were always girls of compassionate spirit who were willing even under clumsy stimulation to descend from the yearnings of the spirit to the passions of the flesh.

Beyond these nocturnal ventures, the days offered even more strenuous challenges. There were marvelous places to swim and explore at the James River, which flowed, or sometimes trickled, past the campground. A low-head rock dam backed up the water to provide a swimming and diving area. The beginners could learn to mud-crawl, to tread water and finally to swim across the shallow stretch of river below the dam. A great old elm tree which reached out over the water offered magnificent diving. When one wished, there were bullheads and catfish to be caught in the river. There were turtles to be picked up as temporary captives, gophers to be trapped, rabbits, squirrels and birds to be observed. But most exciting of all, there was a marvelous cliff to be scaled and descended. I doubt that climbers of Mount Everest experience a more profound thrill than I did when I first scaled the cliff above Holiness Campground and reached the grassy plateau above treetop level where one could lie lazily viewing the prairie skies.

Sometimes, resting in the grass on the back side of the cliff, I would let my mind drift back to bright spring days in Alberta when my mother used to take us out to gather crocuses. She would sit on a blanket with a picnic basket while we scampered over the foothills of the Canadian Rockies to collect the first purple crocuses of the season and then raced back to drop them in her lap. I must have been only four or five years of age, but that experience has remained with me as one of the joyful memories of my childhood.

Mother was a Canadian, born in Ontario and reared in Alberta. She had come to Aberdeen from Calgary to visit her sister, Margaret, who had been keeping house for two bachelor uncles, Abe and Hiram Cummings. Mother was a beautiful, statuesque woman with a lovely voice and gentle nature. I was always proud to have my friends know that this elegant woman was my mother. She was twenty years younger than my father, and although she loved and revered him deeply, I never heard her call him by his first name. I think that to the end she remained in the role of the choir girl who had come under the spell of her minister at Aberdeen.

Her father, Justin McLean, was an enormously strong-willed Scotsman with total self-confidence and blunt-spoken convictions. He had taken his family westward to Calgary and made a modest fortune in frontier farming, cattle raising and real estate. I recall him as an awesome personality with the emotional impact of a giant. Each summer he would buy a new car and drive at top speed the fourteen hundred miles from Calgary to Mitchell. Approximately every third summer he would lose control of his car on a curve or hill and then go rolling across the prairie or hurtling into a telephone pole—his car a total wreck, and Grandpa emerging enraged with a sprained ankle, a broken wrist or a cut over one eye. When my father chided him about his reckless driving, he invariably replied, "What's the use of paying good money for a new car if you're not going to drive it?" He seldom came to a halt at a stop sign, although any indication of disapproval from a passenger would bring a stern grunt from Grandpa: "I observed it." He did in fact observe things, and he observed people, but never to the point of changing what he wished to do at any given moment.

As a small boy I adored my grandmother, but I always felt that she was kept in nearly total subordination to my grandfather. There was no hint of women's liberation in the McLean family. To some extent this relationship existed between my mother and father. My father even purchased the groceries and sometimes prepared the meals.

The McGoverns and the McLeans shared a devotion to thrift and careful purchase. My parents never went grocery shopping without first studying the ads to locate the "specials" at two or three stores. Our clothes were purchased at "sale" time. My mother mended my trousers and extended their length and then altered them to fit my brother. Leftover food was never thrown away. The furniture in our house throughout my years of growing from infancy to manhood never changed. Sometimes it had to be reupholstered, but never replaced. We had the same sofa, the same chairs, the same piano, the same buffet, the same ancient vacuum cleaner, the same old aluminum dipper hanging over the stove.

This economy of life style provided a sense of stability and permanence that became an important fact in my life. I have never been quite comfortable with the affluence, the waste and the built-in obsolescence of today's society. My parents would be appalled by the extravagance of my upper-middle-class life style. And while not seeking to give it up, I myself am uneasy about it. I do not like to see familiar pieces of furniture or appliances break and be replaced. I prefer old houses or churches or public buildings that are built for the ages rather than modern-style structures that quickly deteriorate. I am uncomfortable with any translation of the Bible other than the magnificent King James version.

The summer I graduated from high school, Grandpa McLean came to Mitchell with one of my Canadian cousins, Harold McLean, and the three of us set off for the East Coast in his new Studebaker

Champion. We never stopped at restaurants or hotels; Grandpa didn't believe in spending money for such extravagances. Despite the pleadings of his youthful passengers, he skirted New York City and the World's Fair, then in progress, on the grounds that "carnivals are a waste of money." He had relatives and acquaintances all across the United States and the Canadian provinces and we graced them all at mealtime or for a night's lodging. In many cases we stopped for supper and an overnight stay with some startled distant relative without the slightest warning. But more often than not, Grandpa would pull out his bulging, battered wallet before our departure the next morning and give every member of the family a $20 bill. He loved to give away money, but he hated to spend it—except for new cars—or, at an earlier period, fine horses.

One of his children, my Aunt Alma, rebelled against the authoritarian discipline of Justin McLean. When she disobeyed his warnings and stayed out too late with a man who had aroused his suspicion, Grandpa would lock her out of the house despite the fervent protests of my grandmother. One night when Alma came home in the bitter cold to a locked door, she smashed the storm-door window with her hand. She fled to our house weeping and bleeding profusely from the broken glass, and I listened in horror while my parents discussed with the doctor the need for multiple stitches. Aunt Alma was a frail, beautiful girl who succumbed a few years later to asthma and a weakened heart.

It was the first death in our family that deeply saddened me. I remember the earlier death of my maternal grandmother and the scene of my mother's tears after the long-distance telephone call that brought the news. But Grandma was old and tired, whereas Aunt Alma wilted and died suddenly like a lovely flower cut off from the soil. One expected the old to die and I have never deeply mourned the passing of older people, including my parents. But I weep for those who die young—and especially for those who are still filled with the passion and joy of life. The worst characteristic of war is that it kills the young and the strong and the brave. Likewise, improperly treated illness, bad diet, ugly surroundings and the abuse of children can cripple and kill the young—and that is the tragedy of neglect and deprivation. My mother was imbued with similar feelings.

One day during World War II, Mother read a news story describing an Allied military victory in which tens of thousands of German soldiers were killed. Although I was one of millions of American combat forces locked in deadly battle with the German enemy, my mother's eyes were moistened with tears as she murmured, "Oh dear, there must be so much sadness in Germany tonight with all those boys dying." In a way, my mother was proud of my personal war service, but she regarded war as a horrible folly and her grief knew no national limitations. My parents were patriotic citizens, but they were incapable of rejoicing over the valor of men in arms. I never once heard them say a laudatory word about warfare in any of its forms.

But the revulsion to arms did not extend to the use of firearms for hunting purposes. It was pure joy for my dad to go hunting South Dakota pheasants. He took me to the Montgomery Ward store in Mitchell to purchase my own .16-gauge single-barreled shotgun. He used a Model 97 Winchester .12-gauge pump. Those two guns still stand in my closet—no longer in use but recalling joyous experiences with my dad.

It was on a hunting trip to Art Kendall's farm south of Mitchell in 1932 that I saw clearly the human toll taken by the Depression, drought and dust storm in the 1930s. Art Kendall was a master of the double-barreled shotgun and the art of hunting pheasants. He was also a superb farmer and an unusually good and decent man. One day as we drove into his farmyard we saw Art sitting on the steps of his back porch, tears streaking his dusty face. I had seldom seen an adult cry. Art Kendall explained to my dad that he had just received a check from the stockyards for a year's production of pigs. The check did not cover the cost of trucking the pigs to market.

During the next few years I saw other sad-eyed farmers scanning the skies for rain that did not come. I saw the precious topsoil churned into the air in choking dust storms until noontime became as dark as midnight. I saw hordes of grasshoppers eating the young crops and even chewing their way through hoe handles. I saw banks and stores and farms closing their doors in bankruptcy. It deeply saddened me to see how little hard-working farmers and small merchants received for their labor and investment. It was distressing, too, to see young fathers without jobs—unable to care for their families.

Then came the impact of the New Deal and the radio fireside chats of President Roosevelt.

My parents were Republicans, but without any strong partisan conviction. They approached the problems of society on a personal rather than a sociological or ideological level. I once heard my dad say that he voted for Bill Comstock for Davison County Treasurer despite his Democratic label because "Bill treats the public courteously and efficiently." That made sense to me then and still does. Whether my parents supported Franklin Roosevelt I do not know, but they listened eagerly to his radio messages and I never heard them criticize his efforts.

Frequently, however, I heard other adults scoffing at the WPA,

CCC, AAA, social security, REA and "relief." But even in Republican South Dakota, the Roosevelt measures were accepted by most of the voters. The banks came back under the guarantees of the FDIC. Young men went to work in the CCC camps. Other men and women were employed in public works projects. The farmers saw their prices stabilized and new conservation methods introduced. Social security reduced some of the anxiety in growing old. Shelter belts of trees were planted across the prairies to break the force of wind and erosion. Rural electric cooperatives brought electric lighting and power to the farms and small towns. No state benefited more from these New Deal measures than South Dakota.

Yet by 1940 South Dakota was back in the Republican fold—registering one of the most overwhelming votes against President Roosevelt's re-election of any state in the Union. Some years later I asked Herb Clarkson, an old Democratic banker of Buffalo, South Dakota, how he explained such political behavior. "What can we do to reach South Dakota voters with the fact that they suffered under Republican economic and fiscal policy and prospered under the New Deal?" I asked. Herb, a self-taught student of philosophy and history, peered at me for a moment and replied, "George, as Voltaire once observed, arguing with a man who has renounced his reason is like giving medicine to the dead." I later had an opportunity to demonstrate that Herb Clarkson was too harsh in his judgment as to the rigidity of South Dakota Republicans and too skeptical about the power of argument. Indeed, my own life was transformed by the effort to persuade others.

When I was small, my most serious handicap was a painful bashfulness in the presence of strangers. My first year in school was a nightmare. Although I had learned to read prior to the first grade, I refused to participate in the oral reading exercises. The teacher promptly placed me in the circle of the poorest readers. I remained with that group for the balance of the year, sitting red-faced and silent when it came my turn to read. Nor did I recite in class, or volunteer answers, or ever raise a hand for recognition. I desperately wanted to go unnoticed and to remain silent.

Somehow my teacher sensed, perhaps from my written work, that I was not totally stupid and she passed me "on condition" to the second grade. There I encountered a determined young instructor who first started the process of loosening my tongue. She did it by a rather direct implication that I would either recite in class or be bounced out of school. But this message was given to me in private after school and she kept me with her in these after-school sessions for several days, forcing me to read and recite to her. She was firm and, indeed, insistent, but the slightest stammering response on my part brought words of strong assurance. The shyness continued, but I did begin to participate, however reluctantly, in class recitations. And I was impressed with that concerned, youthful teacher.

Then, in the third grade, I came under the influence of Grace Cooley—a self-confident, witty, dedicated woman who enlivened her courses with stories of her experience in international travel. I desperately wanted to please her, and I believe she detected a few possible indications of intelligence in me.

There were setbacks from time to time in the struggle against shyness. One embarrassing experience occurred in the second grade when I had been postponing a visit to the rest room rather than raise my hand and ask to be excused. After a painful hour of repressing the forces of nature, a trickle appeared on the floor below my desk. This brought an excited shriek from Dorothy Nash, a girl with a high-pitched voice who sat next to me: "Oh, look what he's doing!" I have never been closer to total heart failure.

Looking back to the committed teachers of the Mitchell public-school system, I am convinced that good teachers may be as important in the development of a child as good parents. It was two high school teachers who steered me onto a course that explains much of my subsequent development.

As a high school sophomore I took a course in English composition from Miss Rose Hopfner. She was the first teacher to single me out for high praise combined with specific advice. She told me one day that I had a sensitivity and clarity of expression that was rare for a sophomore. Then she urged me to talk with Bob Pearson, the history teacher and debating coach, about participation in the extracurricular debate program. A few days later I stood up at an evening meeting of the debate squad to refute the proposition "Resolved that the several States should adopt a unicameral legislature." The speech was a disaster. It was supposed to take ten minutes. I spoke for two minutes in barely coherent terms and then sat down humiliated and filled with a sense of failure. But Bob Pearson was soon on his feet giving a serious critique of what I had said and assuring me that it was an adequate first effort. No other person did more to strengthen my confidence and draw out my latent powers of expression than Bob Pearson.

Competitive high school debate literally transformed my personality and my approach to life. I learned to organize my thoughts, to buttress my ideas with evidence and to speak extemporaneously. The practice of debating both the affirmative and negative side of each year's debate proposition forced me into the complexities of major public questions.

The world of academia and debate was, of course, only one factor in growing up in Mitchell. Across the alley from my home at Fifth and Sanborn we dug a marvelous cave in a vacant lot which became an underground clubhouse. It was the meeting place for countless hours of excited discussion over a period of two or three years.

There were daily activities involving rubber guns made with strips of old inner tubes fastened to a clothespin and a crude wooden gun, homemade slingshots, kick-the-can and capture-the-flag games at night, the building of huge snow forts for snowball fights in the wintertime, and the throwing of green tomatoes at passing cars under the cover of darkness.

Movies were off-limits to good Wesleyan Methodists, as were dancing, cardplaying, smoking or drinking. I had no trouble forgoing any of these, except movies. The first taste of a darkened movie theater came when I was taken by a friend to see *Aladdin and His Wonderful Lamp*. I never expect to be closer to heaven than I was in that first forbidden movie experience. From that day on, I hoarded enough pennies to see at least one movie each week at the Paramount or the Roxy. I loved them all, and to this day I remain addicted to movies and those who act in them. In retrospect, I think my parents knew of my transgressions at the theater, but they had too much common sense to enforce this particular phase of the Wesleyan doctrine. Furthermore, I made my escapades more acceptable by financing them from my own earnings and by devoting much of my leisure time to reading books from the local library.

By the time I was through the first four grades at the old wooden Whittier School and had advanced to Central—the brick complex which housed the fifth through the ninth grades—I had become a frequent visitor to Mitchell's Carnegie Library. That building, constructed of ageless Sioux Falls granite, held a fascination for me that grew with the years. Several times a week I would browse through the aisles. A cozy reading room was equipped with oak tables and chairs, as well as racks holding all the current journals and magazines. One section at the front of the library offered new books that the librarian believed to be of special interest. Across from the periodical reading room was a second room containing the library's reference books and encyclopedias. Frequently after school or on Saturdays I went to that room to dig up facts for a school paper or a debate case. During the long summer-vacation months, that library was my treasured and unfailing friend.

The first books I recall borrowing from the library were a series of animal adventure stories, including *Reddy the Fox* and *Bowser the Hound*. Those books brought animals to a human dimension in my mind. Then came two highlights of my reading endeavors—Mark

Twain's *Tom Sawyer* and *Huckleberry Finn*. I raced through those books with delight and wonderment. That experience was one of the lasting joys of my boyhood. Every child should read the books of Mark Twain.

The Altsheler series, recommended to me by my friend Bart Hersey, held my attention for at least two summers. These books of the American frontier, Indian scouts, hunters, trappers and backwoodsmen fired my imagination and curiosity about life in the American West. I literally devoured them. They were reinforced by the novels of Zane Grey, such as *Riders of the Purple Sage*—and other books of exploration, mystery and romance.

The first mind-stretching book I recall borrowing from the library was one also recommended by Bart Hersey, Stuart Chase's *Tyranny of Words*. Bart was several years older than I, but he knew that he and I were the two big readers in the neighborhood. Thus I frequently had the benefit of his suggestions for reading, as well as a friend with whom I could discuss a book once I had finished it.

In later years, serious books were to influence the course of my life. I became a compulsive reader. It has always been important to me to have a book at my bedside, in hotel rooms, on airplanes or trains and on vacation.

If, in cultural enjoyment, books were at the top of my personal value list, music was not far behind. Should I ever be marooned alone on a desert island, the beauty and bounty of nature might sustain me for a while. But books and music would be much more dependable fare. I cannot imagine a world devoid of music. As a small boy I loved to hear our old phonograph player scratching out the sounds of Harry Lauder singing "Roamin' in the gloamin' with mae bonnie by mae side," or a choral group singing "Will the circle be unbroken, bye and bye, in the sky?" On Radio WNAX from Yankton we heard a newly emerging band assembled and directed by a Dakotan with a unique accent, Lawrence Welk. His music was interspersed with that of a lustier group, Happy Jack and His Old Timers.

During church services I came to love such hymns as "Blest Be the Tie That Binds," "I Need Thee Every Hour" and "Amazing Grace." To this day I can sing those old hymns by heart, and often when I'm in my car on the open road I sing them with the gusto of those devout congregations that shaped my life so many years ago. Likewise, hundreds of Biblical passages have remained in my memory. I seldom deliver an extemporaneous speech that is not marked either by a Scriptural reference or a word that has slipped into my vocabulary from the Sunday School classroom, the Summer Bible Schools, or in home and church worship.

I especially enjoyed the great male quartets that visited our church during evangelical meetings, particularly the quartet from Milton-vale College in Kansas. I thought they sang like angels. George Beverly Shea (now with Billy Graham) also found his way to the revival circuit as an evangelistic singer. He was magnificent.

A few years later I found myself singing with the Mitchell Melody Masters—a male quartet assembled by a local preacher to promote the Holiness Campground meetings. We had a superb bass, Everett Walker, but the rest of us—Ellsworth Pooley, Arthur Lutz and I—were never heard from in the musical world again. Our nightly travels to the churches in the Mitchell area were a special joy to me. The sponsoring parson was a big man endowed with a booming voice, a rollicking humor and an insatiable appetite. Money collected from the audiences we tried to inspire was entirely devoted to the purchase of large hamburgers, malts, French fries and other treasures. As our preacher friend would say in ordering a hamburger "with everything": "Man can't live by bread alone." He would occasionally give us a warning not to yield to the temptations of the local females, but I noticed that he usually paused to evaluate their anatomy even while preparing to pray for their souls. I'm sure he thought it necessary to minister to the whole person.

Perhaps most vivid in my mind, however, were the school glee clubs and choruses directed from the first grade through the twelfth by Valentine Preston. She was a perfectionist, totally committed to the teaching and enjoyment of vocal music. It was a delight to sing in the special concerts she directed each year at the Mitchell Corn Palace. We did either Handel's *Messiah* or a varied program of classical and contemporary music.

Nor can I forget the great swing bands of the thirties and forties —Tommy Dorsey, Glenn Miller, Benny Goodman, Duke Ellington and others. Most of them played at least one stand at the Mitchell Corn Palace. This unique building, decorated annually with various colors of corn and grain, offered a week-long festival each September, usually featuring a renowned band. It was a time of gay celebration for the people of Mitchell and the surrounding area. Activities of this kind were ideally suited for family participation. My brother and sisters joined with me in the joys of Mitchell's main street—especially during Corn Palace Week.

As the second child, I had the advantage of learning from my older sister, Olive. No one had a more fiercely loyal sister. An excellent student and an engaging human being, she shared her knowledge with me gladly. From the time I was a small boy until the present day, anyone who criticized me in Olive's presence was vigorously rebuked. Mildred, my younger sister, was quieter and less assertive. A sweet and gentle girl who always avoided family quarrels, Mildred is now a superb professional nurse. The youngest of the family, my brother Larry, was a mischievous, fun-loving boy whose temperament was not compatible with the serious puritanical atmosphere of a Wesleyan Methodist home. I have always regretted that the age difference between us kept us from the kind of "pal" relationship that would have existed between two brothers of similar ages. Larry was later to develop a serious alcohol problem which he resolved only after long struggle. He is now a respected therapist dealing with alcoholics in Illinois.

The number of hours I could devote to music, books and fun was limited by the necessity of helping to support myself and to begin saving for a college education.

My first job, at the age of fourteen, was an invitation from Mrs. Truax to mow her lawn. This elderly neighbor was the perfect first employer. She was endowed with a strong character, a charming personality and a high sense of craftsmanship in any task, however humble. She made me feel that mowing and carefully trimming her grass was a work of art. She paid me ten cents an hour for the first job, but by the end of the summer she had given me a raise to fifteen cents. The following summer I began to mow and weed and trim for a dozen others and was earning twenty or twenty-five cents an hour. My parents continued to provide me with a comfortable home, including my own bedroom, good food and medical care, but all other expenses—clothing, recreation, school costs and incidentals—were financed from my yard work. I do not recall my parents' ever giving me any money after I began high school. My savings account always showed a favorable balance, because except for movies and a craving for chocolate and ice cream, my expenditures were frugal.

Perhaps the most quietly satisfying experience of my early life came on high school graduation day in the spring of 1940. Not only did I graduate third from the top in a class of 140 seniors, but I was given the coveted bronze medal as "The Most Representative Senior Boy." It may not have seemed like a miracle to anyone save my mother and me, but that night we exchanged glances which told of the transformation that had taken place since I passed the first grade "on condition" twelve years earlier.

One day during my junior year at Mitchell High, Bob Pearson had departed from an American History lesson long enough to give us a brief outline of his philosophy of life. I was ready by then to follow his advice on anything—but especially on the meaning of life. The most important goal, he said, is "the service of others." And, he added, the most vital ingredient in a useful and satisfying career is "imagination." It did not require much further stimulus on my part to decide that I wanted to follow Bob Pearson's career of teaching history. My imagination was to extend that initial decision to added dimensions, but my essential course had been set two years before I enrolled at Dakota Wesleyan University on the south side of Mitchell in the fall of 1940.

2

COLLEGE–
MARRIAGE–WAR

It was snowing in Mitchell in mid-February 1943 when the Dakota Wesleyan Varsity Debate Squad returned from the Red River Valley tournament at Fargo-Moorhead. We had just completed several days of competition, followed by an all-day car ride in the snow from Fargo to Mitchell—and we were the champions. Fargo is the home of North Dakota State University. Moorhead, Minnesota, located across the river, is the home of Concordia College. Over the years, these schools had co-hosted one of the most competitive debate tournaments in the nation. University debaters from a ten- or twelve-state area assembled annually to match their skills at "the Red River."

A strong tradition of debate had been gradually developing among the small liberal arts schools of the Plains States and the Upper Midwest. The best debaters in the nation came not from Harvard or Yale, but from colleges such as Nebraska Wesleyan, Augustana (South Dakota), St. Olaf (Minnesota) or Emporia State (Kansas). I had little fear in meeting a debate team from the Ivy League or the Big Ten. But when we were pitted against the University of Nebraska or St. Thomas or the University of South Dakota, I knew the competition would be formidable.

Not only did Matt Smith and I win the 1943 Red River Valley tournament in competition with thirty-two other teams, but Matt was rated the second highest individual speaker and I was rated first. I literally glowed during that entire four-hundred-mile homeward journey.

But when we arrived at the DWU campus, Dean Matthew Smith, Sr.—the father of my debate colleague—was waiting for us with what seemed to me to be a grave demeanor. After congratulating us on our victory, he said that he had a message for me from the Army Air Force. He knew what was inside and so did I; it was a summons to duty for air-force training. I read the official message with mingled feelings of self-importance, anxiety and excitement.

From my first days on campus in the fall of 1940, the war clouds over Europe and the Far East were visible at Dakota Wesleyan. Units of the 147th Field Artillery, to which the South Dakota National Guard was attached, were called up in late 1940. A number of Dakota Wesleyan students had joined the Guard as a means of securing additional income for college expenses. These men were involved in the earliest National Guard call-up. But the war still seemed remote to most of us on that relaxed campus.

At the nearby Mitchell airport, the federal government had inaugurated a program of civilian pilot training—one of many such programs to augment the nation's reserve of pilots with at least introductory training. It was possible to take this course for college credit, including ground school instruction at the college and flight training at the airport. I was persuaded to enroll by Norman Ray, a fellow student and friend from Custer, South Dakota, who was desperate to get the required ten students enrolled so that the course could be offered and he could learn to fly.

Norman Ray loved every minute of it. But if I had known what was ahead, I never would have enrolled. When the instructor opened the throttle for takeoff on my first flight, I was terrified. I was even more terrified in subsequent lessons when he demonstrated spins and stalls. But I hung on, and after eight hours of instruction I made my first solo flight. I was nervous, but I also felt a sense of exhilaration.

On December 7, 1941, I was at home listening to a radio broadcast by the New York Philharmonic. These listening sessions on Sunday afternoon were required of all students participating in Professor Robert Brown's course in Music Appreciation. We were also required to submit a written critique of what we had heard. I was jotting down a few impressions of the concert when an announcer suddenly broke in to report that the Japanese had bombed the American naval base at Pearl Harbor. It did not surprise me to hear President Roosevelt call within a matter of hours for a declaration of war. What surprised me was the awesome skill and power demonstrated by the Japanese in a succession of air and naval victories which followed. But I had been brought up with an unshaken faith that America would prevail in any war we entered and that our cause was absolutely right. We were confronted with totalitarian powers bent upon the destruction of freedom, and that was all I needed to know. I wanted to be a part of that struggle.

A few weeks after Pearl Harbor I made a decision to enlist in the Air Force—hopefully for training as a combat pilot. Perhaps it was the drama of aerial combat that drew me to the Air Force, but I think there was another factor. I had done well in the civilian pilot training program; however, there was still a lingering fear of flying that bothered me, and I was determined to overcome it.

At some point in my life, perhaps during the early struggles to overcome shyness, I had developed an enhanced sense of self-satisfaction from undertaking tasks that were especially difficult for me. So in the spring of 1942 I joined a two-car caravan of Dakota Wesleyan students bound for the Air Force enlistment center at Omaha, Nebraska. Most of us were uncertain about whether we should enter army or naval air training. But shortly after our arrival in Omaha, one of our group reported that someone had told him the Army would give us tickets for a free meal at a local cafeteria while we were in the enlistment process, whereas the Navy would not. On the basis of this unsubstantiated rumor of a meal benefit—probably worth about a dollar—all ten of us joined the Army Air Force.

It was not, however, until that triumphant day in February 1943, following the big debate victory, that Walter Kreimann, the president of the DWU student body, and I were called to begin training at Jefferson Barracks near St. Louis. By then I could look back on two and a half of the most satisfactory years imaginable. There are doubtless some students who thrive better at a large sophisticated university than at a small informal liberal arts school such as Wesleyan. But there is no doubt in my mind that as a somewhat shy small-town boy, I should have attended a school like Wesleyan. Its teachers were so close to the students that we called some of them by their first names.

Each morning I walked the mile from my home to the college, then back home for lunch, or a quick sandwich at the Texaco Café just off campus, and then back for an afternoon of study at the library, or a debate meeting, work on the Phreno-Cosmian, a student government session, or intramural athletics. I even ventured into a college play, *The Bad Man,* directed by Buren C. Robbins. "Robbie" and his assistant, Bernie Enslin, produced superb sets and props for their plays. And they won the affection of their students.

"Robbie" and Bernie were both bachelors who frequently dated coeds. I felt as much at ease with them as I did with other students. One day I confided to Bernie that I was intrigued by the Stegeberg twins, Eleanor and Ila, of Woonsocket. They were well known on campus as cheerleaders and as good students. I had also been impressed by the fact that Eleanor had tied with me for a score of 98 out of a possible 100 in a *Time* magazine current-events test offered in Art Shoemaker's freshman Economics class; the Stegebergs were highly intelligent girls. While very reserved, they exuded a radiant beauty that seemed to come from within. "But," I said to Bernie, "they are so small that I feel awkward around them." To which he snorted, "They may be only five feet tall, but, by God, they're all there and if you don't move, some other guy will."

Bernie's knowledge of women was vastly superior to mine, so in the next few days I took special note of these two lovely girls, who resided at the Graham Hall dormitory. Eleanor worked part-time for Dean Smith. Ila worked for Business Manager Harmon Brown. I would see one of them occasionally as she walked across the campus, or at work, or in the classroom. I was soon able to tell them apart. At an earlier roller-skating party in a Mitchell roller rink, Ila had tagged me during a women's-choice skating number. I remembered her wistful face and her skating grace, and I was pleased that a popular coed would ask me, a freshman, to skate with her in preference to so many impressive upperclassmen. I decided that I might one day ask Ila for a date.

But on that day when Bernie and I discussed the twins, he had, because of their differing schedules, observed Eleanor more than Ila. And it was Eleanor he was urging me to date. The question of which one was resolved when George Flora, a Mitchell friend who had a date with Ila, asked me if I would like to make it a double date by asking Eleanor to see the current Mitchell High School play.

That first date went off pleasantly, and a few days later Eleanor invited me to a dance sponsored by a campus women's organization. I went. Then one beautiful sun-filled April day as Eleanor and I walked across the campus, there was a simple touching of hands, then a slight squeeze of fingers, and I was in love—hopelessly. The rest of that spring was magic.

That was Eleanor's only year at DWU. The next fall she went to work as a secretary for two Mitchell lawyers we both highly admired, former U.S. Senator Herbert Hitchcock and Fred Nichol, whom I persuaded President Kennedy to nominate for a federal judgeship twenty years later. Ila went to the Mayo Clinic in Rochester for nurse's training. There was not sufficient money for both of them to continue their education, so Eleanor urged Ila to go on with her plans to become a graduate nurse, while she earned money in the hope that she could return to college.

I had met Earl Stegeberg, Eleanor's widowed father, under unexpected circumstances that first summer of 1941. I had agreed to pick up Eleanor at her farm home twenty-eight miles northwest of Mitchell and then go to a dance at nearby Ruskin Park. But I was detained in Mitchell and arrived at the Stegeberg residence after the twins had left with Ila's date for the dance. As I approached the darkened house Mr. Stegeberg got up from the porch step and waited for me to explain my delayed arrival. He was a gruff-spoken, desperately lonely man. Eleanor had warned me that he was seldom friendly to visiting boys—all of whom he understandably suspected were lusting after his lovely daughters.

After a few initial grunts he began to talk to me, and an hour later we were engaged in an animated discussion ranging from religion and philosophy to man's desire for women and the ultimate weakness of women in surrendering. "Every man is a devil," he said, "and you will learn that no woman belongs on a pedestal." I went along with that analysis verbally, although I was already elevating Eleanor to a unique pedestal, and it was painfully obvious that this suffering man had kept his own deceased wife on one, too. He was obsessed with her death and the memory of their all-too-few years together. For a decade he had condemned the doctors, the Depression and himself for lovely Marian Stegeberg's death in the Mitchell Methodist Hospital at the age of thirty-four. Eleanor was later to realize that the death of her mother and the circumstances which followed were sources of deep emotional trauma and subsequent conflict in her life.

Eleanor was astonished when I arrived at the Ruskin Park dance two hours late and reported on my conversation with her dad. She could scarcely believe that we had accepted each other so easily. I have always taken special satisfaction in that conversation because Eleanor's family and friends told me that it marked the beginning of a new, more outgoing Earl Stegeberg. But what was most important to me at the time: it elevated me in Eleanor's eyes. Although my dancing was as bad then as it is now, I knew that this mattered less to Eleanor than the approval of her dad.

But Earl Stegeberg was not happy when Eleanor and I decided to be married at the age of twenty-one. We were engaged before I left for air-force training early in 1943 and expected to be married after the war was over. But I was scarcely in service before we decided to advance the date to my graduation from pilot training and the receipt of my wings—expected in the spring of 1944. With each week of separation, we moved the date still closer. We were married by my father on October 31, 1943, on a three-day pass that permitted me to leave primary flight training at Muskogee, Oklahoma, for a hurried train ride to Mitchell. After an informal ceremony at the Woonsocket Methodist Church in Eleanor's hometown, our honeymoon consisted of a night at my home in Mitchell and then a long train ride to Muskogee in a dirty coach equipped with hard straight-backed seats. We arrived after midnight and I reported back to the base ready to fly at six o'clock that morning.

Marriage to Eleanor in those months of aviation training was really a series of hurried Saturday-night dates. We were permitted to leave the bases—Muskogee, then Coffeeville, Kansas, and later Pampa, Texas—for a few hours on Saturday night and during daylight on Sunday.

Then one day after I had moved up to advanced pilot training in a B-24 four-engine bomber, Eleanor discovered that she was pregnant. She was overjoyed. I was not at all sure this was a wise development with overseas duty looming, but I shared Eleanor's excitement. She did not so express herself, but I felt she was desperate to be pregnant before I went into combat because, as she acknowledged years later, she would have a child from our marriage even if I failed to survive the war.

After receiving my pilot wings at twin-engine advanced training in Pampa, I went on to Liberal, Kansas, for training in B-24s. I could scarcely believe it when I read a blackboard notice that my instructor would be Lieutenant Norman Ray, my old friend from Dakota Wesleyan who had persuaded me to take civilian pilot training two years earlier. He gave me no breaks. Indeed, he was especially tough on me to offset any hint of favoritism and also because he wanted to give me the skills to survive in combat.

The B-24 was a difficult plane to fly. It had a wingspan of 110 feet, and this long, narrow Davis wing seemed to defy aerodynamics. The plane—at that time the biggest in the Air Force—did not have the lift of the B-17 Flying Fortress; it ate up every foot of an average runway before lifting off. Nor did it offer the handling ease of the B-17; its controls were stiff and it exhausted its pilots in formation flying. But I was fascinated by these clumsy old Liberators and I developed more and more confidence in their durability and design.

After being checked out as a first pilot, I went to Lincoln, Nebraska, to be assigned the crew that was to go into combat with me after a summer of transitional training at Mountain Home, Idaho. I was worried about whether or not I could convince the crew that they were safe in the hands of a twenty-two-year-old commander. So in the last few weeks before going to Lincoln to meet them, I grew a mustache hoping that it would add a couple of years to my appearance. I felt considerably older and wiser when I was stroking that mustache.

My co-pilot was Bill Rounds of Wichita, Kansas—the son of a wealthy businessman who headed the Rounds and Porter lumber interests. He was a rollicking, fun-loving adventurer whose real desire had been to be a fighter pilot. It would be more accurate to say that he was an early advocate and practitioner of the admonition "Make love, not war." I marveled at the speed with which Bill Rounds could move from an air base to the business of heavy romance with total strangers. I soon learned to listen with one ear to his accounts of spectacular multiple achievements in a single evening that were vastly beyond my area of experience.

On one occasion we were riding down the main street of Boise, Idaho, with Bill driving while I sat in the back seat. Suddenly Bill opened the front door and jumped out of the car in pursuit of two girls—the car still rolling down the street. I cleared the front seat in one diving motion, grabbed the steering wheel and narrowly averted hitting a parked truck. By the time I got the car stopped at the curb, Bill was back with a girl on each arm.

But if Bill awed me with his off-duty feats, I won his respect by a serious effort to master the B-24 and by insisting that every member of the crew maintain a no-nonsense attitude when we were in the plane. After an indifferent start Bill settled down, and within a few weeks he developed into one of the best formation fliers I ever came across. But he did not abandon his quest for adventure on the ground even after we were assigned to a combat base in Italy.

Our squadron was located in an olive grove near the little town of Cerignola. Each crew was given two tents—one for the four officers on the crew and one for the six enlisted men. With the help of Italian workmen we built a cement floor and then assembled the tent. Each tent was also equipped with a crude oil stove that we constructed ourselves. The tents were supported by ropes tied at the four corners to the nearest olive trees. Many of the crews would work for days in their off-duty periods perfecting their canvas homes. The modifications and refinements were limited only by the imagination and energy of the occupants.

It so happened that we were assigned a location between two of the most elaborately constructed tents in the squadron. Both of these dwellings were occupied by combat-weary veterans who were nearing the end of the thirty-five missions we were required to fly before going home. I met the pilot of one of these crews when Bill Rounds, traveling at high speed in a borrowed jeep, caught the corner rope of the lieutenant's tent and simply tore the structure in half. The stove, the hanging uniforms, the shelves of books, magazines and photographs—all of this and more literally flew into the olive grove. And out of this incredible nightmare emerged an aging pilot with heavy circles under his eyes who had to be at least twenty-five. I was horrified as he walked slowly up to the shaken Bill Rounds and me and said, his voice quaking with rage, "You two sons-of-bitches will never make it through combat. I should kill ya right now."

I thought my days were numbered until an even older veteran of twenty-seven, a crack navigator who detested the aggrieved pilot, strolled up and told him to knock it off. We spent the rest of the day humbly assembling a replacement tent for the angry neighbor.

But Bill Rounds was not one to forget such a threat, and he figured out a way to get back at our nervous neighbors. One night he rolled a 30-gallon drum of fuel oil into the parade section of our squadron area, set it on fire and shouted "Enemy raid!" There were screams of panic and anguish on all sides of our tent—accompanied by the muffled laughter of the unstoppable Bill Rounds.

Sam Adams of Milwaukee, my taciturn, sad-eyed navigator, was the complete antithesis to Rounds. No two human beings ever had less in common. Sam was a capable, highly conscientious technician who wanted only to do a competent job and finish his missions as soon as possible. He spent his idle hours in the tent writing long letters, cleaning his equipment, reading, or simply lying silent on his cot—his brow sometimes furrowed in deep thought or perhaps in disapproval of the crude banter between Bill and me.

It was the practice, when a crew first arrived in combat, for the pilot to fly five missions as co-pilot with an experienced crew before taking off for the first time in the pilot's seat with his own crew. This meant that most pilots completed the required thirty-five missions while the rest of the crew still had five missions to go. Sam hated to fly with any pilot other than me. And he was even more disturbed by the thought of being left to fly another five missions after I had gone back to the United States. So midway through our tour of duty he told the squadron commander that he would be willing to substitute as navigator with another crew on any day when I was not scheduled to fly. The second mission of his substitute service, Sam's plane was blown out of the air by Nazi anti-aircraft fire. There were unconfirmed reports of two or three parachutes being seen after the plane exploded, but we never heard another word of this quiet, hollow-cheeked navigator who dreamed of returning to Milwaukee and studying for the Presbyterian ministry. He was simply "missing in action." For the rest of the war, while we depended on substitute navigators, we lived with Sam's empty bunk, his treasured photographs and his neatly hung clothing, waiting for further word that never came.

The oldest member of our crew was our engineer, Mike Valko of Bridgeport, Connecticut. Mike was thirty-three. He had been divorced. He had developed a deep affection for alcohol. And he had a temper that constantly got him into fistfights over seemingly minor provocations. His nose was battered and his face heavily scarred from years of combat on the streets of Bridgeport. At five foot three, Mike was barely tall enough to qualify for the Air Force. I suspect that his small size added to his braggadocio manner and his seeming need to inform me at frequent intervals that he had just "punched some big guy in the nose."

Mike was the only member of our ten-man crew who "cracked" in combat. I watched the unraveling of this man with sadness, anger and dread. There is no tolerance of error in handling any airplane— but especially a four-engine bomber in combat. So the emotional deterioration of our engineer was a matter of deep concern to me and the crew. Mike's problem was triggered by a series of rough missions and difficulties where we came close to death.

On my seventh mission—the second one with my own crew—our plane blew the right-hand tire during takeoff. No member of that crew needed to be told that it was extremely hazardous to land a B-24 with only one operating wheel. The tower officer gave me the option of bailing out or attempting a controlled landing when we returned. I chose the latter and we continued on our mission. But that nine-hour flight to and from the target with the knowledge that we might be returning to a crash-landing drove Mike Valko to the edge of hysteria. He asked me countless times on the long flight back to the field if I really thought I could keep the plane from cartwheeling or skidding into a fiery crash. His face was contorted in fear and his hands were trembling. He desperately needed a drink—many drinks. As we approached the landing field I told Mike and the other members of the crew that if any or all of them wanted to bail out over the field, they should feel no shame in doing so. There were no bailouts and we walked away from the landing.

On the next mission Mike's frayed nerves were further tested. We had flown through barrages of anti-aircraft fire on earlier missions, but thus far our plane had not been hit. Flak to us was a series of large puffs of black smoke at 25,000 feet that were all around us and sometimes sent red-hot metal tearing into the engines or fuselage of other planes. We did not feel its terror until the eighth or ninth mission when a large piece of shrapnel smashed through the windshield and struck a heavy steel girder just inches above my head. It fell to the floor directly in front of Mike Valko, who had been crouched between Bill Rounds and me checking the instrument panel. Mike picked up the jagged piece of shrapnel and said, "Lieutenant, if that had been a few inches lower, it would have taken your head off." Then he looked imploringly at Bill Rounds as if to say, Please become as competent as you can in case anything ever happens to McGovern. Mike needed many more drinks that night before sleep finally came.

Then came a mission to the Skoda ammunition works at Pilsen, Czechoslovakia—a major source of arms for the German war machine. We climbed in formation to about 25,000 feet, cleared the Alps and broke out into the sunlight above the clouds. About an hour short of the target I noticed a rapid loss of oil pressure on the number-two inboard engine. I feathered the prop and then increased the power on the three other engines in an effort to stay with the formation. But as we turned onto the bomb run an hour later, the added strain on the engines had taken its toll and we blew a cylinder on the number-three inboard engine. The loss of oil pressure was so rapid that we were unable to feather the prop and it began windmilling, thus adding to the drag on the plane. We immediately dropped down and out of formation with six hundred miles of enemy territory between us and our home base at Cerignola.

As we lost altitude in the crippled plane Sam Adams navigated a course slightly east of Yugoslavia where the flak was lightest. But by the time we reached the Adriatic Sea we had mushed down to 600 or 700 hundred feet. I ordered everything in the plane to be thrown overboard to lighten the load—flak suits, ammunition, machine guns, oxygen tanks—everything that was loose or could be detached. Then suddenly the windmilling number-three engine caught fire. I remembered reading months before in a B-24 technical manual that when an engine catches fire, the flames will burn through the engine's protective firewall in about five minutes and explode the gasoline wing tanks.

At this moment Sam Adams told me that the Isle of Vis was just off our wing. The British had constructed a short one-way landing strip on this little island for the use of their Spitfires. It was far too short for a safe bomber landing, but we had no other choice. As we turned onto that final approach, we saw the wreckage of other planes that had overshot their landings and piled into a mountain at the far end of the little runway. We knew that we had to hit that runway perfectly and that there was no way to pull up and go around if we missed. We set down in the first few feet of the runway, and Bill Rounds and I rode the brakes all the way to the opposite end. As the big plane groaned to a stop, the crew leaped out and literally kissed the ground.

But Mike Valko was again seriously shaken and had to be grounded for a while. He was back with us, however, when we flew our thirty-fifth and final mission of the war. That mission took us to Linz, Austria, where a portion of Hitler's forces were maneuvering desperately just before their final collapse. Our assignment was to bomb the key rail center at Linz to break up the movement of German forces and equipment. It proved to be our toughest mission.

The anti-aircraft fire was amazingly heavy, concentrated and accurate. Our old B-24 was hit by more than a hundred pieces of shrapnel. Our hydraulic lines were severed in half a dozen places. The electrically heated suits that we wore to keep warm at subzero altitudes went cold and our oxygen supply was disrupted. Worst of all, Tex Ashlock, our big waist gunner, was hit by a piece of shrapnel that traveled up his leg and lodged in his thigh.

That mission all but destroyed Mike Valko. He stood by almost helplessly while we cranked down the landing gear manually and then tied parachutes to girders at the waist hatch which we used to slow the plane once it was on the ground. The hydraulic brakes were gone and I sat helplessly while the plane rolled to the end of the runway and then slowly nosed over into a shallow ditch. It was the end of the war for our crew, and the war itself ended a few days later. Mike Valko was confined to a hospital, mentally ill, for months after the war. Then one day while he was crossing a street near his home in Bridgeport, he failed to see an oncoming truck and his troubled life was ended.

The other members of my crew were boys when we entered combat. They emerged as serious men: Ken Higgins of Virginia, our quietly competent, witty radio operator; Bill McAfee, the tough, disciplined ball-turret gunner from Port Huron, Michigan; our nose gunner, Bob O'Connell, the laconic Irishman from Brattleboro, Vermont; "Tex" Ashlock, our big rangy waist gunner from California who exuded both physical and moral strength; and Isadore Siegel, our tail gunner from Omaha who suffered endless bouts of air sickness while flying backwards in the bouncing tail section of the plane. Our bombardier, Bill Eames of Idaho, was transferred shortly after we arrived for combat because of a new Air Force decision to have all the bombers release their load on signal from the lead-ship bombardier rather than by individual releases.

These men, like hundreds of others, were welded into a highly competent team by their common yearning to survive. Beyond that, our closely intertwined lives in that Italian olive grove built relationships that have lasted through all the years of our separate careers since the war's end.

I flew my crew back to the United States in a B-24 in June of 1945. As we cruised high over the Atlantic during the night, my crew fell asleep and I was alone above a blanket of soft white clouds, beautifully illumined by a full moon, the dark ocean five miles below. My thoughts were beginning to turn from the war so recently ended to my loved ones back in the United States.

In December of 1944 I had received a delayed cable informing me that my father had died instantly of a heart attack which struck him

while he was on a pheasant-hunting trip with my boyhood friend
Eddie Kendall. Eddie was killed by a piece of shrapnel in the final
weeks of the war in Europe. I thought about my father and how
pleased he would have been to welcome me home.

One afternoon on the troop ship that was taking us across the
Atlantic to Italy I had written my father a letter telling him how
much he and our family had meant to me. He replied with an expression of his pride in me and his prayers for my safe return. "But, my
dear boy," he wrote, "these are times when we need to be redeemed
by God's saving grace and you must learn to draw on the spiritual
strength that is available to those who seek it." I knew that my dad
would breathe a prayer for me almost every hour that I was gone.

Mother had gone to Calgary for an extended visit with her aging
father, so I was glad that Eleanor had agreed to stay with Dad during
that first autumn when I was overseas. He was lost without my
mother and had told me in that final letter how much Eleanor eased
his loneliness.

Four months after my dad's death, President Roosevelt died suddenly. The announcement in our squadron area left every man I
knew with a sense of deep personal loss. That night there had been
an unusual consumption of alcohol at the old stone stable we used for
an officers' club. I recall a big red-haired Texan by the name of
Graham saying about Roosevelt's death, "We've just lost the goddamn war." I considered myself a Republican at that time, but I
understood Tex Graham's sentiment. It seemed so paradoxical that
with Allied victory in sight, Roosevelt was dead and Hitler was alive.
Most of us had never really known the United States except with
FDR as President. We did not think of him as a politician. He was that
magnificent voice of the fireside chat, who, along with Winston
Churchill, inspired all those who stood for freedom and decency in
the war. What would the United States be like without him?

Many things had changed for me. On March 14, 1945, I had returned from a bombing mission over Wiener-Neustadt, Austria, with
a new sense of elation, for on that beautiful, sun-drenched day I was
suddenly aware that all the old nagging fears of flying had vanished.
I was enjoying it. Then, on that pleasant day, I was handed a cable
saying that our daughter, Ann Marian, was born. Now, months later,
with the engines droning and the moonlight streaming into the cockpit on that homeward flight, I wondered about that little girl who
would be four months old before I was to see her for the first time.
I thought of Eleanor, whose love had sustained me for so many
months. Bob Brown, a talented young Mitchell photographer, had
produced a superb photo of Eleanor which had been on the night-
stand next to my cot from February 1943 in Jefferson Barracks until

I headed home from Cerignola in late June of 1945. That lovely face was the beginning inspiration of every day and the sweetest ending of each night before I drifted off to sleep. In my billfold I carried a small snapshot of Eleanor that she had given me in 1941. I thought that she was the loveliest creature on earth.

That worn billfold picture of Eleanor was propped up in front of me on the instrument panel and I turned up the cockpit light enough to make out the features without waking the sleeping Bill Rounds. I wondered what it would be like to embrace Eleanor and where we would live and what marriage would be like in peacetime and how I would relate to an infant daughter I was yet to see.

Eleanor had written to me asking if she could meet me in Minneapolis and then make the rest of the trip to Mitchell with me. She was doubtless trying to retrieve the honeymoon we had never had. We met at the Nicollet Hotel and then after a night in Minneapolis boarded the train to Mitchell.

Waiting for us at the old Chicago-Milwaukee rail station, where I had said goodbye to them in February 1943, were my mother, my brother and sisters, and my infant daughter. It was a joyful homecoming. As we drove down the Mitchell main street to our old house at Fifth and Sanborn with that tiny child in my lap, I thought of the continuity of life. Dad was missing, but a granddaughter he had never seen was here. Beyond this, I knew that with the war over for me, I would have to begin planning my life and preparing to take care of a young family.

A few weeks after I came home, dramatic news stories reported that a fantastic new bomb had been dropped on Hiroshima. We were told that an entire city had been incinerated by a single explosion. I had thought that the demolition bombs we had dropped on European cities were devastating, but it was clear now that the A-bomb had drastically changed the dimensions of warfare. Two days later the city of Nagasaki vanished under the mushroom cloud of a second atomic bomb. Then the Japanese surrendered and the war in the Far East was over. I learned later that my friend Norman Ray was one of the B-29 pilots in the Pacific waiting his turn to annihilate another city if the Japanese did not surrender.

Within days, a spate of articles and speeches appeared followed by sobering books which attempted to measure the implications of the atomic secret American scientists and engineers had unleashed. I was convinced that this was a weapon too terrifying for further use. From that day to this I have believed that unless the nuclear monster can be contained, civilization will be destroyed. But I had faith in the newly created United Nations and I believed that the United States would handle its new power with intelligence and restraint.

I wanted to be a part of that postwar effort to build a structure of peace on the smoldering ruins of war. The question was how best to contribute to the peace of the world. As early as the winter of 1941 I had won the South Dakota Intercollegiate Oratory Contest with the subject "My Brother's Keeper." The thesis was that man's inhumanity to man, if not disciplined by the claims of brotherhood, would destroy both our own society and the international community. I spoke of Mussolini's use of bombers against defenseless Ethiopia and the Nazi air raid which killed a thousand people in Coventry. Although I was even then on the verge of becoming a bomber pilot, I was horrified by the vivid descriptions of these events— especially by the boast of Mussolini's son Vittorio that exploding bombs reminded him of the beauty of a flowering rose.

That oration came back to me in the summer of 1945, and a few weeks later, after I returned to finish my college education at Dakota Wesleyan, I wrote my first serious postwar piece, an oration entitled "From Cave to Cave." The title was suggested by a current article proposing that the only escape in the nuclear age was to build the cities underground. My idea, of course, was that history had come full circle from the ancient cave man to modern man condemned by his own weapons to return to the cave.

But writing orations of this kind did not satisfy the questions that had developed in my mind during that summer. I wanted to know more about the historical process, about the nature and destiny of man, about the adequacy of our contemporary value system and the capacity of our institutions to nurture those values.

During the war I had read Charles and Mary Beard's two-thousand-page work, *The Rise of American Civilization*. What the Beards attempted was to reach beyond the traditional historical account of political, military and diplomatic events to achieve an understanding of all the complex forces that shape a developing society. Two hundred years earlier Voltaire had explained: "I wish to write a history, not of wars, but of society; and to ascertain how people lived in the interior of their families and what were the arts they commonly cultivated. . . . I want to know what were the steps by which mankind passed from barbarism to civilization." I underlined this quotation from Voltaire in the preface of the Beard book. I also underlined the thesis of the Beards that "the philosophy of any subject (that is, the truth of it) is not at its center but on the periphery where it impinges on all other sciences." If that were true, I sensed that one must not be devoted so singly to one area of study as to lose sight of its relationships to other areas of knowledge, experience and insight.

Those thoughts were playing in my mind as I pondered the meaning of the new atomic age.

Thus when I enrolled at Dakota Wesleyan in the autumn of 1945 to complete my undergraduate degree, I was a much more thoughtful student than the boy who had left that campus for war two and a half years earlier. I was looking for nothing less than an answer to the ultimate questions of man, society and the universe. It was in that frame of reference that I enrolled, along with half a dozen other GI students, in a class by Professor Don McAninch, "The Making of the Modern Mind." We used a textbook by the same title, authored by John Herman Randall, Jr., of Columbia University. It was McAninch's first course as a professor. He had come to DWU directly from graduate work in philosophy at Boston University, and he was deep into the search for meaning and a dependable value system. The professor, his course, the textbook, the collateral reading, the class discussions—all of these were to have a profound effect on my own intellectual and spiritual development. I chose Hegel's *Philosophy of History* to meet a course requirement for a critical book report and term paper. McAninch's reaction to my paper inspired me to further probing into historical and philosophical works. The question was how to relate these new interests to a constructive career that would not only enable me to delve into the realm of ideas but to serve the needs of my time.

"If the history of a people is a philosophy of the whole social organism in process of becoming, then it ought to furnish material with which discernment can be whetted," observed the Beards. "That is what Emerson must have had in mind when he advised Americans, in search of the full life, to stand fast where they are and work out their destiny in the place allotted to them by history for the fulfillment of their capacities."

I was "in search of the full life." But how could I work out my place in history "for the fulfillment of [my] capacities"? I was to grapple with that question for the next eight years.

The Beards warned that such a challenge, if pursued fearlessly, might end in frustration and disappointment—if not failure. But I accepted their conclusion that "it might be better to be wrecked on an express train bound to a destination than to moulder in a freight car sidetracked in a well-fenced lumber yard." I was later to learn the wisdom of their observation of history that it sometimes becomes the darkest just before the stars come out.

3

CLASSROOM
TO POLITICS

G eorg Wilhelm Friedrich Hegel once la-
mented: "Only one man has understood me and even he has
not." I am not that "one." But in the autumn of 1945 I worked my
way through Hegel's *Philosophy of History* with sufficient comprehension to satisfy Professor McAninch.

In Hegel's view, every individual, every institution and every nation evolves through a dialectical process of continuous change. Each
stage of development (the thesis) encounters a challenge (the antithesis) and this clash of ideas or institutional form leads to a new synthesis. But the resulting synthesis will also be challenged by still another
historical condition, resulting in further evolution. Thus, the process
of historical change is inevitable and continuous. To Hegel, it was the
responsibility of a wise citizen to understand the historical ideas
moving in one's own time and to support and accept change as an
inevitable process of growth. "The history of the world is none other
than the progress of the consciousness of Freedom," he asserted.

But Hegel's notion of Freedom was the freedom to discern and
accept the Divine Spirit, and he came to see that Spirit enshrined in
the State. Whereas in the past the evolving world spirit had been
manifested in the Orient, Greece and Rome, it was in Hegel's day
manifested in the Prussian monarchy of the 1820s. "The State is the
Divine Idea as it exists on earth . . . It is the Idea of Spirit in the

[33]

external manifestation of human will and its Freedom," he wrote.

With such a rationalization of the ultimate claims of the state, Hegel came to be known as the philosophical dictator of Germany. His ideas were to be adapted to their own purposes both by his pupil, Karl Marx, and by the architects of Hitler's national socialism. His theories also contributed to the evolutionary views of Charles Darwin.

I came back to Hegel two years later in graduate studies when I did a lengthy term paper comparing the Hegelian dialectic to the dialectical materialism of Karl Marx. Where Hegel traced the evolution of the ideas and spirit of an individual or an age, Marx was interested in the evolutionary stages of economic organization. He adapted Hegel's concept to his view that the struggle between conflicting economic classes followed a dialectical pattern in which one system produced its own challengers, which would inevitably lead to a differing economic order. The ultimate expression of Marx's dialectical materialism was the triumph of a "dictatorship of the proletariat" which would end the divisions between classes and thus end any further need for the state to exist as a preserver of a dominant class.

The study of these men forced me to think seriously about the political process, but neither of them captured my interest with anything approaching the enthusiasm I experienced in discovering "the Social Gospel." This effort to find in the New Testament and the Hebrew prophets an ethical imperative for a just social order strongly appealed to me. To know that long years of familiarity with the Bible and the idealism nurtured in my public-school years were resources that I could direct to humane political and economic ends was a satisfying discovery. Religion was more than a search for personal salvation, more than an instantaneous expression of God's grace; it could be the essential moral underpinning for a life devoted to the service of one's time. Indeed, one's own salvation depended upon service to others. "Inasmuch as ye have done it unto one of these the least of my brethren, ye have done it unto me," read the New Testament.

Suddenly religion seemed relevant to the world around me. And the man whose writings made it so was Walter Rauschenbusch, whose ideas I first discovered in John H. Randall's *The Making of the Modern Mind*. Rauschenbusch, a professor of church history at the Rochester Theological Seminary, emerged after the turn of the century as America's most noted advocate of the Social Gospel. In two highly influential books—*Christianity and the Social Crisis*, published in 1907, and *Christianizing the Social Order*, published in 1912 —Rauschenbusch set forth the ethical imperatives before twentieth-century humanity. I read these books hungrily as, page by page, they explored the social implications of a creed that seemed eminently right and urgently needed.

The message of Rauschenbusch and the Social Gospel he espoused was that the Kingdom of God is not an ethereal utopia in the eternal heavens, but a just and humane society to be sought after by human beings here on earth. "It is not a matter of getting individuals to heaven, but of transforming the life on earth into the harmony of heaven," he wrote.

"Religion in the past," Rauschenbusch noted, "has always spent a large proportion of its force on doings that were apart from the real business of life, on sacrificing, on endless prayers, on traveling to Mecca, Jerusalem, or Rome, on kissing sacred stones, bathing in sacred rivers, climbing sacred stairs, and a thousand things that had at best only an indirect bearing on the practical social relations between men and their fellows."

The teachings of Jesus command us to love one another, to feed the hungry, to heal the sick, to be the makers of peace. These tasks cannot be achieved in a social and international order guided by greed, discrimination, injustice and the degradation of human personality. "The church must either condemn the world and seek to change it, or tolerate the world and conform to it. In the latter case it surrenders its holiness and its mission," wrote Rauschenbusch. "If a man is satisfied with things as they are, he belongs to the other side."

To Professor Rauschenbusch, the central lines of the Lord's Prayer, inscribed on the dedication page of his first major book, were "Thy Kingdom Come, Thy Will Be Done on *Earth.*" In this volume, *Christianity and the Social Crisis,* Rauschenbusch wrote in 1907: "The religious, political and intellectual revolutions of the past five centuries, which together created the modern world, necessarily had to culminate in an economic and social revolution such as is now upon us ... In politics all issues and methods are undergoing upheaval and realignment as the social movement advances. In the world of thought all the young and serious minds are absorbed in the solution of the social problems."

I thought these concepts were convincing, liberating ideas then; I still do.

I soon discovered that Rauschenbusch was only the most prominent of a whole generation of modern-day religious philosophers who molded the thinking of most liberal Protestants and many Catholics and Jews. I was to encounter similar ideas in the sermons and books of Harry Emerson Fosdick, E. Stanley Jones, Ernest Fremont Tittle and others. I accepted Rauschenbusch's criticism of the excessive trappings of religion, just as I accepted Fosdick's conclusion of

1920 that "we have on the one side appalling human need, and on the other an immense amount of religious motive power and zeal, which are not harnessed to the problems of human welfare." I remember being struck by the words of E. Stanley Jones, who had reported that the great Indian leader, Mahatma Gandhi, had told him, "Bring your Christ, but leave your Christianity at home." I was impressed by George Bernard Shaw's observation: "The only trouble with Christianity is that it has never yet been tried." I believed that Rauschenbusch and Fosdick, Gandhi and Shaw and the others whose words inspired me were all seeking a society—"a Kingdom of God" —that was based on brotherhood, service and the love of others. The writings of these men and the classroom discussions with Professor McAninch were rapidly leading me toward a decision I could not have foreseen when I returned to Wesleyan in that first postwar year. I was beginning to search out some better way to attach idealism and "religious motive power . . . to the problems of human welfare."

With work for my B.A. degree completed in the spring of 1946, I began to think about whether I should pursue my long-time plans for graduate studies in history or enter the clerical career of my father with a Social Gospel orientation.

Albert Einstein and others had warned that unless humanity could change its contemporary thinking, civilization would soon succumb to nuclear holocaust. It seemed to me that a whole chorus of writers and commentators were in effect crying out for an application of the Judeo-Christian ethic to our contemporary crisis if humanity was to be saved.

I realized that it was necessary to test the claims of idealism and faith against the findings of science and my observations of the practical workings of life. But the greatest scientist of our time, Einstein, had observed: "The unleashed power of the atom has changed everything save our modes of thinking, and thus we drift to unparalleled catastrophe."

I came to believe that unless political leaders and diplomats recognized the new demands for a world society based on justice and compassion, neither America nor the world could find peace or security.

For several months I discussed with Eleanor, Don McAninch and others the possibility of enrolling in a seminary where I could learn to articulate my views from the pulpit. Eleanor then, as always, made clear her willingness to support any career decision I made. I detected some anxiety on her part, but she seemed to understand the influences that were leading me to consider such a ministry.

She had become pregnant almost immediately on my return from Italy and our second daughter, Susan, was born on March 27, 1946.

We were living in a small apartment that my dad had designed several years before his death in our old house at Fifth and Sanborn. It was a difficult time for Eleanor. She was caring for two babies—born a year apart—and trying to adjust to a husband she had not seen for a year. I felt a certain obligation to spend some time each day trying to cheer my mother, who still occupied a portion of the house. With the memory of Dad still so much in her mind, these visits meant much to Mother. Eleanor understood them intellectually, but emotionally it was hard for her to await my return from college classes and then have me stop for a chat with Mother before I bounded upstairs to our tiny apartment. I know now that I should have made more effort to assist Eleanor with our children when they were infants. Her mother was only a sad memory and her twin sister was hundreds of miles away. She had suffered from severe and prolonged nausea during the pregnancy periods followed by difficult births.

Every woman needs the most sensitive understanding and support of her husband during pregnancy and in the postnatal period. Eleanor was too gentle and restrained to complain, but it is one of the deep regrets of my life that my own career concerns frequently left Eleanor without the emotional support she needed so desperately. If I had devoted a fraction of the effort to preparing myself to play the role of husband and father that I did preparing for a career, the time would have been infinitely better invested.

We do not properly prepare ourselves for marriage and child care. Many young people devote more time and thought to preparing for their wedding ceremony than to preparing for marriage. We should have some of our best-trained and most imaginative teachers offering classroom instruction in marriage and child care. There should be a counselor available to every neighborhood, especially high-stress areas, to visit the homes and assist families with their special problems. Family services, including day care, should be carefully integrated with the activities in the home. Young parents should be regarded as society's most important concern. They should be made to feel and understand that the rest of us are aware that their contribution is the most difficult challenge facing any person in our society, a task requiring greater intelligence, imagination and wit than any other—the proper rearing of our little citizens.

Marriages in the United States are now dying in the divorce courts at a rate of over one million a year. Millions of children are blighted for life by improper guidance, bad nutrition and ugly surroundings. We pay the price for this neglect not only in unhappy families, but in enormous costs to the nation in the form of juvenile crime, sickness, unemployment and chronic dependency.

*   *   *

In the summer of 1946 I said goodbye to Eleanor and our two infant daughters, Ann and Susan, and headed for Diamond Lake, Illinois. I had decided to enroll at the Garrett Seminary on the campus of Northwestern University in Evanston. Arrangements had been made for me to live temporarily with the Wallace Reidel family in Diamond Lake and to assume the pulpit as a student pastor of the Community Methodist Church that summer. Eleanor and the children were to join me later after I had found a house.

I worked hard on my sermons that summer and began to participate in the life of the little community. Without benefit of seminary education, I turned to the sermons of Fosdick and of Ernest Fremont Tittle, who was then ministering to the prestigious First Methodist Church in nearby Evanston just off the campus of Northwestern University and the Garrett Seminary. I also drew on familiar texts with which I felt comfortable. One of my first sermons was built on the verse "Whosoever will save his life shall lose it; and whosoever will lose his life for my sake shall find it." That verse had intrigued me for years and still does. I called upon the congregation to understand that if we wanted to find meaning and fulfillment in our lives, we had to reach beyond immediate self-serving enrichment to consideration for the well-being of others. Peace among nations depended upon a willingness to subordinate national rivalry and commercial greed to the larger needs of the human family. My audience knew that I had recently been a combat bomber pilot decorated with the Distinguished Flying Cross, but I detected some anxiety when I insisted that nuclear energy had rendered traditional nationalism obsolete. Nevertheless, the congregation generally responded well, and within a few weeks the Sunday attendance had tripled.

After Eleanor arrived, we moved into a comfortable old house in a wooded area not far from the church. I converted our ground-level bedroom into a den lined with books. We shared the big house with Eleanor's sister, Ila, her husband, Bob Pennington, and their infant daughter, Sharon. It was generally a good arrangement. Bob was enrolled in the graduate school of history at Northwestern, and we were able to work out a car-pool arrangement with three of my fellow students at Garrett who were serving nearby student pastorates. Each day we commuted twenty-five miles to the Garrett-Northwestern campus and then returned in the late afternoon or early evening for a shared dinner with the Penningtons.

It was a fairly happy time except for two factors: I was ill-suited temperamentally to the priestly functions of the ministry, and I could not break loose from the old love for historical study. The courses at Garrett Seminary were stimulating, and constructing and delivering a sermon was a challenge that I responded to readily. But baptizing babies, officiating at weddings, administering the communion rituals and presiding at funerals—these tasks left me feeling excessively pious and ill at ease. Also, after three years of zesty language in the service, I was not prepared to experience a sudden hush of reverence when I approached a group of men telling raucous stories or using four-letter words.

Then one afternoon Bob Pennington suggested I visit a lecture course he was taking under Professor Ray Allen Billington, "Intellectual History of the United States." I was transfixed by that eloquent, witty lecture. It whetted all the old appetites for historical study. Beyond this, I knew that Eleanor was increasingly uneasy about her role as "the minister's wife." That was the end of my nine-month experience with seminary and student preaching. I simply moved across campus and without any loss of momentum plunged into the graduate study of history.

The Penningtons and McGoverns were soon located in neighboring apartments at 710 Clark Street in Evanston in an ancient, deteriorating building. Few of the older residents of lovely Evanston would admit that a cockroach had ever penetrated the city. But 710 Clark Street was the base of operations for the pests. Each resident sprayed for cockroaches whenever enough money could be saved to buy a can of roach killer. But since we never coordinated our attacks in a building-wide offensive, the battle-hardened roaches simply transferred to the apartment next door.

Eleanor and I were living on the $120 monthly stipend provided by the GI Bill of Rights, plus some part-time earnings. Our apartment was so small that we converted a closet into a tiny bedroom for Ann and Susan. But with the help of water-base paint, we transformed the walls into a pleasant soft rose color, and Eleanor made attractive slipcovers for the few pieces of secondhand furniture we had acquired. She stretched our food dollars miraculously and made clothing both for herself and the children. I remember Ann and Sue playing day after day with a battered old baby carriage and two small dolls. Frequently we took them to play in a nearby park or along Lake Michigan. Eleanor and I were happy with the Evanston years and so were the children.

During the summer of 1949 our third daughter, Teresa, was born. She was a beautiful baby, and all seemed to go well with her birth. But Eleanor suffered a severe postnatal depression that summer and fall. She struggled bravely to combat it, but much time was to pass before she was able to sort out her life and discern the childhood origins of her emotional stress. She tells of that struggle with remarkable insight and perception in her book, *Uphill.*

As for my studies, I found history fascinating, as I had imagined;

my professors were not only able scholars but in some cases became close, long-time friends. They have since told me that the group of World War II veterans who came to study at Northwestern in the first years after the war were the best graduate students they were to know in a lifetime of teaching.

Ray Billington was a superb lecturer with an especially keen sense of the absurd aspects of history. His own doctoral dissertation had traced the origins and manifestations of the Know-Nothing political movement of mid-nineteenth-century America. No one was more admirably endowed than Ray Billington with that combination of sardonic wit, capacity for ridicule and sense of justice that is required to assign "know-nothings" of every variety to their proper placement in society. I have never known a more effective lancer of stuffed shirts, hypocrites, bigots and buffoons. Beyond the classroom he and his wife, Mable, loved to open their home in the evening to a roister-ous party of graduate students and their wives. Ray once told me that the successful ingredients of a good party were minimal: civilized guests and plenty of cheap booze.

Billington's courses in American Intellectual History and his inter-est in the social impact of the advancing American frontier stimu-lated me to additional reading in the works of Vernon Parrington, Frederick Jackson Turner, De Tocqueville, Lord Bryce, Merle Curti, Arthur Schlesinger, Sr. and Jr., the Beards and numerous others.

The professor I came to know best at Northwestern, however, was Leften Stavrianos, whose specialty was the Balkans but whose inter-ests ranged broadly across the whole spectrum of human civilization. He was a masterly lecturer whose comments were invariably inter-spersed with clippings from the *New York Times* and contemporary journals that he related to the historical subject at hand. He was no apologist for the Soviet Union, but his lectures gave one a more balanced view of the Cold War that was then beginning to develop. Collateral reading stimulated by his courses—Leland Stowe's *While Time Remains,* Edgar Snow's *Red Star Over China,* Howard K. Smith's *The State of Europe,* John King Fairbank's *The United States and China,* Edwin Reischauer's *The United States and Japan,* Ed-ward Hallett Carr's *The Soviet Impact on the Western World,* Theo-dore White's *Thunder Out Of China,* Frederick Schuman's *Interna-tional Politics* and Owen Lattimore's *The Situation in Asia*—all of these and numerous others made it impossible for me to accept the conventional view of American Cold War policy.

I saw the Soviet desire to control the political alignment of its western neighbors—Czechoslovakia, Hungary, Rumania, Poland, Bulgaria, Yugoslavia and East Germany—not as the beginning of a Soviet march across Europe, Hitler-style; rather, it was a Soviet reaction, however regrettable, to two world wars. Twice in the space of a quarter century Russia had been savagely overrun by invading Western armies. No nation had suffered so grievously from World War II. If all of America from the Atlantic seaboard to the Mississippi River had been burned and devastated, with twenty million Americans dead, it would give us some idea of the Soviet experience during the terrible years after 1941.

Beyond this, the Soviet leaders knew of the implacable Western hostility to their Marxist ideology. Following the Bolshevik revolution of World War I, Russia was attacked by counterrevolutionary forces supplied by the Western nations with which they had recently been allied against imperial Germany. Again, after World War II, several Western leaders, including Winston Churchill, were warning of the need to contain the Soviet menace.

Without excusing the aggressive behavior of the Soviets in Eastern Europe after 1945, I have always believed that we not only overreacted to it but indeed helped to trigger it by our own post–World War II fears. "From Stettin in the Baltic to Trieste in the Adriatic, an iron curtain has descended across the continent," Churchill warned in a memorable address at Westminster College in Fulton, Missouri. The new American President, Harry Truman, and his Secretaries of State, James Byrnes and Dean Acheson, shared this view of the Soviet menace. In a matter of months, the globe was divided into "the free world" and "the Communist world." President Truman pledged a "Get Tough" policy to halt Soviet influence in Greece and Turkey. Within two years, the Marshall Plan was formulated to buttress the economies of Western Europe against Soviet penetration. In China we poured in more than $2 billion of military equipment to prevent the triumph of Mao Tse-tung over Chiang Kai-shek. And in an obscure French colony embracing the little states of Vietnam, Laos and Cambodia, we sided with the French colonialists against the revolutionary leader, Ho Chi Minh.

I could not square any of these official American interventions with what I was reading and learning in graduate courses and conversations in the Northwestern history department of the late 1940s. It was especially hard to justify our failing effort to rescue Chiang Kai-shek with what I had read about his corrupt reactionary policies as against the grassroots appeal of Mao's revolutionary cadres. Nor could I comprehend how any American policy maker who had read Owen Lattimore's perceptive *Situation in Asia* could believe that we were serving either American ideals or American interests when we chose to back the French colonialists against the independence movement of Ho Chi Minh. Twenty-five years of misguided and failing American policy in Indochina could have been avoided if men like Lattimore had been heeded instead of hounded to the sidelines.

Writing in 1949, Lattimore reported: "Asia is out of control. From Suez to the Western Pacific we face one problem after another, in one country after another, which we cannot settle either by an American decision or by joint action with countries that we consider our allies.

"From the Arab countries to China, the old forms of ascendancy, protectorate or rule cannot be reasserted by military action. We have already had enough experience to prove that the more modern and highly equipped is the military force that is used, the more expensive is the failure eventually inflicted on it by cheap methods of guerrilla warfare that require no industrial support."

In a brilliant analysis of the twin forces of nationalism and social revolution that were convulsing Asia, Lattimore concluded: "Asia, to sum it up, has become a part of the world where the great powers can no longer lay down the law as they did in the nineteenth and the early part of the twentieth century. We must negotiate; and we can only negotiate successfully if people in Asia are as well satisfied with what they get out of negotiated agreements as we are with what we get out of them. This limitation applies to Russia as well as to the other great powers."

At the time, these words made sense to me as a graduate student; they made it impossible for me to accept the later arguments of the fifties and sixties that Moscow and Peking were controlling the revolutions of Asia and that only American intervention could prevent the "dominoes" from toppling into the lap of the Kremlin. There would have been no American intervention in Vietnam with all its attendant bloodshed and devastation if the views of Lattimore and other competent Asia scholars had been heeded.

I could not accept either for Asia or as a global view in general the bipartisan Cold War rigidity of the late forties. As the first post–World War II presidential election approached (1948) it became clear that President Truman, the Democratic candidate, and Thomas Dewey, the Republican candidate, were in essential agreement on their view of the world. Anti-Communism at any cost was the order of the day. It did not seem to matter what America stood *for;* the guiding concern was what we were *against.* And we were against Russia, against China, against Ho Chi Minh and against any revolutionary nationalistic movement that might in the minds of our policy makers be associated with what they called "international Communism."

All of this was at odds with my view of America as a nation born and nurtured in revolution against the imperial status quo. I did not accept the ideology or the methods of Communism, but neither could I accept American support for the reactionary regimes in China, Korea and Indochina that we were backing.

Thus I was receptive to an alternative to the Truman-Dewey bipartisan policy of 1948. That alternative was provided by former Vice President Henry Wallace. Wallace was a highly respected Iowa businessman and farm operator who had developed hybrid-seed corn plants in Iowa, Illinois, Indiana and Ohio that were selling $4 million worth of seed corn annually by 1933. He had served as Franklin Roosevelt's Secretary of Agriculture and then as his Vice President. He was forced to resign as President Truman's Secretary of Commerce when he took public exception to the Administration's Cold War policies.

When he emerged in 1948 as a third-party presidential candidate on a platform of international cooperation and "people's capitalism," Eleanor and I gave him our support. Indeed, we went as delegates from Illinois to the Progressive Party convention in Philadelphia. My most vivid memory of that convention was the group singing led by Pete Seeger. I also remember encountering a few hard-line Communists whose rigidity and fanaticism I found obnoxious. But most of the delegates were idealistic middle-class Americans who wanted a foreign policy based on restraint and reason, and domestic policies geared to the public interest. Wallace was attacked by his enemies as a "pink" or a "red." He was, in fact, an old-fashioned free-enterprise capitalist and a practical internationalist.

In his book, *Sixty Million Jobs,* published in late 1945, Wallace called for full employment "without a Planned Economy, without disastrous inflation, and without an unbalanced budget that will endanger our national credit." A man of strong character and high intelligence, he believed that a progressive American capitalism and sound federal policies would not only end deprivation and idleness, but in doing so would reduce crime, disease and racial tensions.

Wallace rejected the view that the American economy required a certain level of unemployment to combat inflation, to hold down wages and thereby to increase profits. He believed that unemployed workers meant reduced consumption, reduced production and a sluggish, wasteful economy which would jeopardize not only the system of free enterprise, but also the social health of the nation.

A man of deep humanitarian instincts, Wallace observed: "Men with broken spirits, women waiting at home in endless anguish, children neglected and undernourished—these are the true costs of unemployment . . . No one will ever be able to plumb the depths of tragedy that result when futility and frustration replace human dignity in a man's soul."

Like millions of other Americans who had experienced the deep satisfaction that grew out of a shared national experience in World

War II, Wallace longed for that same feeling in the pursuits of peace-time society. He wrote:

"The most prized asset that any of us can have is the sense of belonging: the feeling that we are a part of something, that we are appreciated, that our efforts do count, that we can look ahead with mutual hope and confidence.

"The impact of war on our security gave this sense of belonging to most of us. It gave us the feeling that we were bound together for survival. The great problem of peace is to make it seem as important and urgent as war.

"We must feel as close to each other in winning the peace as we did in winning the war. We must make peace as challenging—and as exciting—as war."

Wallace viewed the deterioration of Soviet-American relations that began with the ending of the war as a dreadful threat, not only to world peace but to the tranquillity and prosperity of the American people. While rejecting Soviet ideology, he saw no reason for a break-down in peacetime of the cooperative relationship we maintained with the Russians while we were combating Nazi Germany.

Thirty years after I read Wallace's little volume I came across this passage which I had marked in 1946:

There is altogether too much irresponsible defeatist talk about the possibility of war with Russia. In my opinion, such talk, at a time when the blood of our boys shed on the fields of Europe has scarcely dried, is criminal. There are certain people—and they are the rankest kind of un-Americans—who are anxious to see the United States and Russia come to blows. I do not deny that in the past Russia has given the United States some provocation—just as the United States has given provocation to Russia. But anyone who has studied the relations of western Europe and Poland with Soviet Russia after World War I— anyone acquainted with the bungling policy of nonrecognition blindly followed by this country until Franklin Roosevelt ended it in 1933— surely can understand the background of Russian suspicions. However, there is no need here to unearth this past. The job for all of us today is to try to understand the basic historical, geographical, political, and economic facts. Then, I am sure, we would all readily understand the basic lack of conflict between the United States and the USSR—and then there would need be no question about our doing our part toward developing a co-operative and harmonious relationship with Russia. I am assuming, of course, that the Russians will come halfway. I think they will. From what I have learned through long and hard study of the Soviet Russian mind in action—from my own personal acquaint-anceship with a wide range of Russian citizens from officials to factory workers—I firmly believe that the people of Russia have a great admiration and friendship for the people of the United States and that they want to live with us and prosper with us in peace.

Today Harry Truman is being elevated retroactively as a great President, whereas Henry Wallace is largely forgotten. But I believed in the late forties and I believe now that both the domestic health of the nation and the peace of the world would have been better served by the hopeful and compassionate views of Wallace than by the "Get Tough" policy of the Truman Administration.

The Wallace movement that climaxed in 1948, however, was discredited in the eyes of most of the press and the public. Truman won a narrow victory over Dewey, and the Cold War began to gather force.

Joe McCarthy, the obscure junior Senator from Wisconsin, sensing the officially fed fear of a global Communist conspiracy, plunged onto the national stage in early 1950. McCarthy's target was the State Department and especially the Asia experts whom he blamed for the fall of Chiang Kai-shek and the success of the Maoist revolution. It is difficult for anyone who did not live through the McCarthy crusade to realize the damage this unscrupulous demagogue did to American politics and diplomacy. His sensational claims of "card-carrying Communists" in the State Department dominated the airwaves and the press. He whipped up the right wing to the point of hysterical hatred of the State Department. Even such impeccable Cold War advocates as Secretary of State Dean Acheson were branded as "pinkos." The distinguished American general and wartime commander, George Marshall, was labeled "a front man for traitors."

McCarthy's excesses finally brought him an official censure by the United States Senate, but not before he had either forced the resignation or had silenced most of the State Department's knowledgeable Asia experts. "McCarthyism" spread across the American political landscape like an ugly cancer. It fed the already mounting Cold War hysteria and throttled any hope for serious foreign policy debate. I have always thought that it set the stage for our involvement in both Korea and Vietnam.

This was the setting that gave Congressman Richard Nixon his opportunity for national recognition in the House of Representatives. And in the Senate, Karl Mundt was preparing the Mundt-Nixon Bill as a legislative weapon to curb the Communist menace. These two men and their close associates were more adroit than Joe McCarthy in exploiting the "red scare" while avoiding the kind of extreme charges against powerful personalities that eventually destroyed McCarthy. I regarded the Nixon-type demagoguery as the most dangerous form of McCarthyism because it was more cleverly attuned to what Americans were willing to tolerate. It was used by Nixon to defeat first Congressman Jerry Voorhis, and then U.S. Senate candidate Helen Gahagan Douglas.

In his 1946 campaign against Congressman Voorhis, Nixon, following a strategy advocated by Los Angeles lawyer Murray Chotiner, had depicted his opponent as an advocate of Communist principles. Shortly before the election, a Nixon campaign advertisement warned: "Remember, Voorhis is a former registered Socialist and his voting record in Congress is more Socialistic and Communistic than Democratic."

Actually Voorhis, a moderate liberal who had served in the Congress for ten years, had been voted by the Washington press corps as the congressman with the greatest integrity. His own colleagues in the House of Representatives had rated him as the hardest working congressman and second among the 435 members of the House in putting the nation's welfare ahead of personal political interests.

But Nixon's innuendos against Voorhis' patriotism and judgment were enough to defeat the respected incumbent congressman. Two years later Congressman Nixon orchestrated an unusual direct-mail campaign to California Democrats. Postcards carrying his picture bore the salutation "Dear fellow Democrat" and urged the recipient to "re-elect Congressman Nixon." A precursor of his 1972 presidential campaign, in which "Democrats for Nixon" called on their fellow citizens to "Re-elect the President," Nixon's 1948 bid was so cleverly managed that he won the Democratic primary as well as the Republican.

Writing about this election years later, Voorhis observed: "Here we find our first important evidence of a developing source of political strength—a wondrous flexibility. Richard Milhous Nixon could even be—albeit very temporarily—a 'member' of the party he made a practice of accusing of action highly detrimental to the nation, if not actually subversive."

Encouraged by the tactics of deceit and fear-mongering which were so successful for him in 1946 and 1948, Congressman Nixon used the same methods to discredit his congressional colleague Helen Gahagan Douglas in a race for the U.S. Senate in 1950. Nixon was elected after he gave wide circulation to a "pink sheet" purporting to show that Congresswoman Douglas sometimes voted the same way as Vito Marcantonio, a New York City congressman with Communist leanings. He also circulated literature implying that Mrs. Douglas, the wife of screen star Melvyn Douglas, was hiding the fact that her husband was Jewish.

Bolstered by his California victories and his work as a member of the House Un-American Activities Committee leading to the perjury conviction of Alger Hiss, Nixon had become enough of a political force to be considered for the vice-presidential nomination in 1952. He got his place on the national Republican ticket with General Eisenhower by undercutting his California Republican colleague, Governor Earl Warren, when he persuaded many California delegates to switch their allegiance from Warren to Eisenhower. This may be one reason why Warren despised Nixon throughout his public career.

Eisenhower was an affable, somewhat nonpartisan figure who had widespread support from both Democrats and Republicans. But this did not deter Nixon from using the tactics of "smear and fear" that had worked so effectively for him in his California races. In the 1952 presidential campaign he said of Secretary of State Dean Acheson, "Dean Acheson has a form of color blindness—a form of pink eye— toward the Communist threat in the United States."

Of the eloquent, much-admired governor of Illinois, Adlai Stevenson, the Democratic presidential nominee, Nixon said, "Mr. Stevenson has a degree all right—a Ph.D. from the Acheson College of Cowardly Communist Containment." I have loathed Richard Nixon since he first came on the national scene wielding his red brush in 1946, but I especially resented his cheap insults to Adlai Stevenson —my first genuine political hero. It remains the mystery of my life that this unscrupulous man could deceive so many Americans for so long—including two successful campaigns for the vice presidency in 1952 and 1956, a razor-close presidential defeat by John Kennedy in 1960, and victorious presidential campaigns against Hubert Humphrey in 1968 and against me in 1972. Even Ray Billington's lectures on the Know Nothing tradition in American politics had not prepared me for this amazing chronicle of manipulation and deceit.

Nevertheless, my graduate studies at Northwestern had introduced me to some of the rawest aspects of American politics and society. During my final year of residence study in Evanston, Professor Arthur Link, the distinguished biographer of Woodrow Wilson, joined the Northwestern faculty as a professor in Recent American History. I was then searching for an interesting doctoral dissertation topic. Arthur Link suggested one that I accepted: "The Colorado Coal Strike of 1913-14," and imposed a work schedule on me that left no possibility for the kind of procrastination that has produced so many incomplete doctoral careers.

The Colorado Coal Strike, which erupted in September 1913, was one of the bloodiest, bitterest and most widely publicized labor battles in American history. It was a struggle organized by the United Mine Workers to break the virtual serfdom in which the miners were held by John D. Rockefeller's Colorado Fuel and Iron Company and other absentee-owned corporations in the coal fields of southern Colorado. These miners—many of them non-English-speaking immigrants from southern and eastern Europe—lived in company towns along the coal canyons. The homes, the stores, the schools, the churches, the doctors—all of these were owned or controlled by the coal-mine operators. Editors, judges, juries, sheriffs and other county officials frequently took their orders from company officials. Union organizers were harassed, physically assaulted and sometimes driven from the area. The power of the coal operators even reached into the governor's office at Denver.

It was this industrial, legal and political power that ten thousand miners challenged in the strike, which began in September of 1913 and extended to the end of 1914. The climax of the struggle came on April 20, 1914, at Ludlow when gunfire broke out between the Colorado state militia and a tent village set up by the union for the strikers and their families. When the smoke of the battle had cleared, the bodies of a dozen women and children were found huddled in a hole under one of the tents that had been set afire during the battle.

In the days that followed "the Ludlow Massacre," pitched warfare spread across the hills of Colorado involving hundreds of armed miners and militiamen. Finally President Wilson dispatched both federal troops and a federal mediator to Colorado, and the strike was ended.

I traced this story of hard-bitten coal barons, tough labor leaders and intimidated politicians through thousands of pages of testimony taken later by a special Industrial Commission headed by Thomas Walsh and a U.S. House of Representatives Investigating Committee headed by South Carolina Congressman James Byrnes. I searched through the papers of the Wilson Administration. I spent long hours reading newspapers and journals of the period. During most of the summer I poured over the archives of the State of Colorado assisted by the excellent State Archivist, Delores Renze. I worked twelve-hour days at the Library of Congress, the New York Public Library, the Princeton University Library, and at the Federal Archives building in Washington.

Through this research I came to know the life of a courageous labor leader, John Lawson; I studied the career of a brave Colorado senator, Edward P. Costigan; I was moved by the colorful, impassioned charges to the strikers by Mother Jones, who, when introduced as "a great humanitarian," snorted, "I'm no humanitarian, I'm a hell-raiser." And she was. She could spit out a string of four-letter profanity with rare eloquence and righteous indignation.

But the real heroes of the Colorado Coal Strike were the thousands of simple miners, wives and children who bore the long dreary winter months in the meagerly equipped tent villages. They lost most of the objectives they were seeking in the strike, but for the first time in American history, a major strike touched the hearts and consciences of the American people. It was a temporary defeat for the United Mine Workers but a long-term victory for those who were building a public climate willing to accept the notion that coal miners should be represented by a union of their own choosing.

I had completed most of the research for my dissertation between February and September of 1950. I then began teaching history and coaching debate at Dakota Wesleyan while starting to write the first chapter of the dissertation. Week after week I spent my spare hours in my third-floor office on the west side of the old DWU Science Hall. As each chapter was finished I mailed it to Arthur Link for evaluation and criticism. In a few days he would return the manuscript carefully annotated, with a terse note saying that he was expecting the next chapter on a specified date. (The dissertation, which ran nearly five hundred pages, has since been published by Houghton Mifflin with the help of co-author Leonard Guttridge.)

Work on my dissertation left little time for class preparation, but I had almost complete freedom in selecting the courses I wished to teach and the class discussions were usually lively. These were the years of the Korean War and I had serious questions about American involvement in that conflict. But what disturbed me most was the obvious fact that by pressing the American counteroffensive across the 38th parallel all the way to the Yalu River along the Chinese border, General Douglas MacArthur brought Chinese forces into the struggle—one million strong. What began as a seemingly limited police action designed to force the North Koreans back to the 38th parallel became a major international conflict that killed 33,000 young Americans and cost $150 billion.

This unpopular, indecisive war of unclear origins became a major factor in the 1952 presidential election. President Truman had repeatedly rejected the negotiating terms offered by the North Koreans. Thus, the way was open for General Eisenhower to win millions of votes by a pledge that if elected, he would "go to Korea." True to his pledge, the new President did go to Korea and the war ended. But American forces, nearly 40,000 of them, are still deployed along the 38th parallel. And I continue to regret their presence in this divided country where a precipitous move by the dictators of either North or South Korea could immediately involve America in another war on the Asian mainland.

My opposition to the Korean War and my support for Adlai Stevenson in 1952 were not widely endorsed in Republican South Dakota. But I could not resist Stevenson's eloquence. The night he gave his midnight acceptance speech in Chicago, I was painting the living room of our apartment near the DWU campus—Eleanor and the four (our son, Steve, had been born in 1952) children long since asleep. There was a combination of high intelligence, character and common sense in that address which profoundly attracted me. As a student of history I included among my political heroes men of both parties—Republicans Abraham Lincoln, George Norris and Robert La Follette; Democrats Thomas Jefferson, Woodrow Wilson and Franklin Roosevelt—but I had no special attachment to the Democratic Party.

I was particularly taken by Stevenson's conviction that the Democratic Party "will never be indolent as long as it looks forward and not back, as long as it commands the allegiance of the young and the hopeful who dream the dreams and see the visions of a better America and a better world." And I could only say "Amen" when I laid down my paint brush and heard that earnest, articulate voice asserting: "What does concern me, in common with thinking partisans of both parties, is not just winning the election, but how it is won, how well we can take advantage of this great quadrennial opportunity to debate issues sensibly and soberly. I hope and pray that we Democrats, win or lose, can campaign not as a campaign to exterminate the opposing party, as our opponents seem to prefer, but as a great opportunity to educate and elevate a people whose destiny is leadership, not alone of a rich and prosperous, contented country as in the past, but of a world in ferment . . . Better we lose the election than mislead the people; and better we lose than misgovern the people."

That was it. Here was a politician who was willing to combine reason with ambition, who was eager to talk sense and debate the great issues, who would rather lose than win by deceit. I was dedicated to the Stevenson campaign from that moment on. But how could *I* help—an impoverished history professor with no political connections?

I decided that my contribution would begin with a series of articles submitted to my hometown paper, the Mitchell *Daily Republic*, setting forth the historical issues that separated the two major political parties.

The *Daily Republic* was a remarkably good paper for a town the size of Mitchell. Its editor, W. R. Ronald, was in the best tradition of the old-fashioned country editor: fiercely independent, courageous and intelligent. He enriched his editorial page with the syndicated columns of Thomas Stokes, Doris Fleason, Marquis Childs and Drew Pearson. My files bulged with clippings from the editorials and columns of the *Daily Republic* that I had collected over the years.

It was thus with some pride that I saw my series of seven articles appearing in the *Daily Republic* during the summer and fall of 1952. Whether these articles strengthened the Democratic cause in general and the Stevenson campaign in particular in South Dakota, I do not know. But they caught the attention of Ward Clark, a young Canistota lawyer who had recently become the State Democratic Chairman. Ward asked me if I would give a campaign address over WNAX at Yankton, South Dakota's major radio station. I proudly accepted. A few days later, as the 1952 campaign drew to a close, I drove with Ward to Platte to face my first live audience with a campaign speech.

Late that night, over coffee at "Boom's" café in Platte, Ward Clark told me of a plan that had been simmering in his mind for some time.

We were going to be badly beaten in Tuesday's election, he predicted. Stevenson would lose heavily and so would the state Democratic candidates. But he believed that if given attractive candidates backed by a strong grassroots organization, the Democratic Party could make a comeback after the election.

Ward knew that organizing a political party would require the full-time effort of an imaginative, hard-working person. What he proposed was the creation of a state party executive secretary, and he then proceeded to tell me why I should resign my professorship and accept this job. I was at first astounded, but I listened to his arguments until far into the night and then drove back to Mitchell deeply intrigued by this unexpected proposition. I was far from accepting it, but from the beginning it fired my imagination. Could I actually resign as a professor and forensics coach just as I was to complete a dissertation and receive a Ph.D.? Did I dare jeopardize my family's security by giving up a sure, albeit limited income, to accept a job with a party that had no money and no apparent future? Would I look ridiculous trying to work at political organizing as a full-time responsibility? Was it possible to replace the warm relationships with my students and faculty colleagues with new satisfactions in politics? And finally, was the whole idea of building a viable Democratic Party in Republican South Dakota a foolish gamble?

All of these questions were swirling in my mind as I drove down the darkened highway between Platte and Mitchell that night at the end of October 1952.

4

GRASSROOTS

W ard Clark's prophecies about the 1952 election results in South Dakota were accurate; Stevenson and the Democrats were smothered under a Republican landslide. The Republican win even swept Democrats out of the county courthouses and the state legislature. In a state Senate of 35 members, not a single Democrat was elected. Only two Democrats, Frank Lloyd of Platte and Carl Furchner of Plankinton, were elected to the 75-member state House of Representatives. So, when the legislature convened in January, two lonely Democrats faced 108 Republicans—a ratio which many South Dakotans felt was ideal.

I went to the J. C. Penney store in Mitchell to ask manager Bradley Young—a respected, long-time Democrat—his advice about Ward Clark's offer. Bradley snorted, "George, you'd have to be crazy to take that job." He explained that our fellow townsman Joe Robbie (now owner of the Miami Dolphins) had spent two hard years trying to organize the Democrats for what proved to be an unsuccessful race for governor by Robbie in 1950. Other talented, energetic men had also tried and failed. Brad Young thought that trying to build an effective Democratic organization in South Dakota was hopeless. Beyond this, he admired my work at Dakota Wesleyan and did not want me to resign from a position that he believed was important to the college and to the security of my young family.

I got the same advice across the street on the second floor of the Mitchell Commercial Bank building, where Herb Hitchcock and Fred Nichol had their law offices. These men were dear friends to both Eleanor and me. They feared that I would be overwhelmed by the Republican proclivities of South Dakota; yet I thought they were also intrigued by the imaginative challenge of Ward Clark's proposal. I then went down Third Street to the *Daily Republic* to chat with Ez Brady—another respected Democrat. To my surprise Ez, after warning me about the hazards of the job, said that he thought it was worth the risk. As a matter of fact, he had discussed the matter with Ward and had urged him to follow up on his idea.

So while preparing for my final exams leading to a Ph.D. in history at Northwestern in early June 1953, I notified Matthew Smith, Sr., then president of Dakota Wesleyan, that I would resign from the faculty in June to begin organizing the Democratic Party in South Dakota. President Smith, visibly distressed, urged me to reconsider. He had known me for sixteen years as a high school and college debate partner of his son, as a wartime pilot and as a member of his faculty. His eyes were moist that afternoon in old College Hall. But he knew, as I did, that the Republican-dominated college board of trustees would not permit me to work as a political organizer for the Democrats while serving as a professor. So I called Ward Clark and accepted his offer to become the full-time Executive Secretary of the Democratic Party at an annual salary of $6,000.

I started with a small room in the old Western Building that I rented from Harold Grant, a Mitchell insurance man and the director of Mitchell's National Guard Band. I had no secretary, so the party files, the correspondence and the organizational effort all were handled by me with the support of a desk, two chairs and a file drawer, and pictures of Abraham Lincoln, Franklin Roosevelt and Adlai Stevenson.

Ward Clark's office at Canistota, fifty miles away, was the scene of frequent early conferences to plan the organizational effort. Dennis Jensen, a vigorous, imaginative young hardware dealer from nearby Spencer, the party's state treasurer, would often sit in on these sessions. Ward, Dennis and I—sometimes aided by the advice of Ez Brady, Cobb Chase of Watertown, Goldie Wells of Aberdeen, Jim Magness of Miller, Katie Kuhns of Worthing, Jack Weiland of Mitchell and others—developed a general plan of action.

I would spend considerable time on the road locating the county officers who could be depended upon to work their counties, noting those who were ineffective, and recruiting the most attractive possible candidates to seek state and county office in 1954. Eleanor's father was the Sanborn County Democratic chairman, and he offered valuable advice on both the strengths and the weaknesses of Joe Robbie's recent organizational drive. I spent countless hours visiting the homes, shops, farms, classrooms and offices of hundreds of South Dakotans of both parties, drawing them out on the nature of political organization and public issues in the state.

My first formal action was a carefully planned letter to the state's sixty-seven Democratic county chairmen and chairwomen. The letter explained my eagerness to assist them in strengthening their county organizations, filling vacancies among the party officers and recruiting good candidates for 1954. I also asked them to supply an up-to-date list of their county and precinct committee officers and to advise me as to how we could work together in reorganizing the party. Sixty of the county leaders responded to my urgently worded letter by ignoring it. Of the seven who replied, one simply said: "Who the hell are you? I resigned as chairman a year ago when the Democrats tried to run that smart-ass Stevenson against Ike. Don't send me any more of your stuff." Another one told me he had not really been a Democrat "since Roosevelt ran for a third term." Still another said that he was hoping Karl Mundt would nominate his son for West Point and that if this happened, he would have to "go underground for a while." He suggested that if I were to visit his business place, it might be best for me to telephone him first, or else come to the back door.

But the remaining replies came from four feisty, blunt-spoken Democrats whose years of combat with the Republicans had only deepened their resolve. These men and women were typical of thousands of independent-minded South Dakota Democrats whose liberalism had been refined in the fires of opposition, ridicule, and in some cases, the penalty of social and professional discrimination. I learned early that a few committed allies of this kind are better than an army of drifters who go with the prevailing winds. Sometimes the drifters can't even detect a shift in the wind until it has blown past them.

Carl Schneider of Mobridge was no drifter and neither was Jennie O'Hern of nearby Wakpala. They were spirited, fighting Democrats who loved the annual meetings of the State Central Committee, where they could report on their local combat with the Republicans —and sometimes with each other. During my first meeting with the state committee at the Marvin Hughitt Hotel in Huron, Jennie took the floor to protest one of Carl's fund-raising efforts on behalf of the party.

Mobridge, astride the Missouri River near the boundary of North and South Dakota, boasted one of the few flourishing brothels in the state. It was never quite clear to me whether it was a legalized institution or whether "the law" simply developed a convenient case of failing vision. But it was generally accepted by the community—at one time even carrying a sign doubtless posted by a jovial customer: WE GIVE S & H GREEN STAMPS.

In any event, Carl, a retired railroad man and the county committee's treasurer, was inspired to solicit the brothel's comparatively affluent female staff for contributions to the Democratic Party. Jennie, an elderly Catholic of established virtue, was as outraged by this fund-raising inspiration as Carl was delighted. Thus the stage was set for a bitter battle between these two old warriors in the fall of 1953.

Jennie took the floor first and delivered a scathing attack against the very thought of a party founded by Thomas Jefferson and Andrew Jackson being contaminated with money from prostitutes. Carl, whose admiration for Jefferson and Jackson was perhaps more historically informed than Jennie's, indignantly rose to the defense of "those hard-working girls at Mobridge." With eyes burning and lungs pulsating, old Carl thundered that the Democratic Party has always been the party of "all the people." We are, he said, not just a party of "the self-righteous goody-goodies"; we are a people's party with plenty of room for "ordinary" people. "Those girls earn their money, and it's every bit as good as the money of some son-of-a-bitchin' big banker," he roared.

I have never known whether it was a positive reaction to the "hard-working girls" or a negative reaction to the bankers, but Carl drew a burst of applause that ended the argument.

Ward Clark, always the astute chairman, referred the entire matter for further study to a committee of three prominent Democrats who may even yet be pondering the complexities of the issue.

I was deeply involved at the time in an even more earthy problem. The week-long State Fair was in progress at Huron, and I was experiencing my first direct face-to-face competition with the state Republican organization. It had long been customary for the two parties to maintain booths at the fair where the public could meet the major candidates and party officials. This year, in the flush of their smashing victory of the previous November, the Republicans had set up a large tent over a new concrete floor. They were offering free coffee, balloons for the children, shopping bags for the women, an attractive array of posters, photos, free government publications, and tables laden with Republican literature. In front of their headquarters were their two U.S. senators, Karl Mundt and Francis Case, their two congressmen, E. Y. Berry and Harold Lovre, Governor Sigurd Anderson and—most appealing of all—a real live elephant borrowed from an Omaha zoo.

Across the muddy thoroughfare I stood on the wet, cold sod in front of a dismally small tent with no floor, no literature, no coffee, no elected officials—and no counterpart to the GOP elephant.

After a demoralizing day of listening to the rival Republican loud-speaker herding chilled fair-goers into the tent to visit Karl Mundt and Bingo, the elephant, I knew that a counterattack was imperative. Providence intervened at this dark moment in the form of a loyal Democrat who appeared at my tent to inform me that he had a donkey at his gas station in Wolsey, fourteen miles away, that I could borrow. I left immediately in my old Chevy after removing the rear seat to allow room for the donkey. This was the first fateful step in a gathering, multiple disaster.

The donkey's assisted lunge into the car sent a hoof through the window on the opposite side. I slammed the door behind him—an action which inspired the bleeding animal to leave at least one jag-ged splotch of blood on even the most remote areas of the car's interior.

After halting the bleeding, I proceeded to Huron with the thrash-ing beast and finally succeeded in tying him to the main pole support-ing the Democratic tent. To my horror, that scrawny little creature with the apparent strength of an enraged bull jerked the pole for-ward and the tent collapsed in the mud. With derisive Republican laughter in my ears from across the midway, I worked frantically, assisted by two humanitarian onlookers, to reconstruct the tent. While this operation was going forward, I tied the donkey to a sturdy tree. Within minutes he urinated copiously on an innocent nun who had turned her back on him. I pretended not to see this and the disciplined nun slipped away to recover her dignity.

I then began to speak into a scratchy gadget—carelessly described as "the PA System"—urging people to visit Democratic headquarters and, somewhat fearfully, to see the donkey. At this point a child's scream pierced the air and I looked in horror at the scene of a donkey's teeth planted around the chubby hand of a ten- or eleven-year-old girl. I kicked the donkey with sufficient force to jar his jaws and reached for the little girl to take her to the first-aid station. But she broke into a terrified run down the midway with me in full pursuit imagining tetanus, an amputated arm, a massive lawsuit and political disgrace. Child molestation must have crossed the minds of hundreds of spectators watching the frightened girl fleeing before a bloodied, perspiring, wild-looking male. Fortunately the girl ran into her mother's arms, and of equal good fortune, the mother was a Democrat with a cool head. Presently we were at the first-aid station, the donkey bite proved to be only a small nip, and the little girl actually managed a smile when I gave her a couple of dollars for carnival rides. But I have never trusted donkeys since. They deserve to be called asses.

During this first State Fair I hit upon an idea that was much more successful than the Democratic donkey. It was a system that was to become a useful instrument in both my organizational success in South Dakota and my later successful bid for the Democratic presidential nomination in 1972. That valuable instrument was the 3 × 5 card, carefully annotated and filed. Each time I met a person at the fair, in my office or in endless travels around the state, I wrote down the individual's name, address, telephone number and any pertinent information about political affiliation, relatives, special talents and interests. In a shoe box I set up sixty-seven orange-colored tab markers for the sixty-seven counties, with green tab markers for the five or six towns in each county. Into these subdivisions went the annotated name cards in alphabetical order. Within two years I had a file of several thousand names—each one carrying a thumbnail sketch of the individual and a dated notation of each contact by letter or in person that I had with that individual.

That growing box of cards was always on the front seat of my car as I traveled from town to town, and each day I added another batch of cards based on the people I had visited during the day. I learned to drive to a town with one eye on the road and another eye on the names of the people in the card file that I had already met in the community I was about to enter. People were amazed when I saw them again and was able to inquire about daughter Mary at Augustana, or son David at Fort Leonard Wood, or tell them how much I appreciated their helping out at the Democratic dinner the previous summer. They were impressed that I cared enough to remember— and I did care: it is no small task to write a longhand description of every person one meets. No computer can ever duplicate the human feeling that comes to a politician when he makes his own notes and maintains his own files and uses them with the care I gave to that old shoe box. I eventually purchased a double-drawer metal file case, and then a larger one, until my 3 × 5 cards reached a total of more than 40,000 names.

These names enabled me to function with much greater effectiveness as the party's chief organizer. When we needed funds, I could make a direct-mail appeal that more than paid for the postage. When there were county meetings or fund-raising dinners, I could recruit promoters or ticket sellers from my list. In securing candidates for state and local office, I studied the notations on my cards.

Soon after beginning as executive secretary, I became aware that if I were to receive my salary and travel expenses, I would have to raise these funds myself. The party had little income and, indeed, was in debt. This gave birth to a second idea—the Century Club. The purpose was to get 100 people to pledge $100 annually, for a total budget of $10,000 to cover my salary and travel. Within a short time I was able to secure 130 participants in the Century Club, and from that day to the present, the South Dakota Democratic organization has been sustained in considerable part by the $100-a-year contributors. But we have continued to rely on our county dinners of $5 and $10, plus our $15 or $25 state dinners, to raise additional funds. These techniques freed the South Dakota Democratic Party of special-interest contributors. There have been no scandals or questionable deals that I am aware of in the last quarter of a century in our state party finances. Rank-and-file Democrats rightfully feel that the party belongs to them, and it is fiscally strong.

But the key to building an effective political structure in South Dakota was personal association with as many people as my strength and tenacity would permit. I wore out three secondhand cars in those organizational travels of 1953 through 1955. I shook hands at hundreds of receptions, courthouse meetings, visits to private homes, farms, shops and in the streets. Hundreds of phone calls were made that I dialed personally. Tens of thousands of letters, mimeographed or individually written, flowed over the state from my tiny office in Mitchell or from hotel rooms and private homes in all parts of South Dakota. Always I was looking for good county and precinct workers, recruiting candidates for office, raising money, discussing issues and "firing up the troops."

On the average of once a week I constructed a press release which I delivered to the news services with a request that one or more of them file it with the Associated or United Press. Sometimes the releases were critical of the incumbent Republicans; sometimes they were positive statements of Democratic policy.

The first test of these efforts came in November of 1954 when we elected six Democrats to the state Senate and eighteen to the House. The score thus shifted from 108 Republican legislators against 2 Democrats to 86 Republicans opposed to 24 Democrats—not a spectacular gain, but an impressive one. What may have been more impressive was the generally high quality of the twenty-four elected Democratic legislators. They lost no time in charting a vigorous, positive course at Pierre, and I worked closely with them to develop a solid legislative record.

We also scored impressive gains in the courthouses of the state. Kenneth Holum, a Groton farmer, ran a strong campaign for the U.S. Senate against Karl Mundt, while Sioux Falls lawyer Francis Dunn was doing well against Congressman Harold Lovre. They lost, but they won the respect of many South Dakotans.

We were hurt that year by one of those inexplicable quirks of politics that develop in virtually every campaign. Ward Clark believed that the most important office for us to win was the governorship, and he gave his close personal attention to recruiting the strongest possible candidate. The man he settled on was E. F. McKellips, a highly respected country banker from Alcester. McKellips was one of the few bankers in the state who had insisted on paying back his depositors after the bank closings of the 1920s. He used his bank and his knowledge to finance hundreds of farmers, merchants and homeowners in his trade territory. He was a man of impeccable character with moderately liberal views. Ward was overjoyed when McKellips finally consented to be our gubernatorial candidate, and we promptly scheduled a large rally in Mitchell, where he could formally announce his candidacy.

The Republicans were preparing to nominate as their gubernatorial candidate, Joe Foss, a Medal of Honor winner and the nation's top flying ace in the Pacific during World War II. The odds were against us, but both Ward and I believed that McKellips' vastly superior business and professional experience and his thorough knowledge of agriculture might produce an upset over Foss.

But to our amazement, at the banquet for the McKellips announcement an unknown Chamberlain rancher by the name of Ed Martin circulated the word that he was going to challenge the "bosses"—McGovern and Clark—and seek the Democratic gubernatorial nomination. We greeted this development with amused and somewhat puzzled tolerance. No one had ever heard Ed deliver a public utterance, and he was not known to the party leaders or the public at large. Indeed, the first reaction was one of disbelief that anyone would be sufficiently interested in a Democratic nomination to volunteer for it without being cajoled for days, as we had done with McKellips.

But for reasons that were never clear to me, my old friend Ez Brady was persuaded to assist Ed in writing some press releases and running some paid ads in the newspaper. McKellips ignored this seemingly improbable opponent, confident that the nomination would come to him in the June primary by an overwhelming margin. But that was not to be; Ed Martin won handily and "bosses" Clark and McGovern were soundly rebuffed. That was the first painful lesson to me that endorsements and official backing can sometimes be a handicap to a candidate rather than an asset.

Ward Clark was staggered by this unexpected turn of events, but he gamely did his best to help Martin in what proved to be a totally ineffective campaign against Foss. Ed was so reluctant to speak publicly that he would regularly cancel out on meetings at the last moment, leaving Ward or me to take his place. His longest speech of the campaign was under two minutes and only the closest listener could hear what he was saying. So having defeated the two dangerous party bosses, he was overwhelmed by Joe Foss in November.

Ward always saw the humor in situations of this kind, and he was a joyful companion on those occasions when we traveled together. I shall never forget a ten-day tour we made in his big Packard that took us through a series of area meetings in the western half of the state during early 1954. If there is any part of America that has any higher percentage of colorful characters than western South Dakota, I have not visited it. This area, which was once the territory of Wild Bill Hickock, Calamity Jane, Poker Alice, General George Custer, and the Wounded Knee massacre, is the home of rugged individualism. It is difficult to comprehend the sharp cultural differences in that half of the state west of the Missouri River compared to "East River people." When a South Dakotan from the Black Hills, the Badlands or the short-grass country anywhere west of the Missouri speaks of "an East River boy," he does it with a disdain that one might more likely reserve for a suspected visitor from a distant foreign land. Nevertheless, as an "East River boy" I have always loved the people and the land of western South Dakota, especially the Black Hills.

During the 1954 "western safari," as Ward dubbed it, after a brief courthouse forum we would adjourn each night with one or more local characters to talk and drink and eat and laugh until the early hours of the morning. The political yarns, the local gossip, the regional folklore, the hopes, the hates and the anxieties that flowed through these nocturnal sessions deepened my sense of compassion and warmth for these earthy people. No one is qualified for high office until he has tasted the frustrations, the sorrows, the joys, the hopes, the fears, the weaknesses and the strengths of his fellow humans. Politics divorced from basic human experience is not a dependable or satisfying exercise.

One evening when Ward and I arrived at the Peacock Café in Winner for a three-county meeting, I noticed a copy of the Winner *Advocate* carrying a picture of Karl Mundt and the announcement that he would preach the Sunday sermon at the local Methodist Church. As the owner of an Irish name, I was believed by many South Dakotans to be a devout Catholic—certainly not the son of a Methodist clergyman. But turning to a local Democratic woman who was both an ardent Democrat and a confirmed Catholic, I said, "Mrs. Maloney, it strikes me as bad taste for the Methodists to have Karl Mundt occupying the pulpit on Sunday when he is running for re-election."

"Mac," she said, "those damn Methodists will do anything."

Herb Clarkson, a banker in Buffalo, South Dakota, whom we called on several days later, provided us with conversation I shall remember the rest of my life. A recent news item had reported that Herb had given $50,000 to South Dakota State College. Beyond this, we knew that he owned a string of banks in South Dakota, North Dakota and Montana, also that he was an elderly bachelor who had saved and profitably invested ninety-nine cents out of every dollar he had earned for sixty years. We had no doubt that he had amassed millions of dollars—although neither one of us had ever met him.

As we drove from Belle Fourche to Buffalo, Ward mused over the possibility that with skillful persuasion we might talk Clarkson into financing the entire Democratic Party for the next couple of years. If he would give $50,000 to a single college, why not at least that much to the South Dakota Democratic Party? I thought the question was reasonable.

So we headed for Herb's hotel in Buffalo about five o'clock prior to an evening rally with visions of a major victory for Democracy. In the lobby we found a drunken cowboy lying on a battered sofa, beer cans on the floor below his dangling arm. Across the shabby lobby sat an old man in a rumpled suit that did not quite cover his dumpy torso. His eyes were only partly open, but Ward asked him if he knew Herb Clarkson. "I think so," he said.

"Can you give us directions?" Ward inquired.

"You're looking at him," said the ancient figure in the rocking chair.

Herb Clarkson, a younger rancher and his semipermanent female house guest were the only Democrats who appeared at our rally that night. So after an abbreviated address by Ward, we adjourned to the lobby of Clarkson's hotel at about eight-thirty or nine. And until four-thirty the following morning, Herb regaled us with some of the lustiest, most imaginative discourse I have ever experienced. He held forth with genuine enthusiasm over such diverse subjects as the philosophy of Plato, the advantages of a weekend in Chicago with a fancy call girl at the Palmer House as compared to an endless marriage in South Dakota, the naïveté of the Midwestern small business-man who imagines that the same conservative politicians who serve Chase Manhattan are interested in his welfare. These topics, punctuated eloquently with a stream of four-letter words and buttressed by quotations from Voltaire, Jefferson, Victor Hugo, Ben Franklin, Mark Twain, Jesus and Clarence Darrow, kept Ward and me laughing until our stomach muscles literally ached.

I decided that we were getting along so well with Herb that I would gingerly suggest he make a contribution to Dakota Wesleyan —in view of his $50,000 to South Dakota State. "I wouldn't give that damn school a dollar," he said. "I don't like the church connection. When I was at the Louvre in Paris, I found out that the damn Chris-

tians had hacked the testicles off the statues. It's a wonder the bas-
tards didn't hack off the tits too."

Herb Clarkson didn't like popes, or Christians, or churches, or any
of their works. So I dropped the subject of Dakota Wesleyan and let
Ward continue the night-long preparation for a big Democratic "hit"
at the appropriate time. I admired Ward's restraint when he told
Herb at four-thirty that we should go to bed, but that we would like
to take him to breakfast after we all had had some rest. Herb readily
agreed and suggested that we meet across the street at the town café
at seven o'clock. It was near the end of this breakfast that Ward
gracefully went into his pitch for financial support of the Democratic
Party. Herb listened for a few minutes and then said, "You don't
need to sell me. I'm a good Democrat." He then pulled out his
checkbook and with visions of $25,000 or $50,000 in our heads, we
accepted his check for $25.

I have never had any confidence in my fund-raising ability from
that day to this. But as the holder of a Ph.D., I learned a lot about
European philosophy and art from that old South Dakota banker
with his elementary-education certificate. Furthermore, we had no
one to blame but ourselves for believing that a man who was too tight
to have a wife would give non-tax-free money to a losing political
party—and especially to a party headed by two men foolish enough
to devote an entire night to one cynical voter in Buffalo, South
Dakota. Any politician who spends more than thirty minutes trying
to get either a single contribution or a single endorsement deserves
to lose—and probably will.

After our all-night vigil with Herb Clarkson, Ward and I set out for
Mobridge, with brief stops at Lemmon, McIntosh, McLaughlin and
Timber Lake. It was a bitterly cold night when we arrived in Mo-
bridge and we were hungry after a day of receptions fueled only by
coffee and doughnuts. Ward had told me of the delicious steaks at
Serena's Café and I could scarcely wait to get out of the car at the
Brown Hotel and head for Serena's. But we had not reckoned with
Carl Schneider, who was waiting for us in the lobby of the Brown.
Carl insisted first on giving us a personal tour of the suite he had
ordered for us. When Ward expressed amazement over its size, Carl
proudly announced, "Not a damn bit too good for the heads of our
party." But when we told him we were planning to have dinner at
Serena's, he said, "To hell with that. They're the toughest Republicans in town. We'll go to the coffee shop. It's run by a good Democratic railroad man." No Democrat should even walk through
Serena's, he said. Whereupon he guided us to a tiny restaurant that
served us a greasy plate of hamburger and fried potatoes. As Carl

said, "The food's not much, but it's cooked by a damn good Democrat."

Carl then entertained us for most of the rest of the night with stories, philosophy and fervent advice on how to whip the Republicans. His chief interest in life was the poker games that sometimes ran nonstop for more than twenty-four hours—sometimes on his railway run from Aberdeen to Miles City, sometimes in hotel rooms or bars, any place where a half-dozen old cronies could assemble undisturbed.

Carl had two sons, one a high-strung, poker-playing hellion like his dad; the other a conscientious student at the University of Wisconsin. The first son had committed suicide while on a trip to Spain. Carl told us that this boy could draw to an inside straight better than any poker player he ever knew. As for the other boy, "That kid couldn't see a jack rabbit run across the table. He couldn't get his hands out of a flour barrel." He got A's at Wisconsin, but he had "one hell of a lot to learn." When Carl was visiting his son in Wisconsin he was horrified to see him reading the Chicago *Tribune* instead of the Madison *Capital-Times*. "I grabbed that Republican rag and threw it out the window," he said. "I told that kid to either start reading the *'Cap'* *Times* or else get the hell out of college. I'm not working on the railroad to educate some fool who ends up reading the *Tribune,"* he snorted.

It was good for morale to visit the old-line Democrats up and down the main streets and across the farming and ranch country of South Dakota. Frequently one of them would insist with fierce pride that he was the only Democrat in town. It was almost as though he wanted to keep it that way. That splendid loneliness—the image of a single brave man standing against the hordes of Republicanism— was a posture difficult to share with others.

But I knew that political victory in South Dakota depended on appealing beyond the Democratic registration lists to those considerable numbers of South Dakotans who were telling me, "I'm a registered Republican, but I vote for the man. I'm no straight-ticket voter." Many South Dakotans prided themselves on their independence without regard to party appeals. Also, there were younger citizens coming of voting age and still others who had never been sufficiently interested to vote for either party. I decided, after concentrating on the Democrats and party organizational efforts from June 1953 through 1954, that I would shift my attention to capturing the interest and possible support of open-minded Republicans and independents. Thus, in 1955 I began to speak to the Kiwanis, Rotary,

Lions and Sertoma clubs; to the chambers of commerce; to the REA annual meetings, to teachers conventions, to church meetings, and to countless high school and college convocations. I always reserved time at the end of my remarks to field questions from the audience. I frequently issued a carefully worded press release on themes that would not arouse strong partisan reactions.

One weekend I sat down in the small den I had fashioned in the basement of my home at 300 West 4th Avenue in Mitchell and wrote a speech for these nonpartisan audiences that I used with minor modifications countless times. The speech carried three basic themes: first, a simply stated argument that politics is a crucial influence in our society that we neglect only at our peril. From constantly testing this theme I knew I could convince most listeners that there was no escape from the impact of politics—that it touched their businesses, their farm income, their tax returns, their schools, their roadways, and even the question of whether their sons would live or die in peace or war. Second, I pointed out that politics was neither better nor worse than the quality of the voters who participated and the politicians they chose to represent them. I left little doubt that I viewed myself as among the better breed of politicians who deserved their attention, if not their support. Third, I contended that South Dakota was handicapped by a one-party monopoly. Just as we did not want a single business giant to stifle commercial competition on main street or a gigantic corporate agriculture to destroy the independent farmer, neither could we afford the dead hand of political monopoly. Both Democrats and Republicans would function more in the public interest if neither could win too easily.

All across South Dakota I saw heads begin to nod slightly in approval of what I was saying. Soon a few favorable editorials appeared in widely scattered weekly and daily papers.

Beyond this, the South Dakota Republicans were beginning to experience the burdens of federal power. With Democratic Administrations in Washington from 1933 until 1953, South Dakota's Republican congressional delegation could blame all national problems on Franklin Roosevelt or Harry Truman, while the patronage jobs were dispensed through a handful of state Democratic party officers. But with the election of the Eisenhower-Nixon ticket in 1952, the Republican congressmen took on two new political difficulties: (1) they had to decide which South Dakota Republicans, starved of federal patronage for two decades, should receive the limited number of postal and other federal appointments, and (2) they had to defend the policies of their new Republican Administration.

Nothing in politics produces such bitter long-term animosities as a community dispute over which of the seven or eight applicants for the local postmastership is most deserving. A loyal party member deprived of such a prized plum will sometimes carry a grudge to his grave against the harassed congressman or county chairman who has recommended someone else for the appointment. Entire county political organizations have been shattered beyond repair by a single patronage battle. Party members may argue with mutual respect their differing viewpoints on monetary policy, agricultural price supports, social security or American policy toward China. But there is seldom any margin of tolerance or forgiveness in a dispute as to who most deserves to be mail carrier, postmaster, marshal or federal judge. I began to encounter bitterly disillusioned lifelong Republicans who were ready even to accept the despised Democrats rather than support the hapless Republican congressman who had "doublecrossed" them on the post office. I was reminded of the late Senator George Norris' weary observation: "I never appointed a man to office without creating nine enemies and one political ingrate."

But of greater concern to rank-and-file South Dakota Republicans were the unpopular policies of Eisenhower's Secretary of Agriculture, Ezra Taft Benson. Almost from the outset of the new Administration in 1953, Benson began to enunciate agricultural policies that worried and then angered Midwestern farmers. A devout Mormon Apostle from Utah, Benson believed that man should earn his bread by the sweat of his brow, that high farm price supports would disrupt free enterprise and price American products out of foreign markets. He advocated a system of "flexible price supports" designed to reduce the federal role in the agricultural economy and to leave the farmer largely at the mercy of a "free market." In a short time, farm prices started downward and government-held stocks of grain began to rise as farmers opted to leave their grain in government hands rather than pay off their price-support loans. Thus Benson presided over lowering farm prices and increasing farm surpluses—a highly unpopular prospect from the viewpoint of farmers.

The Democrats of the Midwest had their targets: Ezra Taft Benson and declining farm income. At the same time Secretary of the Treasury George Humphrey was encouraging higher interest rates, and Charles Wilson, the Secretary of Defense, was expounding the doctrine "What's good for General Motors is good for the country." Such precepts stirred latent populist sentiments in South Dakota and elsewhere, and I, along with other Democrats, began to sound the alarm.

Walt Ryan, a grizzled old Democrat from Salem, said to me that you can always tell when the Republicans are in power: "Interest rates go up and corn prices come down." I quoted Walt's wisdom on platforms all across South Dakota.

And I began to sound a new theme that has been basic to my entire public career. Why not utilize the farm surpluses that were piling up in government granaries to feed the hungry at home and abroad? "There are two surpluses in the world," I said. "The surplus of grain and milk and edible oils, and the surplus of empty stomachs." We should start to see our agricultural abundance not as a curse, not as an excuse to punish the farmer by reducing his prices, but as a constructive resource that can reduce human hunger, conflict and despair.

I began to sense that it might be possible for a well-organized Democratic candidate to win a major election. I had little desire to be governor of the state, since my interests were primarily centered on national and international issues. Francis Case, the incumbent U.S. senator, was up for election in 1956, but I felt that Ken Holum had first claim on that contest, since he had waged a good campaign against Karl Mundt in 1954. So I decided to run for Congress against Harold Lovre, a three-term, popular representative from Watertown. Lovre had previously served as Republican state chairman, and in 1954 he led the Republican ticket in his winning percentage. He had, along with Senator Karl Mundt, voted against the policies of Agriculture Secretary Benson, but he was too loyal a Republican to break squarely with Benson in a public repudiation.

I knew that the race against Lovre was uphill, but near the end of 1955 I quietly resigned as the party's executive secretary, and on January 4, 1956, announced my candidacy for Congress on a bitterly cold, snow-filled day on the campus of Southern State College at Springfield.

My next step was to study my name files until I had identified a potential working chairman and chairwoman in every town in the First Congressional District. I wrote all of these persons, asking them to name a "McGovern for Congress" committee in their town and the surrounding rural townships. I enclosed a mimeographed sheet of suggested ways that volunteer recruits could help me: talking to their friends about my candidacy, writing letters to the newspapers about the issues of the campaign, raising money, distributing literature, canvassing and registering voters. I also sent each chairperson and volunteer a supply of pocket-size booklets, each one containing ten membership cards in "The McGovern for Congress Club" with an attached stub for the person's name, address and the amount of money contributed. Largely from $1, $5 and $25 contributions, we raised and spent $14,000 in that campaign. Bob Verschoor, a Mitchell Chevrolet dealer, served as campaign finance director—a role he was to handle in all of my subsequent campaigns. There was no paid staff except Pat Buchanan, a strong-willed, capable young journalist and housewife who volunteered her services as a secretary, and George

Cunningham, a University of South Dakota law student who volunteered both his car and his time as a driver. Pat was the wife of a *Daily Republic* reporter who later went to Florida to work for the Miami *Herald*. George has been my top Senate aide and close political adviser for many years.

The campaign schedule of 1956 was a tireless one which attempted to utilize every minute to reach the voters. A typical day would include an early-morning visit to a meat-packing plant where I could shake hands and sometimes visit briefly with every worker. Each person would be handed a small card carrying my name, photograph and the basic principles of my public philosophy. I might then stop for breakfast at a popular restaurant where, before sitting down, I would introduce myself to everyone in the kitchen, the waitresses, the cashier, the manager and all the customers. If additional customers came in while I was eating, I met them before leaving the restaurant. Then I would head for the next town and spend an hour or two going from shop to shop meeting the owners, the clerks and the customers. Perhaps at ten forty-five or eleven I would, after an earlier phone call to the school superintendent, briefly speak to the students and faculty at the high school and then field their questions until time for their noon break. At this point I would either have lunch at the town's most popular restaurant or address the local Rotary, Kiwanis or Lions club.

After lunch I moved on to the next town, or possibly two or three towns depending on their population, to repeat the same process in the afternoon. If I learned of a livestock auction sale, I would stop there to meet the cattle buyers and sellers. Frequently the auctioneer recognized me in the sale-barn audience and would call on me to greet the crowd. In the evening I might be slated for a Democratic dinner, but if not, I looked for a church supper or a bowling alley or a town where the stores were open so I could continue meeting people. There were always a few bars open in the evening where a campaigner could find knots of voters. Bars were sometimes poor places to campaign because there was always the possibility that some character with a big mouth and a befuddled brain would seize on the opportunity to lecture me on what was wrong with the country and how it could be corrected. I have always found drunks hard to take, and especially the ones who get mean or loud. On the other hand, I doubtless collected hundreds of votes from people glowing pleasantly in bars who might not have been as friendly to me if I had met them at a formal meeting in the presence of their Republican friends.

Moving around the state, I always made an effort to call at every newspaper and radio station. Frequently these visits produced a news photo, a printed interview, an appearance on a radio call-in show—all free publicity. As the campaign progressed I equipped my little blue Ford with a portable loudspeaker. Thus armed, I would sometimes stop at the main intersection and address a few remarks curbside to whatever size group of listeners I could bring together. There were days when I spoke in as many as eight or ten towns in a single day.

I was seldom more than a few dollars ahead in the campaign budget. At times I or someone traveling with me, usually George Cunningham, would go up and down the streets selling large campaign buttons for a dollar apiece so that we could get enough money for a tank of gas or a hotel room at the next town. One night George and I were horrified to learn that I had lost a $20 bill that had slipped through a hole in my pocket. We went back to the picnic grounds on Farm Island near Pierre where I believed the bill had been dropped; then, on our hands and knees, equipped with a flashlight, we spent a fruitless hour searching for the missing $20. Fortunately my friend Herb Thomas of Pierre invited me to stay at his apartment that night, and the next morning as I was leaving, he insisted on giving me $20. Men like Herb Thomas and his wife, Freda, were great morale builders in a campaign. They had political courage, but they also had a sense of humor and intelligence that made the whole political effort enjoyable and interesting.

No candidate can maintain his morale without drawing on the energy, laughter and counsel from time to time of an outspoken supporter such as Herb Thomas of Pierre, Si Rogers of Sioux Falls, Margaret Reetz of Webster, Jessie Sanders of Rapid City, and my great old friend at the Lawler Café—Margaret Conlon. Margaret presided over the Lawler Café from early morning until late in the evening. She was a marvelous, indomitable woman who cheered every traveling salesman, every politician and every patron who needed his spirits lifted. She was an ardent Democrat and a devout Catholic, but mostly she was a strong human being with a warm heart and a gay tongue, and she was filled with the enthusiasm of life. Sometimes I dragged into the Lawler Café about closing time, tired and battered, wondering why I could have been so foolish as to give up a comfortable professorship for the exhausting demands of a race for Congress against an incumbent Republican in a Republican state. But Margaret would slide into the booth next to me and sometimes, squeezing my hand, she would say, "You know, George, people are telling me that George McGovern is going to be elected. That's right. George McGovern is going to be elected. Leo Harmon is a Republican and he just said, 'You know, George may just get himself elected.' Slick Draisey, Bruce Stoner and Harry Goldblatt are saying the same thing. Yes sir, that's what Leo and the boys are saying, George McGovern is going to get elected." Suddenly the fatigue and the discouragement would begin to lift, a bowl of soup would appear, Margaret would throw the check into a wastebasket, and I would leave the Lawler convinced that nobody could beat me. I do not know what heaven is like, but I know that wherever saints go after they die, Margaret Conlon has been assigned one of the better dwellings.

I decided in early summer after a long conversation with Mike Schirmer, a Sioux Falls real estate man who was my campaign chairman, that in addition to the long hours of personal campaigning, I would use three other devices in the campaign: (1) one hundred large billboards placed strategically around the state to familiarize people with my name and face; (2) three fifteen-minute TV addresses scheduled during the summer before any other candidates were on the screen, plus six five-minute weekly telecasts during the last six weeks of the campaign; and (3) a letter-size, attractive brochure that could be mailed to every home ten days before the election. These efforts worked beautifully. The timing, the coverage, the impact could scarcely have been better.

In early September a poll commissioned by three daily newspapers showed that I was within a few percentage points of my highly favored opponent. Although he was a seasoned politician, he panicked. He and his aides organized a political front of prominent Republican business and professional men, entitled "The Committee Against the Admission of Red China to the United Nations." Since the collapse of Chiang Kai-shek and the triumph of Mao in 1949 I had been advocating that we should recognize the new Chinese government as the actual government of China. But the new committee, taking my recommendations out of context, constructed a series of full-page ads suggesting that I was, if not a Communist, at least an apologist for the Communists.

These bold-faced ads worried me because I was not sure how the conservative South Dakota electorate would react to them. So I purchased ten minutes' time on television and in a performance which was as emotion-packed as I could make it, I accused Lovre of resorting to the tactics of fear and smear. Referring to my record as a bomber pilot decorated with the Distinguished Flying Cross, I blasted the opposition strategy as cowardly and devious. I went after some of the signers of the ads by name with such telling effect that the next day one of them nervously called me to explain that he had not really intended to hurt my feelings.

But the campaign broke wide open when the highly respected,

well-known Republican clergyman Reverend Frank Lochridge of the Mitchell Methodist Church wrote a letter to the editor of the *Daily Republic* indignantly repudiating the tactics being employed by my opponent. The letter was quickly picked up by the Associated Press and was carried on the front pages of most of the state's daily newspapers. A few days later a prominent signer of the controversial ads, John Ehrstrom of Watertown, went to the press with a public apology for his role in the ad campaign. I could feel the reaction against Lovre setting in across the state as people rejected what they perceived to be an unfair attack.

It was at this stage that we mailed our brochure to every home in eastern South Dakota. It was an affirmative combination of human-interest photos, complimentary statements from respected editors and other recognized personalities, and selected phrases from my speeches and writings. That carefully composed brochure clinched the election. Perhaps we exaggerated the impact of the desperation charges against me. Some indication of this came one afternoon late in the campaign when I stopped at a café in Lennox, where a group of farmers were sitting at the coffee counter. I noticed that one of them was idly looking at one of the full-page ads with my name in four-inch letters and the scurrilous innuendoes against my patriotism printed in smaller type. "I'm George McGovern," I said to the farmer. "What do you think of that ad?" "Oh, hell, I don't know," he drawled. "I just guessed you were some kind of a big shot with an advertisement that big for ya."

Two sad events marred the 1956 campaign. Eleanor's father died suddenly of a heart attack as I was about to do a live telecast in Sioux Falls. I received the news by telephone just a minute or two before I was to go in front of the cameras—with Eleanor and the family at a nearby restaurant planning to meet me afterward. I went ahead with the telecast, picked up my family and then once we were on the road to Mitchell, I told Eleanor of her father's death. She wept quietly as we drove down the darkened highway. Earl Stegeberg, fifty-six, who would have been particularly proud to see me elected to the Congress, never lived to enjoy that experience. But an even sadder death had occurred in Eleanor's family a few weeks earlier. Bob Peterson, a college basketball star and a superb human being who was married to Eleanor's younger sister, Phyllis, died of a ruptured aorta at the Cleveland Clinic following radical surgery to correct a long and baffling illness. He was twenty-nine.

We won the election with a comfortable margin of 11,000 votes. Ken Holum lost his second race, but winner Senator Francis Case's margin was only about 4,000 votes. Ralph Herseth lost a close gubernatorial race to Joe Foss. But in the legislature and the courthouses,

Democrats scored substantial gains and the morale of the party was on the upswing.

In late December, Eleanor and I loaded our five children into a station wagon and headed for Washington. We had received a letter from Hubert and Muriel Humphrey stating that the house next door to them in Chevy Chase, Maryland, was for sale. So arriving in Washington on December 22, we drove past the Humphrey home. It was a dark night and it was snowing. We could see the Humphreys through a large bay window near their Christmas tree. We did not disturb them, but we did look carefully at the darkened, empty house next door. A week later—after Christmas in a vacant apartment at Glass Manor in Southeast Washington located for us by our friend Walt Kreimann—we bought the house on Coquelin Terrace next door to the Humphreys. That house was to be our home in Washington for the next twelve years. We were constantly adding on to it and making it more livable. Eleanor developed a flower-laden backyard that was a place of remarkable beauty. We finally sold the house in 1969 and moved into Washington. But to this day I cannot think about that home on Coquelin Terrace without a tinge of sadness and regret that we are no longer living there. It is adventuresome to buy a new house, but no one should do it without first considering the emotional attachments that have to be broken with the old house. It can be an unexpectedly disconcerting and depressing experience. I was able to withstand it because of the joy our new house brought to Eleanor. But our children have never quite forgiven us for surrendering the home where they spent most of their childhood years.

When we moved into the house on Coquelin, Ann, our eldest daughter, was eleven years old—a pretty, intelligent girl whose ardent champion had been her grandfather. His death a few months earlier was a painful loss to Ann. All children need someone who is unequivocally committed to them, especially when they are experiencing times of difficulty. Earl Stegeberg adored Ann. He felt a special claim on her love, since he was there when she was born while I was overseas in combat. Ann and Earl could carry on a relaxed dialogue for hours, not as an older man speaking down to a small girl, but as two human beings communicating as equals. I think it is much harder for parents and their children to establish such a relationship. Parent-child relations are complicated by the problems of discipline, financial anxieties, concern over the child's development, marital stresses, and in my case the clash between a demanding career and the emotional needs of my children. I let Ann slip from young girlhood to adulthood without realizing the swift, turbulent changes in her life. The hours of relaxation at home for a new congressman are limited, and it was easier to romp with the younger members of the family than to engage in the rambling dialogues Ann once enjoyed with her grandfather. We had some pleasant times together, but all too quickly she was no longer a child. She was in high school, off with her boyfriends, and then college and marriage. She now has two little sons and is a teacher at the Washington Psychiatric Institute.

In retrospect, I wish that on more nights and weekends I had left my briefcase at the office and given time to fun and conversation with my children. Some Saturdays, but not often enough, I would take one or more of them with me for a couple of hours of "clean-up" work at the office and then perhaps a relaxed lunch or a movie or a stroll. I also wish I had taught them to play tennis or to ski or to develop other recreational habits that would have enriched both their lives and mine.

Susan was ten when we moved to Washington. She was quieter than Ann, but of equal intelligence and charm. She had a superior capacity to concentrate on academic work both at home and in the classroom that Ann may have resented. For various reasons, there was sometimes tension between Sue and Ann. They had played together as little girls, incessantly and joyfully, but the sibling rivalries were never far below the surface and they became more obvious in later years.

As an infant Susan was an unusually happy, even-tempered child. She continued as a growing girl to make few demands on us or on her brother and sisters. But she keenly felt the harsh words of others and she needed more perceptive love and attention than she received. There should have been more times when Sue and I went for long walks in the park, or sat and talked in her room about her concerns and interests. She needed to know more about me as a human being, and I needed to listen more in every way to that lovely girl with the large, sometimes hurt eyes that was growing up while I was engrossed in my career. Sue is now married to Jim Rowen, the deputy mayor of Madison, Wisconsin. Like Ann, she is the mother of two little sons.

Our family sometimes went to the park for picnics, or to a movie, or for breakfast or dinner at a nearby restaurant. Sometimes we took short vacation trips together. But there should be occasions in every child's life when he or she is alone under pleasant, unhurried circumstances with a single parent.

Teresa, age seven, was the "character" in the family. She loved to clown, to dress up like a nurse or a mother or an actress. Whereas Ann and Sue were only separated by a single year, Terry was more than three years younger than Sue. Too young for their concerns and resented because of her attention-getting antics, she made her own friends in the neighborhood and she always seemed to be in charge. I had a special joshing relationship with Terry, whom I called "the Bear." When I awakened her for school in the morning, I did it by gently tapping the end of her nose, sometimes after hanging an old teddy bear or a cloth frog just above her head. I think she loved it. But Terry also needed more insight than we perhaps were able to give her. For reasons too diverse and complex for anyone to comprehend fully, she was later to develop a serious emotional depression that she has overcome only by long and persistent effort. A recent graduate of the University of South Dakota with a major in psychology, she is now a mature, thoughtful, endearing personality.

Steve was born during the summer of 1952 in the middle of the presidential campaign. He was named Steven—after Adlai Stevenson. Our only boy, Steve early developed his own play patterns. He had his room filled with toy soldiers, trucks, cars and construction sets. Before starting school, he was fascinated with books about animals, an interest which was soon replaced with a curiosity about the Civil War. I was amazed to hear him listing the names and detailed movements of Union and Southern generals in various battles. He could play alone in his room for hours in perfect contentment.

Each night when I returned from the office, we went through a joyful ritual of Steve running to meet me at the car. Once inside the house, he would climb to the third or fourth step of the stairway and jump into my arms.

I have always thought that Steve was a victim of the wrong kind of school system. The quick, active intelligence and imagination that were so obvious in him as a small boy seemed to be blunted almost from the day he entered school. A shy, quiet, kindly boy, he did not respond well to formalized education and would probably have flourished under the influence of a good tutor. Without wanting to denigrate the public-school system, I have to say that it was quite obviously not suited to his needs. I wonder how many intellectually curious, bright young children are dulled and bored by routine classroom instruction. While Steve may not have received as much of my time as he needed for counseling, recreation and conversation, he always had an abundance of neighborhood friends. Perhaps more than any of our other children, he has been influenced by his friends more than by the family.

It is especially hard on a son to have a well-known father. Steve's relationship to me has been an ambivalent, difficult one. Intellectually he is proud of my political career—especially my nomination as a presidential candidate—but emotionally he would probably have preferred a mechanic or a forest ranger as a father. Steve was terrified at the thought that we might actually move into the White House. To him, that would have been the final, embarrassing end to years of painful experiences over the prominence and sometimes controversial stands of his dad. He would have vastly preferred a more anonymous, private life away from the public limelight for our family. When he learned that I was going to give his high school graduation address, he stayed away from gym class enough times to fail that course so that he would be one credit short of graduation, thus being able to avoid the agony of sitting on the stage at Cole Field House with his classmates while thousands of people watched him as his father delivered the commencement address.

Mary, born in the summer of 1955, was only a year and a half old when we arrived in Washington. She therefore experienced none of the difficulties of changing schools or neighborhoods that faced the other children. She was a happy, delightful baby and little girl. Her older sisters saw no threat in this tiny, laughing little creature. And Steve did not come to the battle stage with her until she was old enough to needle him and crowd him for attention. I usually had a special pet name for each of the children at some stage of their lives. Mary was "the Goofy Gopher," Steve was "Burr Head," Terry was "the Bear," Sue was "Jiglingheimer" and Ann was "Annikens." I never knew whether they liked those names, but they created an affectionate, playful spirit that made me comfortable and relaxed with my children. Mary was and is a sentimental girl. She loved getting the entire family ready for Christmas, writing little notes to people, and being treated like a princess. She has a dramatic, poetic sense that manifested itself from the beginning. She was always arranging elaborate costumes for herself and her friends, staging little plays or writing her thoughts in poetry and essays. Frequently her writings demonstrated remarkable insight into the concerns, the sorrows and the hopes of the people around her. One day, months after John Kennedy was killed, I noticed a slightly loose tile in our bathroom floor. When I picked at it, it came up and underneath was a faded note written by Mary: "I prayed that Kennedy would live, but I failed."

As I write these recollections of my dear children—of the joy, the tears, the pride, the anxiety and the hopes that they have brought to me, I recall the lines of Alexander Laing:

> What else then?
> If our love won't see them through,
> Nothing can.
> We wait knowing time's only waste
> Is want of love.

5

HOUSE
AND SENATE
1956-1968

In early January 1957 I moved into two large empty
rooms in Suite 120 of the Old House Office Building. Three friends
had come with me from South Dakota to work in the new congressional office—Bob Nelson, Jay Larsen and Marie Clark. None of us
had more than a textbook knowledge of the Congress. I spent most
of the first two or three days talking to experienced congressmen
about how to do the job.

Several large boxes of unanswered letters had accumulated since
the election, and additional mail was pouring in. We faced a seemingly endless flood of phone calls and requests for appointments.
Suddenly the first delegation of visitors from South Dakota arrived
to attend a U.S. Chamber of Commerce meeting. After greeting
them among the piles of unpacked boxes in my office, I invited them
to walk over to the Capitol with me for lunch. Somehow I made a
wrong turn in the subterranean passages that link the office buildings
with the Capitol. Trying to cover my mistake, I kept taking turns and
twists until we ended in the boiler rooms. After asking direction from
a Capitol maintenance man, we finally found the House side of the
Capitol, but it was two wrong turns later before we located the
dining room. My guess was that the visiting Chamber of Commerce
types had voted against me—and that they left Washington fully
vindicated in their judgment.

On my third or fourth day in office I learned from a friendly congressman that there was a superb secretary, Frances Donovan, with several years' experience on the House Ways and Means Committee staff who might be interested in changing jobs. After a telephone call from me she arrived at my office for an interview. I wanted desperately to hire her, but she already worked at a salary level that would have strained our limited budget. She told me, however, that her younger sister, Patricia, who was working for Congressman Harold Donohue of Worcester, Massachusetts, might be interested. I was too worried about the paperwork chaos of my own office to have any qualms about raiding another office, so I asked Frances to tell her sister to stop by after working hours that evening. I hired Pat Donovan on the spot. She has been with me ever since. Pat has had a rare ability not only to take dictation and type with incredible speed and accuracy, but to compose letters with a structural, spelling and grammatical dependability that I have never seen equaled on Capitol Hill. She had one other quality that made her invaluable to a new congressman: a self-confidence that enabled her to be bluntly critical of slipshod work on the part of anyone in our office, including me. She was not always right in her judgments, but she seldom hesitated to express them.

My maiden speech on February 21 was an attack on the agricultural politics of Ezra Taft Benson. It was almost standard fare for Democratic congressmen from farm states to sharpen their teeth on Mr. Benson. We ate a piece of him for breakfast every morning. So when I started to deliver my anti-Benson speech, I was asked by various congressmen to yield to them for observations that were considerably harsher than mine. One Montana freshman, LeRoy Anderson, even suggested that the harassed Secretary of Agriculture was "a bloodsucker." This was too much for Nathaniel Hill of Colorado, who rose to an emotional defense of his friend Benson. This in turn provoked Gene McCarthy to observe that while Benson frequently claimed to be acting under providential inspiration, he must be judged by his works, not by his claims of divine guidance.

Knowing that McCarthy was a lifelong Catholic and believing that he was getting close to blasphemy, Hill said, his voice trembling with emotion and anger, "I could mention a lady, if the gentleman would like to know something, who was considered a fool and an upstart, an eighteen-year-old girl, but today she has been canonized by the very people who put her to death. What kind of a man do you think you are to have a right to criticize someone because he happens to believe a little of the unknown which the gentleman professes to know nothing about?"

"If we want to discuss the issue of religion in politics we should get time," McCarthy replied. "I should be glad to talk about it further. In the meantime, I assure him that Joan of Arc was not canonized for advocating flexible price supports."

At this point Congressman Tom Abernethy of Mississippi interjected, "I just want to say that while I have not taken part in this discussion that if, and when, the gentlemen do get time at some later date to discuss this agricultural program from the religious angle, I would like to represent the Methodists in that discussion."

My maiden speech was not especially original, but this colloquy made it—and me—instantly known to most members of the House. A few days later, when a major farm bill was being considered, I boldly offered an amendment calling for 90 percent of parity price supports for basic agricultural commodities. To my surprise, the amendment came within four votes of passing. It immediately established me in the Congress, in the farm press and in my own state as an aggressive congressional champion of the farmer.

As a member of the Committee on Education and Labor, I fell into a useful role in shaping the first major breakthrough in federal aid to education. Such aid had failed in the past, partly because of anxiety over federal interference in the schools, partly because of the separation-of-church-and-state doctrine which blocked federal funds for church-related schools, and partly because of amendments by Congressman Adam Clayton Powell, Jr., barring aid to racially segregated schools.

But in the fall of 1957 the Russians had launched their Sputnik—the first space capsule—and suddenly Americans were concerned about the apparent superiority of Russian academic and scientific methods. How could the Soviets have beaten us into outer space if not through the superiority of their educational and research systems? Soon articles appeared, describing the superior standards of Soviet schools and research centers. These exaggerated accounts set the stage for a worried look by the Congress at the need to invest greater resources in education—for reasons of national security; hence the National Defense Education Act of 1958.

The measure was given a "defense" label to ensure support in the Congress from those politicians who instinctively vote against social spending but who just as instinctively vote for anything called "defense." Ten years before, it must have been a public relations man with at least a working acquaintance with the ways of the Congress who suggested that the war-making branches of our government be named the Defense Department. Now we were using the same psychology in linking education with "defense."

In this spirit, the first version of the bill limited its scope to loans for college students majoring in the physical sciences. I led a successful effort in committee to broaden the legislation to aid college students without regard to their fields of concentration. It seemed to me that the strength of our society called at least as much for students versed in history, philosophy, literature and the arts as in chemistry and physics. The bill was enacted into law, and with subsequent modifications, has operated to the present time. It opened the way for a series of federal acts that help meet the costs of education from the elementary grades through the graduate level.

Agriculture and education were popular back home and so was the role I played—an unusual one for a first-term congressman—in those legislative areas. But that first term also brought a harder test on an issue that easily could pit a liberal South Dakotan against his own constituents—labor reform. South Dakota's senior Senator, Karl Mundt, was a prominent member of the Senate committee investigating union corruption. Since the Teamsters Union had backed selected Republican conservatives, Mundt tried to shift the committee focus from the mess in that union to the alleged "left-wing" political activities of Walter Reuther and the United Auto Workers. I hit hard on the other side, assailing the Becks and the Hoffas while defending honest leaders such as the Reuther brothers.

Senator John F. Kennedy and Senator Irving Ives, a New York Republican, had co-sponsored a labor-reform bill which was generally regarded as "moderate." It was not a union-busting bill; it did not, as many conservatives like Mundt wished, include measures such as antitrust action against unions. The Senate passed the Kennedy-Ives bill, but when it became clear that the House would not have a chance to vote on it in 1958, I went to Congressmen Stewart Udall of Arizona and Frank Thompson of New Jersey—close friends of mine on the Education and Labor Committee—and told them that I felt it was substantively right and politically essential for the House to vote the bill up or down. The three of us then went to Speaker Sam Rayburn to plead our case for putting the bill on the House Calendar. Rayburn agreed and we got our vote on August 18, but the measure went down to defeat, principally because Republicans and Southern Democrats united to oppose it; to them, it wasn't tough enough. The following year, on August 13, 1959, the House approved their tougher version, the substitute Landrum-Griffin bill. I voted against it, but it cleared the House by a 28-vote margin.

It was because of the labor bill that I came to know John Kennedy better. I had first met him at a party in January 1957. He was already being talked of as a presidential possibility, but I wondered whether he was a genuine liberal or just a dilettante benefiting from his father's wealth. He had ducked the McCarthy issue, which I regarded as a key test. His record hardly seemed innovative or courageous. And I bought the conventional view that a young Catholic millionaire probably couldn't win.

I saw little of Kennedy after that party until he met with several of us on the House side to discuss legislative strategy on labor reform. During that fight I was impressed with his grasp of the issue, the depth of his commitment, and his skill. His staff was first-rate, especially Ted Sorensen, who was to become a good friend, and Ralph Dungan, who drafted two hard-hitting speeches for me. I also talked with Bob Kennedy several times on the phone, though I was not to meet him until 1960, when he came over to do a TV spot for my Senate campaign. Bob, who had become famous in his own right as the Senate committee counsel on labor reform, had his own, typically Kennedy script for the spot: "When others ran away, George McGovern stood up on labor reform." I liked him instantly that day, and not just for what he said. He had a kind of appealing earnestness; later, when he was one of my cherished friends, I came to think of it as a rare combination of compassion and toughness.

That first congressional term also marked my first vote against excessive powers of presidential war-making. I joined with 60 other House members to oppose a request by the Eisenhower Administration for a "blank check" to intervene in the Middle East. The resolution also called for $200 million in economic and military aid to the Arab states to strengthen them against Soviet inroads. Although it seemed to me to be a clear abdication of congressional authority over war-making, the measure passed the House by an overwhelming margin, 355–61.

Hubert Humphrey called Congressman Eugene McCarthy and me to urge us not to oppose such a fundamental bipartisan foreign-policy proposal. The Congress should support the President on such questions, he said. It was a preview of the issue that from 1965 to 1972 was to create differences between Hubert and me and eventually to make us opponents inside the Democratic Party. But that was still a long way off. For now, I was a first-term congressman trying not to be a one-termer.

In South Dakota, the Republican leadership was laying plans for my defeat. Governor Joe Foss, a popular Medal of Honor winner and World War II air ace, had announced that he would not seek election to higher office in 1958, but he was under intense party pressure to change his mind. Foss yielded near the end of 1957 and announced that he would oppose my re-election in 1958. My friends in Washington and many in South Dakota immediately assumed that I was doomed to defeat. While Foss had been deliberating, the editor of the Rapid City *Journal* observed that my retirement would be assured beyond doubt if the governor decided to challenge me.

But I had established the basis for a strong campaign. I had emerged as an outspoken advocate of the family farmer and small merchant; I had taken the lead in measures to strengthen education; I had a good record of supporting organized labor while opposing excesses in unions such as the Teamsters. I had also worked hard to serve the individual constituent needs of my state and to stay in close touch with the voters back home. I scheduled an extensive tour of my district during the late autumn and winter recess of 1957. Day in and day out for two months I spoke to scores of service clubs, schools, commercial clubs, farm organizations—every group and constituent I could reach. I hoped the stage was set for a strong defense against the Foss challenge.

Actually, it turned out to be the easiest campaign of my career. Whatever danger I faced evaporated during a debate with Foss sponsored by the League of Women Voters and carried on statewide radio. It was so painfully one-sided that I feared a sympathy reaction for my highly nervous, poorly prepared opponent. A congenial, swashbuckling, winsome man, Foss had won the affection of many South Dakotans, including mine. At one point in the question session when he said he was totally opposed to any form of federal assistance to education, I gently reminded him that we were in the home city of our federal-land-grant college—South Dakota State—and that I was sure he did not intend to say he was opposed to all federal funds for the schools, but only to major new additions. Joe gratefully allowed that this was what he had meant. In any event, word spread across the state of the "slaughter" at Brookings, and Joe was never really in the race after that night. My victory margin increased by 50 percent over 1956.

Almost immediately I began to plan a campaign for the Senate in 1960 against Karl Mundt. I think that I had had my eye on an eventual race with Mundt from the day I entered politics. When it was first announced that I was to give up my professorship to organize the South Dakota Democrats, Mundt had responded that he felt sorry for "that teacher who gave up his job for the Democrats." Now I decided that the time had come for "that teacher" to take the measure of Senator Mundt.

Mundt had built a state and national reputation on "the Red scare." No other politician had so skillfully parlayed to his own political gain the public fear of Communist inroads. Mundt was also an affable, adroit campaigner and an accomplished public speaker. I knew that he would be a formidable opponent who would remind South Dakotans in every possible way that his seniority in the Senate was a precious asset to the state that should not be surrendered to a young rookie still learning the rules of the House.

But I was confident—overconfident—that Mundt could be beaten. In defeating Harold Lovre in 1956 and Joe Foss in 1958, I had already eliminated two of the most popular Republican vote getters in the state. Furthermore, a privately commissioned poll showed me leading Mundt 60 to 40.

With the cooperation of the Sioux Falls *Argus-Leader* and the Omaha *World-Herald*—two papers that were totally committed to Mundt—he had orchestrated a scenario as effective as it was deceptive. He first suggested to the *World-Herald* that it ask Dave Beck, president of the Teamsters Union, whom he was backing in the South Dakota Senate race. Knowing how damaging his endorsement would be in Republican South Dakota, Beck dutifully replied that he was supporting me. This phony endorsement was a double delight for Beck. It repaid Mundt for his efforts to divert the labor investigation from the Teamsters to the Auto Workers—and punished me for the harsh attacks I had directed on the House floor against Teamster corruption. The *World-Herald* and the *Argus-Leader* carried prominent stories: BECK SUPPORTS MCGOVERN.

While I was reeling from this blow, Mundt arranged for his old friend Fred Christopherson, editor of the *Argus-Leader,* to write a letter to J. Edgar Hoover asking him what members of the Congress had been most effective in protecting America from the Communists. Hoover, in bipartisan style, replied that there were four men he considered outstanding defenders of America: Republican Senators Karl Mundt and Styles Bridges, and Democratic Representatives John McCormack and John Rooney. Only Mundt was faced with a hard race in 1960. Only he benefited from Hoover's endorsement— an endorsement which Hoover would never admit was a departure from his no-endorsement rule. And true to form, the *Argus* carried a front-page story with a bold head: J. EDGAR HOOVER LAUDS MUNDT IN ANTI-RED FIGHT.

Then came a series of political advertisements across the state: HOOVER ENDORSES MUNDT; BECK ENDORSES MCGOVERN. It was the most devious propaganda used against me in my public career with one exception—the television spots in 1972 ordered and paid for by "Democrats for Nixon."

But an even more serious problem in 1960 was the impact on all South Dakota Democratic races of the Kennedy presidential candidacy. In the early campaigning I openly supported my neighbor and friend Hubert Humphrey; I had enlisted a group of young liberal congressmen to declare for him. He seemed more liberal than Kennedy and he had befriended me as a young congressman in many ways. In addition, he was a native of South Dakota whose brother, sisters and mother were my constituents—operating a drugstore in Huron.

But after the Kennedy landslide in the West Virginia primary, Humphrey told me that he was dropping out of the race and releasing his supporters. Kennedy had stayed in contact following the labor-reform fight. Ted Sorensen had called me occasionally; Kennedy himself told people I was "one of the real comers in the House," and the word of that filtered back, as I think it was supposed to. Now the choice was down to Kennedy; Lyndon Johnson, Stuart Symington of Missouri and possibly Adlai Stevenson. I had been enthusiastic for Stevenson twice, but I doubted that he could win. So I called Kennedy and arranged to meet him at his Senate office—an office I was later to occupy. Over a cup of tea I agreed to endorse him; it was hardly the same as getting Mayor Daley, but John Kennedy went after every vote. As we left the office he invited me to drive with him to a reception with Democratic congressmen in the House Office Building. Noticing the name "Bonneville" on the instrument panel of his car, I kidded him about a presidential candidate driving a foreign car. It was the first time I witnessed Jack Kennedy's capacity to respond to a stupid comment by saying nothing. It was not until I saw a newspaper advertisement several days later that I learned of Pontiac's new model—"the Bonneville." Perhaps as an act of contrition, the next car I purchased was a Bonneville.

I recall one other aspect of that meeting with Kennedy. After a quick description of his strategy, he clenched the steering wheel and said coldly, "If I win that nomination, I'll knock the jock off Nixon."

Despite the contrary urging of my campaign advisers, I publicly campaigned for the Kennedy-Johnson ticket in South Dakota while carrying on my own race for the Senate. When Kennedy appeared at the National Plowing Contest near Sioux Falls for the major agricultural speech of his campaign, I introduced him to a crowd of 50,000 farmers. It was a windy, rainy day and Kennedy was uncomfortable with the prepared text, which he read with surprising awkwardness. Karl Mundt was standing with the farmers in the front row sucking on his pipe, smiling through the speech and the tepid crowd reaction.

But later that day Kennedy found his agricultural theme speaking extemporaneously to a wildly cheering, jam-packed audience at the Corn Palace in my hometown of Mitchell. "I don't regard the . . . agricultural surplus as a problem," he said. "I regard it as an opportunity . . . not only for our own people, but for people all around the world. . . . I think the farmers can bring more credit, more lasting good will, more chance for freedom, more chance for peace, than almost any other group of Americans in the next ten years, if we recognize that food is strength, and food is peace, and food is freedom, and food is a helping hand to people around the world whose good will and friendship we want."

These were the themes I had spoken of for years on countless platforms in South Dakota. Kennedy and I had talked of them on the ride from Sioux Falls to Mitchell. They struck a highly favorable response there. But Richard Nixon carried South Dakota in a landslide, as he did virtually every farm state in the land. Kennedy's Catholicism hurt him all across rural America. Nixon's Republican rhetoric was attuned to the conservative Protestant voters of the prairie states.

I lost the race to Mundt by a single percentage point, and while I carefully avoided any public hint that the reaction against Kennedy had contributed to my loss, the realities were clear to every observer. Even our highly popular Democratic governor, Ralph Herseth, was swept out of office by the Nixon landslide in the state. The entire Democratic slate from the courthouses to the U.S. Senate race was laboring under a virtually impossible handicap.

No one understood this better than the victorious John Kennedy. After his South Dakota campaign appearance, he had said of me to his brother Bob, "I think we just cost that nice guy a Senate seat." Bob determined that if I was to bear the burden, at least I would have the benefit of a Kennedy presence, so the last week of the campaign he had spent a day stumping South Dakota for me. One night after the election Eleanor and I were having dinner at our long-time Mitchell neighbors', Delvan Becker and his wife, Dobie, when the phone rang. Dobie answered and then said it was a long-distance call for me. I picked up the receiver expecting another consolation from a South Dakota friend. But the accent at the other end was unmistakable. "Hi, George, this is Jack. I'm terribly sorry that I cost you that election in South Dakota." I politely protested that it wasn't Kennedy's fault, but he said, "I know what happened. I just called to ask if you would talk to me before you make any plans."

The next few weeks were a heady time. Somebody close to Kennedy tipped off *Life* magazine that Stewart Udall was to be Interior Secretary and I was to be Agriculture Secretary; *Life* called for a picture-taking session. Bob Kennedy was pushing for my appointment; so were Arthur Schlesinger, Jr., and John Kenneth Galbraith. Kennedy's counsel Mike Feldman and Sarge Shriver, who was directing the talent hunt, favored defeated Minnesota Governor Orville Freeman. One afternoon Ted Sorensen called; the thing was pretty well set. Had they cleared it, I wondered, with Senate Agriculture chairman Allen Ellender and House chairman Harold Cooley? No, but they were about to. Ellender thought it was fine, but Cooley hit the roof. He wanted to be Agriculture Secretary himself, but what he said was that I was just a youngster, I had only been on the committee for two years, it would be an insult to senior members. Cooley had no chance for the post, but his reaction tipped the balance of President Kennedy's judgment to Freeman.

So I was not to be Secretary of Agriculture. At the time I thought that perhaps I did myself in by raising the question of Cooley's clearance with Sorensen. I rationalized that the Kennedy staff would have thought of it anyway. As it turned out, if my own question was my undoing, it was also my salvation: the Secretary of Agriculture post would have been a political burial ground for me as surely as it was for Freeman.

Kennedy called me to his Georgetown home on N Street to offer a consolation prize—director of the newly created White House office of "Food for Peace." He announced this and Freeman's appointment simultaneously from his front porch on a crisp December evening. He said that he regarded Food for Peace as the forefront of a maximum battle against world hunger. It would have the highest priority; thus my job was to be of "virtual Cabinet rank."

Bob Kennedy said I was better off there anyway. Not only was the Secretary of Agriculture post politically difficult, but Food for Peace was a concept that appealed to everybody. I had been saying for years that such a program was good for farmers, industry, the nation and the world's hungry. Now I was to discover personally how right that was. For the farmers, Food for Peace provided an outlet for farm surpluses that would otherwise depress prices. For the hard-pressed American merchant fleet it was a godsend, since the law required that 50 percent or more of all Food for Peace shipments move in American vessels. And it appealed to humanitarian and religious groups—and to the general American sense of compassion.

President Kennedy's commitment to the Food for Peace idea was genuine, but he didn't have to establish a special office for it in the White House. He did so largely as a favor to me, to keep me in a visible and favorable position for another campaign in South Dakota. Neither he nor I had any clear idea at the outset of how the office should be structured, staffed, financed—or even where it should be located. The only authority I had was an executive order of the President creating the office and calling on me to exercise "affirmative leadership and continuous supervision over the various activities" involved in our overseas food operations.

Before the new President was even inaugurated, I paid a visit to the old Executive Office Building, which adjoins the White House. Accompanied by Nelson Post, who was to be my key assistant, and by my secretary, Pat Donovan, I located the custodian of the building and asked him to show me a suite with the capacity to house the Food for Peace office. The man showed me several suites. I selected a commodious, attractive one on the west side of the building and simply told the obliging custodian to "hold those rooms for Food for Peace." To my surprise, he readily agreed. I moved in and began to assemble a small staff, about the size of a senator's. I chose James Symington, son of Senator Stuart Symington, later to be a congressman from Missouri, as my deputy, and we were in business.

Shortly after we had moved into our new offices, the custodian appeared and somewhat apologetically told me that the new Vice President, Lyndon Johnson, had also requested a suite in the Executive Office Building and that mine seemed to be the best one available. Would I consider moving to other quarters, perhaps at the State Department or the Department of Agriculture? In a flash of inspiration I gravely asked the man to come into my private office and close the door. In hushed tones I told him that I personally had no objections to giving up my office to the Vice President. But, I explained, the President had defeated Senator Symington in his bid for the presidential nomination and was now trying to heal the wounds opened in that effort. Thus, I said, we might be injuring the President and Senator Symington if after just employing the senator's son, we expelled him from his office. It was low-grade bluff but it seemed to terrify the custodian, and he never again appeared except to make certain that we were fully satisfied with the accommodations and the equipment.

During the next year and a half there were several efforts made by the State Department to absorb Food for Peace into the foreign-aid bureaucracy, by the Department of Agriculture to place the program under its jurisdiction, and by the Budget office to consolidate our small staff somewhere, anywhere outside the White House complex. But whenever disaster seemed imminent I would call Evelyn Lincoln, the President's secretary, and go to see him. He would list all the groups pressuring him to give them Food for Peace, then listen to my standard answers, smile and send me back to work. Kennedy was a politician; he knew exactly what he was doing. Food for Peace had turned out to be one of the brighter stars in the Kennedy record. Nor would it serve the purpose of helping me politically to submerge the agency in some vast bureaucracy, where it might become both invisible and ineffective.

Freeman was particularly disappointed about losing these skirmishes. Originally he had hoped to be Secretary of Defense. When that went to Robert McNamara, he set his aim on Health, Education and Welfare. When Ribicoff took that post, Freeman settled for Agriculture, which at first he had sworn not to accept. He changed his mind after farm-cooperative leaders persuaded him that he could be the new Herbert Hoover, the man who saved the world from famine after World War I. Freeman never gave up trying to get Food for Peace, but after my departure and President Kennedy's assassination, the agency was transferred to the State Department, where it soon lost much of its visibility and initiative.

An independent office was not structurally neat—it didn't fit well amid the lines and boxes of the charts—but it was, by all accounts, even more effective than Kennedy and I had hoped it could be. The first priority was to give the program a better public image. We stopped using the term "surplus disposal," which had been the familiar one for the operations of Public Law 480—the legislative authority for Food for Peace. In news releases, speeches, memoranda and government communications I always interpreted America's agricultural abundance not as a problem to be disposed of, but as a valuable resource offering new hope and strength to the world. We also worked to give substance to the image. We cut through the red tape that required a squad of government agencies to approve each food agreement. Sometimes a proposal would be stalled by a dispute between the State Department and the Department of Agriculture. Then I would intervene as a mediator until the conflicting views were resolved.

I put special emphasis on two of the most appealing aspects of Food for Peace: the overseas school-lunch programs and the "food for work" projects. The latter were small-scale reforestation, road building and other construction projects in which a portion of the wages were paid in the form of American food. We expanded these "food for work" operations into twenty-two developing countries. In some cases they were supervised by local government personnel; in other cases by American voluntary agencies such as CARE, Church World Service, Lutheran World Relief or Catholic Relief Services. This same combination of private charitable organizations and local governments was used to expand the school-lunch program to tens of millions of children in the poorest nations of the world. Wherever such programs were organized, there were dramatic improvements in the physical and mental health of the children. In the Puno area of Peru, for example, school attendance increased by 40 percent and academic performance jumped noticeably.

Shortly after the inauguration, the President asked department and agency heads to suggest ideas that might be proposed in his first State of the Union address. I sent back a memorandum advocating that Food for Peace missions be sent to Latin America, Africa and Asia to survey food needs there. The next I heard of the suggestion was in the State of the Union message when Kennedy announced that he was sending a Food for Peace mission to Latin America immediately. A few days later he called me to say that he was asking Arthur Schlesinger, Jr., then one of his Special Assistants, to accompany me. I was later to learn that Arthur's mission was to get some feeling about the impact of Fidel Castro on Latin American journalists, writers, students and political leaders.

This was the first overseas mission dispatched by the new Kennedy Administration. We confined our trip to Argentina and Brazil, especially the drought-stricken northeastern sector of Brazil. There I saw children dying from malnutrition. I saw weary, undernourished mothers trying desperately to keep their families alive. In one hut I saw the mother sitting on the dirt floor with two children lying across her lap. A seven-year-old boy had died the day before, and it did not appear that the two emaciated creatures lying listlessly before us could make it through that night. "She is the symbol of the underdeveloped country," said Dr. Celso Furtado, the Brazilian economist who watched me staring at the shapeless little mother sitting there in her despair.

I saw that scene duplicated countless times in other parts of the world during the year and a half that I served as Food for Peace director. These experiences gave stark witness to words I had written in a newsletter during my second congressional term:

> "Give us this day our daily bread" is still the prayer of human beings in the far corners of the earth. For most Americans, it is the prayer of gratitude for ample food. But for more than a billion human beings it is the cry of hunger—the feeble plea of the old man begging on the streets of Cairo, the child whimpering for milk in Bombay, the weary African mother trying to convert a few scraps into an evening meal for her family.

Now that I had a minor part of a national Administration's power, I was determined to have America do as much as possible to provide more than those scraps. By the end of my service as director of Food for Peace, over a third of all American overseas economic aid was in agricultural products. While other kinds of foreign aid were under heavy attack, we managed to make up a large part of the gap with food. Food for Peace increased from an annual average of $891 million from 1954 to 1961, to an average level of $1.4 billion for the three years following mid-1961. Twenty-seven percent of all U.S. food exports were moving through Food for Peace when I left the program. Two thirds of our wheat exports were through Food for Peace. In twenty-two countries, 700,000 workers were being paid part of their wages in American food. More than 100 million people were receiving direct food donations under the program, and several times that number were benefiting from reduced price sales.

The Latin American trip had one side effect which contributed to my later decision to leave Food for Peace. In the summer I was stricken with hepatitis. The doctors discovered that I had contracted the disease from a yellow-fever inoculation in the White House dispensary prior to the trip. The dispensary wasn't using disposable needles, but reusing old ones, a practice modern medicine had abandoned years before. President Kennedy was furious and the dispensary changed in a hurry. At least I had the satisfaction of knowing that I brought safe needles to the White House!

The price was a serious illness, the first one of my life, and long days in bed at the Georgetown University Hospital. During those days, for the first time in a long while, I had time to read, think and occasionally dream apparently far-fetched hopes. One of the books I read was Theodore White's *Making of the President 1960,* the brilliantly written anecdotal description of that campaign which stirred a new kind of political journalism (not all of it, including White's own subsequent efforts, nearly as good as his first try). The book also stirred some feelings in me. It recalled how much electoral politics had come to mean to me as an opportunity to lead and to affect the course of events, however marginally, for the better. I started looking ahead to another try for the Senate in 1962. And there were the first faint and very private stirrings in my mind that perhaps one day I might seek the presidency. It was no flash of insight, just a matter-of-fact possibility. That confinement in the hospital prompted a new determination on my part to live life to the fullest—which I thought might mean a national campaign for me sooner or later.

The following spring I went through a difficult internal debate about whether to challenge the incumbent senator, Francis Case, or remain with Food for Peace. When I discussed the race with Bob Kennedy he urged me, in view of my bout with hepatitis, not to make it. "We think that you've done a great job with Food for Peace. It has helped the President and it has helped people around the world. Why don't you stay with us and let somebody else go after Case?"

This seemed like good advice for several days. But the restlessness persisted. I shared the excitement about the Kennedy Administration. It was a time of hope, the last one for years to come. But while it was a privilege to be part of that, I kept thinking that I might do as much or more in the Senate. I could support the President there, but I could also be an independent voice. And realistically, what else could I accomplish in Food for Peace other than to delay slightly the inevitable bureaucratic takeover? I might be able to advance the program better as a senator, especially if I had, as I thought I would, a seat on the Agriculture Committee and possibly on Foreign Relations. So a few days after my discussion with Bob Kennedy I went to the Oval Office to talk over my decision with his brother.

"Can you win?" John Kennedy asked crisply. "If you can, go after Case; if you can't, stay where you are."

I told the President that Case would be hard to defeat, that he was admired not only by Republicans but by many Democrats, including me. "If that's true," he said, "I don't think you should run, but you make the decision and whatever it is, I'll be with you."

A few days later I announced my resignation from the Food for Peace program and my candidacy for the Senate. Before I could begin any serious campaigning, the race was transformed. Francis Case died suddenly of a heart attack. Lieutenant Governor Joe Bottum, former Republican state chairman, was appointed by the governor to fill the remaining six months of Case's term. After a hard convention fight Bottum also won the Republican senatorial nomination.

The campaign moved along well through early September. Bottum charged that I was simply a tool of the Kennedys sent back to South Dakota at their bidding. I replied that I was proud to be a friend of the President and the Attorney General. "Is it really a handicap to South Dakota to have a senator who is close to the President of the United States?" I asked repeatedly.

I challenged Bottum to a series of public debates, which he persistently declined. But he could not avoid the traditional joint appearance of the major candidates at the State Corn Picking Contest on October 4, a month before the election. I was particularly eager for this confrontation, since it would provide an opportunity for me to engage Bottum on my best ground—food and agriculture.

That morning as I literally struggled out of bed after a few hours' sleep at my home in Mitchell, I knew something was seriously wrong. Lawn Thompson, my Washington doctor and friend, had warned me not to press hard in the first year after my hepatitis attack. But in the excitement and quickening pace of the campaign I had inevitably ignored his advice. Now I realized that I was ill, very ill, with a recurrence of the disease.

As anyone who has ever experienced it knows, hepatitis drains all energy from its victim until it is difficult even to raise a hand. But I was determined to have that debate with Bottum. So Eleanor put a mattress in our station wagon and we took off for the corn-picking site near Madison, seventy-five miles away. I lay in the car and listened to Bottum give the opening speech. Then as I heard the master of ceremonies begin introducing me, I walked slowly to the platform. The angels—or the adrenaline—were with me that day: for the next twenty minutes, operating purely on nerve, I gave what had to be one of the most effective public performances of my life. At least that is how I remember it. By the end of the exchange I knew why Bottum had so studiously avoided a face-to-face debate, and I knew that he had been thoroughly embarrassed on statewide radio and before the huge crowd at the corn-picking contest.

I also knew that I was dreadfully ill. But in an effort to minimize publicity over the fact, I arranged through friends to enter a Sioux City, Iowa, hospital under the care of their family doctor. In a feeble effort at anonymity I checked into the hospital using my first initial and full middle name, "G. Stanley McGovern," but before I could even get to my room I was recognized by one of the nurses. That evening David Schoumacher, then working for a Sioux City television station, called me. The news was out. Years later Schoumacher said, laughing, to a friend, "Signing in as G. Stanley McGovern instead of George McGovern is about as close as McGovern can get to telling a lie." There were some tough moments in 1972 and afterward when I especially treasured this good-natured compliment from a respected veteran journalist, by then an ABC national correspondent, who knew me when we were both largely unknown outside South Dakota and Iowa.

I spent most of the rest of the 1962 campaign recovering in the hospital and at home in Mitchell. Eleanor picked up my campaign schedule with the help of friends such as John Lindley of Chamberlain and Ken Holum, who himself had almost won the same Senate seat in 1956 and who later served as Assistant Secretary of the Interior in the Kennedy-Johnson years. In the closing days before the election I mustered enough strength for a series of evening call-in programs on television. Thank God for TV make-up! I got by without looking completely corpselike.

Hubert Humphrey came into the state and stumped hard for me. He fires up South Dakota audiences as few other political figures ever have. Ethel Kennedy also provided an assist shortly before the election, flying out from Washington for brief appearances in Aberdeen, Rapid City and Sioux Falls. Since I was being attacked as a friend of the Kennedys, I was grateful for Ethel's help. I could not have escaped the Kennedy identification if I had wished to, and I sensed that John Kennedy was now far more popular in South Dakota than he had been in 1960. His presidency had answered the religious fears; his charisma was more appealing on the Great Plains than Karl Mundt and the South Dakota GOP had assumed, and it was just days after the Cuban missile crisis. We had a strenuous schedule ready for Ethel, and though she was pregnant, she stuck with it. Two years earlier, in 1960, Bob Kennedy had taken the Friday night before the election to barnstorm the state for me, though he was in the midst of the last-minute crises of managing his brother's presidential effort. For years afterward Ethel teased Bob that she had won for me in 1962, while he had lost it for me in 1960.

After the Cuban missile crisis broke on October 25 I flew to Washington despite my run-down condition. In retrospect I'm not exactly sure why I went. It was partly the impulse to be where the action was, as I had been for the previous two years. Partly it was politics. But within hours of the flight to Washington I felt foolish; I returned to Minneapolis the same night. M. W. Thatcher, the long-time general manager of the Grain Terminal Association, persuaded me to rest quietly at his home for a while; two of his sons were chiropractors. They and an older doctor treated me and I left for South Dakota for the final campaign days with a sense of renewed well-being.

When the returns came in, I had won the election by a disputed margin of only about 200 votes. The next morning, not having slept through the long election night, I was in the public library reading about recounts. Understandably, my opponent called for one, and for the next month we waited out the slow, torturous review of approximately 250,000 ballots. Under the guidance of Sioux Falls lawyer Holton Davenport we quickly prepared volunteer lawyers and others in all parts of the state to assist in the recount. President Kennedy was watching the situation closely; halfway through the process he saw to it that the Senate Rules Committee sent Jim Duffy to South Dakota to consult with us. With Davenport and his associates donating the legal expenses, we were able to monitor the recount carefully in every county. Finally I was declared the winner by a margin of 597 votes—less than one third of one vote in each of the state's 1,800 voting precincts, though I didn't quite believe the news until George Cunningham got out of his car in front of my house waving the official certificate of election signed by the Republican governor and secretary of state.

My first seatmate in the Senate was Ted Kennedy. I suppose that in early 1963 I shared the common reaction that the President's kid brother had come to the Senate. I liked the Kennedys but didn't expect much of Ted. I quickly got over that misimpression. Ted was determined to be a good senator; he has become one of the best. Right away he put together a brilliant staff. He worked hard, debated well and displayed an increasing mastery of complicated issues such as tax reform.

Perhaps my most vivid memory of that first year in the Senate was the day President Kennedy was killed. I heard the news of the shooting in my office and went immediately to the Senate floor. Entering through the swinging doors beside the rostrum, I saw that Ted was presiding over the Senate, one of the small tasks of being a freshman. Someone was whispering in his ear. He motioned to me. It was obvious he had just been told. He asked me quietly to relieve him. "Something has happened," he added, his voice on edge, but controlled. As I took the chair he touched my arm, said "Thank you" and hurried off.

In the coming weeks I sat next to Ted in the last row of the Senate while he listened to the eulogies for his brother. He was present at all of them; he sighed occasionally, but kept his composure. You could sense his internal weeping; you had to admire him. We talked one afternoon about the strength of his mother. He said, "Well, my mother is the key to it. She has this deep religious faith that sustains us all. She doesn't waiver. It's her faith and serenity . . ." He was to say much the same to me four and a half years later, when his brother Bobby was shot.

From the outset I set goals for myself in the Senate: first, to use it as a national forum on major foreign-policy issues; second, to build a solid record of legislative achievement in the fields of agriculture, food and nutrition; and third, to provide good service for South Dakota. For years George Cunningham and our chief constituent caseworker, Barbara Giles, have arrived at the office by five-thirty, and much of the day's work has been laid out before dawn.

Ben Stong, an agricultural expert and experienced legislative craftsman, was the initial key to my successful efforts as a legislator on agriculture. With his help I soon emerged as a major force on the issue, authoring the Voluntary Wheat Certificate Plan of 1964 which became the basic wheat program of the 1960s. I also sponsored and secured the passage of Resolution 88, which put the Senate on record against any federal reduction in farm income.

However, I have never believed that the sole use of my time in the Senate should be as a legislative technician, nor could I be comfortable heeding Sam Rayburn's advice to "get along by going along." Temperamentally, I am not a very good temporizer. I have never been a safe party man. Instead I have tried to offer forthright leadership on the great issues of war, peace and public priorities. Yet the first great issue to come to the Senate in my first term, the civil rights bill, was not one on which I already had deep feelings. Intellectually I had been for civil rights, but it was not until the spring of 1963 that the commitment became a matter of heart as well as head. Like many others, I was infuriated when police dogs and fire hoses were loosed on children in Birmingham. I thought, Is this happening in America? It's like Nazi Germany. Bull Connor, the segregationist enforcer of Birmingham, was inadvertently the perfect advocate of Martin Luther King's cause. He was right out of Hollywood casting.

During the filibuster over the civil rights bill, I presided over the Senate through enough long-winded pronounciamentos to compose the first draft of my book on Food for Peace, *War Against Want.* (One night-to-morning session I was in the chair at four-thirty when Senator Bob Byrd, then one of the filibusterers, now Senate Majority Leader, read a poem he had written in honor of my daughter Teresa's fifteenth birthday.) The struggle, in which I played just a supporting role, left me with a new certainty that civil rights was a decisive test for America. At the political hard points, such as busing during the 1972 campaign, I have tried to keep the promise I made to myself to stand fast on civil rights. I have come to see it as more than a matter of my own conscience. The issue seemed easier, almost simple, in 1964. As it has become more intricate and difficult, pretending easy ways to evade the demands of equality only shakes the already fragile faith of people in the political system. Thus I knew it would be unpopular to say at the Democratic Issues Convention in Louisville in 1975 that busing was there to stay—that no matter what the candidates appeared to promise, they could not change that fact. I didn't like to say it, but I thought someone had to.

The topic of my maiden Senate speech, on March 15, 1963, was "Our Castro Fixation versus the Alliance for Progress." The thesis of the speech was that the Administration and the Congress were so absorbed in their fears of Fidel Castro that they were overlooking the real challenge to the United States in Latin America—"the economic, political and social ills" of the nations to the south of us. I described the misery and political instability of Latin America as "a smoldering blockbuster on our doorstep . . . a continent cursed by a social system that concentrates enormous wealth in the hands of the few and consigns the many to lives of desperate poverty." I contended that "the appeal of Castroism and Communism in other parts of the hemisphere springs from the same corruption and social injustice that paved the way for the collapse of Batista and the triumph of Castro.

"Sometimes the hand of Providence moves in strange ways," I said. "There can be no mistaking the fact that much of Castro's appeal to the oppressed rests on the knowledge that his presence has forced every government in the hemisphere to take a new and more searching look at the crying needs of the great masses of human beings."

In this, as in later foreign-policy speeches, I emphasized the impact of foreign policy on the standards of American life. I concluded:

We dare not let our preoccupation with Mr. Castro and other irritants abroad blind us to our domestic responsibilities. If America is to fulfill its promise both at home and around the globe, we must move ahead on vital domestic fronts. We have a gigantic agricultural plant to be nurtured and stabilized; we are faced with the necessity of creating new job, educational, and recreational opportunities for our young people; our older citizens are confronted by rising medical and hospital costs; we need to consider seriously the relationship of our tax and fiscal policies to a sluggish national economy—these and many other mounting challenges call for clear minds and steadfast spirits. It is no longer possible to separate America's domestic health from our position in world affairs.

This speech attracted favorable comment from several colleagues, including Majority Leader Mike Mansfield, and also from journalists and foreign-policy experts. The *New York Times Magazine* asked me to expand it into a lead article. I dug out a quote from Theodore Roosevelt that demonstrated how little American overreactions to Cuba had changed since 1906. I began the article with Roosevelt's complaint, which, except for its distinctive style, could have come from the most ardent apostles of a cold war in the Caribbean. Roosevelt had written:

Just at the moment, I am so angry with that infernal little Cuban Republic that I would like to wipe its people off the face of the earth. All that we wanted from them was that they would behave themselves and be prosperous and happy so that we would not have to interfere. And now, lo and behold, they have started an utterly unjustifiable and pointless revolution and may get things into such a snarl that we have no alternative save to intervene—which will at once convince the suspicious idiots in South America that we do wish to interfere after all . . .

Nineteen sixty-three, the year I started in the Senate, also brought a brighter side of foreign policy. Following the missile crisis of the previous October, Washington and Moscow seemed to be moving toward détente. Through skillful but potentially catastrophic diplomacy and naval deployment, President Kennedy had persuaded Khrushchev to withdraw Russian missiles from Cuba in return for assurances that the United States would not invade the island. The two superpowers looked into the nuclear grave and backed away with a new appreciation of the need for peaceful accommodation. As Admiral Hyman Rickover put it: "The cold war turned a corner in October, 1962, and it has never been the same since."

On June 10, 1963, at the commencement ceremonies of American University, President Kennedy explicitly invited Soviet-American détente and in effect declared the beginning of the end of the Cold War. In what I regard as his greatest speech, he called for a "world safe for diversity." Kennedy announced that the United States was stopping the atmospheric testing of nuclear weapons and would not resume it unless other powers continued it.

The speech set the stage for the treaty banning the testing of nuclear weapons in the atmosphere. Other steps were taken that summer to improve Soviet-American relations, including a "hot line" between the White House and the Kremlin. In October, Kennedy offered to trade American wheat for Russian gold as "one more hopeful sign that a more peaceful world is both possible and beneficial to us all." But after modest initial wheat sales, U.S. shipping restrictions, aggravated by the refusal of maritime unions to load the wheat, ended the exchange.

I had long believed that Soviet-American relations could be improved by positive steps on our part designed to elicit a Soviet response. I believed that we could not only improve the chances for peace and enhance our international leadership but strengthen our own society by reducing the enormous burden of military hardware. From the perspective of 1963, the prospect did not seem hopeful. (Which is not to say that it does now.) For two decades, military appropriations had sailed through the Congress virtually without floor debate or discussion; indeed, the Congress would frequently force more appropriations on the Defense Department than it had requested. Whereas modest requests for funds for education, health or conservation were scrutinized, debated and discussed for days, and then finally passed in reduced form or rejected on a close vote, billions of dollars for the military were approved unanimously, often in a few minutes' time.

I took the Senate floor on August 2, 1963, to call for new and broader criteria of American security and national strength. Proposing a reduction of $5 billion in a military budget of $53.6 billion, I suggested that we were wasting funds on "overkill" that were urgently needed in other areas of our national life. This speech laid the basis for the foreign-policy views I was to press in the Senate and in two presidential campaigns over the next decade. To my surprise, the speech received front-page coverage in the *New York Times,* which characterized it as a break from the assumptions that had prevailed since 1945. "The Great Powers," I said, "are spending over a hundred billion dollars yearly on arms—each side justifying its investment in the name of 'defense.' Yet modern science supports the ancient biblical wisdom, 'There is no place to hide.' "

In the ensuing thirteen years we have seen the global arms budget climb to $300 billion annually, but the world, America included, feels no more secure today than when I took to the Senate floor in August of 1963. What I said then applies now without changing a word:

> I share the conviction that America ought to have a defense force that is second to none. But has the time not come to question the assumption that we are adding to defense and security by adding more and more to the nuclear stockpile? I suggest that we need to examine carefully the assumptions on which our military budget rests.
>
> Have we remembered that the defense of a great nation depends not only upon the quality of its arms, but also on the quality of its economic, political, and moral fabric?
>
> Is the size of our military budget the chief criterion of effective international leadership and national strength in today's world?

I contended that while we had achieved nuclear superiority over the Soviet Union, it was irrelevant: either side was capable of destroying the other.

> When a nuclear exchange of a few minutes' duration means instant death and indescribable devastation to both sides, what consolation is there to the dazed survivors to know that there remains under the poisoned skies amidst the rubble some unused "overkill" capacity?

I proposed that the Senate consider a $1 billion reduction in the Atomic Energy Commission's weapons procurement, and an additional $4 billion cut in the Pentagon budget. I proposed that these savings be invested in an expanded program of vocational and technical training for unemployed youth. Referring to the racial tensions then building in the country, I argued that the shortage of constructive jobs, good schools and decent neighborhoods was contributing to racial and urban tensions. Beyond this, we were using most of our scientific and technical talent in research and development for war at a time when American society urgently needed to divert some of this talent to the reconstruction of our cities and the strengthening of our environment. Why not a planned conversion of surplus military investment to job-creating enterprises? I asked.

On September 24 I moved on the Senate floor to implement the recommendations of that speech. The Senate was considering a military research, development and procurement bill of $23 billion. I offered an amendment to reduce the amount by 10 percent. Today such an amendment might win the support of one fourth to one third of the Senate, but in September of 1963, when the roll was called, the only senator who voted with me was Jennings Randolph of West

Virginia. Senator Randolph was fighting hard to secure funds for his economically depressed Appalachian constituents, and he saw my amendment as a source of additional funds for jobs, housing and rural renewal. But other senators dutifully voted the Pentagon line. Some of them, I am sure, thought I was simply an upstart freshman who would soon learn to mend his heresies.

Included in that September 1963 speech was a passage which to the best of my knowledge was the first dissent in the Senate from our deepening military involvement in Vietnam. "The current dilemma in Vietnam is a clear demonstration of the limitations of military power," I said. "This is scarcely a policy of 'victory'; it is not even a policy of 'stalemate.' It is a policy of moral debacle and political defeat. It is a policy that demonstrates that our expenditures for more and more 'special forces' are as useless and dangerous as our expenditures for more and more nuclear capability." I concluded that "the failure in Vietnam will not remain confined to Vietnam. The trap we have fallen into there will haunt us in every corner of this revolutionary world if we do not properly appraise its lessons."

Very early in my efforts to cut out some of the more obvious fat in military spending, my colleagues let me know that the "fat" represented military payrolls in their states—a vote to reduce military spending would mean fewer jobs for their constituents. Professor Seymour Melman of Columbia University had anticipated this concern and had talked with me on several occasions of the need for economic conversion planning. Melman convinced me that with proper planning and wise public investment we could actually increase the number of jobs by reallocating excessive arms spending to housing, transportation and urban development. I was also persuaded that such alternative investment would be less inflationary than arms spending because it would create goods and services to absorb the purchasing power of employed workers. By contrast, nuclear bombs or aircraft carriers are not consumer items. The production of such items actually diverted materials from the civilian market while creating wage earners whose purchasing power tended to drive up prices on other goods.

Working with Melman and others, I drafted the National Economic Conversion Act and introduced it in the Senate on October 31, 1963. The measure won the co-sponsorship of thirty-one other senators and the support of prominent editors, labor leaders and business groups. It would have set in motion planning mechanisms at the federal, state and local levels to assist in the transition from war to peacetime production. It would also have required defense contractors to allocate a portion of their own budgets to planning their own contingencies in case of conversion.

But by January 1964 it was clear that the Johnson Administration was cool toward the conversion bill. Senior members of the Senate —especially those who long had supported all military appropriations—seemed nervous about the legislation. Under considerable pressure from me, the Senate Commerce Committee did hold two days of hearings on the measure in the spring of 1964. But as the war in Vietnam escalated and arms spending soared, it was easy to forget conversion planning altogether.

Years later the war in Vietnam finally did end. But for the first time in our history, military spending went up in a postwar period. The military budget, which was $53 billion when I first urged its reduction in 1963, has now climbed to over $100 billion. When President Eisenhower offered his farewell warning in 1961 about the mounting danger of the "military-industrial complex," its cost was less than $50 billion. As I write these lines in 1977, it would seem that there is less interest in preparing our economy for rational reductions in excessive military outlays than was the case in 1963 or 1960. A conversion capability, I have concluded, will come only after a genuine commitment of presidential leadership to pressing for it.

During my years in the Senate, in a long list of weapons boondoggles, the most patently foolish one was the antiballistic missile. I described it in 1968, the year it was initiated, as "the most costly, wasteful and transparently futile 'defense' program of the decade." For years the Eisenhower, Kennedy and Johnson Administrations had resisted Pentagon pressures to build the ABM. All three Administrations had insisted that the ABM would add nothing to our national security—that indeed it would accelerate the arms race.

The ABM became a weapon in search of a rationale—or rationalization. In 1966 there were reports that the Russians were building an antiballistic-missile defense around Moscow. This stimulated a new drive for an American response, resulting in the Johnson Administration's reluctant decision to advocate a modest ABM system capable of countering not a Soviet attack, but the very limited nuclear capability that the Chinese were believed to be building. This ABM admittedly was worthless against a large-scale missile barrage and no one could explain why the Chinese might risk certain annihilation by popping a comparatively weak fusillade at the United States.

To me, the key argument against the ABM system was that defensive missiles could always be overwhelmed by simply targeting more offensive weapons on a city than there were defensive missiles to shoot them down. Suppose we were to build a battery of antiballistic missiles around New York or Los Angeles capable of knocking down fifteen or twenty incoming missiles: the obvious Soviet response would be to target more offensive missiles on each of these cities, thus nullifying the ABM system.

The Johnson Administration, concerned with Republican charges of weakness on defense, authorized a limited ABM go-ahead in 1967. A short time later the Senate approved by a single vote a modified "Safeguard" ABM system concentrated in North Dakota. After the expenditure of $5.5 billion on this useless contraption, even the Pentagon was prepared to admit that the ABM was a waste of tax dollars, energy and technical skills.

Long before Vietnam I felt that except in time of major war, the United States should rely on a voluntary system for military manpower. Many of the migrants to America came here to avoid conscription. The Declaration of Independence and the Constitution both embody a repugnance to large standing armies and forced conscription in peacetime. But Vietnam gave urgency to the question. As the conflict escalated, I also saw ending the draft as a means of curtailing American involvement. It did not seem to me that this war ever could attract massive numbers of volunteers.

Paradoxically, the abolition of the draft came under Richard Nixon. A long-time advocate of the Vietnam war, Nixon nevertheless was politically shrewd enough to see that it had destroyed the Johnson Administration and would have to be ended, won quickly or sharply reduced. Part of the Nixon strategy was to mute some of the outcry against the war by ending the draft, which was possible if Vietnamization permitted the withdrawal of most American troops. However, I never accepted the argument that the Nixon ploy proved that the draft was pro-peace because it assured student protest in the event of the wrong war. Without the draft President Johnson simply could not have raised the troop commitment in Vietnam by 500,000 in less than three years. Nor has the volunteer army met its opponents' other fear—that it would be too pliable a tool of the professional military, in effect a praetorian guard. Instead the enlisters of the "new" Army (or Navy, Air Force, or for that matter, even the Marine Corps) seem ready and able to assert their own rights; since they have a choice, they also have an opportunity to insist on better treatment. This, I suspect, is why the Pentagon is now making noises that the volunteer army is too expensive—that it costs perhaps an extra billion dollars a year. An extra billion is something the Pentagon normally spends, or wastes, with hardly a question; an arsenal of technocratic explanations awaits any critic of the usual cost overruns.

An issue which I thought even riper for redefinition than military conscription was American policy toward mainland China. As a graduate student at Northwestern in the late forties, as a teacher at Wesleyan in the fifties and as a Senator in the sixties, I found our China policy unrealistic and self-defeating. I had advocated recognition of China in lectures at Dakota Wesleyan in 1951. It was the middle of the Korean War, and my comments stirred a local controversy. I defended them in a letter to the Mitchell *Daily Republic* and a speech to the Mitchall Kiwanis Club. What I said then I still believed twenty-five years later. It was unrealistic to ignore 800 million human beings in the world's most populous nation while clinging to the myth that a deposed former war lord could one day reassert his control from the island refuge of Taiwan.

It was this myth, and the policy based on it, that I attacked on the Senate floor on May 3, 1966. I had worked on the speech for several weeks. It was intended as an article for *Look* magazine with the understanding that I would not release it until the article was published. Shortly before the piece was to appear, however, I received a call from Ted Kennedy explaining that before he learned about my article, he had planned to speak on the same subject the next day. I concluded that even though it would cost me the opportunity to publish a major article in *Look,* the impact would be greater nationwide if Kennedy and I spoke for a new policy the same day in the Senate. In fact the speeches did command wide attention.

I followed my China speech with a serious effort to arrange a visit to mainland China. Over the next few years I attempted to arrange that visit through the State Department, foreign embassies and the personal intervention of Edgar Snow, the American journalist and author who had a long association with Mao and the Chinese leadership. One day in 1971 I received a postcard from Peking written in longhand by Snow saying that he was pressing hard for my admission, but he added that a prominent member of the Nixon Administration was also asking to go to China. I have always been amazed that this open-faced postcard with its broad hint of one of the Administration's most closely guarded secrets, the impending Kissinger visit, had come through the mails with apparent ease. Only later, after the revelations of CIA mail covers, did I assume that it had been Xeroxed along the way.

It is one of the ironies of history that Richard Nixon, once the quintessential Cold Warrior, the friend of Chiang Kai-shek and the China lobby, the politician who accused Dean Acheson of "losing" China, became the President who opened American relations with the mainland regime. The surprise visit of Henry Kissinger to Peking via Pakistan in July 1971, followed by President Nixon's visit in February 1972, established a relationship which, except for the opposition of Nixon, Joseph McCarthy and their ilk, could and should have started as early as 1949. Then there might never have been wars in either Korea or Vietnam. At least one of the major reasons for our involvement in those wars—the specter of Communist Chinese expansionism—would have been a minor factor. I believe that the Nixon rapprochement with China, though belated, will prove to be his most constructive achievement.

Shortly before my 1966 Senate speech on China, Bob Kennedy asked me to his house for a discussion of the issue with a group of China experts, including Doak Barnet. Bob had come to the Senate in January 1965. We had liked each other before and we soon became close friends. More and more our conversation focused on Vietnam. For a long time he was obviously torn. It was hard for him to break with the officials whom his brother had appointed and who were executing what were arguably his brother's policies. Defense Secretary McNamara and General Maxwell Taylor kept turning Bob around on the war; he would see them, then pepper me with a host of new questions. But his doubts steadily mounted and, as he told me, he instinctively distrusted the primary agents of the war policy: the Joint Chiefs, the State Department, the military experts. "They gave us all the wrong advice during the Bay of Pigs and the missile crisis," he said over a hot-fudge sundae, his regular dessert at lunch in the Senate Dining Room.

The general view is that Bob changed from a ruthless, heedless campaign manager and Attorney General into a sensitive tribune of change by 1968. There is some truth in that, but as I knew him, the qualities that finally led Bob to the challenge of 1968 were always there. While President Kennedy was alive, those qualities tended to manifest themselves in personal relations more than public policy. He was a loyal, empathetic friend. Policy was right because his brother wanted it that way. He did not think about it then as much on his own as he later would; after he came to the Senate, the compassion and feeling he had given to friends brought him, now on his own, to a deepening passion about policy for its own sake. His instinctive reaction to an issue was, how would it affect the weak and the poor—the draftees and the villagers of Vietnam? Old politics sometimes pulled him the other way, but the "Good Bobby," as Jules Feiffer called him, was the friend I came to know better and better.

With others, like Maryland Senator Joe Tydings, he talked more of civil rights or the Great Society. He and I had the usual small talk—for example, the perennial joke that Ethel won for me in 1962 and he lost it in 1960; the constant questions about how I could be so liberal and win in South Dakota—but increasingly Vietnam dominated our discussions. Certainly that was partly my doing. I wanted him on the antiwar side. In addition, I was so convinced that Vietnam was a looming catastrophe that for me it became what one staff member described as "a magnificent obsession." From 1965 until the last American soldier left Vietnam in April 1975, the war was never far from my thoughts. My anguish over this issue was the driving force of my public career and the constant topic of my private conversation for an entire decade.

After several brief warnings against our involvement in Vietnam in the autumn of 1963 I decided, following the assassination of President Kennedy, to avoid further mention of the war until after the 1964 presidential election. It appeared likely that the Republican nominee would be Senator Barry Goldwater, who was openly and strenuously pressing for a much greater American military effort in Vietnam. Goldwater believed, I think sincerely, that the United States could quickly win the war if we would unleash a massive bombing attack against North Vietnam along with an accelerated offensive in the South.

Lyndon Johnson seemed to resist this approach; he told the Kennedy Cabinet and the White House officials he had inherited to continue the limited intervention in Vietnam. I believe that at the time of his death Jack Kennedy was beginning to see the hopelessness of containing an Asian political revolution with an alien military force. I became convinced that Johnson would try to hold the line in Vietnam until the 1964 election and would then move to extricate our military forces. It was hardly a direct approach, but I thought Kennedy would have handled it similarly. Being politic seemed understandable, given the more extreme position of Goldwater. (I have decided, in light of the subsequent tragedy of Vietnam, that the country is better off when candidates face such issues squarely, even if it is hard for them to do so. It is too risky to bet on a candidate's secret plans—or intentions. The deception also tends to be self-destructive, as the fates of Johnson and Nixon both testify.)

My assessment of Johnson's intentions was partly based on a conversation with him on a flight in December 1963 to the funeral of former Senator Herbert Lehman of New York, one of the great progressives of the twentieth century. I barely knew Johnson. We had seen each other at large parties and exchanged casual conversation around the Senate. In 1960, when I was running against Karl Mundt, then Majority Leader Johnson had spoken at a fund-raising luncheon for me in Washington, along with John Kennedy and Hubert Humphrey. Johnson had praised me in generous superlatives: one of "the ablest men in Washington; I want him elected." Johnson orated of someone whose hand he had shaken perhaps half a dozen times. With a gracious self-deprecating aside to me, the big Texas senator said, "George, I'll come to South Dakota and campaign for you or against you—whichever you think will get you the most votes."

From a distance, there was an exuberance I liked in Johnson, a skill I respected, even as I wondered about his wheeling and dealing for the sheer joy of it. But it was a distant, impersonal relationship, so I was surprised when the White House called and asked me to accompany the President to Senator Lehman's funeral. As soon as I boarded *Air Force One* I knew I was on the "liberal flight." Senators Joe Clark and Gaylord Nelson were there; so was ADA co-founder Joe Rauh, perhaps the most persistent of all the lawyers who have litigated for civil rights, civil liberties and other liberal goals. Johnson summoned us in groups to his cabin. He told Nelson, Clark and me, "The military has about four times as much of everything they need. Whether you're talking about missiles or submarines or bombers or aircraft carriers, they quadruple everything." He complained that the waste in the Pentagon was "incredible." At last, he assured us, we had a President who was on to the military.

That conversation was one reason I withheld my criticism on Vietnam through the next year. In August 1964, when word reached Washington that two American destroyers had been attacked in the Gulf of Tonkin, Johnson responded with a bomber strike against the North Vietnamese PT-boat base and then requested a congressional resolution endorsing resistance to "aggression" in Indochina. I was uneasy about the request, despite private assurances that it was primarily a ploy to defuse the Vietnam issue during the presidential campaign. As I walked to the Senate floor with Gaylord Nelson he showed me an amendment which said in effect that nothing in the resolution should be construed as changing the American policy of limited intervention. Nelson and I went to see Senator J. William Fulbright, the chairman of the Foreign Relations Committee and the floor manager of the resolution. Fulbright reiterated the plea that we had to help Johnson against Goldwater. We were just backing the President on his Tonkin response, not giving him a blank check for war. The resolution was "harmless," Fulbright insisted. It would have to go to conference if there was an amendment and that would frustrate Johnson's purpose—"to pull the rug out from under Goldwater." Nelson agreed to withdraw his amendment in return for a colloquy on the floor in which Fulbright emphasized the resolution's limited effect.

I accepted this scenario, though I was still disturbed. Only Senators Wayne Morse and Ernest Gruening voted against the Tonkin Resolution; they truly were right from the very start. My vote for the resolution is the one I most regret during my public career. It violated my own record against the Eisenhower resolution authorizing American action at presidential discretion in the Middle East. I should have known better than to be rationalized out of my convictions in the Tonkin case. Later I commiserated with Bill Fulbright; he was just telling Nelson and me what Johnson had told him. He was more than to make up for his own mistake in the turbulent years ahead. The lesson the Tonkin vote taught me—never to trade what I see as the truth for a winking assurance in a back room—probably explains why I now have a habit of speaking out publicly what some of my colleagues in the Senate prefer to say privately.

Not until long after Tonkin did the Congress and the country learn that the alleged attacks on the American destroyers were vastly exaggerated or flatly concocted as a pretext for a bombing strike and for the resolution, which, it came out, had been drafted weeks before the incident. These revelations added to the credibility gap which the Johnson Administration had already dug for itself. It was part of a pattern of deception which, in its culmination under Richard Nixon, alienated Americans from the political system. Presidents seemed to be manipulators.

After Johnson's election in 1964 I soon came to the view that he had never meant his campaign promise that "American boys are not going to be sent to do the job of Asian boys." Early in 1965 Senator Frank Church and I called for a negotiated settlement of the war. Perhaps naïvely, we still hoped that by avoiding direct attacks on the Administration and pressing instead for a negotiated settlement, we might persuade the President to modify his course. Bombing attacks had started against both South and North Vietnam in February 1965. But the Administration insisted that they were restrained and carefully controlled. Johnson just closed his ears to anyone who seemed to oppose him as well as the war. So for the last time I attempted an approach through channels. I called Johnson aide Bill Moyers and asked for an appointment with the President. It was scheduled for seven o'clock that night. Sitting in the Oval Office, I reviewed my concern that the war was escalating out of control. Johnson replied, "I'm going up old Ho Chi Minh's leg an inch at a time."

"Well, Mr. President," I said, "sometimes when we go up a leg we get slapped."

"I don't let those planes hit so much as a shithouse without my personal approval," he answered.

I had prepared a brief memorandum setting forth the reasons why the continuing American military involvement was mistaken militarily, politically, economically and morally. When I referred to it, Johnson said, "Don't give me another goddamn history lesson. I've got a drawerful of memos from Mansfield. I don't need a lecture on where we went wrong. I've got to deal with where we are now."

For the balance of my half-hour with the President, we discussed the assumptions of official policy. He insisted that if we did not stop "Communist aggression" in Vietnam, America would lose its influence elsewhere around the globe, including Latin America. Driving out the White House gate that night, I literally trembled for the future of the nation. I was not angry at Lyndon Johnson. I was filled with sadness and foreboding that this powerful, well-meaning man who wanted so desperately to be a great President was heading down the road to disaster.

After 1965, Johnson never invited me back to the White House. Nor was I ever there during Richard Nixon's term. It was unusual treatment for a senator, but it was the least of my concerns. As Joe Rauh has said, "The conversation isn't very good anyway." By coincidence, the first time I was in the White House in a decade was for a small stag dinner given by President Ford for King Hussein of Jordan on April 25, 1975, the day Saigon fell. He noted that it was the first time I had seen him there, but added that of course I was familiar with the White House. I answered that I hadn't been there in ten years and explained why. He seemed shocked; it was not Jerry Ford's way to exile his political opponents. Though we had disagreed about further military aid in the preceding weeks, he said, "Well, I'm glad you're here the day the war finally ended."

Shortly after my private meeting with Johnson in the spring of 1965, Hubert and Muriel Humphrey came over to the house for breakfast after we had all attended the Sunday-morning service at the Chevy Chase Methodist Church. Hubert had been Vice President for only a few weeks and we were still close friends. I told him of my deep misgivings about the war. I said that though it might be necessary for the Vice President to support the policy, I hoped he could do it without excessive enthusiasm and with as little personal identification with it as possible. This set off the first real argument Hubert and I had had in a decade as neighbors and friends. He replied heatedly that he believed in the policy—that we had to stop the Communists in Vietnam or they would take all of Asia. He continued that if I heard others say he wasn't with the President all the way, they weren't doing him any favor—it wasn't true. He had been fighting Communists, he added, ever since he had helped drive them out of the Democratic Farmer-Labor Party in Minnesota in the forties; liberals had to be anti-Communist and Vietnam was the test.

I thought back to his support for the Eisenhower resolution and to a conversation Hubert and I had on the way to work in 1961. (He would drop me at the White House, then continue to Capitol Hill.) One morning, in the midst of trouble over Berlin, shortly after the

Kennedy-Khrushchev summit in Vienna, I asked Hubert what he thought the President should do. "Quietly add a few billion to the military budget," he replied—which is exactly what Kennedy did.

Through 1965 Hubert continued to discuss Vietnam with me. He arranged one meeting in his office with Frank Church and Johnson's National Security Adviser McGeorge Bundy. Bundy intently read the draft of a speech Church was planning to deliver that week. He appeared subdued and calmly asked us not to dissent: "Americans have to present a united front." I wanted to know whether we were in Vietnam because of a fear of the Chinese or of Communism in Vietnam. He replied with some hesitation, "I think it's both." "Do you mean," I said, "that we're going to use American forces to stop Communism everywhere?" He remonstrated that he hadn't said that —in Vietnam, the Chinese were a factor. What, I continued, if the Vietcong were not Communists? Would we still be fighting Chinese expansion in Vietnam? Bundy was unsure. (When I saw Robert McNamara shortly afterward I decided to ask him the same question; one never got an ambivalent answer out of McNamara. "It's not Vietnamese Communism," he answered crisply. "We wouldn't be there if it weren't for aggression supported by the Chinese." The persistence of "the Chinese threat" as a justification for the Vietnam war was one of the factors that persuaded me to deliver that 1966 speech on China policy.)

Through the discussion with Bundy, Hubert sat silent and attentive. It was becoming obvious that he could not convert Church or me—that we were as hopeless as Morse and Gruening. As time went on, Hubert and I stopped talking about Vietnam. We tried to remain friends, but the war was "off-limits" in conversations between our families. Gradually we saw less of each other. There were no harsh words. It was just quietly understood that it might be awkward to spend much time together, though Hubert did invite Eleanor and me to spend a weekend at Greenbrier in late 1967. He knew that I was for Bob Kennedy in 1968; though I never formally endorsed him, I encouraged my supporters in South Dakota to work for Kennedy.

Hubert and I were to feel many strains on our friendship between 1965 and 1972. But it has been one of the best friendships of my life and in the end it withstood the strains. We are good friends now; maybe we always were, even through our awkward silences during the war. In most respects, Hubert would have been a great President. It was the country's tragedy as well as his that an instinctive anti-Communist globalism leading to the Vietnam trap denied him the White House.

Late in 1965 I took my first trip to Vietnam, accompanied by Joe

Floyd, a broadcaster and friend from South Dakota. That trip answered any lingering doubts about the rightness of my opposition to the war. My first flight over the jungle terrain left me wondering how any military strategist could seriously argue that this was a viable battleground for American forces. A visit to an American military hospital made me sick at heart as I met young Americans without legs, or arms, or faces, or genitals—all of them victims of land mines, booby traps or sniper fire. One handsome young lieutenant, his face twisted in pain, had just received a Purple Heart; both of his feet were missing. I was at a loss for words; I congratulated him for winning the Purple Heart. He looked at me and replied evenly, "Senator, that's easy to get in this damn place." We talked awhile about the war. He became the first of an endless stream of Vietnam veterans who were to tell me in the next few years of their disillusionment and disbelief. The next night I stayed with Marine General Lewis Walt at Da Nang. Listening to him talk earnestly long past midnight of his love for the Vietnamese people and his faith in the justice of American intervention, I thought how sad it was that devoted and capable men had been drawn into such a tragic misreading of reality.

While in Da Nang, on a tip from an American reporter, I requested permission to visit a hospital for civilian casualties. The scene will stay in my memory as long as I live. A decrepit, unbelievably overcrowded building staffed by several young Danish doctors and Vietnamese nurses was filled with savagely wounded men, women and children of all ages. Patients were lying on the lawn around the hospital, on the veranda, and two to a cot in the wards inside. One large open ward was jammed with two hundred patients who had been mangled by shrapnel from American bombs and artillery. As I walked from bed to bed, the room was absolutely silent. I reached out to shake the hand of a teen-age boy, but he recoiled in fear and pain. When I attempted to take a picture of an infant girl whose head was wrapped in bloody bandages, her mother smiled bravely, wiped some of the blood from the child's face and held her proudly before the camera. I left that hospital determined to redouble my efforts against the war. I was ready not merely to dissent, but to crusade— to join peace marches, sign petitions, lecture across the nation, appear on television, to do whatever might persuade the Congress and the American people to stop the horror.

6
1968:
A YEAR
OF DECISION

I n early 1968, after years of Administration predictions that the war in Vietnam was moving toward a victorious conclusion for "our side," the Vietcong staged a carefully planned offensive that actually carried them into the American embassy in Saigon. No matter how many statistics Administration spokesmen cited to prove that the Tet offensive had failed, it dealt a lethal blow to the American public's already declining faith in the war. From that time on, it was just a question of *how* our policy makers would liquidate their failing enterprise in Vietnam. The hopes for victory or even for a stalemate were dying, except in the minds of a few long-time advocates who were never able to face up to the realities of Southeast Asia.

By the summer of 1967, eighteen or twenty senators were openly opposing American involvement in the war. On numerous college campuses, in some of the churches, and among some business and professional leaders, opposition to the war had been building since 1964. The antiwar effort has frequently been seen largely as a campus movement. It was vastly more than that. Antiwar sentiment developed on a broad base that cut into all sections of society. But if any one institution instigated and then focused the opposition to the war, it was the United States Senate. The speeches of Ernest Gruening and Wayne Morse in 1964 were as intellectually sound and as morally indignant as any of the campus antiwar "teach-ins" that began a year or two later. Senate debate on the war and hearings before the Foreign Relations Committee between 1965 and 1968 led the way in the gathering evidence and protest against the war. As for the campuses, I recall receiving a mixed reaction to antiwar speeches in 1965 and 1966. Many students and professors were opposed to the war, but antiwar senators who sometimes tested sentiment on campus by calling for a show of hands would find students nearly as divided on the issue as their elders.

By 1967, however, the campuses and other elements of the American populace were either morally repelled or politically disillusioned over the escalating slaughter and destruction in Vietnam. Beyond considerations of humanity was the inflationary, deficit-producing economic waste of the war which destroyed Lyndon Johnson's hopes for "a Great Society." The war against poverty, the rebuilding of our cities, and the improvement of health and educational efforts—all of these were undercut by the emotional and economic drain into the Southeast Asia sinkhole.

Perhaps most costly of all was the loss of government credibility based on the widening chasm between Administration rhetoric and Vietnamese realities. For the first time in their lives, millions of Americans were beginning to realize that their own government had involved them in a mistaken war and was compounding the error with misleading public pronouncements and a deepening military entrapment. I kept recalling a boyhood experience when I turned my car into a muddy side road while hunting pheasants. After momentarily considering the possibility of stopping the car and backing up, I decided to accelerate through the muddy stretch to a gravel road at the next intersection. But the mud deepened, and my wheels were soon spinning into the mire up to the axles. That was Vietnam —even before the Tet offensive of 1968 erased any remaining doubts.

Any understanding of the politics of 1968 and of 1972 must begin with Vietnam. That conflict divided the American people as it had not been divided since the Civil War. The war tore the Democratic Party asunder. In differing ways, this issue so shattered Democratic ranks that it gave Richard Nixon his opportunity for victory both in 1968 and 1972.

It was against this Vietnam backdrop that a few individuals approached me in mid-1967 on the possibility that I would challenge President Johnson for the Democratic nomination in 1968. Antiwar activists Al Lowenstein, Marcus Raskin and Richard Barnet, after conversations among themselves, came to my Senate office on two or three occasions in the summer of 1967—first Raskin and Barnet together and then Lowenstein alone—urging me to enter the race. I knew that at least Lowenstein had previously tried to persuade Robert Kennedy to challenge Johnson. It was his view, as it was mine, that Kennedy had the best chance of either unseating Johnson or coming close enough to force an abandonment of the war policy. I had been privately urging Kennedy to run for the past two years. He seemed intrigued by the idea and yet, I became convinced, as did Lowenstein and others, that he was too "practical" to challenge an incumbent Democratic President. His reluctance may have been compounded by the knowledge that Johnson had inherited the Vietnam involvement from the Kennedy Administration.

Johnson's chief advisers on Vietnam were three Kennedy Administration holdovers: Secretary of Defense Robert McNamara, Secretary of State Dean Rusk, and presidential assistant Walt Rostow. These men all saw the war as an extension of Chinese and Soviet Communist power in Asia. They interpreted the conflict as "aggression from the North" despite the fact that the main fighting forces in the South were South Vietnamese guerrillas. They came to view the war as a test of American resolve against Communist "wars of liberation." Thus the beginning of systematic bombing of North and South Vietnam in February 1965, the assignment of 100,000 American troops that year, and a steady build-up to half a million Americans by 1967. This was the policy of "graduated response" that was supposed to bring North Vietnam to its knees or to the conference table. It was viewed by the Administration as a "limited" war, but it produced a near-total response from the Vietcong and the North Vietnamese. No matter how limited each new increment of American power might seem to Johnson and his advisers, it served only to deepen the resolve of the other side. That this strategy was devised by men selected by his assassinated brother doubtless made it more difficult for Robert Kennedy to challenge the President who was directing the war.

I was intrigued by the earnest young men who were urging me to challenge the President. My reservations were of a different dimension than Kennedy's. First of all, I did not have the national name recognition and political drawing power of a Kennedy. In addition, I was faced with a tough campaign for re-election to the Senate in South Dakota. To run for the presidential nomination would have involved asking the South Dakota Democrats to secure another nominee for my Senate seat. There was no liberal, antiwar candidate in sight that I thought could win the Senate seat if I gave it up. And even Lowenstein was concerned about the prospect of losing my voice in the Senate in a presidential nomination bid which might very well fail.

So there was little protest when I pointed out that it might make more sense to seek out a senator who was not faced with a re-election campaign in 1968. Looking down the list of Democratic senators in the *Congressional Directory,* we were struck by the fact that so many of the antiwar senators—Church, Fulbright, Morse, Clark, Nelson— were like me faced with Senate elections. I checked the names of Lee Metcalf and Gene McCarthy and suggested to my young friends that they visit these men. A short time later I encountered Gene in the Senate chamber and offered a light-hearted apology to him for sending the presidential mission to his office. I was startled when he replied in a casual but clearly serious manner, "Not at all. I think I may do it." I swallowed my surprise and said that I was glad to learn that he would consider it. "Well, somebody has to raise the flag," he said. I did not know then that his children and others had been urging him to challenge Johnson on the war. But it seemed to me that he had all but decided to do it.

Later that afternoon I received a call from Arthur Schlesinger, who had been conferring with Joe Rauh—both men long associated with the Americans for Democratic Action—about the possibility of a peace plank in the 1968 Democratic platform. Near the end of the conversation I told Arthur that I thought Gene McCarthy was going to run for President as an antiwar candidate. Within an hour Bob Kennedy called and asked to discuss the matter with me. He was highly agitated and pressed me on how certain I was about the information I had given Schlesinger. It was clear that he was deeply distressed by the possibility of a McCarthy candidacy. Bob and Gene had a cool, somewhat strained personal relationship—a continuance of a similar relationship between Gene and John Kennedy. But more to the point, Bob was forced to realize that his own option to enter the race at some later date would be seriously complicated by an earlier McCarthy candidacy. While indicating no plans to become a candidate, he urged me and other senators to think carefully before making any commitment to Gene.

But neither Gene McCarthy, nor Bob Kennedy, nor I, nor anyone else known to me was prepared for the outpouring of support that the McCarthy candidacy generated, with only a modest effort on the candidate's part. If I had sensed that such a groundswell of support were possible, I would have entered the race—even at the sacrifice of my Senate seat. Bob Kennedy was later quoted in several publications, including *Look* magazine, as saying that if I had done so, he would not have become a candidate.

But as the first strong McCarthy returns came in from the March 12 New Hampshire primary, Kennedy could not resist the temptation to plunge into the contest. Two days following his near-victory in

New Hampshire, McCarthy had accepted an invitation for a noon luncheon at my office with then Secretary of the Interior Stewart Udall, Congressman Frank Thompson of New Jersey, and Senator Lee Metcalf. Having worked together in the House of Representatives during the 1950s, the five of us would meet from time to time for lunch. This luncheon was to celebrate Gene's "moral victory" in New Hampshire. But Gene failed to attend the luncheon and his office seemed unable to provide even a clue as to his whereabouts.

As we were lingering over a final cup of coffee the phone rang; it was Bob Kennedy calling to ask if he and Ted Sorensen might drop by for a chat. When I told him who was in the office, he asked if they would all stay until he arrived. For the next two hours Bobby struggled with the presidential decision. He paced the office. He offered arguments pro and con. His face was that of a suffering man trying desperately to reach a solution to an enormously complicated problem. I think he wanted us to urge him into the fray, but we were reluctant to do that at a time when McCarthy was beginning to gather momentum.

Bobby spent that night grappling with the problem at his Hickory Hill home, where a number of his aides and advisers had gathered. By the end of the week, he was in the race for the nomination.

The rest of that spring was a succession of shock waves emanating from the Vietnam war and the domestic racial and political crisis.

On March 31 Lyndon Johnson went before the television cameras to deliver a speech which ended with a political explosion: "I have concluded that I should not permit the presidency to become involved in the partisan divisions that are developing in this political year. Accordingly, I shall not seek, and I will not accept, the nomination of my party for another term as your President."

Johnson's announcement came in the context of three factors. He was about to be defeated by Gene McCarthy in the April second Wisconsin primary—with Kennedy and McCarthy preparing to challenge him in other primaries all the way to the Chicago convention. Second, his new Secretary of Defense, Clark Clifford, had concluded that the war in Vietnam was not headed for victory. General Westmoreland was requesting at least 200,000 additional troops beyond the half million already there—with no assurance that this would turn the tide. In any event, all indications were that neither congressional nor public opinion would sustain such a major escalation. Third, Johnson viewed the gathering racial tensions and antiwar protests with deep concern, knowing that they jeopardized his presidential authority and his capacity to govern.

His surprise announcement came just in time to reduce serious embarrassment to the White House over McCarthy's victory in Wisconsin forty-eight hours later. Then, two days after the Wisconsin results, Martin Luther King, Jr., was assassinated on the balcony of a Memphis motel. Thousands of blacks erupted in an outbreak of pillage, looting and burning in major cities across the country. A few steps from the White House, Fourteenth Street went up in flames, and in Chicago, Mayor Richard Daley issued a police order: "Shoot to kill arsonists, and shoot to maim looters." Riots in more than a hundred cities killed thirty-seven people within a few days of King's death. The Situation Room in the basement of the White House was now monitoring serious trouble in America, as well as the deepening war in Southeast Asia.

Robert Kennedy, who learned of King's death en route to a street rally in Indianapolis, broke the news to a group of waiting blacks and then quoted Aeschylus: " 'Even in our sleep, pain which cannot forget falls drop by drop upon the heart, until in our despair, against our own will, comes wisdom through the awful grace of God.' "

As for Richard Nixon, the three British journalists who wrote the best book on the 1968 election reported that prior to Johnson's announcement that he would not seek re-election, Nixon had been planning a major speech on Vietnam in which he intended to moderate his position. "He had felt the strength of the desire for peace that swept the country after the Tet offensive. The reason he gave for canceling his speech was a foretaste of the cautious technique he was to use all year long. He did not wish, he said, to embarrass 'our negotiators' in Paris."

Nixon attended the King funeral, but his Southern regional campaign director devoted the day to reassuring telephone calls to Southern political leaders explaining that it was "something the candidate felt he had to do." The British reporters noted that this "instinctive professionalism was all too prophetic of the price that Nixon would pay for the Presidency."

Vice President Hubert Humphrey was in the presidential race shortly after Johnson's withdrawal statement, but his path to the nomination differed sharply from McCarthy's and Kennedy's. Humphrey ran as the heir apparent to the presidency and went after the delegates already pledged to Johnson or those to be selected in the caucuses and conventions of the nonprimary states. McCarthy and Kennedy slugged it out in the primaries—Indiana, Nebraska, Oregon, South Dakota and California.

Although I was pleased that both McCarthy and Kennedy were challenging the Johnson-Humphrey war policies, I made a decision to avoid being drawn formally into the presidential nominating contests and instead to concentrate on my re-election to the Senate. I told each of the three candidates that I would avoid formal endorsements but would be pleased to host all of them in South Dakota. I did in fact warmly introduce McCarthy to a large Sioux Falls rally that spring. When Humphrey came to Huron, his former hometown, I was on hand to greet him and to introduce him as an old friend and neighbor. But in introducing Robert Kennedy in Sioux Falls, Rapid City and Mitchell, I left little doubt that he was my choice. This was not an easy decision, because of my long-time personal affection for Hubert and my appreciation for McCarthy's early effort in New Hampshire and Wisconsin. I had hoped at various times after 1965 that Hubert was secretly opposed to the war and was only going along with the policy because of his role as Vice President. But he took pains to make clear to me and other old friends in the Senate that he was a convinced believer in American policy in Vietnam. I had no reason to doubt that in 1968, but I thought there was a strong possibility that he would emerge as the Democratic presidential nominee in any event and I did not want to cripple him for the race against Nixon in the fall. I knew that Hubert had a good record on civil rights and domestic economic issues, and however objectionable his position on the war might be, it could be no worse than Nixon's. Indeed, in 1954 while men like Lyndon Johnson and Hubert Humphrey were warning against another American involvement in an Asian land war, Vice President Richard Nixon told reporters on the eve of the French defeat by Ho Chi Minh that the United States "must face up to the situation and dispatch forces." It is one of the maddening paradoxes of politics that Richard Nixon, who had long supported American military intervention in Asia, should ride into the presidency in 1968 because of the unpopularity of that intervention. To compound the irony, four years later he was to be re-elected in part because of his "winding down" of the Vietnam war and his rapprochement with China—policies which he had long opposed and which I as his Democratic opponent had long advocated.

In any event, when Robert Kennedy landed at Sioux Falls on April 16, I introduced him as follows:

> For reasons that most of you understand, I have seen fit not to take sides in the current presidential contest for the Democratic nomination. I feel that my fellow South Dakotans should make their own decision.
>
> All three men now being considered as candidates—Senators Kennedy and McCarthy and Vice President Humphrey—are close and treasured friends of mine. Each of them would serve our nation well. Each of them would have my cooperation as President. Each of them knows that situations might develop where I would disagree with him.
>
> And may I add that President Johnson has taken on new stature and

dignity by the magnanimous manner in which he placed his view of the Vietnam issue above his desires for re-election.

But I do want to say to my fellow South Dakotans in the presence of our distinguished guest that if he is elected President of the United States, he will, in my judgment, become one of the three or four greatest Presidents in our national history.

I have heard the talk about his ruthlessness and his long hair. But he isn't as ruthless as was the great Theodore Roosevelt, and his hair isn't half as long as Thomas Jefferson's, and unlike Abraham Lincoln, he has no beard at all.

What he does have is the absolute personal honesty of a Woodrow Wilson, the stirring passion for leadership of Andrew Jackson, and the profound acquaintance with personal tragedy of Lincoln.

Recently, one of our nation's most eloquent preachers was slain at Memphis. In one of his finest sermons, he took for his text the words of the Great Teacher: "Be ye therefore wise as serpents and harmless as doves."

"We must," said Dr. King, "combine the toughness of the serpent and the softness of the dove, a tough mind and a tender heart."

One of the reasons, I suspect, that some people are puzzled by Senator Kennedy is that he is a tough-minded man with a tender heart.

He is, to borrow Dr. King's fitting description of the good life, "a creative synthesis of opposites."

The presidency is a sobering office that calls forth the seeds of greatness. Many a man whose talents were undetected or misinterpreted took on new stature in the White House. I think that was true of the late John F. Kennedy who became a greater man with each passing month he lived in the presidential office.

You people know the affection and the esteem I held for President Kennedy, but it is my carefully measured conviction that Senator Robert Kennedy, even more than our late beloved President, would now bring to the presidency a deeper measure of experience and a more profound capacity to lead our troubled land into the light of a new day.

So while I decline to endorse any presidential candidate prior to the national convention, I do speak from the heart about a gallant friend and colleague whom I now present with pride to you—Senator Robert Kennedy.

Bob loved that introduction and so did his campaign aides. "We'll take non-endorsements like that any day," said his press secretary, Frank Mankiewicz. Bill vandenHeuvel, a New York friend and campaign aide to Kennedy, was so moved by the introduction that he ordered it to be reprinted and distributed nationally. The next day Ethel Kennedy called me to thank me profusely for what I had said.

Kennedy returned to South Dakota on May 10. I met him in Omaha as he was nailing down a victory in the Nebraska primary, and we flew together to my hometown, where he was to speak and remain overnight. He was plainly exhausted. I introduced him to a large crowd at the Corn Palace in Mitchell and he responded with a warm tribute to me. "There is no one I feel more genuinely about, whether we are in politics together or not—about the importance of their contribution and the importance of their understanding and feeling —than George McGovern. Of all my colleagues in the United States Senate, the person who has the most feeling and does things in the most genuine way, without that affecting his life, is George McGovern. He is so highly admired by all his colleagues, not just for his ability but because of the kind of man he is. That is truer of him than of any man in the United States Senate." He then proceeded to ramble in a disconnected, repetitious manner for nearly forty-five minutes. Finally, in an effort to salvage a tired and failing performance, he threw the meeting open to questions from the floor. One or two slightly hostile questions cut through his fatigue to his smoldering temper, and he finished off his interrogators with a strong retort that fired up his supporters.

After the rally I went with him to the Lawler Café for a late-night snack with my old friend and Kennedy admirer, Margaret Conlon. As we ate, Margaret saw a small spaniel and went storming across the room: "Get that dog out of this café." When someone whispered to her that it was Kennedy's dog, she reached out and petted him, inquiring sweetly, "Isn't he the nicest dog you ever saw in your life?"

In presenting Bob to the Corn Palace crowd, I had quoted from the popular song "The Impossible Dream." As we sat around the old Lawler round table, where I had spent countless hours in political conversation during the past fifteen years, Bob wistfully asked, "Do you think it is impossible?"

The next morning I drove with him to the Mitchell airport prior to his departure for a rally at Brookings. There was a note of loneliness about him as he boarded his small chartered plane that left me with a vague sadness. I never saw him again.

A few days later Kennedy defeated McCarthy by a narrow margin in the June 5 California primary. And on the same day he won a sweeping victory in South Dakota. McCarthy received 20 percent of the South Dakota vote, a slate committed to Humphrey garnered 30 percent, and Kennedy took the remaining 50 percent of the vote. It was the largest election margin he had won in any state. His victory was all the more remarkable in that he had been pulled into the South Dakota race somewhat against his will. Bill Dougherty of Sioux Falls had simply filed a Kennedy delegate slate and forced the candidate's hand. Now Dougherty was jubilantly savoring the Kennedy victory at campaign headquarters in Sioux Falls.

I was at my home in Washington that night, and not wishing to add to Bob's hectic circumstances in Los Angeles, I decided to call his brother, Ted, in San Francisco with congratulations on the victories in South Dakota and California. But Ted told me that his brother was about to go down to the ballroom of the Ambassador Hotel in Los Angeles to make his victory statement and would want to talk to me immediately. In a moment I was on the phone with the victorious candidate and we discussed his strong showing in South Dakota. He was especially pleased to learn that some of the Sioux Indian precincts had given him 100 percent of their vote. The notes of this telephone conversation were included with the scribblings that he took to the rostrum for his victory statement a few minutes later.

It was already very late, Washington time, so after completing the telephone chat to Los Angeles, I went to bed. I had scarcely fallen asleep when I was awakened by a phone call from my state field representative in South Dakota, Pat McKeever, who told me between sobs, "Bobby Kennedy has just been shot in Los Angeles."

I reacted with anger rather than grief. Somehow I did not immediately believe that a tough young battler such as Bob would die from a bullet wound. But I was furious that another Kennedy had been shot down just at the moment of his greatest triumph. The next day Frank Mankiewicz was on television announcing that Bob Kennedy was dead. "He was forty-two."

On the funeral train slowly working its way from New York to Washington's Union Station, my grief was compounded by a recurring thought. If I had entered the presidential race in late 1967 as Raskin, Barnet, Lowenstein and others had urged, perhaps Robert Kennedy would still be alive. Did he mean it when he told reporters he would not have become a candidate if "someone like George McGovern" had been in first?

As I pondered this question Bill Dougherty tapped me on the shoulder and said that we had to start thinking about "a replacement for Bobby." Bill was and is one of my dearest political allies, but I was irritated that he should initiate such a discussion on a funeral train bearing the grieving Kennedy family. Yet I knew he was as saddened over Kennedy's death as I was. Indeed, it was his devotion to Kennedy that led him to talk not only to me, but to California's Jesse Unruh and other political leaders about the urgency of securing a candidate who could lead the Kennedy delegates to the Democratic National Convention.

Bill was convinced that the heated exchanges between McCarthy and Kennedy during the primaries would preclude a shift of the Kennedy delegates to McCarthy. Humphrey's support for the Administration war policy would rule him out for most of the grieving delegates. "I think it's up to you," Dougherty said.

Before the long train ride was over, other Kennedy supporters were making the same observation to me. Messages reached me from the young Kennedy legislative aides, Adam Walinsky and Peter Edelman. Soon telephone calls came from Frank Mankiewicz and Joe Dolan urging me to pick up the banner of their fallen leader. I was pleased by the confidence of the Kennedy aides, but I felt they were acting prematurely. It seemed to me that if anyone was to enter the race at that point, it should be Bob's surviving brother, Ted, and that he should be given time to compose his thoughts.

I also felt that Gene McCarthy, despite the recent frictions, should inherit the Kennedy delegates. Early in July I encountered Gene on the Senate floor and decided that I should talk to him about a rumored report that he was preparing to go to Hanoi on a peace-seeking mission. I said that such a move might destroy his candidacy —that his political enemies would miss no opportunity to blame him for prolonging the war. McCarthy agreed that the mission was politically hazardous in the middle of an election, but, he said, "I really don't care about that. The nomination is already sewed up. Hubert's got it. I'll probably keep going to keep up the spirits of my supporters, but it's all over."

I was astounded. It seemed to me that having invested months of his own time and effort and that of thousands of idealistic supporters, Gene would be moving hard to secure the Kennedy delegates, as well as those still uncommitted across the country. In retrospect, however, I think his assessment was not entirely unrealistic. A large portion of the delegates to the 1968 convention were picked by party leaders loyal to the Johnson-Humphrey Administration. Some of these leaders and delegates had worked for John Kennedy in the early sixties, and as such might have responded to a direct appeal from a Kennedy. But they did not look kindly on the McCarthy candidacy. Many of these same orthodox Democrats were hostile to me four years later. In short, the delegate-selection system was stacked against a reform candidate running against an incumbent Democratic Administration. McCarthy may have given up too soon, but I doubt that either he or Kennedy could have denied Humphrey the nomination in 1968.

I was nonetheless convinced that every effort should be made to maximize the impact of the antiwar effort at the coming convention. And Bill Dougherty and his colleagues were convinced that the only sure way to get the Kennedy delegates to the convention was to rally them around my candidacy. My Senate staff was alarmed by this prospect because they viewed any such effort as a near-fatal blow to my hopes for re-election to the Senate that fall. This concern did not deter Dougherty.

On July 13 he organized a Robert Kennedy memorial dinner at Huron, South Dakota. At the head table that night he assembled Governor Pat Lucey of Wisconsin, Ted Sorensen, Jesse Unruh and Richard Goodwin. A sizable contingent of the national press corps also flocked into Huron for the dinner. Sorensen, meeting with the Kennedy delegates after the dinner, extracted a pledge that they would remain uncommitted to either McCarthy or Humphrey until further efforts were made to persuade me to be their standard-bearer.

Eleanor and I were at that time attending the World Council of Churches convocation in Uppsala, Sweden. We had heard vague reports of the Huron meeting, but I was still of the view that if there was to be a late presidential entry, it should be Ted. Following my return from Sweden, I went to Los Angeles to address a meeting of a newly formed group called the Kennedy Action Corps. Unaware that the meeting had been organized to encourage me to become a candidate, I spoke quietly to the crowd on the need to advance the ideals of social justice and peace represented by RFK. "I do not speak for Robert Kennedy . . .," I said. "But perhaps from the meaning of his life we can take a new measure of conviction, a new courage, a new resolve that he shall not have died in vain; and that . . . we can yet serve the end he so tenderly sought for us all—'to tame the savageness of man, and make gentle the life of the world.' "

I was unprepared for the sustained standing ovation and the cries of "We want McGovern" which filled the hall.

Actually, I had delivered that speech in a deeply troubled mood. During the previous night I had been awakened by a long-distance call from Eleanor to the Beverly Hills home of Louis and Miriam Licht, where I was spending the night. Eleanor told me that our nineteen-year-old daughter, Terry, a freshman at Dakota Wesleyan, had just been arrested and jailed in Rapid City on a marijuana-possession charge. She had been canvassing for my re-election in the Black Hills with a group of young volunteers when a woman employee at the motel where they were staying discovered a small container of marijuana in their room. The woman, a devout Republican, reported her find to local Republican leaders, who in turn notified the Attorney General's office at Pierre. The suspected marijuana was quickly flown to the State University for identification, and that night the Rapid City police, armed with an arrest warrant signed by an interim judge, arrested Terry and lodged her in jail. The South Dakota Legislature had only a few weeks earlier passed an incredibly tough marijuana law calling for a mandatory prison sentence of not less than five years for a first offense.

I was familiar with the new law and I was sick at heart when I read the story of Terry's arrest in the morning edition of the Los Angeles *Times*. Lou Licht drove me to the Kennedy meeting and made arrangements for me to fly to Rapid City immediately after my speech. I walked from the auditorium with the shouts of "We want McGovern" ringing in my ears, but the McGovern on my mind was 1,500 miles away and she was in jail.

I had called my attorney friend George Bangs of Rapid City during the night and by the time I arrived in the Black Hills, Terry and Eleanor were waiting for me in his office. I expected the worst in the emotion-charged atmosphere of election year, but to my pleasant surprise, people all across South Dakota poured out their sympathy to our family. When wire photos appeared showing me with Terry in court, the messages of sympathy and support increased. Even conservative Republicans telephoned to tell me that the new law was too harsh and that they were worried about their own children being caught in its web. Several judges told me privately that the law was a legal outrage.

Fortunately, "Archie" Bangs and his partner, Wallace McCullen, were able lawyers who spotted a discrepancy in Terry's arrest. The commission of the interim judge who had signed the warrant had expired two hours and twenty-eight minutes before he attached his signature. The case was thrown out of court on grounds of "inadmissible evidence." I was overjoyed—except for one haunting thought: How many young people were sitting in prisons across the land for similar offenses who were not so well represented in court? I wondered if my daughter would have escaped if her father had not been a United States senator with able legal friends. But as I campaigned across the state that summer and fall, I discovered that the prevailing view was that my daughter had been singled out for arrest *because* she was the daughter of a United States senator. Whether or not that was the case I do not know, but I shall always be proud of the tolerance and understanding of my South Dakota constituents— Democrats and Republicans alike—who stood with us when their understanding was so important to our family. Strange as it may seem, that unfortunate arrest became a political plus in the 1968 re-election campaign.

Following Terry's release, I took my family to a secluded Black Hills cabin near Hisega to relax. But the calls from the relentless Dougherty continued. After several days, not wanting to burden Ted Kennedy, I called his brother-in-law Steve Smith and asked him if there was any chance Ted might enter the race as a stand-in for Bob. "I see no chance of that," Smith said.

That night, while having dinner at a beautiful restaurant operated by a Republican friend, Carl Burgess, I asked Burgess somewhat nervously how he would react if I decided to run for President. Carl looked at me for a moment and then pulled out his checkbook. He scrawled something on a check and handed it to me in the dim glow of the lantern on the table. "McGovern for President—$5,000." That was it. I knew I would be in the race.

When I called Owen Donley, my administrative assistant in Washington, to tell him to prepare for a news conference on Saturday, he inquired only half jokingly, "Are you still at Hisega or have you put your head upon Mount Rushmore?" Eleanor was nearly as stunned as Owen, although she knew I had been wrestling with the matter for days.

So the following Saturday, August 10, just a fortnight before the Democratic National Convention was to open in Chicago, I walked into the Senate Caucus Room with George Cunningham and announced:

> I wear no claim to the Kennedy mantle, but I believe deeply in the twin goals for which Robert Kennedy gave his life—an end to the war in Vietnam and a passionate commitment to heal the divisions in our own society. . . . If I have any special asset for national leadership, it is, I believe, a sense of history—an understanding of the forces that have brought this country to a position of power and influence in the world and an appreciation of what is important in our own time. For five years I have warned against our deepening involvement in Vietnam—the most disastrous political and military blunder in our national experience. That war must be ended now—not next year or the year following, but now. . . . Beyond this, we need to harness the full spiritual and political resources of this nation to put an end to the shameful remnants of racism and poverty that still afflict our land. Just as brotherhood is the condition of survival in a nuclear world, so it is the condition of peace in America. . . . It is for these purposes that I declare myself a candidate for the presidential nomination.

There was little time for anything other than a few public appearances, press interviews and a few brief trips in an American Airlines Electra that we engaged. Hurried trips were arranged to New York City; Kearney, Nebraska; Huron, South Dakota; Valparaiso, Indiana; Cleveland; and on to Chicago.

Bill Dougherty, Don O'Brien of Sioux City and Dave Harrison of Massachusetts quickly opened up a small delegate-courting operation at the Blackstone Hotel in Chicago. Professor Richard Wade, a fellow historian at the University of Chicago, organized a volunteer operation that was coordinated with the Dougherty delegate hunt. Stan Kaplan of Charlotte, North Carolina, loaned us $17,000 to pay for the telephones and other convention-hall expenses. Gloria Steinem, the New York feminist, not only raised money but guided me around the national-media world concentrated in New York.

High atop the Time-Life Building in New York, I was nearing the end of a lengthy off-the-record luncheon discussion with the editors of *Time* and *Life*. Gloria had arranged the meeting, and she and Pierre Salinger were obviously pleased with the way the dialogue had progressed. Then editor in chief Hedley Donovan asked what he said would be the final question: "Senator, I have heard from some people that you're too nice a guy to be President. Let me put it this way. They think it takes a real son-of-a-bitch to be a good President. Are you a son-of-a-bitch?"

I could see that this was no idle question, as every person around the table leaned forward. "Well," I said, "I don't know whether it takes a son-of-a-bitch to be President, but it does seem to me that we've given that thesis a generous test in recent years."

The meeting broke up in laughter, but as we stepped into the elevator Pierre said, "George, that was a great answer, but they'll never keep that 'off the record'; it's too juicy to hold."

The feeling that I was "too nice" or "too decent" or "not tough enough" was a recurring concern about me, both in 1968 and 1972. It was a superficial observation. Deep in my soul I believed that much of the world's "toughness" was a thin cover for the insecurity, lack of self-confidence and even paranoia that marked many men in public life. I have normally been "soft" on people and "tough" on issues. There was no doubt in my mind about my capacity to be a "tough" President on the matters that affected the national interest. For starters, I believed that I could quickly end the war in Vietnam on terms acceptable to the American people, that I could call for a declaration of war if and when circumstances required and that I could just as quickly withdraw American forces when circumstances so indicated. I had no fear of standing up to the Joint Chiefs against excessive military outlays or ill-advised interventions. It was my closest friend and later my 1972 campaign finance director, Henry Kimelman, who said affectionately: "George McGovern is the most modest, self-effacing egomaniac I ever knew."

It takes a rather large ego to propel a man into a race for the most powerful office in the world. And it takes a generous supply of toughness even to get close to a presidential nomination. Some of the journalists who were worried about how much toughness there was in me never seemed to realize that it requires no toughness to wound a politician with a pen or a tongue, but it takes considerable toughness to receive those barbs while keeping a calm heart and a clear eye.

There was no chance for me to win the presidential nomination in 1968. But I did keep calm and steady. So did Eleanor and my family. This was the year that gentle Eleanor first displayed to the nation her essential strength. She handled press conferences, television interviews and public appearances as well as any candidate's partner I ever knew. Millions of Americans remembered the graceful intelligence she manifested in that brief effort.

Three experiences are still vivid in my mind from the 1968 convention: a three-way, nationally televised debate with Humphrey and McCarthy before the California delegation; Abe Ribicoff's nominating speech on the night of the Chicago street riots; and my appearance with the victorious Humphrey at the speaker's rostrum following his acceptance speech.

The debate was arranged by Jesse Unruh, who headed the huge California delegation. It took place at the LaSalle Hotel on Tuesday morning, the day before the nomination was to be decided. Each of the three candidates spoke for ten minutes, followed by questions from the delegates. Although Gene and Hubert are two of the nimblest debaters in public life, neither of them were impressive in that crucial test. Gene was in an irritable mood and used a considerable portion of his time in defensive statements aimed at me rather than the central war issue that had given force to his campaign. Hubert spoke as a defender of Administration policy, opening himself to easy refutation. I have never been more wildly cheered by an audience that previously knew little about me. It was a satisfying triumph by any standard. As I worked my way through the crowd of happy faces and outstretched hands after the debate, I could hear the exclamations: "Where did *he* come from?" "Why wasn't he in earlier?" "McGovern for President!" It was a unique experience for a junior Senator from South Dakota to know that he had bested two highly talented colleagues before the television viewers of the nation. I confess that thoughts of a future bid for the presidency entered my mind as I drove back to the Blackstone Hotel that day.

Abe Ribicoff's nominating speech started off ordinarily enough the following night. But in the holding room off the convention floor, Abe had been watching an incredible pitched battle between the Chicago police and young demonstrators. Discarding his prepared text, Abe displayed a forceful indignation as he said, "With George McGovern, we wouldn't have Gestapo tactics in the streets of Chicago." The great hall was momentarily hushed under the shock of these words. Then came a deafening roar of approval from hundreds of delegates, while hundreds of others, led by Mayor Daley, exploded in an angry blast at Ribicoff. Abe stood quietly until the shouting subsided. Then with a faint smile he looked squarely into the Chicago mayor's face and said, "How hard it is to accept the truth. How hard it is."

I was watching the proceedings with a doctor friend, Lawn Thompson, in my suite at the Blackstone. We had just viewed the sickening scene on the street below my fourth-floor window as helmeted, club-wielding police closed in on the young antiwar demonstrators. It was not a pleasant experience. The conservative Lawn Thompson, who a few minutes before had expressed some irritation with the youthful demonstrators, was now saying, "Can you believe what those sons-of-bitches are doing to those kids?"

I could believe it because I knew how deeply the war had polarized the American people. The explosion on Michigan Avenue was not fundamentally the fault of the police or of Mayor Daley or the zeal of the young. It was the outgrowth of a miserable war and deceptive national leadership that infuriated young idealists whose demonstrations in turn offended the patriotism of many Americans who assumed that their leaders were representing the nation's interest.

As I pondered the violence in the streets and the shouting contest at the convention—all of this symbolized by the stand-off between two former political allies, Daley and Ribicoff—I felt more sadness than anger. Earlier that week, Abe and I had gone through a pleasant conversation with the Chicago mayor in which we had urged his support for my candidacy. But now Abe and the mayor were shouting at each other and I knew the Democratic Party was being torn asunder. I was to see that same disruptive force rip the party again in 1972 after four years of negative, divisive manipulation by the Nixon-Agnew team.

I had gone into the Chicago convention resolved to support the nominee of our party, whether it was McCarthy or Humphrey. For a brief period of time there were rumors that Ted Kennedy might fly to Chicago as a last-minute candidate. I never at any time believed Ted would enter the competition, although I knew that some people —possibly including Daley—were hoping that he would do so. But as I prepared to speak to a group of delegates at the Chicago Club on Wednesday morning, the day of the nominating speeches, Ted telephoned to assure me that he would not be a candidate. He indicated that if Daley and others had publicly committed their support, he might have entered the competition, but he was unwilling to come to Chicago in the absence of announced support from influential party leaders, including Daley.

As it became clear to me that Humphrey would be the nominee, my major interest was in securing the strongest possible platform on ending the war in Vietnam. Serious efforts were made by McCarthy and McGovern representatives to strike a Vietnam plank compromise with Humphrey. But each time we thought an agreement could be reached, it was blocked by representatives of President Johnson. On Tuesday morning Walter Reuther, Norman Cousins and Clark Kerr—all Humphrey backers—came to my suite for breakfast to gain my agreement to a Vietnam plank that was acceptable to Humphrey. After reading their draft carefully, I told them that while it did not go as far as I would like, it was a plank that I could accept. They secured the same assurance from McCarthy and jubilantly reported back to Humphrey. Their joy was short-lived. Hubert found the proposal acceptable and was delighted that Gene and I could endorse it, but when he checked it with the White House, he got a blunt rebuke—to which he quickly yielded.

The rejection of the compromise Vietnam plank was a political tragedy. Its acceptance would have given McCarthy's supporters the satisfaction of knowing that they had won on the central issue of 1968 despite losing their presidential bid. The Kennedy-McGovern forces would have been equally cheered. But this was not to be and the cost to Democratic unity behind Humphrey was fatal.

Considering the wishes of much of his constituency, McCarthy refused even to attend the final session of the convention as Humphrey gave his acceptance address. Eleanor and I accepted Hubert's invitation to be in a guest box as he spoke, and we joined him at the rostrum following his speech. There was a deafening roar from the delegates as Hubert and I stood together at the rostrum. As I turned to leave, I almost collided with Douglas, the youngest Humphrey son, whom I had watched growing up next door to us on Coquelin Terrace. His eyes were glistening as he said to me, "Thanks for standing with my dad tonight." Sometimes in politics the personal factor can loom large.

Late the next forenoon, at a final press conference in Chicago, I expressed the hope that there would be no "drop-outs from the effort to end the war in Vietnam. I hope we won't withdraw to the sidelines in despair because we didn't get the plank that we wanted . . . or the . . . nominee." I then fielded questions from the press, including a query as to whether or not the street violence had hurt the Democratic Party. "I think all of America has suffered from what has taken place. Every citizen in this land wants to see law and order restored, but we can't do it by the kind of methods that were used on the streets of Michigan Avenue here last night. I hope and pray that kind of exhibition will not be repeated anywhere else in America, because if it is, instead of contributing to the cause of law and order and hope in this country, it will contribute to disorder and despair."

Then, as I terminated the press conference, something unusual happened. The press, with their reputation for being hard-boiled and unemotional, stood and applauded as Eleanor and I walked from the auditorium.

It was a good feeling. We had run an eighteen-day campaign for the presidency with a total expenditure of about $80,000. We had no debts. Familiar names from the Kennedy campaigns had given their help—Pierre Salinger, Frank Mankiewicz, Pat Riley, Joe Dolan, Ted Sorensen, Adam Walinsky, Arthur Schlesinger, Dick Wade, Ed McDermott, Shirley MacLaine, Gloria Steinem, and, of course, the nonstop workers Dougherty, O'Brien and Harrison. But much of the difficult behind-the-scenes work of the campaign, including the convention scheduling, had been carried by my Senate staff—George Cunningham, Patricia Donovan, Owen Donley, John Holum, Barbara Giles and Beverly Tobin. These six staffers are still working in my Senate office a decade later. There were countless volunteers who flocked in to work at the Chicago headquarters or in my Senate office whom I did not know. One of the first was a pleasant girl by the name of Mary Jo Kopechne.

That night, after my family flew back to Washington, I boarded a plane for South Dakota to resume my interrupted campaign for re-election to the Senate. A few weeks before, I had stood at 70 percent in a public-opinion poll against the former governor who was my opponent, Archie Gubbrud of Alcester. But what would I find now after the turbulence of Chicago and the absence from South Dakota? I had already begun to hear reports of nasty attacks from the opposition. A new poll was soon to show that the reaction to my sympathy for the young antiwar demonstrators and my criticism of the way they were handled by the police had dropped my poll rating to 48 percent—just two points above Archie Gubbrud.

But I went straight from Chicago to the South Dakota State Fair then in progress at Huron—and plunged into the Senate race. When I was introduced at the grandstand, 10,000 people gave me the loudest applause I have ever experienced in South Dakota. For the next three days I scarcely sat down even to eat as I shook the hands and accepted the comments and questions of thousands of State Fair visitors. Two matters were clear to me by the end of that marathon at the fair: first, I had been hurt by the negative public reaction to the Chicago disorders; second, I was confident we were going to win re-election.

I eased the anxieties on the first matter by affirming the fact that most of the Chicago police and officials had handled their duties responsibly. I also kept a Chicago speaking date in mid-September at a fund-raising dinner for Illinois Attorney General Bill Clark, who had supported my brief presidential bid even as he was launching a race for the U.S. Senate. Prior to the dinner I paid a courtesy call to the mayor and told him that all of us had to heal the wounds opened at the Chicago convention. "Yes," he said, "that is important because I think our presidential nominee in '72 will either be you or young Kennedy."

By the time I had returned from the brief trip to Chicago, the outline of the campaign against me in South Dakota was clear. It was to be a negative attack charging me with being at war with "South Dakota thinking." A mean-spirited, narrow-gauged youthful climber from Sioux Falls, Jerry Simmons, had moved into the Gubbrud camp to design the negative advertising campaign. Simmons and his cohorts developed a series of newspaper ads carrying an unflattering profile of me that was always done in black—a rather vivid likeness of the devil.

Each ad carried a text that twisted my words out of context. Legislation which I had introduced to provide tax incentives in rural states such as South Dakota to slow the migration of job-seeking youths from the small towns and farms to metropolitan areas was interpreted as a plan on my part to import "50,000 big-city Negroes" to South Dakota.

When these ads first began to appear, I reacted angrily to their crude distortions. But soon I found myself laughing at one of the ads and a quiet confidence emerged as I recognized the desperate character of the opposition campaign. As they had done so many times before, the opposition strategists were overplaying their hand. The more strident they became, the more I sought to sound a positive note of restraint and reason.

In the end, the people of South Dakota gave me a resounding victory—by nearly 40,000 votes. For a senator who had been elected six years earlier on a recount margin of 597 votes, 1968 was "a very good year."

7
REFORM

The presidential campaign of 1968 left me with the strong impression that a Democratic presidential candidate closely identified with the Vietnam war policy would have great difficulty in being elected. Perhaps the reverse was equally true: an all-out antiwar Democratic candidate would also have had considerable difficulty being elected.

Hubert Humphrey was an unusually articulate, vigorous candidate. For years he had crisscrossed the nation speaking on behalf of Democratic candidates and causes. He had served tirelessly as a U.S. senator and as Vice President of the United States. He was running as the candidate of the majority party. On the other hand, his opponent, Richard Nixon, had been narrowly defeated by John Kennedy in the 1960 presidential race and then defeated decisively by Governor Pat Brown in the California gubernatorial race two years later. He had assured reporters after his second defeat that they "won't have Richard Nixon to kick around anymore."

But Nixon, after an eight-year absence from public office, came back in 1968 to be elected over the seemingly much more winsome Humphrey. He did so despite the fact that an independent third-party candidacy by Alabama Governor George Wallace probably siphoned off more potential votes from Nixon than from Humphrey.

The 1968 Nixon victory is explained at least in part by Humphrey's reluctance to break with the unpopular war policies of the Johnson Administration. Early in his campaign he made an evening appearance with me at the Coliseum in Sioux Falls. In that speech, at my urging, he inserted a single line pledging an end to the war in Vietnam if he was elected. That line brought a sustained standing ovation from the South Dakota crowd. I thought that the Sioux Falls experience would inspire Hubert to continue on a similar course for the rest of the campaign. But it was difficult for him to break publicly with the man who had selected him as his Vice President. He offered no further critique of the war until he reached Salt Lake City on September 30, 1968. There he expressed a more carefully phrased, lengthier exposition of the necessity to end the war. This speech was not only warmly applauded in Salt Lake City, but was well received nationally. Again, under White House pressure, however, Humphrey backed away from any posture approaching a clear break with his old mentor, Lyndon Johnson.

Meanwhile, Nixon was cleverly straddling and down-playing the Vietnam issue. He excused himself from discussing the war policy by suggesting that he did not wish to complicate any negotiations President Johnson had under way. But he clearly implied that if elected, he had a private plan to bring a quick and satisfactory end to the war.

Humphrey might have been elected in 1968 if he had either accepted the compromise peace plank on Vietnam at the Chicago convention, or if he had held to the restrained peace theme expressed briefly at Sioux Falls and Salt Lake City. But the Vietnam war made it hard for any Democratic candidate to win either in 1968 or 1972. So long as the war continued, it would shatter the Democratic Party. The debate between "hawks and doves" was largely a conflict between Democrats. A "hawkish" Democratic presidential candidate risked alienating the "dovish" faction; likewise, a "dovish" candidate would alienate many of the "hawks."

But it seemed clear to me that no matter what the political risks might be, the Democratic challenger of 1972 would have to take a clear position against both the Vietnam war and the distorted national-security assumptions that had carried us into that conflict. Furthermore, I saw another lesson from the 1960s and the Democratic defeat in 1968: the need to restore political credibility to Democratic leadership. Trying to rationalize an irrational war had seriously eroded public confidence in the White House. It seemed clear to me that if the Democrats wished to hold Mr. Nixon to a single term—a feat seldom accomplished in American history against incumbent Presidents—they would have to force an end to the war in Southeast Asia and close the credibility gap that was alienating millions of voters from the political process. The most obvious and fundamental corrective for the credibility disease was for national leaders to confront reality and tell the truth.

A more complicated aspect of the credibility problem was the conviction of many citizens that the political process was weighted against candidates and voters who sought meaningful change in public policy. Many of the most active supporters of Gene McCarthy and Robert Kennedy, and later of me, believed that the Democratic presidential nominating process was dominated by party wheel horses, entrenched officeholders and local bosses. They believed that despite the strong popular showing of McCarthy and Kennedy in primary elections, a majority of the convention delegates were selected in a manner that favored the so-called "establishment" candidates. Indeed, nominating conventions did tend to be dominated by comfortable white upper-middle-class middle-aged males. Women, youth, minorities and independent-minded voters, who comprised an important part of the antiwar reform forces in the country, were not adequately represented in the nominating conventions, nor were millions of other Americans who somehow saw themselves by-passed in the political decision-making system.

At the turbulent Chicago convention of 1968, only 14 percent of the delegates were women; only 2 percent were under thirty years of age; only 5 percent were blacks—despite the fact that blacks comprised 11 percent of the nation's population and provided 20 percent of the Democratic vote in presidential elections. Also, more than a third of the delegates to the Chicago convention were selected by procedures that were already irreversible by the time Lyndon Johnson announced he would not seek re-election and before it became clear that the Vietnam war would be the dominant issue.

Other abuses had weakened the delegate selection process. In some cases there were no written state party rules to guide the selection of delegates. In some states the so-called unit rule made it impossible for candidates who got less than a majority of the vote in a caucus, convention or primary election to receive any delegates at all. In other states, delegates were picked by one or more party leaders at unpublicized meetings or in caucuses where a single party leader might hold enough proxy votes to determine the outcome. In still other states, filing fees or party "hospitality" charges reaching as high as $500 per delegate excluded less affluent citizens from serving as delegates.

Considerable frustration over these procedures erupted at the 1968 Chicago convention, especially among the youthful supporters of Gene McCarthy. They were convinced that the nomination of 1968 was prejudiced by the system—that their man was defeated even before he began the grassroots organizing effort that carried him to victory in several state primary elections. A number of these disappointed backers of McCarthy, joined by some of those who had supported first Robert Kennedy and then me in 1968, were ready to challenge the Democratic Party to reform its presidential selection process or else face the prospect of a new party or a large number of alienated dropouts from the entire political system. They took their first steps toward reform even before the Chicago convention convened.

The demands of blacks for greater participation in the 1960s, and the growing antiwar activism of the young, were joined by the movement for women's rights. In 1966 the National Organization for Women was founded by a group of women, including author Betty Friedan and Congresswoman Martha Griffiths. In 1971 the National Women's Political Caucus was started through the efforts of Congresswomen Bella Abzug and Shirley Chisholm, Gloria Steinem, Elizabeth Carpenter and others.

As early as the 1964 Democratic convention in Atlantic City, the party had initiated efforts to create more democratic procedures in delegate selection. This effort centered on the claims of fair representation for black voters in the South. A stunning credentials challenge to all the delegates chosen by Mississippi's regular Democratic organization forced the convention to consider the question of racial discrimination in delegate selection. In acting to ensure equal opportunity for racial minorities, the convention laid down precedents for more comprehensive reform. Thus, long after the national government had assumed a more powerful role than the states, the national Democratic Party began to set standards once determined entirely by the states and their party organizations.

In 1964 the struggle for civil rights in states of the Deep South gave rise to the Mississippi Freedom Democratic Party, a rival to the state's regular Democratic organization. The party was organized by local black activists, including Aaron Henry and Fannie Lou Hamer, assisted by Northern white civil rights workers, including Washington attorney Joseph Rauh. Leaders of the Freedom Party claimed that their racially integrated party truly represented the loyal Democrats of Mississippi. They charged that the Mississippi State Democratic Party was dominated by white racists, only nominally loyal to the Democratic Party.

At the 1964 convention the Freedom faction challenged the Mississippi delegation, demanding that their representatives be seated in place of the regulars. The Freedom Democrats argued that the regulars supported segregation, that they had previously bolted the party ticket and remained unwilling to pledge their loyalty, and that the regulars systematically excluded blacks from participation in party affairs, including the process of choosing convention delegates. The arguments of the Freedom delegates were extremely persuasive. Questions of loyalty had previously been brought before Democratic conventions, and delegates had been unseated on this ground. But the new twist in 1964 was the party's deep commitment to civil rights and its unwillingness to tolerate discrimination within its own ranks.

Ultimately a compromise proposal on the Mississippi challenge was suggested by President Johnson and vice-presidential aspirant Hubert Humphrey, and was ratified by the convention. The compromise provided for seating all regular delegates who signed a loyalty oath to the Democratic Party; welcoming the Freedom Party delegates as "honored guests" of the convention; seating two leaders of the Freedom Party, Aaron Henry and Edwin King, as "delegates at large"; and most significant, mandating that delegates be selected for the 1968 convention without regard to race, creed, color or national origins, with a special committee to fulfill its mandate.

The Mississippi challenge aroused more interest than any other event of an otherwise predictable convention. The delegates' response to the challenge not only placed the party on record against racial, ethnic or religious discrimination in delegate selection, but also established precedents for a thorough overhaul of the delegate selection process. The antidiscrimination resolution passed by the convention implied that all Democrats should be able to participate in the process of selecting convention delegates. If practices that discriminated against ethnic, racial or religious groups were unacceptable, how could the party countenance other practices that closed the delegate selection process to potential participants? The convention also exercised its power to set forth standards for delegate selection that were binding on each state party, regardless of state law, party rules or traditional practices. At the risk of its convention seats, each state party was enjoined to eliminate discrimination in the selection of delegates; no exceptions were permitted. Previous standards adopted by national conventions had related only to the question of how delegates should behave after being selected—more specifically, their loyalty to the Democratic national ticket. Never before had the convention intervened in the process of delegate selection. Moreover, by seating Henry and King as delegates at large, the convention recognized the legitimacy of credentials challenges that pertained neither to loyalty nor to the conformity with state party rules. No one argued that the regular state party had violated either state law or party procedure.

Finally, the delegates assembled at Atlantic City created, for the first time, a body to act as its agent in fulfilling the requirements set forth for the upcoming convention. Mandated to "aid the states" in adhering to the Call to the Convention of 1968, a Special Equal Rights Committee, chaired by Governor Richard Hughes of New Jersey, had the power to interpret the convention's resolution against discrimination, to investigate the selection procedures of individual state parties, and to inform the states of their obligations for 1968. Although the committee had no power to enforce its interpretations of the convention's intentions, its findings and recommendations could have a decisive influence on the outcome of credentials challenges at the 1968 convention.

The Hughes Committee broadly construed its authority, assuming that as an agent of the 1964 convention, it could unilaterally interpret the convention's resolution against discrimination. In a letter of July 26, 1967, to all members of the Democratic National Committee and state chairmen, Hughes set forth six basic requirements that each state must meet. Should a state fail these requirements, warned Hughes, "this committee will recommend that the Credentials Committee declare the seats to be vacant and fill those seats." Hughes did not first clear these requirements through National Chairman John Bailey.

The Hughes Committee, however, confined its investigation only to the delegate selection process of Mississippi. It thus forfeited its power to exert broad influence on credentials challenges in 1968, or to monitor compliance with its guidelines. In response to a committee request, only two states ever submitted plans for compliance with the six basic elements required by the committee. But the committee's Mississippi investigation led to a recommendation that the regular delegation be unseated and replaced by Freedom Party delegates. When the 1968 convention accepted that recommendation, it fulfilled Lyndon Johnson's pledge of 1964 that the party would not tolerate racial discrimination in the selection of convention delegates.

Just prior to the 1968 Chicago convention a group of McCarthy supporters, including Eli Segal, Geoffrey Cowan and Anne Wexler, launched an ad hoc group to study the whole presidential nominating process. Congressman Don Fraser of Minnesota, a highly regarded, reform-minded Humphrey supporter, and Fred Dutton, a well-known Kennedy campaign aide, also joined the group. Governor Harold Hughes of Iowa served as chairman. Aided by a small staff, this ad hoc commission issued a report one week before the Chicago convention, highlighting some of the injustices in the current delegate selection process.

The reformers succeeded by a close vote of 1,305 to 1,206 in winning adoption by the Chicago convention of the Minority Report of the Committee on Rules, which called for specific reforms in delegate selection to be included in the official Call of the 1972 national convention. That convention-approved action clearly stated that the 1972 convention call would declare: "It is understood that a State Democratic Party, in selecting and certifying delegates to the national convention, thereby undertakes a process in which all Democratic voters have had full and timely opportunity to participate . . . All feasible efforts [must be] made to assure that delegates are selected through . . . procedures open to public participation within the calendar year of the national convention." This mandate could not have been approved at the Chicago convention without the votes of many Humphrey supporters, as well as those delegates pledged to McCarthy, Kennedy and me. Also, the Credentials Committee of 1968, under the chairmanship of Governor Hughes of New Jersey, secured acceptance of its majority report, which declared that all Democrats must have "meaningful and timely opportunities to participate fully" in delegate selection. The report also called upon the chairman of the Democratic National Committee to establish a "Special Committee to study the delegate selection processes in effect in the various states," to "recommend improvements in the delegate selection process," to "aid the state Democratic parties" in changing state laws and party rules, and to "report its findings and recommendations to the Democratic National Committee." Finally, the Majority Report called for the establishment of yet another special committee "to aid the states in fully meeting the responsibilities and assurances required for inclusion in the call for the 1972 Democratic National Convention."

The report of the Special Equal Rights Committee, also adopted by the convention, added yet another call for party reform. In part, the report recommended that "a Commission on Party Structure should be created to study the relationship between the National Democratic Party and its constituent State Democratic Parties, in order that full participation of all Democrats without regard to race, color, creed or national origin may be facilitated by uniform standards for structure and operation."

For many of the dissidents who followed Gene McCarthy, the resolutions mandating reform of the Democratic Party were the only favorable results of the Chicago convention. Those alienated from the party felt that it could be saved only by major reform. During the next few years, party reform was second only to the Vietnam war as an issue put forth by the dissidents to distinguish themselves from party regulars.

On January 14, 1969, the Democratic National Committee authorized its chairman to appoint two reform bodies—one combining the issues of delegate selection and party structure, the other on party rules. The Commission on Party Structure and Delegate Selection was enjoined "to devise means to carry out (1) the language of the minority Rules Report adopted by the 1968 Convention, which out-laws the unit rule in delegate selection and urges that Convention delegates be selected democratically in the year of the Convention; (2) the language of the Credentials Committee report adopted by the 1968 Convention which urges, in more general terms, reform of the delegate selection process to make it more open and democratic; and (3) the language of the Special Equal Rights Committee report to the 1968 Convention, which creates a commission to study and recommend uniform, democratic standards for delegate selection."

To the new Democratic National Chairman, Senator Fred Harris of Oklahoma, fell the task of appointing members of the reform bodies. A co-chairman along with Senator Walter Mondale of the Humphrey campaign, Harris had not yet begun to establish his later reputation as a populist reformer. But he was young and ambitious for higher office and his work on the Kerner Commission had already earned him liberal credentials he was anxious to maintain. On February 3, 1969, he met with leaders of the New Democratic Coalition, an organization formed in October 1968 by antiwar Democrats who were pressing for a more responsive Democratic Party. He assured the coalition that he would promptly appoint the new reform body and that it would be composed of people who supported the mandate of the 1968 convention. He declined, however, to tip his hand on the choice of a chairman for the reform committee. Coalition leaders and other advocates of reform were pressing for the selection of Harold Hughes, the newly elected senator from Iowa, who had continued to speak out in behalf of party reform.

But to Humphrey supporters, Hughes was seen as the angry man who had nominated McCarthy at the divisive Chicago convention. Support for the Humphrey-Muskie ticket was a touchstone of party loyalty, and members of the Humphrey wing considered Hughes's support to have been sullen or lukewarm, at best. The Democrats who coalesced around Hubert Humphrey believed that under Hughes's leadership, the reform committee would be a continuing threat to their role in the Democratic Party and possibly to the party itself.

Rejecting the selection either of Harold Hughes or a pronounced Humphrey supporter, Chairman Harris turned to me. As a strong antiwar critic and a late entrant in the Democratic presidential competition of 1968 who supported Humphrey after he was nominated, I was seen by both Harris and Humphrey as a moderate acceptable to both regulars and reformers.

When Fred Harris telephoned me to offer the chairmanship, he

insisted that I was the one person of stature within the party acceptable to all major factions. Harris had checked with Hubert Humphrey, Walter Reuther and others, all of whom thought that I was an
acceptable choice. But I was not particularly interested in the
procedural details of party reform. I asked for a day or two to think
it over and then consulted a few close friends. The prevailing opinion
seemed to be that the chairmanship of the reform commission was
a no-win position that could destroy any presidential hopes I might
have. Richard Wade, a distinguished professor of history at the University of Chicago, offered contrary advice. He thought that while
the job was "risky" and could lead to the charge that I was "factional-
izing the party," it was also "an opportunity both to play a unifier role
and to meet people, reformers and regulars."

I began to feel an obligation to accept the chairmanship because
I believed that I could bridge the gap between the Humphrey and
the McCarthy-Kennedy elements of the party and ensure effective
reforms and a more unified Democratic Party. To me, reform was a
device for strengthening the party. I was convinced that the Democrats could not withstand another convention like 1968 and that
reform was the only way to regain the loyalties of young people,
women, minority groups and the antiwar citizens. Still, it was with
some anxiety that I accepted Fred Harris' assignment. Along with me
as chairman, Harris appointed twenty-seven other commissioners,
whose opinions varied but whose general tendency was moderately
liberal. Sixteen of the commissioners had supported Humphrey in
1968, nine had supported Kennedy, and one had favored McCarthy.
Not a single member of the commission had supported my eleventh-
hour stand-in for the presidential nomination following Robert
Kennedy's death.

The commission included two other possible presidential candidates—Hughes and Senator Birch Bayh of Indiana. As likely contenders for the party nomination, both Ted Kennedy and Edmund
Muskie were asked to name a commissioner. Muskie chose George
Mitchell, national committeeman from his home state of Maine;
Kennedy chose Fred Dutton. Senator Henry Jackson of Washington,
another potential candidate in 1972, had no representative on the
commission, but his staff carefully monitored its activities, alert for
any hint of favoritism.*

---

*Don Fraser was the only congressman on the commission; Bayh, Hughes and I
were its only senators. Also included were one governor, Calvin Rampton of Utah; one
former governor, LeRoy Collins of Florida; and two representatives of organized
labor, William Dodds, director of the Community Action Department of the United
Auto Workers, and I. W. Abel, president of the United Steel Workers of America.
Dodds was appointed to the commission after UAW president Walter Reuther had

Neither the moderate cast of the commission's membership nor my appointment as chairman pleased the more ardent reformers. To reassure this group, I appointed Hughes vice chairman of the commission, over the objections of Fred Harris, and gave him a role in the selection of staff members.

My early decisions as commission chairman reflected both my commitment to reform and my belief that reformers had to proceed cautiously. We had to convince the party reformers that we were carrying out substantive reform; we had to be prudent enough to bring the party regulars along; we had to convince the press and the public that we were a serious, responsible body.

In public statements, speeches and interviews, I drove home the contention that the Democratic Party had but two choices: reform or death. In the past, I noted, political parties, when confronted with the need for change, chose death rather than change. I did not want the Democratic Party to die. I wanted our party to choose the path of change and vitality. That was the function of the reforms. The theme of "reform or die" was a well-chosen persuasive device. Without being belligerent or tendentious, this metaphor conveyed to regulars the warning that unless they cooperated on reform, many party activists would desert the political arena. The reformers now had the momentum. Any attempt to stop them risked destroying the Democratic Party.

I chose Robert Nelson as staff director. He had served as my administrative assistant in the House and I knew him to be a reliable, intelligent man with a pleasing personality that would not prove abrasive to the Democratic regulars. His role was not to fashion the substance of reform; rather, I saw him as an effective spokesman to interpret the commission's efforts to the public and especially to regular Democrats across the country. With Nelson as staff director, I had more political latitude in enlisting the help of the known re-

---

declined to serve. A majority of the other members were either state or party officials: Adlai Stevenson III, State Treasurer of Illinois; Katherine Peden, former Secretary of Commerce for Kentucky; Oscar Mauzy and Albert Pena, state legislators from Texas; Will Davis, state chairman of Texas; Aaron Henry, state chairman of Mississippi and a founder of the Mississippi Freedom Democratic Party; Bert Bennett, former state chairman of North Carolina; Patti Knox, vice chairman of Michigan; John English, national committeeman for New York; George Mitchell, national committeeman for Maine; Carmen Warschaw, national committeewoman for California; Louis E. Martin, former deputy chairman of the Minorities Division of the Democratic National Committee; Fred Dutton and Earl Graves, both former aides to Robert Kennedy; Austin Ranney and Samuel Beer, both professors of political science; Warren Christopher, former Deputy Attorney General; Peter Garcia, former director of the Community Action Program in San Francisco; David Mixner, co-director of the Vietnam Moratorium Committee; and John Hooker, gubernatorial candidate from Tennessee, rounded out the commission.

form activists without creating an unfavorable reaction among more orthodox Democrats.

Following the recommendation of Harold Hughes, I asked Eli Segal to become counsel of the commission—a rare opportunity for a twenty-six-year-old lawyer. Ken Bode, a thirty-year-old political-science professor whom I had come to know when he was president of the Young Democrats at the University of South Dakota, was named as research director. Professor Alexander Bickel of the Yale Law School, Professor Richard Wade of the University of Chicago, and Anne Wexler of Connecticut were engaged as consultants.

In all these personnel decisions, I was seeking to build the credibility of the commission in the eyes of both reformers and regulars. In bringing in a Harold Hughes on the one hand and a Bob Nelson on the other, and following Hughes's suggestion on Segal and my own knowledge of Ken Bode, plus the addition of three able consultants, I thought we had assembled a team that would be impregnable against charges of rigidity or superficiality.

Before beginning the reform effort, the commission had to find operating funds, develop a *modus operandi* and clarify its mandate. We decided to devote all of 1969 to the problem of reforming delegate selection and to leave the examination of party structure to 1970. The staff was assigned responsibility for researching the delegate selection procedures in all states and identifying the problems in various states in getting action on the commission's eventual recommendations. We also decided that the commission would conduct public hearings throughout the nation to secure greater citizen involvement in the reform effort.

Funding posed a special problem for the fledgling commission. Besides salaries, we needed $50,000 to operate the commission, including the cost of hearings, research and publications. But the national committee was mired in debt and could offer no assistance beyond salaries for Bob Nelson, Eli Segal and a secretary. So I decided to undertake a fund-raising effort on my own.

In June 1969 I went to New York to meet with thirty-five wealthy, reform-minded contributors who could have given the necessary $50,000 with no strain. I stressed that reform might heal the wounds of the party and that the commission's hearings would enable people to make their voices heard. Silence. Then a major philanthropist asked a question. If the movement for reform faltered, would George McGovern be willing to lead a fourth party? I wasn't interested in a fourth party, nor did I want the impression to be given that the reformers contemplated bolting the party. I tried as best I could to convince those in the room that the Democratic Party was worth trying to save. But the meeting yielded only $5,200—pocket change for the multimillionaires in attendance. These financial luminaries shared neither my concern for the Democratic Party nor my faith that it could be reformed. They would open their checkbooks only if I denounced the party's leadership and agreed to desert the party unless it was radically transformed.

By midsummer the commission was in desperate financial straits. In these circumstances, I loaned the commission $15,000—virtually my entire savings. The commission also raised money through direct-mail appeals, and with the cooperation of Adlai Stevenson III organized a benefit rally at the Stevenson family farm in Libertyville, Illinois. The Libertyville rally brought together every faction of the Illinois Democratic Party, including Mayor Daley and the Reverend Jesse Jackson.

By the time I resigned the chairmanship in January 1971 we had raised nearly $70,000, and we had no debts.

The almost cryptic mandate of the Chicago convention left many questions unresolved. (1) What did the 1968 convention mean when it called on state parties to "make all feasible efforts" to achieve timely and democratic procedures for delegate selection? (2) Was the commission authorized to *require* or simply to *recommend* delegate selection rules? (3) Did the commission's guidelines have to be approved by the Democratic National Committee?

The commission decided that the call to the 1972 convention *required* the states to eliminate all selection procedures that made participation in the delegate selection process impossible, difficult or confusing for Democratic voters. The commission would assume responsibility for drafting specific guidelines to "aid the states" in meeting new requirements.

The commission endorsed rank-and-file participatory democracy not only as a matter of principle but also as a strategy for unifying the party and achieving success in presidential contests. Some Democrats argued that democracy within the party leads to the nomination of whichever candidate commands the most dedicated, activist faction of the Democratic Party. This system, they contended, produces candidates unrepresentative of the party as a whole and unappealing to the general electorate. In contrast, advocates of the reform position stressed that greater rank-and-file participation in nominating the presidential candidate would broaden the base of the Democratic Party, bringing in millions of young people, women, minorities and others yearning for a meaningful role. They further suggested that the party would only unite behind a nominee selected democratically by rank and file Democrats. Never again would the Democrats accept a candidate hand-picked by oligarchs of the party.

Two activities occupied the commission during the spring and summer of 1969: the public hearings and the task of analyzing each state's procedures for delegate selection. The first regional hearing was scheduled in Washington, D.C., and included such party luminaries as Kennedy and Muskie. For each regional hearing, the staff recruited a local coordinator. At minimum, the coordinator was asked to choose a hearing room, arrange for transportation, contact the local media and invite witnesses representing a broad range of views and interests. Several members of the commission attended each of the regional hearings.

I sent letters to local politicians informing them of plans to hold a hearing in their bailiwick and requesting their cooperation. The commission did not ask for permission before scheduling a hearing, since we had decided that any such attempt might undermine the commission's independent status. Some protests over these procedures, primarily from Southern Democrats, hit the national committee and were leaked to the press.

Hostility to the commission broke into the open at the regional hearing in Atlanta (covering the five states of Virginia, North Carolina, South Carolina, Florida and Georgia). Local leaders largely boycotted the hearing, Georgia Governor Lester Maddox condemning the commission as "an arm of the socialist wing of the Democratic Party."

The hearing in Chicago also produced an unfortunate incident. The most youthful commissioner, David Mixner, was anxious to confront Mayor Daley on the violence at the 1968 convention and the resulting criminal charges against both antiwar demonstrators and the police. Mixner wanted a statement by the commission condemning the Chicago violence and calling on Mayor Daley to drop the subsequent charges. To head off what I knew would be an explosion, I persuaded Mixner to permit me to suggest at the hearing the dropping of charges against both police and demonstrators.

Mayor Daley was the first witness and his statement supported reform, suggesting that all delegates to the national convention be elected in binding state-level primaries. After thanking the mayor for his testimony, I noted that the confrontation between the police and the antiwar demonstrators, plus the resulting legal indictments, had opened "raw wounds" in the Democratic Party. Would the mayor not think it wise to use his influence to "alleviate the situation and put the events behind us, end the anguish and heal the wounds?" Daley exploded. He defended the city's actions and assailed the demonstrators as troublemakers trying to destroy the party. "If you're asking for amnesty for violations of the law, I'll never be a part of it," he declared. Then he made an observation with which I profoundly agreed: it wasn't, he said, the Chicago police who broke up the Chicago convention of 1968—it was "that war in Vietnam." The next day's headlines and stories in the Chicago papers told how the mayor had rebuffed the reformers. Lost in the accounts was the substance of the hearings and the mayor's reform-minded testimony.

It would have been better simply to commend the mayor for endorsing our reform efforts and leave the matter of how to handle the Chicago disturbances to local authorities.

Although the hearings generated controversy, they also protected the commission from charges that it was an elite group isolated in Washington, out of touch with grassroots Democrats. Testimony from more than five hundred witnesses in seventeen cities, representing every element of the party, not only gave us valuable insights but also publicized the work of the commission. News reports on the hearings helped to inform Democrats of the commission's objectives and convince them that the party seriously meant to put its own house in order. Although less important than the staff's own systematic research, information obtained in the hearings helped guide the commission in its examination of practices that inhibited rank-and-file participation in the presidential nominating procedures. Public testimony about abuses shocked nearly every member of the commission, helping to convince them that reform was an urgent priority. George Mitchell, a constructive, pragmatic Democrat, confessed that the hearings "opened my eyes to things of which I had no perception."

Most so-called regulars ignored the commission, assuming perhaps that it was laboring in vain. As Commissioner Patti Knox expressed it: "The McGovern Commission was an orphan of the party. The big power blocs didn't pay any attention to what was going on right under their noses." Those who later complained most loudly about what the commission had wrought were those who had forfeited their opportunity to influence its deliberations.

The AFL-CIO boycotted all our activities. Bill Dodds of the UAW was one of the most active commissioners and a consistent exponent of reform. But I. W. Abel, the AFL-CIO's representative on the commission, did not attend a single meeting. James C. O'Brien, political-action director of the United Steelworkers, who personally supported reform, attended the first meeting in Abel's stead. Neither O'Brien nor any other representative of the union appeared at any other meeting. I called Abel and urged him to participate in commission affairs, but he was noncommittal. Later, when I again tried to reach him by telephone, I could not get past a rather curt secretary. Officials of the AFL-CIO generally refused to testify at regional hearings, often responding with the same litany: "The party which nominated Roosevelt and Truman does not need reforming."

By remaining aloof from the reform effort, labor not only forfeited its considerable influence but also helped maintain the divisions within the party that had opened in 1968. Labor kept itself isolated from what had become the dynamic mainstream of the party and encouraged others to ignore or oppose reform.

At its March first meeting, the commission authorized the staff to explore delegate selection in each state party. Both Richard Wade and Alexander Bickel had written to me stressing that state-by-state research must be the commission's first priority. A "book of the states" detailing rules for delegate selection and documenting actual practices would do more than provide information for drafting guidelines. More than anything else, verified examples of abuses in the delegate selection process would motivate commissioners to support reform measures and help sell reform to the party at large. Information on individual states would also enable the commission to approach the state parties from a position of strength. "We had to convince the state chairman that we had a fair description of the delegate selection process," observed Wade. "Otherwise, we would be eaten up alive."

In the spring of 1969 the commission hired a group of young interns to explore the selection procedures of state parties. The commission had received letters from undergraduates, graduate students and law students asking for temporary employment. For an estimated total salary cost of $10,000, we were able to hire ten interns —including Rick Stearns, who was later to play a key role in my 1972 presidential bid. Under Ken Bode's direction, each intern was assigned responsibility for studying the procedures of five or six state parties. They prepared reports which included a description of the delegate selection process and party structure of each state, as well as a "behaviorial report" of how the delegate selection system actually operated in the state. The interns worked with a preset format which indicated the types of issues they were to explore. The checklist included intrastate apportionment of convention delegates, the timing of the delegate selection process, the status of party rules, mechanisms for ballot listing, quorum and proxy rules, and eligibility requirements for voting.

The interns relied on multiple sources of information. They scrutinized state laws and party rules where available. They scanned local newspapers, communicated with academicians and citizens groups, and interviewed state chairmen over the telephone. These state reports were to form a volume of 3,000 pages. No such information on delegate selection had ever been collected by the Democratic National Committee.

After months of public hearings, painstaking research and lengthy discussion sessions of both the executive committee and the full commission, the commission issued its report, *Mandate for Reform,* in the spring of 1970. The report was a tightly drawn set of eighteen guidelines—some of them requirements and some recommendations—which were to set the ground rules for the selection of delegates to the 1972 Democratic National Convention.

Following the instructions of the 1968 convention, the guidelines required that no part of the delegate selection process could begin prior to the calendar year of the convention. Because so many states had no published rules governing delegate selection, we recommended that all states adopt a set of explicit, well-publicized rules so that persons wishing to be selected as delegates would know in advance the procedures they must follow. The adoption of specific, written rules by a state would also provide a clear basis for measuring state procedures against the guidelines laid down by our commission.

We also made proxy voting illegal and required that all delegate selection meetings be held on an officially designated date and time and in a place easily accessible to any interested Democrat. We required that adequate public notice be provided for public meetings so that there would be no danger of closed or secret sessions designed to exclude rank-and-file Democrats.

The commission also barred the use of the unit rule by committees or conventions. This step was designed to end the practice of requiring all delegates to support the presidential candidate agreed upon by the majority of a local or state meeting. Here again, the commission was adhering closely to the mandate of the 1968 convention.

One issue that prompted considerable discussion among the commissioners was the question of whether a state Democratic committee should be permitted to select a portion of the state's convention delegates. Some commissioners believed that such a procedure placed too much power in the hands of state party officials. Others argued that selecting a portion of the delegates would give deserved recognition to party leadership and would enable the state leadership to provide places on the convention delegation for worthy Democrats who for various reasons were not included. The commission finally settled on a compromise by authorizing state committees to select up to 10 percent of the state's delegation.

The two most heated issues before the commission were representation for women, youth and minorities and the winner-take-all primary—most notably the California primary.

On the first of these questions, the commission decided against the imposition of percentage quotas as a means of ensuring fair representation of all groups. Instead we proposed that state parties "overcome the effects of past discrimination by affirmative steps to encourage representation on the national convention delegations of minority groups, young people and women in reasonable relationship to their presence in the population of the state."

To make certain that this language would not be interpreted as a call for percentage quotas based on sex, age or race, the commission unanimously adopted an amendment offered by former Florida Governor LeRoy Collins, as follows: "It is the understanding of the commission that this is not to be accomplished by the mandatory imposition of quotas."

Despite this seemingly clear statement against a percentage quota system, the impression developed that quotas were mandated by the commission. To understand how this impression evolved and was eventually ordered by the Democratic national chairman, Lawrence O'Brien, it is necessary to trace the commission's proceedings and subsequent actions by my successor as commission chairman.

These so-called "quota" requirements became a telling political issue in the election of 1972 and in the eyes of many critics have loomed larger than all else the commission has done. To Theodore White, the commission's "quotas" symbolized what was wrong with liberal politics and my quest for the presidency in 1972.

Yet the final guidelines on minorities, women and youth were not recommended either by me or by the professional staff I had selected. They were proposed and pushed forward primarily by commission members Austin Ranney, Birch Bayh and Fred Dutton. Regarding discrimination against women, youth and minorities, the commission urged the state parties to adopt programs of affirmative action designed to give more reasonable representation to all of the affected groups. Guaranteed representation through the imposition of quotas was rejected unanimously.

The debate over minority representation within the commission reflected an ongoing controversy within American society. In the early 1960s the civil rights movement struggled against segregation and discrimination. Civil rights partisans fought for integrated schools and accommodations, color-blind justice, open housing, equality of opportunity in jobs and voting. By the middle sixties the emphasis had shifted. "Black power" had supplanted civil rights; affirmative action to overcome the effects of past discrimination had become a major demand of racial minorities. Many national leaders agreed that simply unlocking the chains that had shackled people for generations would not enable the oppressed to compete equally with everyone else. But how does society help people overcome the effects of past discrimination without trampling the rights of others?

Proponents of quotas argued that in the short run, in such areas as employment and education, the effects of past discrimination could be overcome only by assigning percentages to ensure the participation of minority groups. Quotas merely rectified an imbalance that had been created by decades of discrimination. Opponents of quotas argued that such systems produced an insidious form of reverse discrimination that gave certain groups special advantages.

The legislative history of the guidelines on minorities, women and youth was long and tortuous, consuming hours of debate and generating disagreement among the commissioners as to what their motions really meant. Those who spoke out in favor of the language that was ultimately adopted persistently denied that they were advocating a quota system. Others insisted that regardless of what the commissioners thought they meant, their language in effect imposed quotas on the state parties.

Professor Austin Ranney first opened what he later called "Pandora's Box":

> I had the very strong feeling that in many of the testimonies that our black fellow Democrats feel that something more is needed than a no discrimination rule, that at least for the time being they would like some assurance that there will be blacks on the delegation in at least some reasonable proportion to blacks in the Democratic party . . . I wanted to try the idea . . . that the Commission make every effort to see that there be included as members of the delegation adequate, fair, whatever the word may be, representation of minority groups in the population.

I hastened to inform Ranney that in an earlier meeting the commission had "unanimously decided after some discussion that it was not feasible to go on record for a quota system." But Ranney insisted that the commission should "at least *urge* . . . that members of minority groups be adequately, fairly . . . represented." He added, though, that the commission should not *require* such representation "because that would mean quota."

I then asked the staff to draft language reflecting Ranney's concerns. They produced a rather innocuous sentence: "We urge that state parties make every effort to secure adequate representation of minority groups." At this point Senator Bayh argued that the commission needed stronger language to "keep our party moving forward in this matter of racial equality." He contended that there should be "some reasonable relationship between the representation of delegates and the representation of minority groups in the population of the state in question."

Professor Samuel Beer then offered a compromise in the spirit of both Ranney's and Bayh's proposals. "I would suggest," he said, "that we add so that it reads as follows: '*requires* that state parties overcome the effects of past discrimination by affirmative steps to encourage minority group participation and representation on delegations to the National Convention.'"

Bayh still insisted "that such membership bear a reasonable . . . relationship to their representation in the population at large in the state." Nobody noticed that by tying the original Bayh proposal to the tail end of Beer's motion, the commission would now be *requiring* rather than *urging* state parties to encourage the representation of minority groups "in reasonable representation to their proportion in the population." Had the commission merely urged such encouragement, it would have been extremely difficult to base any credentials challenges on the guideline. Actions *urged* by the commission were defined as "desirable" but not mandatory. Ranney, who later denounced the notion of imposing quotas, accepted the combined Beer-Bayh motion as "better than . . . what I originally proposed."

I directed the commission to vote first on the Beer motion and then on the Bayh amendment. Beer's motion passed overwhelmingly, and Bayh's by a squeaker of 10–9. Harold Hughes, however, had voted against both the motion and the amendment because he did not think they were emphatic enough. As chairman I did not vote, but I supported Bayh's initiative. I never favored the percentage quota system, but I believed that we needed to make a reasonable effort to see that all elements were fairly represented.

When the commission turned to the guideline on women and youth, Fred Dutton immediately proposed that the language they had just adopted on racial, religious and ethnic minorities be extended to women and young people as well. Beer and Ranney now balked. They distinguished between racial minorities and other groups on the grounds that racial minorities had experienced the greatest discrimination. And they launched a general assault on "quota" systems of representation, claiming that quotas prescribed the results of delegate selection and thus contradicted the objective of promoting open politics.

Dutton responded that discrimination against women and young people was also severe, and that it was very important to bring these groups into the party fold. He further noted that the motion did not guarantee the results of delegate selection, but only required the parties to redress the imbalances that had made it impossible for women and young people to participate equally with middle-aged males. Indeed, the motion imposed no requirements on the voter at all, only on the slate makers.

DUTTON: What we're trying to handle here is slate making in primary states and the county and state conventions. It is basically the situation where voters don't have a chance now and the reason we can keep the heavy domination by men is because the voters don't get involved in the act . . . I personally believe that historically there has been just as much discrimination against women as there has been against blacks . . . we've got to provide the symbols . . . to have the redistribution of power which will activate women . . . which will activate young people.

During the debate over women and youth, members of the commission began to realize the implications of using the word "require" rather than "urge" in the guideline they had already adopted and the one now being considered. In the interests of harmony, I suggested that before voting the guideline on women and young people, the commission consider changing the word "require" to "urge." Just as I was calling for the vote on this suggestion, Katherine Peden interrupted:

PEDEN: I realize that you've called for the question, but as a matter of principle before we take the vote moving from require to urge, we all need to look at the make-up of this commission; only 11% are women, only 1 person is under 30 years of age, less than 10% are black . . . to back down on the position of women in the Democratic Party would be just as substantive a mistake as we would make if we had backed down on the race, creed, or national origin.

I responded that I was not "proposing a backdown," that I had "no problem voting for the strongest possible language." But Peden's remarks forestalled a vote on the suggestion to substitute "urges" for "requires," and the commission voted 13–7 for the motion in its original form.

Threading through the discussion was a dispute over what the two guidelines really required. Beer, Mitchell, Davis and Ranney contended that the commission had adopted a quota system in which delegations were required to represent minorities, women and young people in proportion to their presence in a state's population.

RANNEY: Again I have the feeling, with Senator Bayh's assistance I opened Pandora's Box . . . if we pass this motion now, we're going to have a quota system.

Bayh, Dutton, Governors Rampton and Collins and I all responded that the commission was not requiring quotas per se. It was requiring only that state parties act affirmatively to overcome past discrimination so that minorities, women and blacks might achieve reasonable representation. Governor Rampton of Utah had departed from the September meeting with the admonition that he and other governors at the Democratic Governors' Caucus were "absolutely opposed to any quota system that would be imposed, either based upon ethnic considerations or ideological considerations." But he now defended the commission's actions, contending that it had not adopted quotas. It remained for Governor Collins to spell out the legal implications of what the commission had done:

> COLLINS: I would say that . . . we have set up standards which if not met raise a presumption on prima facie evidence of failure to encourage the participation of minority groups. . . . the fact that we had not tied ourselves to hard and fast percentages would indicate pretty well, I think, that we're not demanding a quota, but demanding that a reasonable effort be made to secure better representation.

Thus the failure of a state delegation to include minorities, women and young people "in reasonable proportion" to their percentage in the state's population would shift the burden of proof to the state party. To escape successful challenge, it would have to show that despite the composition of the delegation, it actually had acted affirmatively to secure better representation.

Realizing the adverse political implications of a charge that the commission had adopted quotas, I proposed, after the lunch break, that "we go on record as saying that these two steps that we took this morning do not envision the imposition of a quota system." The commission endorsed this suggestion without dissent and adopted as an amendment to the representation guideline the amendment offered by Governor Collins ruling out the imposition of quotas. Harold Hughes, as well as Beer, Mitchell, Ranney and Davis, were not convinced, however. "I have no objections to what you put in," said Hughes, "but I just want it clearly understood that no matter what we call what we have done and say it isn't a quota system, in essence it does say that we have to recognize certain standards that mean something that I would call a quota."

The next day newspapers all over the country reported that the commission had adopted quotas.

Whatever the commission originally intended, in administering the guidelines on minorities, women and young people, it eventually moved very close to adopting a de facto quota system. Although an imbalance in its demographic composition would not automatically disqualify a state delegation, no state party wanted to assume the burden of proving that it had adopted an adequate program of affirmative action. In his verbal advice to state leaders, staff director Bob Nelson suggested that "to avoid challenges, they should adhere as closely as possible to the breakdowns that were spelled out in the guidelines." In late 1971 the commission and the chairman of the Democratic National Committee (then Lawrence O'Brien) issued official interpretations of the antidiscrimination guidelines that further encouraged the state parties to balance convention delegations. In a memo sent to all state party leaders on October 18, 1971, Don Fraser, my successor as chairman of the reform commission, stated that "whenever an organized group meets to recommend, or nominate or otherwise engage in procedures for the purpose of selecting delegates, it is reasonable to impose on such groups the burden of seeking to achieve reasonable representation." He also outlined "a number of affirmative steps that state parties can take to meet [the] guidelines." One month later O'Brien wrote to party officers underscoring "the importance of each state's taking specific, affirmative actions to encourage the representation and involvement of women, minorities and young people."

These instructions, followed by later rulings on the part of Chairman O'Brien and his legal advisers, in effect meant that state delegations which did not at least approach a reasonable percentage of women, youth and blacks in their delegations would be assumed to be out of compliance with the party's guidelines.

The guidelines as a whole were taken seriously by virtually all of the state parties. As a consequence the percentage of women at the 1972 national convention rose from 14 percent in 1968 to 36 percent in 1972; the percentage of youthful delegates under thirty went up from 2 percent to 23 percent; and blacks increased their percentage from a little over 5 to 14 percent.

The major criticism leveled at the commission centered on the charge that we gave too much effort to increase the representation of groups heretofore neglected in the selection process. To George Meany and some of his associates, this process was tantamount to elevating "hippies," "women liberationists," "gays," "kooks" and "draft dodgers." Beyond this, other critics genuinely detested the so-called quotas as a violation of established democratic competition.

The other guideline which caused extensive argument among the members of our commission was the issue of the winner-take-all primary. California, the state that would send the largest delegation to the national convention, was the major example of a winner-take-all primary system. Under the California system, the presidential contender winning the most votes in the primary election was entitled to all of California's delegates.

Some members of our commission and many other Democrats believed this system was unfair in that it denied convention representation to all California voters except those fortunate enough to have backed the winner of the state's primary. Therefore, in a situation where Candidate A won 51 percent of the state's primary vote to 49 percent for Candidate B, Candidate A would be entitled to the entire delegation—thus denying any representation at the convention to delegates pledged to Candidate B even though state voter sentiment was closely divided between the two candidates. Some of our commission members argued that it was inconsistent to ban use of the unit rule in those states selecting delegates by convention or committee systems while retaining it in California and other winner-take-all primary states.

A strenuous counter argument was led by Fred Dutton, who pressed the merits of the California primary system. Dutton built his argument on the contention that political parties should take every feasible step to increase participation in the political process by rank-and-file voters. What better method to accomplish this than offering presidential candidates and their supporters a grand prize in the form of an entire state delegation if they campaigned vigorously enough to come in first in the winner-take-all competition in California and other states.

Privately Dutton reminded party liberals and antiwar leaders that in 1972 California would probably support a presidential contender representing their strongest concerns. Thus, it was important not to dilute California's impact in the presidential nominating process by breaking up its winner-take-all system.

The commission debated this issue at some length and finally decided on a split vote to permit winner-take-all primaries to continue through 1972. But we also urged the party to take steps beyond 1972 to replace the winner-take-all system with a method giving delegate representation to the candidates in proportion to the percentage of their vote in a primary, as well as in the convention and committee systems.

Another guideline of special importance determined that in those cases where state parties apportion their delegation to the national convention, the apportionment would be based on a formula giving equal consideration to population and to the Democratic vote in the previous presidential election.

The guideline on slate making held that every effort must be made to ensure that all interested Democrats be given an opportunity to participate in the slate-making process. The commission emphasized that "whenever slates are presented to caucuses, meetings, conventions, committees, or to voters in a primary, the commission requires

The McGoverns in our living room in Mitchell, 1934; sisters Mildred and Olive, seated at the piano; my father and mother; my younger brother smiles while I look at an apparently serious book.

Flanking me in front of the tent where we lived in an Italian olive grove for a year is my co-pilot, Bill Rounds of Wichita *(left)*, and my navigator, Sam Adams, Milwaukee, who was killed on a bombing raid in 1945.

The McGoverns at the National 4-H Center, Washington, D.C., 1960. *Left to right:* Teresa, Susan, Ann, Eleanor, George, Steven, Mary.

With President Kennedy in the Oval Office in the first days of Food for Peace, 1961.

George Cunningham, administrative assistant *(back to camera)*, Pat Donovan, secretary, and John Holum, legislative assistant, listen to my intentions to seek the Presidency, 1970.

Study tour of Vietnam, November 1965.

A light moment during a heavy convention, 1968, in my suite at the Blackstone in Chicago with *(left to right)* Dick Wade, Arthur Schlesinger and Bill vandenHeuvel.

With Eagleton following his nomination as Vice President — Democratic National Convention, Miami, July 1972.

In the West Virginia coal towns, 1971.

Speech-writing at 35,000 feet on the campaign trail, 1972.

Irish power in Chicago — Daley and Teddy, September 1972.

Running mate Sargent Shriver in Texas, August 1972.

Shirley MacLaine, the actress, and her actor brother, Warren Beatty, both participated extensively in the campaign. Shirley is pictured here at a 1971 discussion of the party reform guidelines.

With Gloria and Bella, Women's Caucus, Miami, July 1972.

A "full disclosure" press conference on campaign finances with *(left to right)* Marian Pearlman, finance assistant; Morris Dees, direct-mail expert; and Henry Kimelman, campaign finance director, 1972.

One year after the Miami nomination victory of 1972, we celebrate at my home in Washington. *Left to right:* Jeff Smith, Frank Mankiewicz, Gary Hart and Rick Stearns.

Visiting with Prime Minister Yitzhak Rabin at his home in Tel Aviv, April 1975.

Touring Cuba with Premier Fidel Castro; Barbara Walters in foreground, Eleanor behind
Castro with interpreter, May 1975.

Conferring with Vietnamese Premier Pham Van Dong under the portrait of the late Ho Chi Minh, Hanoi, January 1976.

state parties to adopt procedures which assure that . . . the bodies making up the slates have been elected, assembled, or appointed for the slate-making task with adequate public notice . . ." In states utilizing the primary election system, the guidelines required that any slate offered in the name of a presidential candidate must "be assembled with due consultation with the presidential candidate or his representative."

In its closing peroration, *Mandate for Reform* reiterated the theme that the Democratic Party faced dire consequences if it squandered the opportunity for reform.

> We believe that popular participation is more than a proud heritage of our party, more than a first principle. We believe that popular control of the Democratic Party is necessary for its survival . . .
>
> If we are not an open party; if we do not represent the demands of change, then the danger is not that people will go to the Republican Party; it is that there will no longer be a way for people committed to orderly change to fulfill their needs and desires within our traditional political system. It is that they will turn to third and fourth party politics or the anti-politics of the street.

Reform or else, the commission told the party.

Two events in early 1970 virtually guaranteed the Democratic National Committee's endorsement of the proposed guidelines. First, Lawrence O'Brien personally endorsed the commission's efforts and sponsored them before the Democratic National Committee. O'Brien had made the same decision I had—that reform was the only way to hold the party together. As one of the party's most seasoned professionals, his support gave reform solid credibility and meant that the Democratic National Committee would be spurning the party's new chairman if it tried to dilute the guidelines. Second, an advisory legal opinion from Joseph Califano, counsel to the Democratic National Committee, sustained our interpretation of the guidelines.

In May 1970 the executive committee of the Democratic National Committee endorsed the proposed guidelines. In February 1971, with little discussion, the national committee incorporated the guidelines into the Call to the 1972 convention. Only a minor guideline eliminating automatic delegate seats for national-committee members stirred any controversy.

In early 1970 we began the long, tedious process of shepherding the guidelines through the state parties. Compliance letters, sent to all state chairmen, consisted of three parts: (1) a cover letter from me explaining the purpose of the document; (2) a statement of what the commission had *required, urged* or *recommended* in its eighteen guidelines; and (3) an analysis of rules and procedures in the state in question that violated commission requirements. Right from the start, state chairmen were being told what had to be changed in their party's delegate selection process. Not a single state was in full compliance with the commission's requirements. Several states were out of compliance with ten or more requirements.

When Segal and Bode left the commission in early 1970, Bob Nelson and Carol Casey took command of the compliance effort. During the remainder of the year, they spent most of their time working behind the scenes with state chairpersons and state reform commissions. Close, well-informed communication with each of the state parties helped to ensure widespread acceptance of the new guidelines.

In January 1971 I formally announced my candidacy for the presidential nomination. Recognizing that it would have been improper for a presidential candidate to be trying to enforce party rules that he had helped shape, I resigned as commission chairman and recommended Congressman Don Fraser as my successor. Respected by staff members and commissioners, he had served on both the Harold Hughes and the McGovern commissions and was thoroughly familiar with the details and philosophy of party reform. I had talked to him on two or three occasions about the whole matter of party structure, and I knew that Minnesota had a strong Democratic Party in which he had been actively involved. His moderate, yet firm manner made him an ideal choice.

Under Fraser's direction, the pace of compliance activities picked up in 1971. He was happy with the team of Nelson and Casey, recalling Nelson as "a superb diplomat" and Carol Casey as "very strong on the technical details." Fraser became an active chairman, immersing himself in the details of compliance work and becoming involved in negotiations with the state chairpersons. He also became the driving force behind the joint efforts of our commission and the O'Hara Commission to revamp party structure. More than any other individual, he was responsible for the proposed party charter offered to the delegates at the 1972 convention and adopted with modifications at a Kansas City convention in December 1974.

Under Fraser's prodding, reform proceeded slowly but thoroughly. Following strenuous activity in late 1971 and early 1972, he could announce in April 1972 that state parties had complied with 99 percent of the guidelines. Compliance in some states was more difficult to achieve than in others. The pace of compliance seemed to depend most on factors unique to each state party. Although some Southern Democrats had initially expressed the greatest hostility to the reform commission, compliance in the South proceeded more swiftly than in most other regions of the nation.

Not a single state party openly defied the guidelines. To do so was to risk expulsion from the 1972 convention. Moreover, the reform tide was flowing. The work of the reform commission both influenced and reflected that trend.

Our commission guidelines ended domination of the presidential nomination by those who controlled state and local organizations of the Democratic Party. The guidelines opened a pathway to the nomination for candidates outside the party establishment. In every state, candidates could now vie fairly for delegates, either in caucuses and conventions or in primary elections of delegate slates. No longer could insiders wrap up delegate votes through procedures begun long before election years, secret meetings, unit rules, last-minute changes in procedure, preferential treatment of delegate slates, and elections in which presidential preferences were not listed on the ballot. Moreover, the number of states selecting delegates through primaries increased from 16 to 22 between 1968 and 1972, and from 22 to 30 between 1972 and 1976. This quantum leap in primary contests was part of a reform tide that has swept the Democratic Party since 1968. In part it was a response to our commission guidelines. By adopting primary systems, state parties could most easily comply with the guidelines without having to revamp their internal organization.

My successful bid for the nomination in 1972 was based in part on the opportunity which the new rules offered to a candidate willing to take his case directly to rank-and-file voters rather than depending on big-name endorsements. A brokered convention would probably not have turned to me as an outspoken opponent of the war in Vietnam and an advocate of changed national priorities. Some commentators have put these facts together and concluded that I shaped the reform guidelines to advance my own candidacy for the party's nomination. Although an interesting backward projection of the events of 1972, this interpretation bears no resemblance to the actual work of our commission.

Millions more Democrats participated in delegate selection for the 1972 convention following the new guidelines than for the convention of 1968. Most of these participants voted in primary elections, but several hundred thousand also attended the party meetings that elected representatives to state conventions.

The McGovern Commission guidelines have for the most part withstood the tests of time and trial. The successor commission, headed by Baltimore City Councilwoman Barbara Mikulski, was created by the 1972 convention to reconsider party rules on delegate selection. This commission reaffirmed the substance of most of the

1972 reform guidelines. Among its more important actions, the Mikulski Commission emphasized that the party did not require a quota system. The new commission also modified the slate-making guideline, authorizing "any candidate or individual" to put together and endorse a slate of delegations. Violations of the slate-making guideline had been primarily responsible for the ouster of Mayor Daley's delegation from the 1972 convention. Revision of the McGovern Commission's prescription for open slate making clearly was a concession to party regulars. Following the recommendation of our commission, the Mikulski Commission also required the proportional representation of minority presidential preferences. It outlawed winner-take-all primaries at the state level, but ruled that winner-take-all primaries at the local district level provided adequate representation for minority preferences. These so-called loophole primaries were outlawed by the 1976 convention, but some party leaders plan to fight for their restoration at the midterm convention of 1978.

The guidelines of the McGovern Commission wedded the Democratic Party to the principle of participatory democracy. Participation was not to be a reward for faithful service or a privilege of the entrenched and the experienced. Rather, it was a right to be guaranteed all those willing to vote in a primary or attend a party meeting. Unlike previous efforts at party reform, the work of our commission did not flow from sectional conflict within the party or focus on racial discrimination or party loyalty. The commission's guidelines fell within a tradition of progressive reform dating from the early twentieth century, when reformers sought to ground the nominating process in popular consent through the mechanism of direct primaries.

Yet reform of the nominating process during the progressive era had been an effort that proceeded state by state. Change could take place only when reformers gained control of the state party or the state government. Our commission imposed its guidelines on the state parties. To oppose them would have been to challenge the party's central authority and risk losing a voice in the nominating process. Just as civil rights statutes enabled the national government to change the laws and practices of individual state governments, the reform guidelines enabled the national party to change the laws and practices of the individual state parties. The strongest opponents of reform were those who still upheld the banner of "states' rights." The strongest supporters of reform were those who favored the forceful assertion of national-party discipline, designed to give every Democrat a voice in the most important function of the party—the nomination of a candidate for the presidency of the world's most powerful nation.

8
THE NOMINATION

I n the opening days of 1971 "Jimmy the Greek" Sny-
der, the nation's most celebrated odds-maker, announced that the
odds against George McGovern winning the Democratic presidential nomination were 200 to 1. A year later, early in 1972, Jimmy listed
the odds as follows:

ED MUSKIE	2 to 5
HUBERT HUMPHREY	4 to 1
HENRY JACKSON	5 to 1
TED KENNEDY	20 to 1
GEORGE McGOVERN	50 to 1
JOHN LINDSAY	50 to 1
GEORGE WALLACE	50 to 1
WILBUR MILLS	200 to 1
EUGENE McCARTHY	200 to 1
VANCE HARTKE	200 to 1
SAM YORTY	500 to 1
SHIRLEY CHISHOLM	500 to 1
DARK HORSE	50 to 1

Thus, after a year of campaigning I had moved from 200 to 1 to 50
to 1—the same odds assigned to John Lindsay, George Wallace and
a possible "dark horse."

When the January 1971 odds placing me as a 200 to 1 long shot were published, a friend of mine was visiting the Desert Inn in Las Vegas. While there, he encountered a bookie in the casino who was willing to bet against me at 100-to-1 odds. My friend produced a thousand dollars in chips and said, "You're on." In the long, hectic months that followed, the bet was forgotten. But one day, after I had won the presidential nomination, a man in a dark suit appeared at my friend's office carrying a brown paper bag. He had all the characteristics of an underworld "hit man." Why was he scowling? Did he have a gun in the bag? What he had in the bag was $100,000 in cash, which he left on the desk and then departed without a word.

There were obvious reasons why Jimmy the Greek's odds found few takers. To begin with, most "McGovern types" did not have surplus cash that they could afford to gamble away on long shots. Beyond this, why should anyone suppose that a junior senator from the sparsely settled prairies of South Dakota would ever be taken seriously as a presidential contender? Never in the history of the state had any South Dakota politician been given more than a good-natured mention as either a presidential or vice-presidential contender.

If any South Dakotan was to be considered "presidential," it would obviously be a former resident of the state who had grown up there as a boy—Minnesota's senior senator and the former Vice President of the United States, Hubert Humphrey. After all, Hubert had come within half a million votes of winning the presidency in 1968 and he was a sure winner for re-election to the Senate in 1970, since Gene McCarthy had decided not to seek re-election.

But aside from Humphrey, two other choices loomed in the minds of Democratic functionaries and press pundits—Senators Ted Kennedy and Ed Muskie. As the only surviving Kennedy brother, Ted was seen by many as the heir apparent to his two fallen brothers. Furthermore, he was a talented, attractive political personality with a capable staff and a capacity to call out the assistance of many of the nation's best political organizers and advisers. It was the conventional view and the verdict of the public-opinion analysts that the nomination was his for the asking.

Ed Muskie of Maine was seen as the man for the nomination should Kennedy decide not to seek it. As Humphrey's running mate in 1968, he had acquired none of the scars inevitably inflicted on a defeated presidential contender. He seemed to have no enemies in the party or among the press.

After Ted's accident at Chappaquiddick, however, which virtually removed him as a presidential possibility, a number of Democratic presidential aspirants emerged: Senators Fred Harris of Oklahoma,

Birch Bayh of Indiana, Scoop Jackson of Washington, Harold Hughes of Iowa and Vance Hartke of Indiana, Governor Terry Sanford of North Carolina, Congressman Wilbur Mills of Arkansas, Congresswoman Shirley Chisholm of Brooklyn, Mayors Sam Yorty of Los Angeles and John Lindsay of New York City, and Gene McCarthy of Minnesota.

There was, of course, another man who was to play a crucial role in the politics of 1972—Alabama's Governor George Wallace. He had won nearly ten million votes as an Independent presidential contender in 1968, and he was growing stronger as he combined continuous campaigning with a flare for attracting the press.

In the wake of 1968 it seemed that the big three for 1972 would be Humphrey, Kennedy and Muskie, with the probability that George Wallace would control the "right wing" of the party and Gene McCarthy, if he wished, playing a role on the "left" as the first major antiwar candidate of 1968.

Thus, Jimmy the Greek's odds on McGovern: 200 to 1.

I never accepted these odds. Indeed, from the time of the California debate with Humphrey and McCarthy at the national convention of 1968, I had begun to think that my chances of winning the nomination in 1972 were anything but hopeless. I agreed with Mayor Daley's private aside to me shortly after the 1968 convention: ". . . I think our presidential nominee in '72 will either be you or young Kennedy."

By the end of 1968 I was already seriously thinking about a bid for the presidency. Recognizing that Ted was the most likely nominee, I felt that he might not make the race in view of the trauma associated with the death of his brothers and the anxiety he and his family must have been experiencing over future security threats. It seemed to me that the intense crosscurrents moving in American society were such that any one of us identified with a controversial issue could be the victim of violence. With the memory of John and Robert Kennedy's deaths so painfully etched in my mind, it seemed to me that if Ted and I were in the race as friendly rivals with similar views, the chances were better that one of us would make it to the nomination should either of us fall during the long bid before the convention.

With his vast family-name recognition combined with a charismatic personality, Ted could delay any open bid for the nomination until a time of his own choosing. But in my case, since I was a comparatively unknown contender with a subdued public image, an early, systematic, all-out effort would be required.

From the outset, it seemed to me that the road to the White House in 1972 consisted of several essential ingredients: first, a candidate positioned on the issues, especially Vietnam, who could coalesce the activists supporting Robert Kennedy and Gene McCarthy in 1968; second, a strong grassroots organization capable of identifying supporters at the neighborhood level and then enlisting their help, their votes and their funds; third, a constant reaching out to party regulars, blue-collar workers and others outside the McCarthy-Kennedy complex; fourth, once having won the Democratic nomination, it should be comparatively easy to defeat Richard Nixon by appealing to the decency and common sense of the American people. I believed, doubtless naïvely, that almost any Democratic nominee would defeat Nixon once voters had experienced four years of his presidency. I was right about the three steps required to win the nomination. I was wrong in my estimate that Nixon would be discredited in four years; that required five years.

Eleanor and I were at the home of Henry and Charlotte Kimelman in the Virgin Islands on July 19, 1969, enjoying a party marking my forty-seventh birthday when "Scottie" Fitzgerald Smith, a Washington friend, arrived and told us of radio reports that Ted Kennedy had experienced a serious accident. His car had gone off a bridge and a young woman riding with him was dead—apparently drowned. (As I mentioned earlier, Mary Jo Kopechne had worked briefly in my office as a volunteer during the previous summer.) Henry and I had been talking for several days about how I might enter the forthcoming presidential competition. We had also talked frequently of the strong bid Ted Kennedy might be expected to make. We both held a long-time affection and admiration for the Kennedy family, and the news of Ted's accident depressed us. I remember thinking in the context of all that had happened to the Kennedys that this was too much tragedy for any single family to bear. I tried to call Ted, but was unable to reach him. That night I sat for several hours in the moonlight around the Kimelmans' beautiful pool thinking alternately about Ted, about my own future and about the American space men—Neil Armstrong, Edwin Aldrin and Michael Collins—who were about to reach the moon. The next morning when I awakened late with the sun streaming in my face, I experienced a vague feeling that I might well be the Democratic presidential nominee in 1972.

The first public indication of my intention came as the result of a dinner at the Kimelman home on California Street in Washington in the fall of 1969. Present at this informal stag dinner were my friend Senator Abe Ribicoff, who had nominated me at the 1968 convention, Stewart and Mo Udall, Fred Dutton, film-maker Charles Guggenheim, Gene McCarthy's 1968 manager Blair Clark, former White House counsel of the Kennedy Administration Myer Feldman, Allard Lowenstein and several others. The purpose of the dinner was to consider whether or not I should seek the presidency in 1972. Most of those present thought that the autumn of 1969 was far too early to be thinking about the presidential politics of 1972. One of them leaked the story of the evening's discussion to the press—much to my embarrassment.

I decided that for the time being, instead of any more such rambling, speculative discussions of the national political scene, my activities should be concentrated on three substantive concerns: (1) the public protest against continued American involvement in Vietnam; (2) my responsibilities to lead the effort to end hunger in America as the chairman of the Senate Select Committee on Nutrition and Human Needs; and (3) my work as chairman of the Democratic Reform Commission. These were three interests that not only held my deep personal commitment but provided platforms and committed followers on which a presidential campaign could be built.

By this time I was already closely identified in the minds of millions of Americans as a leading critic of the war policy. On March 17, 1969, two months after Nixon assumed the presidency, I had delivered a major speech on the floor of the Senate attacking the Administration for continuing the war. Even my Democratic fellow senators who had taken issue with the Johnson war policies told me that my criticism of Nixon was premature—that the new President was entitled to more time. I disagreed, and so did the activists in the American peace movement who were familiar with Nixon's long time advocacy of American military involvement in Asia. So while my colleagues were telling me to go slow on antiwar statements, the mail and telephone calls coming into my office were saying "Right on!"

During the rest of the year I was much in demand as a speaker on college campuses. With three daughters in college—Ann at George Washington University, Susan at the University of Wisconsin and Teresa at the University of Virginia—I was impressed with two considerations: the growing revulsion to the Vietnam folly among the young, and my own practical need to finance the education of three daughters. The college lecture circuit not only financed the education of my daughters, it became my entrée to the thinking of some of America's most sensitive and perceptive young people.

Throughout 1969 and 1970 I made more university appearances than any senator in recent history. Always I spoke on the war, on the excessive outlays for military overkill, on the widening arms race, on the neglect of our central cities, the contamination of our environment, and the need to employ more of our people in such enterprises as the building of a modern rail and mass-transit system. Always the questions would follow, sometimes for as long as an hour or more—occasionally moving into give-and-take talk sessions until far into the night, with me sitting in a circle of students on the floor in a college dormitory or lounge. What right did we have to invade Vietnam or to bomb Vietnamese villages? What did I think of the CIA? Who *really* assassinated President Kennedy and why? What were my views on amnesty for those genuinely repulsed by the war in Vietnam? Why should alcohol be legal and "grass" illegal? Did I not think alcoholism in America was a more serious problem than pot-smoking? Why should male politicians, worried about their own political hides, require a woman to complete a pregnancy she did not want? Was American policy supporting or opposing racism in Africa? Why didn't education come to grips with the real issues of society? Why were so many professors more interested in publishing articles than in working with students? Can capitalism *really* cope with the problems of the poor, the unemployed and the Third World? Does the American political process *really* work? What can one citizen *really* do?

These were the questions, and many others, that I grappled with from the college lecture platforms and lounges across America. Usually my answers drew cheers, but sometimes the response was muted or marked by hisses; sometimes I was even applauded for the candor of a reply, if not for its content.

Thus, on the legalization of marijuana: No, I did not favor the legalization of marijuana. The fact that alcohol is destructive when used to excess does not justify putting a legal stamp on another substance about which we know even less. I would, however, favor decriminalizing the use of marijuana—of prohibiting its use under penalty of a fine rather than imprisonment. Yes, it is hypocritical for an adult tipsy on a third martini to be sitting in self-righteous judgment on a juvenile experience with pot. But as for the "hard stuff" —heroin and the like—I would throw the book at the racketeers and I would press for mandatory treatment of all users. Sometimes I would add that even if research had demonstrated that marijuana was harmless, I would not recommend its legalization in the middle of a political campaign lest it might defeat me. The legal use of marijuana might be pleasant for some, but it was more important to end the war in Vietnam and restore a measure of sanity to our national-security policies. I could not risk these other objectives by getting sidetracked on a crusade to legalize pot. This answer invariably drew delayed but highly gratifying applause mingled with a delightful glow of political insight on the faces of my young listeners.

On federal action to override state laws on abortion: No, I would not recommend the intrusion of the federal government into this highly sensitive area. It did not seem to me to be an issue that should be involved in a presidential campaign. Recognizing the depth of public feeling on the matter, it was my view that the federal government should not tamper with existing state law but that any remedy should come through action at the state level. I had not anticipated a federal court ruling after the 1972 election setting aside state anti-abortion laws. My answer frequently drew a few quiet murmurs of dissatisfaction from students, just as my refusal to advocate the legalization of marijuana produced some hisses.

On amnesty: At first I took the view that although the war was wrong, those who opposed it by disobeying the draft laws should be willing to accept imprisonment or exile as the price of preserving conscience against law. But after a trip to Vietnam in the fall of 1971 I was so grieved and repulsed by the broken bodies and disillusioned minds I found among our troops that my own opposition to the war took on an even more intense character.

One handsome young officer with both feet blown off by a land mine clung to my hand in a military hospital near Saigon and imploringly demanded of me, "Senator, what the hell are we doing out here?" Driving away from that hospital a few minutes later, I encountered a flatbed truck carrying the coffins of a dozen young Americans that were tagged for return to the United States: a corporal from Oklahoma, a lieutenant from California, a private from West Virginia. As I looked at those coffins glistening in the sun—mute testimony to the insanity of war—I wondered if I could not be doing more to prevent other boys from that needless fate. I was not prepared to support war-crimes trials for those who had engineered our entrance into this misery. But I could no longer condemn those who refused to participate. So at the University of Hawaii en route back from Vietnam, when asked if I would support amnesty for those opposing the war, I said, "Yes, with the understanding that such an amnesty would have to await the ending of the war—a process that would be completed within ninety days or less if I become President." I then added that in contrast to draft resisters, who could be covered by a blanket amnesty, deserters would have to be evaluated on a case-by-case basis. This answer brought a tumultuous, sustained standing ovation in the jam-packed University of Hawaii auditorium. From that point on, that position separated me from the other Democratic candidates in the minds of hundreds of thousands of young Americans and their parents.

But at the hands of some of my political rivals, abetted by contrived or careless commentary from such pontifical journalists as Rowland Evans, Robert Novak and James Reston, these essentially cautious, qualified positions on drugs, abortion and amnesty were made to appear as ill-conceived, radical nostrums. It remained for Senator Hugh Scott, the Republican leader in the Senate, to brand me in a statement to the national press as "the candidate of the 3 A's: acid, abortion and amnesty." Some critics referred to me privately in even cruder terms as the candidate of "grass, ass and amnesty."

In relationship to these issues one instructive, amusing incident remains in my mind from the Nebraska primary. Nebraska's marvelous, big, blunt-spoken former governor, Frank Morrison, and his wife, Maxine, were two of the most effective people in the country campaigning on my behalf. They became worried about the charges of "acid" and "abortion on demand" emanating against me from the Jackson and Humphrey political camps. At Frank's suggestion, a public rally was scheduled in a large Catholic high school auditorium in Omaha with the understanding that Frank would answer the "smears" against me and then introduce me to speak on "the real issues" of Vietnam, tax reform, agriculture, jobs, the Pentagon, etc.

The auditorium was packed to a dimension that terrified the fire marshal and the police. But big Frank lumbered up to the microphone, and in a mighty voice quivering with indignation, he began, "We have in our state tonight one of the finest young men in America. He is a great patriot, a highly decorated war hero who loves his country and wants to serve us as President. But he has been subjected to a vicious campaign of smears and innuendo." Then Frank launched his first salvo: "They say that George McGovern is for the legalization of marijuana, but I say—"

Before Frank could complete his denial of the charge, there was a thunderous burst of applause from at least the more youthful members of the audience. Frank looked puzzled and slightly stunned, but as the applause died away he completed his statement: "I tell you that George McGovern does not advocate the legalization of marijuana." This declaration drew no applause, only murmurs of regret.

In an even more powerful second salvo, Frank boomed, "They say George McGovern is for abortion on demand, but I tell you—"

Again Frank was interrupted by deafening applause. Waiting somewhat more puzzled for the clapping and cheering to cease, Frank went on bravely, "But I say to you that George McGovern is *against* tampering with our state laws on abortion."

Again no applause, only the sighs of regret.

At this point Frank made clear that neither he nor I was "radicals" and then introduced "the next President of the United States."

After the rally, as we drove back to the hotel, Frank said after a few moments of reflective silence, "George, maybe I'm too old to understand this new generation. I'll get the oldsters for you, and you take care of the young ones as you think best. We're going to have a tough time beating Hubert in Nebraska."

We won the Nebraska primary.

But to return to my account of the campus odyssey of 1969 and 1970 that preceded the political rallies of 1971 and 1972, I never once spoke during that period without taking on any and all questions. Later, as an announced presidential contender, I was to find that virtually every press conference and press interview was a piece of cake compared to the grueling, probing questions of America's university students. Sometimes, in contrast, the concerns raised by members of the press seemed superficial—the inevitable personality clashes and squabbles among campaign staff members, or whether I was a stalking horse for Ted Kennedy, or whether I was "too decent" to be President, or too lacking in charisma. And above all, how could I be taken seriously when I was so low in the polls? But most of the questions from the press were serious, legitimate concerns, and if in the main I answered them satisfactorily during the hundreds of days that the nation's journalists took turns traveling the country with me, it was in considerable part because of the prior years of interrogation by earnest, idealistic, sometimes cynical, sometimes paranoid, sometimes intensely pragmatic young Americans.

In addition, I was slowly assembling a nationwide army of student supporters who, in turn, recruited their brothers and sisters, fathers and mothers, aunts and uncles, grandparents and friends. At the same time, I was meeting an endless chain of airline ticket-sellers, stewardesses, hotel clerks, waiters, taxi drivers, policemen, entertainers, and curious Democratic local officials who sometimes observed me from the rear of college and high school auditoriums.

As the 1970 congressional elections approached, I took an increasingly active role in Democratic Party functions. During the summer and fall I campaigned on behalf of a number of congressional candidates in selected states. My staff was also alert to state and local party dinners and fund-raisers that provided an opportunity to make an impression on party leaders and workers.

Simultaneously I lent my name to a direct-mail fund-raising effort organized by George Agree on behalf of Democratic senators who were running for re-election. Not only did this effort, which produced over a million dollars for Democratic Senate campaigns, contribute substantially to the re-election effort of a number of senators, it also provided me with a list of 40,000 proven contributors.

During my travels to campuses and party functions, I jotted down the names of potential campaign workers and turned them over to Jeff Smith at my Senate office. Jeff had begun assembling the all-important 3 × 5 name files as soon as the 1968 campaign ended. He began with the Kennedy, McCarthy and McGovern delegates to the Chicago convention, adding other potential supporters from every available source. The thousands of names compiled from the Agree mailings were added to these files. The best source of names for the Jeff Smith index files, however, came to us through my efforts to end the war, and to a lesser extent from my leadership of the hunger and political-reform battles.

From 1965 to 1970 I had been concentrating my opposition to the war on pressing the Administration to begin negotiations, to halt the bombing and to stop the escalation of all forms of military activity. I continued to vote for military appropriations on the grounds that while I was opposed to the government's policy, I did not want to deprive our troops of support as long as they were in the field. It was my view that the proper role of the Congress was to urge a change in Administration policy, while recognizing that the conduct of policy rested with the executive branch.

By early 1970, however, I was coming to the conclusion that appeals to the Administration from the Senate floor and through the public mass demonstrations which I had joined were falling on stony ground. The only real power the Congress had to reverse a recalcitrant Administration policy was to cut off the appropriations that sustained the policy.

Thus, on April 30, 1970, I introduced to the Senate the McGovern-Hatfield Amendment to End the War. The amendment was drafted at my request by John Holum, my long-time legislative assistant, with the legal advice of friends at Harvard and elsewhere. Believing that the proposal would go nowhere without bipartisan support, I called on Oregon's Republican Senator Mark Hatfield and he enthusiastically agreed to become the major co-sponsor.

We introduced the proposed action as an amendment to the Military Procurement Authorization Act. The amendment called for the systematic withdrawal of American forces and an end to all U.S. military operations in or over Vietnam, Cambodia and Laos no later than December 31, 1971. A safety valve to ensure release of American prisoners was included in a proviso authorizing the President to extend the withdrawal deadline by sixty days, during which time he could ask the Congress to establish an alternative withdrawal date.

At the end of 1969, New York Republican Senator Charles Goodell, who had been appointed by Governor Nelson Rockefeller to complete the term of Robert Kennedy, had introduced a resolution to end funding of the war. The weakness of the Goodell proposal was that it was offered as a separate bill with no visible bipartisan base. It could thus be easily shunted aside in the Armed Services Committee.

The McGovern-Hatfield Amendment would inevitably be voted on since it was attached to the military-authorization bill. But even more significant, with a fateful break in timing, our amendment was introduced on the day before President Nixon announced that American forces had invaded Cambodia. This announcement, in the form of a televised address to the nation, set off an outcry of major proportions in the Congress and among the American people. Nixon had acted completely without congressional authorization to invade an independent country, supposedly to destroy its use as a staging area by the Vietcong and the North Vietnamese. He said that our troops were going into Cambodia to wipe out the central command headquarters of the enemy forces.

As it turned out, our troops found no command center. Indeed, they found little or nothing except frightened Cambodians trying to get out of the way. The President told the nation that we had stoutly resisted any previous move against Cambodia despite the repeated attacks from that area by enemy forces. It was later discovered that the Nixon Administration had been secretly bombing Cambodia for fourteen months prior to the ground invasion. These attacks were concealed by fake Air Force records.

The whole Cambodian invasion and the prior bombing were ill-advised, unauthorized and illegal enterprises of shocking proportions. One of the enduring tragedies of our involvement in Vietnam is that far from protecting the neighboring "dominoes"—Cambodia and Laos—our military operations spilled across Indochina to destroy the government of Prince Sihanouk in Cambodia and to lay waste much of Laos. Nothing the Vietcong or the North Vietnamese could have done would have been so devastating as the massive American aerial attacks and internal disruption organized by our war planners to the detriment of Laos and Cambodia. (So strong was the public outcry against the Cambodian "incursion" that Nixon was forced to withdraw our forces by the end of June. Campuses erupted across the nation. Conservative professional and business leaders banded together in large numbers in many cities to protest the invasion and the continuance of the war. I addressed one rally of Wall Street lawyers, brokers and bankers that must have included over a thousand men. All across the nation, groups of every kind were moved to anguish and protest.)

When students at Kent State University in Ohio gathered in protest on May 4, the governor stupidly ordered out National Guard units equipped with high-powered rifles and live ammunition. In some fashion as yet undetermined, the guardsmen opened fire on the unarmed students and four of them fell dead. This shocking incident added to the growing furor over the continued killing in Indochina. The next day I decided that the time had come for a major televised attack on the Nixon war policies. My office asked all three networks for free time to answer the Nixon Cambodia speech. All three turned me down on the grounds that neither I nor anyone else was an officially designated spokesman for the antiwar effort. So I set out to raise $60,000 to finance the purchase of a half-hour on one of the three networks. CBS and ABC both denied my request to purchase time, but NBC told me they would sell the 7:30 P.M. time ordinarily reserved for *I Dream of Jeannie* if I could produce the money within three days.

When David Brinkley mentioned on the evening news that I was trying to raise money for the telecast, a large number of telephone pledges reached my office, and with the help of the Council for A Livable World, we raised $25,000. Earlier, I had told a Washington news source that I was prepared to mortgage my home to secure the additional $35,000. But before this became necessary, Stewart Mott, a generous young New York philanthropist, gave $5,000 and loaned the remaining $30,000. Fifteen minutes before the five o'clock deadline, Mott's representative walked into the NBC office in New York with a $35,000 check, and Gordon Weil, my hard-driving assistant, delivered the balance from Washington.

My friend Charles Guggenheim, with a film-maker's bias against television speeches, suggested that I instead invite Hatfield to join with me in a dialogue covering the issues of the war. The idea made sense to me, and Hatfield readily accepted. Meanwhile, word of my effort had gotten to the offices of Senators Goodell and Hughes. They indicated some degree of anxiety that I might be assuming the leadership role against the war to their exclusion, so they were added to the dialogue. It then occurred to me that none of the four of us were members of the Foreign Relations Committee, so in deference to that body, I asked the highly articulate Senator Frank Church if he would join the panel.

All day Sunday, under the direction of Guggenheim, these five senators—Republicans Hatfield and Goodell and Democrats Church, Hughes and I—worked on the filming of a half-hour discussion of the war. The program went out to the nation on Tuesday evening, May 12, opening and ending with a summary statement by me plus a brief appeal for funds by Church to pay off the loan for the telecast.

To my amazement, nearly half a million dollars poured into our office from across the country. We not only repaid Stewart Mott's loan a few days after the broadcast; we had a considerable sum of money for additional television and radio spots urging support for the Amendment to End the War. In addition, we had a list of 50,000 names of Americans who cared enough about their nation to invest in an effort that would extricate us from the Indochina nightmare. Many of them were soon to become contributors and workers in a presidential campaign.

Presently the McGovern-Hatfield Amendment became the rally-ing point against the war. All during the summer of 1970 a steady procession of antiwar delegations poured into Washington lobbying their senators and congressmen to support our Amendment to End the War. These delegations, representing every stratum of American society, had an unmistakable impact on many senators. Their efforts reached a climax on the morning of Tuesday, September 1, 1970, when I rose in the Senate to give the concluding speech in support of the amendment. It was the hardest-hitting speech I had ever delivered to my colleagues. Nearly the entire Senate was there to hear it.

> Mr. President, the vote we are about to cast could be one of the most significant votes Senators will ever cast.
>
> I have lived with this vote night and day since last April 30—the day before the Cambodia invasion—the day this amendment was first sub-mitted. . . .
>
> What is the choice it presents us? It presents us with an opportunity to end a war we never should have entered. It presents us with an opportunity to revitalize constitutional government in America by restoring the war powers the Founding Fathers obliged the Congress to carry.
>
> Every Senator in this Chamber is partly responsible for sending 50,000 young Americans to an early grave. This Chamber reeks of blood.
>
> Every Senator here is partly responsible for that human wreckage at Walter Reed and Bethesda Naval and all across our land—young men without legs, or arms, or genitals, or faces, or hopes.
>
> There are not very many of these blasted and broken boys who think this war is a glorious venture.
>
> Do not talk to them about bugging out, or national honor, or cour-age.
>
> It does not take any courage at all for a Congressman, or a Senator, or a President to wrap himself in the flag and say we are staying in Vietnam, because it is not our blood that is being shed.
>
> But we are responsible for those young men and their lives and their hopes.
>
> And if we do not end this damnable war, those young men will some day curse us for our pitiful willingness to let the Executive carry the burden that the Constitution places on us.

These words angered some senators, but they also put the entire Senate on trial. The vote was 39 in favor of the amendment and 55 against. To some, that seemed like a defeat; to me, it was a victory. For the first time in American history, more than a third of the Senate had publicly voted to terminate a war which the Commander in Chief was most anxious to continue. (Ironically, the 39 percent of the Senate that stood with me on this issue was the same percentage of the national electorate that was to support me for the presidency against Richard Nixon two years later.)

As the battle to end the war was moving forward, another battle was gathering force—against hunger in America. Inspired by a CBS television documentary on the extent and nature of malnutrition in the United States, I secured passage in the Senate of a resolution to create a Select Committee on Nutrition and Human Needs. I was then named as chairman of this committee, with Senator Jacob Javits of New York as the ranking Republican. In a series of well-staged public hearings in Washington and other parts of the nation, the new committee quickly became the nerve center in the effort to end hunger in America. Over the next few years this committee effort led the way in a dramatic acceleration of nutritional efforts. The number of Americans assisted by the food-stamp program increased from 3 million in 1968 to 12 million by 1972. With increasing unemployment after 1973, the number of low-income Americans assisted by food stamps in maintaining a nutritionally sound diet increased to 19 million in 1975.

Our committee also spearheaded the effort to improve the nutritional health of children. In 1969, fewer than 4 million children were benefiting from free or reduced-price school lunches. That number was more than doubled by 1972. In addition to these major efforts, our committee was largely responsible for effective new nutrition programs for the elderly, for nursing mothers and for children needing special foods. We have also demonstrated the need for better education in the nutritional field.

One of the most remarkable aspects of the select committee's achievements on the hunger front was a series of legislative battles that we won over the opposition of the Senate Committee on Agriculture, chaired by the able, highly regarded Allen Ellender of Louisiana. Senator Ellender was an old-fashioned Southern conservative who generally resisted increasing federal expenditures for social programs. But he loved children and he did not believe anyone should go hungry. Furthermore, he was uneasy about a new committee headed by a junior Senator from South Dakota encroaching on the legislative jurisdiction of his prestigious Committee on Agriculture.

For all these reasons he made certain that he also became a member of my Select Committee on Nutrition and Human Needs, and he participated in our first field hearings in the migrant-labor areas of western Florida. He was disturbed by the housing, health and nutritional conditions we encountered, but all day he maintained the gruff posture of a hard-boiled interrogator while grilling witnesses as to why the federal government had any increased obligation to deal with "a local situation."

The next morning Ellender and I were having breakfast in the motel coffee shop when we were joined by CBS newsman Daniel Schorr. The Louisiana senator, who had recently returned from the Soviet Union with recommendations that the United States should make greater efforts to understand and cooperate with the Russians, began to outline these views to Schorr. He then turned to the danger of Washington doing too much to resolve the kind of human needs we were encountering in Florida. To all of this Schorr finally responded, "Senator, I'd like to ask you a question. Why are you so soft on Russians and so hard on Americans?"

That is one of the best, most appropriately phrased questions I have ever heard directed to a politician. It was perfectly designed to disturb Ellender's political and personal peace of mind. He continued to oppose the increased tempo of the battle against malnutrition our select committee was waging, but he did it without the passion he gave to other Senate fights and he lost on several crucial occasions. In fairness to Senator Ellender, it should be noted that he was the earlier architect of several of the nation's solid nutritional programs.

Taken all together, the effort led by the select committee to end malnutrition in America has been, in the words of Tufts University president and former Harvard University professor of nutrition Jean Mayer, "the most successful single advance on the social front since the passage of the Social Security Act in 1935."

As the party-reform, end-the-war and nutritional efforts moved forward in 1969 and 1970, we began laying the organizational base for a presidential-nomination bid. On March 21, 1970, I flew to Denver, Colorado, to address a large statewide Jefferson-Jackson Day dinner. I had written the text of that address earlier in the week at my home in Washington. It bore the title "Come Home, America"—a theme suggested by Eleanor from some remarks she had read by Martin Luther King, Jr. The speech represented ideas I had been evolving for months calling upon the American people and their leaders to return to the enduring ideals with which the nation began. America needed a leadership that not only sought the truth but would speak candidly to the American people. In the Denver speech I called the nation to come home from the wilderness of needless war and excessive militarism to build a society in which we cared about one another—especially the old, the sick, the hungry, the jobless, the homeless. It was an idealistic speech, but it was also born of common sense and the bitter pain visited on the nation as a consequence of ill-conceived policies, both foreign and domestic.

The Denver speech was repeatedly interrupted by applause, and I received a sustained standing ovation as I reiterated the "Come Home, America" theme in a cadenced conclusion:

> From the politics of manipulation . . . to the politics of hope and reconciliation, Come home, America.
>
> From boasts of a silent majority to the higher ground of conscience and responsibility, Come home, America.
>
> From the hunger of little children, from the loneliness of the aging poor, from the despair of the homeless, the jobless, the uncared-for sick to a society that cherishes the human spirit, Come home, America.
>
> Come home, prodigal America, to the land of your fathers where we can rebuild our cities, revitalize our farms and towns, reclaim our rivers and streams.
>
> Come home, America, to that sense of community that opened our country and gave us nationhood. For what we need most of all is the assurance that each one of us is a part of a nation where we care about each other.

That theme was to become the centerpiece of my bid for the nomination and for the presidency. Audiences in all parts of the nation warmly responded to it as a restatement of America's most treasured values.

The Denver trip coincided with an interesting, albeit minor political development. Earlier in the week the report of President Nixon's Commission on Pornography had been released with a news summary indicating that pornographic literature has no deleterious effects on adults and only minimal impact on children. The report was immediately assailed, not only by the Administration, but by the Congress. Indeed, the Senate voted to condemn it—with only five dissenting votes. I refused to condemn the report for what seemed to me to be a compelling reason: the document was several hundred pages in length and none of us had read it at the time the vote was taken. But Richard Nixon, not to be outdone by the Senate majority on the purity front, timed a blast at his own commission for the Sunday morning press.

I awakened that morning in a Denver hotel suite to the sound of the Sunday Denver *Post* being pushed under my door. It carried a bold headline, NIXON TO FIGHT SMUT, above a story detailing the President's deep concern over the reckless findings of his commission. Attached to the paper was a note from Colorado State Democratic Chairman Dan Lynch reminding me that half a century before, Utah's Senator Daniel Smoot had led a well-publicized campaign against pornography which had inspired these lines by Ogden Nash:

> Smite Smoot
> Be rough and tough
> For smut when smitten
> Is front page stuff.

Then Lynch added, "I liked your vote on this foolishness and I liked your speech last night."

At a breakfast with party leaders an hour later, I learned that my lonely vote against the Senate censure of the Commission on Pornography had won the appreciation of several other influential Colorado activists. This reaction confirmed my own instinct that sometimes what appears to be an unpopular vote gains valuable support from people grown weary of political posturing and hypocrisy.

One of those who was impressed both by my speech of the night before and by humorous references to the Ogden Nash couplet at the breakfast was Gary Hart, a young Denver attorney who coordinated my visit to his city. As my father would have put it, "I liked the cut of his jib." He impressed me as a quiet, competent, practical-minded man with a capacity for idealism, humor and imagination. I was also much impressed by his wife, Lee.

Like me, Gary had considered briefly being a minister and had completed work for a divinity degree at Yale. Also like me, he realized that he was not emotionally suited for the life of a clergyman. After securing a law degree at Yale, he worked briefly for Stewart Udall in the Department of the Interior during the Kennedy Administration. He also was a volunteer in Robert Kennedy's campaign of 1968 and had then opened his own law office in Denver. At the breakfast following my Denver speech I told him of my plans to seek the presidency and asked him if he would take on the task of organizing the Western states, working for the time being out of his Denver office. In the weeks that followed I inquired into Gary Hart's background, his personality, his staying power, his talents. The reports were uniformly good. I was also encouraged by his enthusiastic response to his first visits to the Western states. With these impressions in mind, I asked him to come to Washington and assume the management of the national campaign. He remained in that post for both the nomination and the general election. Two years later he was elected to the United States Senate—one of scores of Americans now holding public office who cut their political teeth in the 1972 campaign.

Following Gary's arrival in Washington and the opening of a small campaign headquarters near the Senate Office Building, we added what was to be the nucleus of a small but highly effective campaign staff: Rick Stearns to direct the bid for delegates in the non-primary states; Joe Grandmaison to organize his home state, New Hampshire, and Massachusetts; Gene Pokorny to organize Wisconsin and his home state, Nebraska; Yancey Martin to give special attention to the concerns of black voters; Jeff Smith to build the lists of potential volunteers and contributors; Amanda Smith to "sensitize" all of us on women's concerns. John Holum and Gordon Weil of my Senate office staff handled a combination of research, writing, press and general campaign activities.

Then, after vigorous pressure from me and from his remarkable wife, Holly, Frank Mankiewicz came on board as political director of the campaign. Frank had given up his California law practice to become a Peace Corps official in the Kennedy Administration; had later served as Robert Kennedy's press secretary, and then had developed a syndicated column with his friend Tom Braden. With Gary building a field organization in the early-primary states, I knew that Frank could give added stature, appeal and content to the campaign as it was perceived by the press and the public. He also added a rare wit that became indispensable to an uphill struggle toward the White House. No single person on the national campaign staff played a more significant role than Mankiewicz.

Frank was soon joined by Ted Van Dyk, a highly energetic veteran of earlier Humphrey campaigns who was to serve us in a broad range of tasks. Then came Steve Robbins and his superb "advance" team, who handled scheduling and promotion of my public appearances. Working without pay was the indomitable Henry Kimelman as finance director, assisted by a paid deputy, Marian Pearlman. I also had the free advice and constant help of Professor Richard Wade and Washington lawyer John Douglas, perhaps my most creative advisers. We were later to be joined by the brilliant direct-mail expert, Morris Dees of Montgomery, Alabama, and by Miles and Nancy Rubin of California, who worked tirelessly to give us the advantage of computer and management skills. Our basic media effort was developed by Charles Guggenheim, Tom Collins and Stan Rapp of New York, Merv Weston of New Hampshire, Stan Kaplan of North Carolina and Elizabeth Stevens of Washington, D.C.

Almost from the beginning we were assisted by some of the nation's most talented and well-known personalities, including Shirley MacLaine, who campaigned virtually nonstop for two years, and her brother, Warren Beatty, who broke new ground in raising funds by well-planned benefit concerts utilizing the drawing power of such talented artists as Barbra Streisand, Dionne Warwick, James Taylor,

Andy Williams, Carole King, Henry Mancini, Peter, Paul and Mary, Simon and Garfunkel, and many others. At his highly successful star-studded concerts, Warren arranged for the ushering to be done by such celebrities as Jack Nicholson, Julie Christie, Goldie Hawn, Paul Newman and Burt Lancaster. Dennis Weaver and Leonard Nimoy, sometimes joined by Candice Bergen and Marlo Thomas, campaigned tirelessly, sometimes with me, sometimes alone, as did President Kennedy's indomitable press secretary and the former Senator from California, Pierre Salinger. We were assisted, too, by over a hundred of the nation's best-known professional football players, a group organized by Ray Schoenke of the Washington Redskins.

I did not pressure any member of the family to campaign. They responded of their own initiative because they believed in the issues I stood for and because of their love for me.

Eleanor is barely five feet tall and weighs less than a hundred pounds, but she was a giant throughout the entire campaign. She traveled the country on her own, speaking day after day to audiences big and small. She handled with intelligence, skill and good humor countless interviews on radio, television and in the press. We never had to brief her on the issues. She did her own research, improvised her own speeches and delivered them with such effectiveness that people in all parts of the nation were warmed by her presence. She was a constant source of inspiration, insight and power throughout the campaign.

As for my daughters, they, too, campaigned on their own with little or no briefing. I was constantly amazed and pleased to learn of what they had said in extemporaneous appearances and in interviews with the press. One early morning in a Detroit hotel room, as I watched them doing a lengthy television interview in New York with the *Today* show's Barbara Walters, I was moved to tears by their plain-spoken honesty and eloquence.

Only my son, Steve, declined a role in the campaign. I later learned why. He genuinely feared the prospect of life in the White House. He did not want to be the son of the President of the United States. Indeed, he confided to Eleanor after the campaign that had he known I would lose, he would have campaigned for me despite his shyness and love of privacy. But Steve was conditioned to believe that his dad never lost and he wanted no part of a McGovern victory, which he saw as the end of his hopes for a normal life.

Beyond all of the more frequently mentioned campaign personalities were the countless dedicated, highly motivated, self-starting volunteers in all parts of the nation. Obviously such a citizen's army would generate some personal frictions—between Gary and Frank at the top, between the national headquarters and state organizers such as Grandmaison and Pokorny, between the unpaid fund-raisers and the paid fund-spenders; between the newly arrived campaign staff and long-time Senate aides who were frequently convinced that the campaign staffers would sooner or later destroy me.

We were, nonetheless, building far and away the best grassroots organization in the country; we had the best-motivated paid staff and unpaid volunteers; we were right on the issues that counted; and we managed a highly effective, well-orchestrated drive for the Democratic presidential nomination, one that may have been unprecedented in American history. We could not have won the nomination without the highly motivated grassroots army that our campaign inspired in growing force across the nation. Suffice it to say that this largely self-starting, deeply committed multitude of supporters from New Hampshire to California were the heroes of 1972. They won ten important primary elections, including a complete sweep in three of the largest states—California, New York and New Jersey; they raised $7 million for the nomination effort; they forced the Nixon Administration to end the war in Vietnam; they changed the rules and the dynamics of the Democratic Party; they captured a presidential nomination and wrote a constructive, intelligent agenda for the nation. In the end, they did not prevail at the ballot box, but their methods and their ideals were essentially right, and over the long term, what they stood for will prevail if the American political process is to prevail.

My formal declaration for the presidential nomination effort broke new ground in American politics. Virtually all previous presidential campaign announcements were made either at the beginning of the election year or at the end of the previous year. I made my announcement almost a full two years prior to the November 6, 1972, election. It was the earliest presidential announcement in American history, although several candidates, including Jimmy Carter, were to follow that course for 1976.

The decision to announce a year ahead of the normal time was part of a strategy worked out at a small all-day meeting at Cedar Point, our family farmhouse near St. Michaels on Maryland's Eastern Shore. The group which met on that sun-filled July 25 forenoon included, in addition to Eleanor and me, George Cunningham, Pat Donovan, Dick Wade, Rick Stearns and our newly arrived campaign manager, Gary Hart.

I opened the discussion with the observation that the Democratic Party had been floundering since the 1968 election and was not providing a clearly focused opposition to the Nixon policies. Following his defeat in 1968, the Democratic standard-bearer, Hubert Humphrey, had returned to Minnesota for two years of college teaching and preparation for a Senate campaign in 1970. The Democratic National Committee was virtually paralyzed with a debt of $9 million from the recent presidential campaign. I argued that the first Democratic presidential candidate to enter the race would move into a leadership vacuum.

Monday, January 18, 1971, Eleanor and I went to the KELO-TV studio on Phillips Avenue in Sioux Falls, South Dakota, where we had been making television appearances since 1956, and announced my candidacy. That opening statement was carefully worded with the assistance of Richard Goodwin to set the tone for the kind of campaign I wanted to run:

> I seek the presidency because I believe deeply in the American promise and can no longer accept the diminishing of that promise. . . . Thoughtful Americans understand that the highest patriotism is not a blind acceptance of official policy, but a love of one's country deep enough to call her to a higher standard . . . we must undertake a re-examination of our ideas, institutions and the actual conditions of our lives which is as fundamental as the discussions of the founding fathers two centuries ago. . . .
>
> A public figure today can perform no greater service than to lay bare the proven malfunctions of our society, try honestly to confront our problems in all their complexity, and stimulate the search for solutions. This is my intention in this campaign.
>
> The kind of campaign I intend to run will rest on candor and reason; it will be rooted not in the manipulation of our fears and divisions, but in a national dialogue on mutual respect and common hope.
>
> The people are not centrist or liberal or conservative. Rather, they seek a way out of the wilderness. But if we who seek their trust, trust them; if we try to evoke the "better angels of our nature," the people will find their own way. We are the children of those who built a great and free nation. And we are no less than that. We must now decide whether our courage and imagination are equal to our talents. If they are, as I believe, then future generations will continue to love America, not simply because it is theirs, but for what it has become—for what, indeed, we have made it.

I then flew to Washington and the next forenoon at eleven o'clock walked into the Capitol Caucus Room to announce my presidential intentions and to field the questions of the national press corps. To these men and women—most of whom were highly skeptical about the practicality of so early a presidential announcement by one with so little chance of winning—I said:

> Americans have never believed that simply to talk about problems was to solve them. We need action, and I intend action.

But surely our failure to act must also reflect a larger loss of spirit and confidence—almost as if citizens felt that the conditions and quality of their lives were beyond their influence. And it is this, in my judgment, that is the heart of the matter. From participatory democracy to women's liberation and citizens' conservation councils, we see an increasing assertion of the individual, a desire not simply to have things done, but to do them.

We want to matter as individuals—all of us. The task of future leadership is not to rule people's lives. It is to change the institutions of our society so the citizens may shape their own lives.

I do not intend to assert that these are simple problems or that the answers are obvious. I do know that we must look for new policies and procedures rather than rush to enact new programs which are simply modified versions of old failures. But we cannot begin even this task unless we reverse the growing corruption of public life which views individuals as objects to be deceived or manipulated, and which regards the art of leadership as a capacity to follow the latest public-opinion poll. . . .

I undertake this quest for the presidency primarily to call the nation home to the liberating ideals that gave us birth. . . .

As for today, let me begin with one pledge above all others—to speak the truth about the hard questions fully and openly.

The closing lines of the announcement were the ones I most wanted to emphasize—"to speak the truth." I believed that the American people were becoming doubtful, if not hostile, toward political leaders. "The credibility gap" was a painful fact of life. So many lies, distortions and cover-ups had been offered in an effort to rationalize the Vietnam war that both the press and the public were in a mood of suspicion and resentment toward the political process. I strongly wanted to find the right answers to the nation's problems and then have the courage to express those answers openly and clearly. Within the limits of my ability, I determined to answer every question from the press or from the voters with maximum candor and bluntness. That was a pledge I did the best I could to keep throughout the campaign and it was an essential part of the formula that enabled me to win the Democratic presidential nomination.

Fortifying the pledge of candor and truthfulness was a second decision reached early in the nomination effort to make the campaign procedures, including all financial arrangements, as open to the public as possible.

Sandy d'Alemberte, a talented young Miami lawyer and former member of the Florida Legislature, had been a leader in the enactment of Florida's so-called Sunshine Law. The purpose of this statute was to open up all Florida legislative business to public scrutiny—no more private, behind-the-scenes committee sessions or closed-door meetings between lobbyists and state officials.

Aware of the favorable reaction to this statute in Florida, Sandy called John Douglas and suggested that we construct a completely "open" campaign. We would begin by publishing the names and amounts given of all contributors. We would file a public report of my personal assets, liabilities and sources of income. We would pledge regular conferences with the press, a desire to meet all other candidates in open debate, and a willingness to answer questions from any audience I addressed. If elected, I pledged regular presidential press conferences, some Cabinet meetings opened to the press, publicized records of all meetings between lobbyists and government officials, specific efforts to expose the presidential office to direct input from citizens of all kinds.

As the first primary got under way in New Hampshire, I pressed the other candidates to be equally "open." Releasing all of my campaign contributors' list, I built increasing pressure on the other contenders to do the same. This became a significant factor, especially in New Hampshire.

Ed Muskie, a decent and honest man, was campaigning on the slogan "Trust Muskie." By implication I suggested repeatedly that a man asking to be trusted with the highest office in the land should be willing to publish both his personal financial records and his campaign financial sources. The problem for Ed was that he had received a substantial number of contributions from anti-Nixon Republicans who believed that he would be the Democratic presidential nominee, but who did not want it known that they were backing him. There may also have been other contributions that Ed was reluctant to publicize. In any event, I later learned that my constant challenges to debate and to open up the financial records was a major worry to Muskie as the front runner. He finally accepted both challenges, but not before I had emerged as the leading advocate of "open" politics.

In pioneering the concepts of "openness" and "disclosure," we set a pattern that nearly all other candidates have since found it wise to follow. Indeed, federal statutes now require the kind of disclosure of campaign contributions which we made voluntarily in 1972.

No part of my successful bid for the Democratic nomination was better handled than the raising and public disclosure of campaign finances. We relied more directly on large numbers of small contributions through mail appeals than any presidential campaign in history. The average contribution in the period leading up to the nomination was about $10. The campaign was actually "kicked off" by a seven-page letter prepared by New York public relations expert Tom Collins and Morris Dees, which was sent to our entire mailing list of nearly 250,000 people. The lengthy letter set forth in some detail the reasons I was seeking the presidency and my dreams for the nation if elected. It ended with a strong appeal for contributions, which resulted in more than $300,000 in funds.

Two dozen additional mail appeals were made in the next year and a half between the time of my announcement and the nomination in Miami. Dees supplemented his regular fund appeals by calling on the first contributors to pledge $10 a month for the balance of the campaign. By the end of 1971, these monthly contributions had reached $40,000 per month. All in all, the mail efforts directed by Morris Dees and assisted by Jeff Smith and Tom Collins generated $5 million—$4 million in net profits—during the eighteen-month period leading up to the nomination.

Supplementing the direct-mail campaign were the highly successful benefit concerts organized by Warren Beatty. A single star-studded concert featuring Barbra Streisand at the Los Angeles Forum netted $300,000. Scores of additional innovative fund-raising efforts were generated by local supporters, including the baking and sale of homemade bread by Louisa Thomas, wife of a professor at Lynchburg, Virginia. Her bread became known as "McGovern Bread" and is still in demand in the Lynchburg area. Helen Parker, from Montgomery County, Maryland, who owned a huge overweight pet cat, painted a homemade banner carrying the words "George McGovern's Only Fatcat." Day after day Helen took her "fat cat" to shopping centers, soliciting small contributions from amused shoppers. Such committed supporters made possible one of the most successful fund-raising operations in our national political history.

Under the close scrutiny of Henry Kimelman, our national finance director, money was not only raised effectively; it was disbursed effectively and prudently. We never went deep into debt; we never contracted for services, materials and personnel without knowing that these expenditures could be covered. We did, I confess, learn how long it would take for a check to be sent to a West Coast organizer and be cashed before it bounced in Washington. But for the most part our checks did not bounce, and when they did, Henry quickly improvised payment.

There were no scandals or dishonesty in our 1972 campaign from beginning to end. I think we set a new standard for the financing and public disclosure of presidential campaigns—and for sound fiscal management—free largely of deficits and waste.

From the outset I was aware that not only my funding but also my workers would have to come from rank-and-file voters. In every sense we were to depend on the grassroots. The "big names" were committed to the front runners, especially to Muskie. For me, this was both an asset and a liability. It was an asset in that it saved countless hours of telephone calls, private meetings in hotel rooms and other time-consuming efforts involved in securing "big name" endorsements and then keeping them "on board." Ed Muskie must have devoted hundreds of hours to winning, and announcing in time-consuming press conferences, an endless procession of endorsements. Meanwhile I was free to meet the voters and to recruit workers in a fast-moving daily schedule that included pre-dawn visits to factories, countless coffee gatherings, high school and college assemblies and informal chats with people at shopping centers, veterans clubs, union halls, farmers meetings, bowling alleys and church suppers.

At one crucial point during the Wisconsin primary, Bill Dixon, my Wisconsin coordinator, learned that Muskie would be coming into the state for two important days of campaigning. Knowing the high premium Ed placed on prestigious endorsements, Dixon concocted a memorandum to me stating that two Wisconsin legislators previously committed to Muskie were wavering toward me. The memorandum suggested that I devote my next Wisconsin trip to cultivating all Democratic members of the Wisconsin Legislature. Dixon "accidentally" dropped a copy of the memo in Muskie headquarters and disposed of the original. I knew nothing of this escapade until months after the campaign. But it produced the results Dixon intended. Ed and his staff were so worried about the alleged defections that they canceled his planned schedule and devoted most of two days to strenuous cultivation of a handful of legislators already safely within the Muskie camp.

In a more fundamental (and honorable!) way, we turned other Muskie advantages into advantages for us. Whereas Ed had the resources to launch campaigns in many states, we targeted our meager funds on New Hampshire and Wisconsin with subsequent plans for major efforts in Massachusetts, Nebraska, Oregon, California and New York. Of the first ninety days in 1972, I devoted twenty days to New Hampshire and twenty-one to Wisconsin, while Muskie was scattering his visits to a score of states. Joe Grandmaison in New Hampshire and Gene Pokorny in Wisconsin had my total confidence and full backing. I regarded these two young coordinators and the army of volunteers they were recruiting as crucial to my nomination bid. I instructed our national office to give them every dollar we could possibly divert to these two states. They responded in kind with a painstaking step-by-step construction of a superb grassroots organization. In every dispute involving Joe or Gene and the national office, I invariably came down on the side of these two irrepressible state organizers.

Only in rare instances did I challenge their knowledge of how I could best use my time. One such case came in New Hampshire when in mid-February I began to sense that we were not giving sufficient attention to blue-collar workers, including those in the shoe factories of Manchester. Joe felt that these workers probably "belonged" to other candidates and that I should concentrate on more promising vineyards. But on February 18 we visited the first shoe plant in Manchester, and I was warmly received by the men and women in this factory and in dozens of others that we subsequently visited across the state. This tactical shift came in time to win thousands of votes that might have gone to other candidates.

As the New Hampshire campaign drew to a close, Muskie and his staff became aware that we were fast closing the gap that once promised to give them a landslide victory. Ed hurriedly flew into the state, tired and harassed from a lengthy tour of other parts of the country. Upon his arrival he mounted a truck in front of the Manchester *Union-Leader* office and began denouncing the publisher for a scurrilous editorial attack on his wife, Jane, that had appeared at an earlier date. As he delivered his denunciation, his voice choked and he appeared to be in tears.

Many members of the press thought that this so-called crying incident hurt Ed's presidential chances. I have always been convinced that it did not. In thousands of contacts with New Hampshire voters afterward, I never encountered a single person who was turned against Ed by this experience. Indeed, my polling consultants, Pat Caddell and John Gorman, discovered that Muskie's tearful attack actually improved his position with New Hampshire voters. Gorman estimated that it gave Muskie 3 or 4 additional percentage points in the final state tally. That finding supported the conclusion I was reaching from my own visits with voters. The notion that this event ended Muskie's presidential drive was a myth concocted in the fertile minds of a few journalists looking for an easy story.

What seriously weakened the Muskie presidential bid was the New Hampshire campaign as a whole. We outworked Ed in every corner of the state. We were also better positioned on the issues that moved the voters: jobs, tax reform, the war, openness in government and political reform. Beyond all of this, hundreds of young volunteers flocked into the state from campuses in the Boston area, from other New England colleges and from campuses across the nation. By election day, nearly every New Hampshire voter had been appealed to by one or more of these eager, idealistic young Americans urging a vote for George McGovern. Many of these volunteers were to move on to the next primary, and the next, and all the way to California.

On March 7 the New Hampshire results rolled in; it was Muskie 48 percent and McGovern 37 percent—not a numerical victory, but a smashing moral and psychological victory in a state that the national press had decided must give Muskie at least 50 if not 60 percent of the vote to avoid a setback to the Maine senator's campaign. Ed's state coordinator strengthened this perception by announcing before the election that if they got anything less than 50 percent, she would "feel like killing myself." Of course, she didn't do that, but the comparatively close results drastically changed the national dynamics of the presidential race. From then on, Ed Muskie was seen as the fading favorite and I was perceived as the rising Cinderella of 1972.

Wisconsin was the next crucial test. This historic primary state was the one where we expected to win our first numerical as well as moral victory. That we did so was explained in part by the superior grassroots organization built so carefully by Pokorny, Dixon and their associates. It was also verification that we were hitting the issues well. Senator Gaylord Nelson, a close personal friend and my seatmate in the Senate, had carefully briefed me on the urgent need of property-tax relief in Wisconsin. He had developed legislation to reduce the local tax burden by direct federal assistance to education financed from reductions in military outlays. I joined in co-sponsoring the Nelson-McGovern Property Tax Relief Act, and I discussed it night and day in Wisconsin—second only to hammering against the continued war in Vietnam and the waste in excessive military spending. For the first time I was also the beneficiary of unexpected, albeit indirect, endorsements. Wisconsin's senior Senator, Bill Proxmire, announced two days before the election that he had cast his vote for me by absentee ballot because of his respect for me as a person and because of my stubborn fight to eliminate needless fat in the Pentagon budget. The next day Governor Pat Lucey told reporters that while he would not make any formal endorsements, he thought I would win the Wisconsin primary.

I not only won the election; I carried seven of the nine districts in the state, losing the other two to Humphrey—one in Milwaukee and the other along the Minnesota boundary. George Wallace came in second to me in statewide percentages, Humphrey third, and Muskie fourth. I even carried the blue-collar wards of Milwaukee that were believed to be safe Muskie supporters. From that point on, I was sure that we would win the presidential nomination. Three weeks later I was even more certain when we won a landslide victory in Massachusetts. For the balance of the nomination bid, I was the front runner.

Meanwhile, we were making hurried side trips to the nonprimary states where delegates were picked by caucus or convention: Iowa,

Arizona, Minnesota, Washington and even such unlikely McGovern fields as Georgia, Louisiana and Mississippi. We won delegates in all of these states—some 300 in the nonprimary states. It was a well-directed effort that was essential to our final nomination victory.

While we continued to press the campaign in trips across the nation, we picked up new momentum and national stature after Wisconsin that enabled us to extend our media campaign. Not only was it then possible to expand our mass-media appeals, but we began to generate greater press coverage, including by early May the first cover stories in *Time, Newsweek* and other national news organs. There is an intoxicating quality surrounding a winning campaign; it adds an accelerating momentum that at some point becomes unstoppable. That force was first apparent in New Hampshire; it gathered new strength in Wisconsin; it reached takeoff speed in Massachusetts.

The path to the Democratic nomination was, however, strewn with pitfalls, booby traps and dangerous crosscurrents that were difficult, if not impossible, to traverse without injury—perhaps fatal injury.

One of those hazards was the nature and make-up of the Democratic Party, its constituency, its brokers and its leaders. The Democratic Party is not a cohesive movement of idealists committed to the public good. It includes such people in remarkably large numbers, but it also includes powerful special factions that tend to be frightened by a candidate and by political workers who appear to challenge the status quo too directly. There is, for example, organized labor—many of whose leaders expect deferential attention from a Democratic candidate and his aides. We tried to develop a working relationship with labor leaders at every level, but some of them felt threatened by the party reforms associated with my name; others were offended by my outspoken opposition to the war; some feared that the cuts in military spending I was recommending would result in the loss of war-related jobs. Still others were turned off by the life styles of many of the young people and "liberated" women who worked in my campaign.

The Democratic Party of 1972 also included a large and vocal Wallace faction. George Wallace's army was a potent force held together by a variety of fears and frustrations: anger over the growing irritations of the federal bureaucracy; anxiety over the demands and increasing power of black Americans; a sense of powerlessness in the face of big government, big corporations and big labor unions. Many of the Wallace supporters regarded criticism of the Vietnam war and advocacy of amnesty for draft resisters as tantamount to treason. They were also offended by talk of "abortion on demand" or "legalizing marijuana."

On the night of Governor Wallace's smashing primary victory in Florida, Ed Muskie bitterly assailed the results as a triumph of racism. Perhaps it was that. But it seemed to me to demonstrate a more complex range of alienated voters whose concerns had to be understood if the Democratic Party were to win in 1972. I addressed myself to these concerns; to some Wallace voters I appeared as an anti-establishment candidate with whom they could identify. I tried to interpret the concerns of Wallace voters when I addressed the nation the night of the Florida primary victory by Wallace. I again called on the nation to understand and to direct along constructive lines the Wallace frustrations with a speech to the Milwaukee clergy as we launched the Wisconsin primary. But in the end, most Wallace voters and their leader found it difficult to identify with a liberal, Northern, antiwar Democrat surrounded by advocates of new styles of life and social behavior.

I tried to appeal not only to the alienated blue-collar workers but also to the antiwar idealists in the nation in a hard-hitting speech delivered at the Jefferson-Jackson Day dinner in Detroit on April 15. Replying to the contention that the next President would be the one who stood most nearly in the established center of the political spectrum, I said that "most Americans see the establishment center as an empty, decaying void that commands neither their confidence nor their love." I went on:

> It is the establishment center that has led us into the stupidest and cruelest war in all history . . . the establishment center has constructed a vast military colossus based on the paychecks of the American worker . . . It is the establishment center that tells us we can afford an ABM but we can't afford good health care for the American people . . . It is the establishment center that says we can afford a $250 million guaranteed loan to Lockheed but we can't afford a decent retirement income for our senior citizens. . . . It is the establishment center that says it's okay to tell the American people one thing in public, while plotting a different thing in private . . . The present center has drifted so far from our founding ideals that it bears little resemblance to the dependable values of the Declaration of Independence and the Constitution. I want America to come home from the alien world of power politics, militarism, deception, racism and special privilege . . .

This speech was designed to appeal to those voters—right, left and center—who were dissatisfied with our present political condition. It was as effective with the Detroit audience as it was with other Americans, but it further aroused the resentment and fear of some established political leaders and party functionaries.

The path to the nomination was all the more difficult because of the considerable number of highly ambitious, talented candidates who were as eager as I was to be President of the United States. Some of them—Humphrey, Muskie, Jackson—were senior to me and firmly believed that they had a more legitimate claim to the presidency. This was especially true of my friend Hubert Humphrey, who doubtless saw me as one of his prodigies who should have been working in the HHH vineyard rather than walking off with the grapes. Hubert, I believe, underestimated the gathering momentum of my campaign and he misjudged the dynamics of the political process. He saw me check Ed Muskie in New Hampshire with a surprisingly strong second-place showing. That suited the Humphrey purposes well because it weakened Ed's hold as the front runner. But my victory over both Humphrey and Muskie in Wisconsin, including clear victories in the blue-collar Polish wards of Milwaukee, was a serious defeat to Muskie and a jolting setback to Humphrey. Then came a series of blows to Humphrey: my overwhelming win in Massachusetts and a near-upset in Ohio, followed by victories in Nebraska, Oregon and Rhode Island.

By the time we reached the California primary it was clear that Humphrey's only chance of obtaining the nomination was to win the huge California winner-take-all primary. But in California we were better organized than Humphrey and our victories in other states had given us a momentum that was attracting considerably more funds for television than Humphrey could afford.

All during 1972 I had been challenging the other Democratic candidates to meet me in public debate. These efforts were just as stoutly resisted by them—including Humphrey, who would never agree to risk his established name and prestige against a junior challenger. But with his campaign treasury exhausted and his chances for the nomination slipping away, Hubert suddenly challenged me to a series of televised debates in the closing days of the California primary.

At that point I had nothing to gain from a heated exchange on network television with a Democratic contender, and I had much to lose. The competition for the nomination was ending and it was time for Democrats to be uniting for the big battle against Nixon. We were nearing the time when the voters should have been offered a debate between the Democratic challenger and the incumbent President on the issues before the nation.

Nevertheless, I accepted the Humphrey challenge. Hubert came into the debate determined to knock me out of the race by discrediting my past record and frightening the voters as to my present positions on major issues. I approached the debate as the virtual nominee of the party needing the support of Humphrey and his followers if I were to defeat Nixon. I had no interest in attacking Hubert or in embarrassing him. Quite the contrary, I was chiefly concerned about doing nothing that might anger his supporters. Thus the stage was set for a damaging last-minute Humphrey attack without adequate rejoinder on my part. Though I won the California primary and three others the same day (New Jersey, South Dakota and New Mexico) and two weeks later captured the entire delegation from New York, millions of voters had seen me, a new figure in American politics, being slashed and blasted by one of the most experienced, best-known figures in American politics—a former Vice President of the United States, our recent Democratic presidential standard-bearer and a long-time hero of American liberalism. The fears, anxieties and wounds opened in those debates were sweet music to the Nixon strategists, and from that time on they set the strategy of their campaign: "Democrats for Nixon"—Democrats who feared the positions of George McGovern as interpreted by Hubert Humphrey. I look back on those fateful days without bitterness because I know the desperation that was in Hubert's mind as his long-sought goal—the White House—eluded his grasp. I also know that Hubert in retrospect came to share my regret that those destructive encounters ever took place.

But the debates were only the beginning of our troubles with the other Democratic candidates. Far more harmful was the totally unjustified and suicidal California challenge launched by the other Democratic contenders, including Humphrey, Jackson, Muskie, Wallace, Chisholm and McCarthy. Born of jealousy, pique and frustration over their pending defeat in the scramble for the nomination, the other candidates conceived the notion that they could at least prevent me from receiving the nomination at our forthcoming national convention if they could arrange an *ex post facto* change in the rules that would deprive me of a sizable portion of the delegates won in California. I believe that challenge destroyed any hopes for a Democratic victory in 1972. It was so outrageously unfair that if it had prevailed, I would have left the Democratic Party and led a third-party movement in 1972. The challenge failed, but it left me with a divided party, an exhausted campaign staff and a shaky nomination.

The stated basis of the challenge was that California had no right to award all of its delegates to the winner of its primary. This matter had long before been resolved by the Democratic Commission on Delegate Selection. The commission, after lengthy debate, gave its approval to the California winner-take-all system for 1972. This recommendation was approved by the Democratic National Committee, and all candidates planned their strategies with full knowledge of the California system. Humphrey was counting especially on gaining the nomination by capturing the entire California delegation via the winner-take-all rule. He so explained his dedication to the California rules in a CBS network discussion with Walter Cronkite just a few days before the votes were tabulated in California. He scoffed at the notion that he might challenge the California law if he lost the election. "That would be changing the rules after the ball game is over," he cried.

Thus the challenge that would have given 120 of my California delegates to Humphrey based on his percentage of the California primary vote was based not on law, or precedent or party rules. It succeeded, however, in lining up a majority of the delegates on the Credentials Committee, but was reversed by the delegates at the national convention in Miami Beach.

Its effects, however, were devastating. Instead of five weeks of much-needed time following the June 6 California primary to prepare for the national convention, to heal the wounds and to select a suitable running mate, my staff and I had to use every minute of this time to turn back the California challenge. It was impossible to make the healing telephone calls and personal visits that were needed, because the people I wanted to call remained locked in bitter combat over the California question. It was difficult to think about a vice-presidential selection, since a number of the most likely choices were also caught up in the challenge. Little time was left for rest, contemplation or constructive effort of any kind.

A further consequence of the challenge was a retaliatory move by McGovern delegates that I did my best to prevent, which led to the expulsion of Mayor Daley and his Illinois delegates to the Miami convention.

All in all, there were no winners in the divisive California battle, only losers: the Democratic Party, the Democratic nominee and the hopes for a unified, constructive campaign against Richard Nixon.

Another major loss to our campaign occurred when my acceptance speech at the national convention was delayed by convention horseplay until nearly three o'clock in the morning—long after the nation's voters had gone to bed. It was probably the best speech I was to give in the entire campaign and I delivered it with the passion and confidence that comes from winning a difficult, uphill struggle for a presidential nomination. But all of this was confined to the delegates in the convention hall and those few Americans who were willing to sit through the night by their television sets. I believe that if the address could have been seen and heard by the sixty or seventy million Americans who were at their TV sets the previous evening, it might have created a public acceptance of my candidacy that we never again had the opportunity to inspire.

But this was not to be. We were caught in a series of damaging events that began with the ill-fated debates in California and continued through the challenge to our California delegation, the expulsion of the Daley delegation, and the incredibly bad timing that denied me the full impact of an acceptance speech. Hidden from view as the tragedy unfolded was an even more deadly complication that was to convert what may already have been certain defeat into a landslide. That final element took its place in the scenario the moment I selected Missouri's attractive young senator, Tom Eagleton, as my vice-presidential running mate. From that moment on, the 1972 presidential results were determined. Richard Nixon and Spiro Agnew were home free.

9

"THE ROCK
IN THE
LANDSLIDE"

"McGovern never recovered from the wounds he inflicted on himself for reversing his own decision; people who have had drinking and mental problems comprise two of the largest groups in the country, and McGovern offended both when he panicked and dropped Eagleton."

Eliot Janeway's post-mortem, four years after the event, expressed the views of many people after I asked Tom Eagleton to withdraw as my running mate.

The editorial view at the time a decision had to be made was not so settled. A cross section shows the range of conflicting reactions:

> ... the fact that stands out starkly in Sen. Eagleton's story is his avowed failure to tell Democratic nominee George McGovern the whole truth before he was designated for the Vice Presidency. . . .
> ... the tragic reality is that his lack of candor in the period preceding his selection has cast fatal doubt on the credibility of his candidacy. His continuance on the ticket can only produce cruel, diversionary conflicts in a year when the real issues should be sharply defined and debated.
>
> —New York *Post,* July 26, 1972

The sad revelation yesterday of Sen. Thomas Eagleton's emotional problems (hospitalized three times for a total of two months) is more damaging to George McGovern than Eagleton.

The young Senator from Missouri couldn't help being sick. But the Democratic Party's presidential nominee certainly didn't have to choose him as his running mate.

—Arkansas *Democrat,* July 26

The really crucial issue is that Sen. Eagleton . . . blandly admitted that he failed to inform the Democratic nominee for President of his past when George McGovern asked him if it contained anything potentially damaging.

He said there was not and Sen. McGovern took him at his word. The fact is that both are certainly experienced enough to know that any shadow of mental illness—however temporary or subsequently cured —is or should be automatic grounds for disbarment to the second most important position in the nation.

—Boston *Herald Traveler,* July 28

. . . he [Eagleton] sensibly sought professional help, underwent treatment and since 1966 has apparently made adjustments indicative of an intelligent, evolving human being. . . . Eagleton's medical history, therefore, basically suggests strength, not weakness. Whether citizens see it that way in the coming days will be a major test of America's maturity.

—Milwaukee *Journal,* July 27

There is another aspect of this astonishing episode which as we see it overrides the question of health. It is the record of deceit over 12 years which grows more damning as the story unfolds.

In 1960, 1962 and 1966 Eagleton did not tell the truth about the reason for his hospitalizations. The files of the St. Louis *Post-Dispatch* show that in each of these instances a physical ailment was given as the reason. . . .

. . . He practiced calculated deceit and is paying the consequences.

—Omaha *World-Herald,* July 28

It seems to us beyond question that taken together, the unanswerable question concerning Senator Eagleton's condition and the answerable question concerning his performance in this matter have created—and will continue to create—an enormous, probably crippling, burden for Senator McGovern's candidacy. . . .

For it is our judgment that the burden imposed by the presence of Senator Eagleton on the ticket can only be removed by his withdrawal as a candidate.

—Washington *Post,* July 27

Replacing Mr. Eagleton might be a blow to the ticket from which Mr. McGovern and his new running mate would have difficulty recovering. And would it not reflect on Mr. McGovern, as to his ability to make decisions and stick to them? Would it not risk a defection by intellectuals and young people, who lack medieval notions about nervous ailments and who regard Mr. McGovern as a man of compassion and high moral caliber?

—St. Louis *Post-Dispatch,* July 31

We believe that the only way the campaign can be turned back into a true test of the programs and leadership qualifications of President Nixon and his Democratic rival, Senator McGovern, is through the voluntary withdrawal of Senator Eagleton from the McGovern ticket.

—*New York Times,* July 28

Since the days immediately preceding the Democratic Convention to Miami Beach, followed by the convention proceedings and culminating now in Senator McGovern's callous, devious and autocratic firing of Sen. Thomas F. Eagleton as the vice presidential candidate, even a casual political observer must conclude that McGovern is a grievous threat to the nation and the Democratic Party.

—St. Louis *Globe-Democrat,* August 1

Sen. Thomas Eagleton should resign promptly from the Democratic ticket.

The Democratic National Committee should choose another candidate who is compatible with the views of Presidential nominee George McGovern.

Then this Presidential campaign should proceed on the issues, not on the alleged frailties of one candidate.

McGovern has stood up like a man in defending Eagleton. He has won respect by not bowing to the pressures to dump the Missouri senator. . . .

This nation is not, however, so poor in administrative talent that it must take a risk of this magnitude.

Compassion compels the nation to wish Eagleton well.

Necessity requires him to withdraw from the vice presidential candidacy.

—Atlanta *Constitution,* July 29

The editorial battle was a fair reflection of the fierce arguments inside our campaign headquarters. Outside, the debate engaged high school students and leading psychiatrists. The painful truth is that no one really knew what was the proper course to follow after the Eagleton disclosure. There was no obvious or trouble-free solution.

I find it painful to relate the Eagleton story from my own point of view. I am still not free of conflicting emotions about that complicated political tragedy. My personal convictions about it were both deeply felt and somewhat contradictory.

First, I believe that the selection of Tom Eagleton as my running mate was made with as much care and reason as traditionally was applied to the selection of vice-presidential candidates. In 1952, for example, Adlai Stevenson selected Senator John Sparkman of Alabama as his running mate almost as an afterthought following a late-night celebration of his own nomination. Sparkman was telephoned following a few minutes' casual conversation among Stevenson and his aides without any background check or even a question to the senator. (Because of the Eagleton affair, of course, Jimmy Carter did it differently in 1976; so will future nominees.)

Second, I believe that my initial decision to back Eagleton after listening to his moving account of how he had overcome mental illness was a natural, human response. But both I and my staff were remiss during the period preceding that decision. We were slow to grasp the implications of the early reports we received about Eagleton's health. We did not make a systematic effort to analyze the decision thoroughly before it was made. We should have insisted absolutely that Eagleton provide a full, documented medical history instead of relying on his own verbal assurances. If it had accomplished nothing else, insisting on seeing the written records before arriving at a public judgment would have provided time for a more dispassionate decision.

Third, I believe that my later judgment after agonizing reconsideration that Eagleton should give up the vice-presidential nomination was a rational decision made with integrity and in the national interest.

Fourth, I believe that Tom Eagleton is a talented and capable senator. The events of 1972 strengthened him, at least with his Missouri constituents. They saw him as a gallant martyr, the victim of a heavy-handed, callous and conniving McGovern campaign. That was surely the view, at the time, of many other Americans.

Fifth, I believe that either through a failure on my part to handle these developments with sufficient skill or through a failure of the press to discern the issue fairly, the Eagleton affair destroyed any chance I had of being elected President in 1972. Perhaps neither I nor any other Democratic challenger could have defeated Nixon in 1972, but the theretofore publicly concealed mental illness of Eagleton, my handling of the problem, and the press reaction combined to give Richard Nixon not only his expected victory but a landslide. The regrettable aspect of the Eagleton problem for me personally was that it clouded and confused my own previous public credibility so that I was defeated as well as diminished in the eyes of many people. This contributed to the overwhelming degree of defeat in 1972, and it also complicated my re-election to the Senate in 1974 and removed me as a possible presidential candidate in 1976 despite the outcome of Watergate, Vietnam and other issues, such as the economy and energy, where events seemed to bear out the positions of the 1972 Democratic campaign. Even a casual backward glance at the attention given to the Eagleton matter leaves no doubt that it became the number one news and editorial development of that campaign. It overshadowed the Watergate scandal as a subject of journalistic concern. It—not Watergate, not Vietnam, not the American economy—was *the* political story of 1972.

My thoughts go back to an exhibition football game at Robert F. Kennedy Stadium in Washington in August 1972. That night Eleanor and I were the guests of Redskins owner Ed Williams during the first half, and of Dolphins owner Joe Robbie during the second half— Robbie is a former South Dakotan, an old family friend from my hometown.

It was the first appearance Eleanor and I had made at a large public gathering since the decision that Eagleton should step down as my vice-presidential choice. As we came out of Ed Williams' private lounge to enter his box just prior to game time, we were greeted by boos and clenched fists from a sizable portion of the crowd. It is not unheard of for politicians introduced at sporting events to be playfully booed by a crowd, but we were not introduced—we were walking quietly to our seats. And that crowd was not in a playful mood. There were a few cheers and smiles, but there were many angry faces. When Eleanor and I moved to Joe Robbie's box at half time, we again encountered the fury of booing fans. The experience hurt, for a stadium of football fans who ordinarily might have applauded a presidential nominee and at worst would have expressed a good-natured partisanship, were hissing out their fury. At about the same time, Senator Eagleton was introduced in Kansas City before a game between the Kansas City Chiefs and the St. Louis Cardinals —and the crowd gave him a rousing standing ovation.

The contrast illustrated how the Eagleton affair had derailed the fall campaign before it ever really started. It brought back the words of an unknown youth who had shouted at me in the Senate Caucus Room the night I announced Senator Eagleton's departure from the ticket: "George, you've just lost the election."

I first met Tom Eagleton the day he was sworn in as a new senator in January 1969, the same day I was sworn in for my second term. I met him at an afternoon reception he gave for his friends, staff members and other senators. It was an uneventful meeting which left me with a vague impression of him as exuberant and energetic. Some months later Tom and I were both at a dinner party at Henry

Kimelman's, but I came away with no certain impression of his qualities as an individual. He was not assigned to any of the committees
on which I served and I seldom encountered him either in the Senate
or socially.

At the end of 1971 Eagleton engineered a triple endorsement of Ed
Muskie involving himself and his Missouri colleagues, Senator Stuart
Symington and Governor Warren Hearnes. Although I knew little of
his activities, I later learned that he made a number of campaign
speeches for Muskie across the country. His name was never one of
those that passed through my mind as a running mate during the
long months leading up to the nomination. And for his part, he saw
little, if any, chance that I would be the party's nomonee.

I had decided long before that if I won the nomination, I would
press Ted Kennedy to be my running mate. It seemed sensible to me,
both from my standpoint and his.

I knew that the conventional wisdom precluded a Kennedy settling for a second place, but there were several factors, it appeared,
that made for a different attitude in 1972. First, Ted was obviously
concerned about the continuing impact of the Chappaquiddick incident. I believed that he had responded badly during the tragedy, but
I also felt that his own admission of his "incomprehensible" conduct
provided a basis for public forgiveness. I know Ted to be a person of
integrity. I think he would be an exceptional President. In 1972, I was
sure, he would also be my strongest choice for a running mate. From
his perspective, a willingness to accept second place would have
permitted him to hold national office while providing a cooling-off
period for the Chappaquiddick issue. Second, I thought that the
danger of a third Kennedy assassination would be reduced sharply if
Ted was the candidate for Vice President rather than President. I
intended to assure him, and at the time did so, that we could carefully
plan his public appearances, maximize security and rely heavily on
television and radio to bring him to the voters. It seemed to me that
these tactics might even make him less vulnerable to an assassination
effort than he was on the campaign trail for other candidates. Finally,
I believed that while Kennedy would insist that he would refuse the
vice presidency prior to my winning the presidential nomination, he
might respond at that point to a direct appeal from me to his sense
of the national interest in a Democratic victory.

Indeed, he did not seem to be totally decided on the matter. Flying
from Washington to Boston with Boston *Globe* political writer Marty
Nolan, Kennedy had a conversation that encouraged me to believe
he might accept. Nolan conveyed that impression to me in my room
at the New York Biltmore Hotel during the closing days of the New
York primary campaign in June. Ted later told me in a visit off the

Senate floor that responsibilities to his family as the only surviving Kennedy brother made it difficult for him to think of either the presidency or the vice presidency. Nevertheless, I never heard the door slam entirely shut.

However, recognizing the possibility of a Kennedy rejection, there were other alternatives in my mind. Governor Reubin Askew of Florida was a man frequently cited when I was asked in early 1972 whom I might select if I won the nomination. Senators Abe Ribicoff and Frank Church were others I had in mind. Ed Muskie would be a possibility if he was interested in a second vice-presidential bid.

Shortly before the convention Eleanor suggested that United Auto Workers President Leonard Woodcock would be a good choice. I was intrigued by the idea and invited Woodcock to my home after telling his assistant, Bill Dodds, the purpose of the meeting. Woodcock was pleased by the inquiry and plainly interested, although he talked modestly of his political limitations. I began leaning to Woodcock as an alternative in the event of a Kennedy turndown. Not an office-holder or professional politician, he was hardly a conventional choice, but our campaign had broken a lot of senseless conventions already.

But in a matter of days, most of the alternatives faded. Governor Askew sent an aide to my headquarters at the Doral just before the convention opened in Miami to say that while he appreciated my kind words about him, he did not feel that he could give up the governorship of Florida after less than two years' service. Simultaneously, we were running into opposition to Woodcock from his fellow labor leaders. The long-standing friction between the United Auto Workers and the AFL-CIO was one problem, but we still hoped for the support of George Meany and his giant labor federation. But the decisive factor was the privately expressed reservations of some of Woodcock's own longtime associates in the UAW. Meanwhile Abe Ribicoff told me privately that under no conditions would he accept the vice presidency. Abe, a former congressman, governor and Cabinet official, genuinely loved the Senate. He said that he would not trade his Senate seat for an eight-year stint as Vice President.

With Askew, Woodcock and Ribicoff out of it, the list of possibilities was curtailed. I was not seriously concerned because there were obvious alternatives, including Church, Muskie, Sargent Shriver, Senator Walter Mondale, Wisconsin Governor Pat Lucey, and National Chairman Larry O'Brien.

Thorough consideration of the vice presidency had been deferred because of the California challenge. With all the other candidates from Shirley Chisholm to George Wallace ganging up in a last-ditch effort to take away our California victory, every ounce of energy in the McGovern camp was concentrated to fight off the challenge. We lost a precious six-weeks "breather" that we needed between the June 6 California primary and the opening of the Miami convention. Save for the challenge, we could have used that period not only to rest but to evaluate the vice-presidential possibilities and plan the general election.

Two days after the California primary I met with Muskie in his Capitol hideaway office for a discussion which both his top aides and mine believed would produce a Muskie endorsement. I thanked Ed for the fair manner in which he had conducted his campaign, noting the contrast with the divisive tactics of some of the other candidates. I told him that I needed and wanted his endorsement to nail down the nomination without further bloodletting among Democrats. He expressed mild apprehension about some of my views, including my call for a reduction in military expenditures and my proposals for welfare reform. I answered his questions as fully as I could and emphasized that at least on the question of welfare reform, I would accept what I believed would be a modified plank in the forthcoming Democratic platform. I left the meeting fully convinced that Ed Muskie was about to endorse me. I then intended to determine whether he was available for the vice presidency.

But after a night of soul-searching and conflicting advice from his staff and friends, Ed announced in a speech at the National Press Club that he was remaining in the race. He would use his continued candidacy, he said, to pressure me into modifying some of my positions on key issues.

The history of 1972 might have been significantly changed if Ed Muskie had endorsed me on June 9. That would have killed the possibility of the California challenge and ended the Democratic in-fighting. In all probability Ed would have been my running mate. Instead, the McGovern campaign was forced to devote the next thirty days to an exhausting effort to nail down the New York primary, convert uncommitted delegates, and keep the California delegates we had won already in that primary. By the time it was over, we had little enthusiasm for selecting as a running mate a man who could have averted the California challenge, but instead participated in it to the bitter end. In retrospect, our reaction, perhaps understandable, was to prove another in a costly series of missteps on the vice presidency.

Early in July, shortly before the convention, Gary Hart came to my home in Washington. We discussed vice-presidential possibilities briefly, but both of us were preoccupied with the California problem. If we lost there, there would be no chance to pick a Vice President. But if we lacked the time to attend to that choice, we should have asked others to do so. I should have instructed Gary to set up a small group of trusted people to recommend and check out the backgrounds of vice-presidential possibilities. Why wasn't this done? Fatigue, the California worry, the feeling that there were enough attractive options—that certainly we would not have trouble finding an able and willing candidate. During the California primary, Alan Baron and Bob Shrum, who were to become close associates in subsequent years, had written a memo to Gary urging a systematic review of the vice-presidential decision. I never saw that memo.

On July 10 we won our California delegates—for the second time, first in the primary, now on the convention floor. On July 12, shortly before midnight, the Illinois delegation cast 119 votes for me. Those votes marked the victory: we had won the presidential nomination. I was watching the proceedings on television in my room at the Doral with a few close friends and aides. Eleanor and my family were in the convention hall.

After some jubilant handshaking and embraces, I sat down with Fred Dutton and Dick Dougherty and talked over the reasons why Ted Kennedy should accept the vice-presidential nomination. I then went to my bedroom, called Ted in Hyannisport and made my case. After listing the reasons, I added that I was painfully aware of the great sacrifices his brothers and his family had made, but that I felt he owed it to the nation to help me turn the country in a more constructive direction. He seemed both tempted and troubled, but after a fifteen-minute discussion said that he did not feel he could accept. He agreed to sleep on it and call me in the morning if he changed his mind. But the next morning he told reporters at Hyannisport that he had turned down the nomination.

After making courtesy calls to Ed Muskie and Hubert Humphrey, to enlist their support in the campaign, I asked Gary and Frank Mankiewicz to meet with the top campaign staff in the morning and draw up a list of recommended nominees. Shortly before noon they came to my room with Jean Westwood and Pierre Salinger. They offered seven names: Mayor Kevin White of Boston, a surprise to me; Senator Walter Mondale; Abe Ribicoff; Governor Pat Lucey; Sargent Shriver; Larry O'Brien, who had presided so effectively over the convention; and Tom Eagleton, who was another surprise. I was told that Eagleton was eager for the nomination; he had appeal as an urban Catholic and a border-state senator with good ties to labor and the Muskie camp. John Holum, one of my most trusted, long-time aides, was favorably inclined toward Eagleton in part because of his admiration for the Missouri senator's staff—especially Doug Bennet, now a highly regarded State Department official. Muskie himself was not on the list; that, as I have explained, was a short-sighted after-effect of the California challenge. And for reasons that now seem superficial to me, Frank Church, a trusted colleague and friend, was also unlisted. I checked out the list for more than an hour with a broad cross section of Democratic leaders. Many of them gave the highest marks to Mondale, White and Eagleton.

At approximately one-thirty I called a larger group of advisers together and decided to make the first offer to Mondale. I didn't want to embarrass either him or myself by a rejection of the offer, so I asked him if his race for the Senate that fall precluded his accepting the vice-presidential nomination. He replied that he was pleased by my interest but that he did not wish to jeopardize his almost certain re-election to the Senate by an uphill fight for national office against strong odds. When I asked him about other possibilities, he strongly recommended Tom Eagleton, with whom he had worked closely in the Senate.

I then called Kevin White and told him that we were seriously considering him for the vice presidency. Would he be interested? He gave me a definite yes, but understood when I told him that in view of our limited association, I wanted to check the choice out further. I was impressed by the arguments Gary Hart and others had made on White's behalf, but it was a suggestion so new to me that I was having difficulty accepting it quickly.

Elizabeth Stevens, a friend of the Kennedy family, had called Senator Kennedy at my suggestion earlier that forenoon to learn his reaction to the White possibility. She reported that Ted had no objection. I felt, however, that I could not select a Massachusetts political figure without a personal call to him. When I got Ted on the phone, he raised some serious questions about White and urged that I consider other candidates, including Ribicoff, Eagleton or Wilbur Mills. He could not campaign for the ticket with as much enthusiasm if White was on it. He seemed to feel so strongly that I asked if he would reconsider his own decision. He said he would. Knowing that we had only an hour and a half left before the filing deadline, he promised to call back in thirty or forty minutes.

During that time I confirmed that neither Askew nor Ribicoff was available. Frank Church's name, although not on the submitted list, was raised and then dropped. The argument, which now strikes me as silly, was that a McGovern-Church ticket would lack nationwide appeal because it would combine two antiwar senators from sparsely settled Western states. Wilbur Mills was passed over because many of his views—including those on tax reform and the war—were too far from mine to put him in a position to succeed to the presidency if something should happen to me. Sargent Shriver was eliminated after Pierre Salinger reported that he was in the Soviet Union on legal business and could not be reached. Fred Dutton had told Sarge before the convention that he might be picked. He was anxious to run, but chary of being disappointed again. (LBJ had almost selected him in 1964, as had Hubert Humphrey in 1968.) So Sarge went to Moscow, as scheduled. Chairman O'Brien and Governor Lucey were both entitled to more consideration than they received. The objection to O'Brien was that he might be seen as too much of a professional politician. The objection to Lucey was his wife's blunt outspokenness, a small irony in light of the situation Eagleton's nondisclosure was soon to create.

While we were waiting for Ted Kennedy's final answer Ken Galbraith telephoned my room to say that the Massachusetts delegation was up in arms over the possibility of Kevin White because of the mayor's strong opposition to the McGovern delegates during the Massachusetts primary. He told me that he and Father Robert Drinan—both Massachusetts delegates—believed the delegation would walk off the floor if I selected White. A few minutes later Kennedy called with his final refusal. He added, "I guess you should go with Kevin White. If you want, he can fly to Miami with me on the family plane." I then told Ted that I had decided against the mayor—because of the opposition of the Massachusetts delegation and Kennedy's own earlier reservations.

Time was running out. With a number of advisers urging me to select Eagleton, I turned to the staff and said, "No, I just don't know enough about Tom. I'm going to ask Gaylord Nelson. He's a trusted friend. I've sat next to him in the Senate for ten years. I know his strengths and his weaknesses and he knows mine." I located Nelson on the phone in Washington and told him I needed him as my running mate. Typically Nelson, he replied, "George, I don't want that damn job. If I was sure you would lose, I might take the nomination, but I think you might win and then I'd be stuck in that office for four years and probably eight." Then he added, "You know the guy who wants it is Tom Eagleton, and personally, he's the guy I would pick if I were in your shoes."

So Kennedy, Mondale and Nelson—three of the most astute politicians in the Senate and all personal friends—were pushing for Eagleton.

By this time it was only minutes before the 4 P.M. deadline for the vice-presidential filing. I was still worried by my lack of knowledge or real feeling about Eagleton. Eleanor and Henry Kimelman were opposed to him, but all through the day, favorable reactions had mounted. I wish now that I had called Larry O'Brien and told him that I would make my acceptance speech that night in prime time, and that we would hold the convention over until the following morning for the vice-presidential nomination.

Instead, I picked up the phone and called Tom Eagleton. I knew that Tom fervently wanted the nomination. None of those who knew him best in the Senate had even hinted at anything other than his ideal qualifications. Rather than asking him any questions, I simply said that I wanted him to be my running mate and that I hoped he would accept. "George, I'm going to say yes before you change your mind," he said jubilantly. I told him Frank Mankiewicz was with me and asked him to speak with Frank for a moment. He assured Frank that there was nothing in his background that would be embarrassing to the national ticket. With that, I went to the next room and resumed working on my acceptance speech.

I did not quiz Eagleton about his personal life. Frank would do that, and I also knew that during the day Gordon Weil had inquired into rumors about his excessive drinking, which, Gordon reported, were groundless. During his four years of service in the Senate, no senator had ever expressed any concern over Tom's personal history. Nor had any such matter been raised in any discussions that day with those familiar with Missouri politics. Charles Guggenheim—a friend and my media director who had worked closely with Eagleton in his Senate campaign and who, like Eagleton, had resided for years in St. Louis—strongly urged him as an ideal running mate. Eagleton, in short, seemed like the perfect choice.

Shortly after my call, Eagleton came to my room and my doubts about the decision lessened. He was warm and dynamic and he had something which by then I had come to appreciate—enthusiasm for the job. Senate Majority Leader Mike Mansfield told me I couldn't have made a better choice. Only Abe Ribicoff among my friends shared the instinctive uneasiness I felt about Eagleton. And as fate would have it, Abe was one trusted adviser I had failed to check with.

Much has been made of how specifically Mankiewicz interrogated Eagleton on the phone about his past. I think that controversy misses the point. Eagleton's history of mental illness and electric-shock treatment was a chapter in his life carefully hidden from the people of Missouri. Even veteran political reporters there knew nothing of it. When he left for the Mayo Clinic in 1966 in a serious mental depression that resulted in weeks of hospitalization and electric-shock treatment, the story his office released was that he was at the Johns Hopkins Hospital in Baltimore for treatment of a gastric disturbance. Then and later, even long-time Eagleton associates did not suspect the truth. A few people did know something and would have told me, but I never discussed him with them.

After Eagleton was dropped from the ticket, Ramsey Clark, who had been in Vietnam during the controversy, told me that as Attorney General he had seen an FBI file on Eagleton's hospital history that was "devastating." But he had not forewarned me because he had not believed Eagleton would be considered for the national ticket. Also, Loye Miller of the Knight newspapers and Matt Reese, a Washington-based political consultant, both remember mentioning to one and possibly two of my staff aides that Eagleton had a troubling medical record. But the staff was so numbed by fatigue after several sleepless nights that the reports did not really register with them, especially since at the time they heard them, they regarded the selection of Eagleton as a remote possibility.

Eagleton was later to tell reporters as well as Eleanor and me that he and his wife had debated whether or not he should reveal his mental history if he was offered the vice-presidential nomination. He decided not to, he said, because he feared that it would keep him off the ticket. If the matter became known after he was nominated, he believed that he could ride out any adverse reaction. Eagleton sincerely felt, he explained, that he had overcome his earlier medical problems and was fit to serve as Vice President or assume the presidency. He may have thought that his medical history would foreclose all prospects of higher office, for a reason he believed to be completely invalid. Though he may have harbored no doubts about his mental stability, others obviously would not share his confidence. But as a *fait accompli*, after he was on the ticket, he might be able to withstand the reaction. In fact, that was probably the only way for him to have a chance at national office.

With the exception of the review President Johnson ordered of Hubert Humphrey in 1964, I know of no investigation of potential Vice Presidents prior to the Eagleton problem. Certainly, Lyndon Johnson was not interrogated by John Kennedy in 1960. Nor were Harry Truman, Alben Barkley, John Sparkman or Estes Kefauver questioned about their backgrounds. Franklin Roosevelt apparently did not check into the character and background of John Nance Garner in 1932. And, it should be noted, Richard Nixon selected Spiro Agnew not once but twice for the vice presidency. Even with the resources of the FBI at his disposal, Nixon apparently knew nothing of the incidents in Agnew's past which forced him to resign less than a year after the 1972 election.

John Sparkman told me after the Eagleton affair that he just assumed, in 1952, that anyone asked to be Vice President would tell the presidential nominee of any difficulties in his background. Sparkman said he would have been insulted if Adlai Stevenson or one of his aides had raised the issue. A man in that position, Sparkman thought, had an obligation to volunteer the truth. Silence meant there was nothing to worry about.

My first knowledge of possible trouble over Eagleton came with a phone call from Mankiewicz the weekend after the convention. I was in Washington, and Frank and Gary Hart were at the Virgin Islands home of Henry and Charlotte Kimelman for a few days' rest. Frank told me that there might be a news story about the hospitalization of Eagleton for exhaustion or depression. The report appeared to be a typical political rumor or, at worst, a minor matter of little consequence. I told Frank to advise me of any further information.

I later learned that in the pre-dawn hours of Friday night, July 14, while we were celebrating at a reception in the Doral Hotel after the acceptance speeches, Gordon Weil had mentioned to Doug Bennet of Eagleton's staff that we had heard rumors of a drinking problem but found them to be groundless. Bennet reassured Weil that the rumors were false, but, he continued, his boss had been hospitalized for exhaustion. When this information was relayed to Mankiewicz, he talked with Bennet and suggested that if the question was raised during Eagleton's scheduled appearance on *Face the Nation* the following Sunday, he could reply simply that he was such a dedicated campaigner that he had campaigned himself right into the hospital. (The rumors of alcoholism actually diverted attention at the time from other considerations. Bennet's assurance on this issue was actually strengthened in the mind of my staff when the hospitalization for exhaustion was mentioned. It was not until days later that the full import of this latter problem was to emerge in the minds of either my staff or Eagleton's.)

The next afternoon Mankiewicz got a call from Bennet saying that the proposed exhaustion answer wouldn't work because Eagleton had been hospitalized twice—not just for exhaustion, but for depression. The next night Eagleton, who was preparing in Washington for *Face the Nation,* called Frank and discussed his medical history, but with no real details. Frank reported this conversation to me but there was only a vague, guarded expression of concern. His wife, Holly, one of the most honest and straightforward persons I have ever known and a treasured friend, was upset and urged Frank to convey her genuine alarm to me. Apparently believing that a long-distance telephone call from the Virgin Islands was not the way to do this, or perhaps not fully sharing her alarm, Frank never conveyed Holly's message. More than a week was to pass before Eagleton and I met to discuss his medical difficulties. Even by then, no real professional advice had been sought and no group convened to assist in reaching a careful judgment. Close advisers such as Henry Kimelman, Dick Wade, John Douglas, Morris Dees and Miles Rubin were never informed that there was a problem.

On Monday, July 17, I left for a brief rest at Sylvan Lake in the

Black Hills of South Dakota. That same morning Susan Garro, a volunteer in the Washington campaign headquarters, answered a call from a man who said that Senator Eagleton had been hospitalized on three different occasions for mental illness and had received electric-shock treatments at least twice. The caller claimed to be a McGovern supporter and said that he had received the information from an indisputable source who had direct knowledge of the shock treatments. He added that he had given the information to the Knight newspapers, a claim which was soon to be verified. (The call to the Detroit *Free Press* was taken by John S. Knight III, the grandson of the publisher, who was told by the informant that a medical report from the Renard Psychiatric Division of the Barnes Hospital in St. Louis showed that Tom Eagleton had been in a "manic-depressive state with suicidal tendencies.") Marcia Johnston, Gary Hart's secretary, telephoned the warning to Gary, who discounted it because of its anonymous nature.

The next day the caller repeated the story to Pat Broun, Frank Mankiewicz's secretary. With that, Frank and Gary called Senator Eagleton from St. Thomas and asked that he meet them for breakfast in the Senate Dining Room the next morning, Thursday, July 20. Gary made notes of this meeting as follows:

> Senator Eagleton, Doug Bennet, Frank and I met in the Senate dining room from about 8:30 to 10:00 A.M. The exchange was direct. How many hospitalizations? Three. Where were they? The first was in 1960 at the Barnes Hospital in St. Louis. What kind of hospital is that? Private hospital with a special unit called the Renard Psychiatric Division. Then where were the others? Mayo Clinic in Rochester, Minnesota. Two? Yes, 1964 and 1966. Both after campaigns? No, let's see, '60 and '66 were, but '64 was around the holidays, around Christmas. Frank winced visibly. (During the campaign despondency of late December 1971, I recalled Frank's delivering a homily one night in the office about the Christmas season's being the statistical peak period for psychological and emotional problems and suicide attempts. So now, we were clearly dealing with more than mere post-campaign fatigue, or even post-campaign depression.) What treatment was used? Rest, some medication. But mostly rest. Professional help, psychiatrists? Yes, one or two had been brought in. But they were mostly trying to figure out the reasons for this depression and melancholy, whether it was related to physical fatigue and so forth. Anything else, anything like shock therapy, electro-shock treatment? Yes. In 1960 at Barnes and 1966 at Mayo. But not very much on either occasion.
>
> I then brought up the point Frank had made in the second telephone conversation from the islands. We have to presume this information is, or shortly will be, in the hands of the Committee to Re-elect the

President. John Mitchell was its chairman. The same John Mitchell who, as Attorney General, had authority over the F.B.I. In any case, it was naïve to presume, particularly since Lyndon Johnson had proved so many times to the contrary, that the President didn't have access to every bit of information in the Bureau's records. If the full Eagleton medical history wasn't in those records now, it soon would be, and from there it would go to Nixon's desk. What do those records show? What words are used? What is the diagnosis? What should we expect? Mostly just depression and melancholy. But won't there be some more technical terms that unfriendly experts can twist and turn? The only way to find out, the only way for McGovern to be fully protected, is to know what they say.

Eagleton agreed. He himself had never seen the files, he said, but he would send a staff member to get them. He knew the doctors and he was sure they would cooperate. He would get someone, a name was mentioned, out to St. Louis and to Rochester in the next couple of days. Since McGovern, Frank and I were headed to South Dakota the following day, it was agreed the files should be sent there as quickly as possible for our evaluation. Eagleton then indicated he would be headed West on Tuesday and planned to stop over in the Black Hills. It was agreed in conclusion that nothing would be done until we got the records and the two candidates met on Tuesday.

While the breakfast was in progress with Eagleton, I was flying back from Custer to vote that afternoon on the minimum-wage bill, a vote which would have ended in a tie had I not returned. I saw Tom briefly on the Senate floor, but as yet had no report on the breakfast conversation. Gary did advise me that the meeting had been held and we agreed to discuss it flying back to Custer the next day. That was a mistake. I should have insisted on being fully briefed as quickly as possible, and the return to Custer should have been delayed so Eagleton and I could have had a long discussion right there with the best-qualified advisers we could assemble in Washington.

Instead I waited until the next morning, still assuming that the difficulty was minor. On board the plane Gary and Frank, speaking in hushed voices so as not to be overheard by the reporters sitting a few feet behind my compartment, gave me their report on the breakfast session with Eagleton. I experienced the first feeling that we were in fundamental trouble. Eleanor, who was about to have her first rest in months, listened and tried, but not very successfully, to conceal her concern.

I was tired, too, from the hurried flight to Washington for the minimum-wage vote. Gary, Frank and I agreed to wait out the weekend—it was Friday afternoon—until I talked personally with Eagleton. He was due to arrive Monday night. That wait was the next

mistake: that weekend there was time—the last time, as it turned out
—to consider the issue carefully. Instead I spent it with a recurring,
nagging worry, but still assuming that we would have a chance to
consider the problem carefully after Eagleton and I met.

But by the time he arrived at midnight Monday, the Knight newspapers had the story. Frank had persuaded them to hold it—but only
briefly. Suddenly, an immediate decision had to be made.

Tuesday morning Eagleton and his wife, Barbara, and Eleanor and
I had breakfast in our cabin. He quickly plunged into the story of his
medical history. He told me he was sorry that he had not informed
me of his mental disturbances before accepting the nomination. He
frankly related the conversation he and Barbara had in which they
debated whether he should divulge his medical history if he was
tapped for the national ticket.

He was over the problem now, he added; his doctors had given him
a clean bill of health. He emphatically added something that
weighed very heavily with me in that moment of decision, but which
he was to cast aside within seventy-two hours. Looking first at me and
then at Eleanor and saying it twice for emphasis, he volunteered, "If
my being on the ticket causes any trouble, I'll leave of my own accord
either now or tomorrow or next week or any other day right up until
the election." He said that he would do it on his own, if either he or
I concluded that was best: I would never have to push him publicly.

I believed him. He had omitted the truth at the convention, but
Eleanor and I understood how anxious he had been to close a painful
series of events in his life that he believed belonged to the past. For
several years we had lived with a deep emotional disturbance involving one of our children. We saw the same tormented look on Tom's
face as he told his story and, as Eleanor described it, "We literally
reached out our arms to him." We were now confronted with a
problem that was about to break as the first big story since the
convention. I recalled all the people who had toiled for long back-
breaking months to win the nomination for me—and for the sake of
deep beliefs about the country. Now Eagleton's problems threatened
to damage or destroy their efforts.

But there seemed to be a course that was both endurable politically and fair to Tom. I decided that we should go ahead with a
scheduled press conference that forenoon, tell the whole story, and
then do our best to explain it to the public. At this point I accepted
Eagleton's assurance that his mental instability was a thing of the
past. He promised me, as he had Frank and Gary, that he would
provide a copy of his medical records so we could be sure. I knew that
if he was to have a chance with the public, I could not be ambiguous
in supporting him. I saw no course other than to accept his resigna-

tion then and there or fully endorse him with the hope that the public would accept the situation. My approach was a gamble, but it appeared to be relatively safe; it was the one way, I thought, to give Eagleton his chance while protecting the public interest and Democratic prospects. If evidence emerged that he should not serve as Vice President or that the ticket could not win, I had his voluntary and unqualified assurance that he would take complete responsibility for stepping down. It was the crucial factor in my decision that morning.

I believed then and I believe now that Tom Eagleton realized by the time of the Custer meeting that his background could gravely jeopardize the national campaign. I believed then and I believe now that he meant his pledge to step down on his own, with no pressure from me, if we encountered significant trouble. But a series of events soon transpired which led him to make it as difficult as possible for me to reconsider my decision. One after another, events following the Custer meeting narrowed my options; finally it became impossible for the national ticket to go unscathed with or without Eagleton. For the first time in twenty years of political life I was to find myself in a credibility gap—due to a curious transference in the handling of another man's credibility.

Throughout my political career, there is one strength I have placed above all others and that is a willingness to speak my real convictions to the press and to the public. There have been a few departures from this rule and I have regretted each one of them. I have also made errors in judgment and compromised needlessly on a few occasions. But on the truly important public issues—even ones fraught with great political hazard—I think my record has generally been one of competence and constancy.

Then came the Eagleton affair, and suddenly a campaign launched a year and a half earlier on a pledge "to seek and speak the truth" was challenged on grounds of both credibility and competence. And doubtless both charges have at least a measure of validity. It was the worst political week of the campaign or, indeed, of my political life. It left me a sadder but wiser man, one determined never again to equivocate even to protect the feelings or career of another person.

After breakfast with the Eagletons I called in Frank Mankiewicz and Dick Dougherty, both experienced journalists and men of considerable maturity and imagination. After inviting in two of his assistants, Doug Bennet and Mike Kelly, Eagleton recounted his story again, concluding, according to Dick Dougherty's notes, as follows:

> Looking at me again, Eagleton said: "I've told George and Eleanor that I know I was wrong not to speak up about this before, Dick, but the

reason I didn't was that I'd put it all so much behind me. To me it was something over and done. I knew my health was sound, that I'd had no trouble for the last six years, and I guess I'd just wiped it from my mind. I've also told George that if he wants me to I'll get off the ticket this second, this minute, this hour, today, this week—any time that he concludes that my presence on the ticket is an embarrassment or a hindrance to his chances of election. I'm prepared to do anything, anything at all that he decides I should do."

Dougherty's notes then have me speaking for the first time: "I've told Tom I'm prepared to stand by him in this. I think we can ride it through."

I asked for the reaction of the four men. Neither Dougherty nor Mankiewicz raised any serious objections, although Frank suggested mildly that it might be better to withhold the decision for a day or two. Mike Kelly suggested with somewhat more force that the announcement be delayed until Eagleton had returned from a trip to Hawaii and the West Coast and we were both back in Washington. He believed that this would avoid repeated inquiries about the story while Eagleton was on his first speaking tour, and would place us both in a more desirable setting to make a carefully timed revelation.

I was impressed by the logic of arguments for delay—that was my own instinctive preference—but they overlooked one serious difficulty: the fact that the Knight newspapers had the story. Knight reporters Bob Boyd and Clark Hoyt had already done considerable checking; they were in Custer pressing Mankiewicz hard to comment whether we had any knowledge of the alleged Eagleton medical history. And we did not know how much they really knew. They might, for example, have had the entire medical record. Furthermore, *Time* magazine was on to the story, which made Boyd and Hoyt increasingly anxious to break it. I could see a situation developing where either the Eagleton camp or my own or both would have to duck the press, refuse comment or make evasive statements that might later compromise the integrity of the campaign.

Moreover, we all assumed that a full-disclosure press conference would put the issue to rest early in the campaign. Long after the event Doug Bennet told me, "I will never forget my astonishment and sense of being cheated when Eagleton got off the plane in Los Angeles that night after the disclosure, told reporters that he would have no further comment, and discovered that no one wanted to ask him about anything except his illness. The only explanation for our underestimation of the publicity consequences of Eagleton's illness was our certainty that he was cured plus a creditable human compassion on your part and others' which simply obscured consequences that people not so intimately involved might have seen."

So the press conference was held, Eagleton made a statement of his medical history, and then the questions came. David Schoumacher of CBS asked Eagleton how I had reacted to the news of his mental problems. With more bravado than common sense, I intervened to answer the question:

> I am fully satisfied on the basis of everything I've learned about these brief hospital visits that what is manifest on Senator Eagleton's part was the good judgment to seek out medical care when he was exhausted. I have watched him in the United States Senate for the past four years. As far as I am concerned, there is no member of that Senate who is any sounder in mind, body and spirit than Tom Eagleton. I am fully satisfied and if I had known every detail that he told me this morning, which is exactly what he has just told you here now, he would still have been my choice for the vice presidency of the United States.

That was a regrettable answer on my part. The strategy of supporting Eagleton all out had already led me to be inaccurate on two points. First of all, neither I nor anyone else really thought that Tom's medical history was so insignificant that it was not "worth discussing with me." I knew that even if he was healthy now, Eagleton had suffered three mental breakdowns serious enough to require hospitalization. Second, neither I nor anyone else really thought that if I had known all the facts of Tom's medical history and its earlier cover-up, "he would still have been my choice for the vice presidency of the United States." But the moment seemed to demand a total commitment to Eagleton if he was to have any chance at all.

Following the press conference at Custer, Tom told me that he would never forget how supportive I had been: "Now that this is all out in the open, I feel as though a burden I have been carrying in secret for twelve years has rolled off my back." I thought the burden was now on my back, but I did not know then what a grievous load I had assumed.

Clearly, I should have been less supportive. Not only should I have tempered my own remarks, but perhaps I should have let the press break the story of Eagleton's health. I could then have said, "Yes, I'm looking into the matter; we're now trying to assess the situation, to see how serious it is." I probably could have gained a few days for reflection, consultation and evaluation of the public reaction. Whatever my decision, I could have carefully planned how best to present it to the press and public.

As it was, almost before the last press-conference question was answered and the stories were filed, the reaction set in across the nation, and it was devastating. Many who had worked tirelessly for my nomination complained that Eagleton had engaged in a cover-up. Some of them applauded my compassion in deciding to stay with him, but they believed that if I did not reconsider this decision, the election was hopelessly lost.

In New York, several well-known Democrats said publicly that because Eagleton had concealed his mental history, he had to leave the ticket, or be forced off if necessary. They overlooked the fact that the only man who could legally remove Eagleton from the ticket was Eagleton himself.

Then came a grim conference call from my key finance directors: Henry Kimelman and Miles Rubin. They told me that Morris Dees —our direct-mail fund-raising expert—had already left for his home in Montgomery, Alabama, in disgust at Eagleton's cover-up and would not return until I reconsidered my decision. Miles Rubin said that it would be a betrayal of everything our campaign stood for if I retained a man who had so seriously eroded the campaign's reputation for credibility. Henry Kimelman spoke more bluntly and angrily than at any time in my experience with him: campaign finances had dried up completely, and it would be impossible to finance the campaign with Eagleton on the ticket. He relayed the same judgment from nearly all the major contributors to the campaign.

The editorial consensus was that while it was personally commendable for me to show compassion for Eagleton, the decision should be reconsidered for two reasons: first, his concealment of his mental problems raised serious questions about his credibility; second, and more significant, I owed it to the nation not to place a man a heartbeat away from the presidency if there was any danger of serious emotional imbalance.

Two days later Jack Anderson reported that as a Missouri state officeholder, Eagleton had been arrested repeatedly for drunk driving. Tom struck back at this charge with ferocity. He seemed confident that Anderson could not prove it. He attacked the columnist for inciting undocumented scandal.

Back in Custer, I was still convinced that with time, the reactions might cool. Carl Leubsdorf of the Associated Press tracked me down on a tennis court and asked me what I thought the public reaction to Eagleton's disclosure would be. I answered truthfully, and I thought, harmlessly, by saying, "We'll have to wait and see." The Leubsdorf story was filed accurately enough, but the headline on the story in some papers was typified by this one: McGOVERN RECONSIDERING EAGLETON DECISION.

Gary Hart called me from Washington in distress about what ap-

peared to be a weakening of our public position. I was furious when
he told me that the Leubsdorf story indicated that I was reconsidering the Eagleton decision, not realizing that it was an improper
headline rather than an inaccurate story. I angrily called Dick
Dougherty and ordered him to tell the press that the Leubsdorf story
was false and that I was backing Eagleton "a thousand percent."

Meanwhile, the Jack Anderson episode was fundamentally altering
the situation. The allegations created sympathy for Eagleton as an
embattled candidate fighting for his political life against false and
perhaps even malicious accusations. Later Anderson partially apolo-
gized for releasing the story without adequately verifying its details.
And after Eagleton had withdrawn from the ticket, the television
cameras showed the columnist appearing in Eagleton's office retract-
ing his story. The charges planted the suspicion, subsequently nurtured by Eagleton, that unscrupulous people were out to get him, to
drive him from the ticket. He was also angered by press speculation
that some members of my staff were trying to "dump" him. Most
important, the Anderson accusations gave Eagleton an opportunity
to seize the offensive and to capture the public's sympathy. From
that moment on, his earlier chastened mood shifted toward an aggressive, angry defense against all charges. Eventually he was telling
reporters that he was on the national ticket to stay—that there was
no way he would leave unless I personally requested it and that even
then, he might refuse to withdraw. Speaking to reporters who accompanied him from South Dakota to a labor convention in Hawaii,
he said of the Anderson charge, "I have never been more determined in my life about any issue than I am today about remaining
on this ticket. I'm not going to bow to Mr. Anderson. I'm not going
to let a lie drive me from the ticket." He argued that for him to
withdraw would give credence to Anderson's accusations, to "scar
me and my family . . . No, you're not going to get me out of this race.
Never."

But the pressure to ask for Tom's withdrawal continued to mount.
Two days after his departure from Custer, I telephoned Gaylord
Nelson and asked him for his judgment. He told me that he, too,
regarded the reaction as severely negative, both in the press and
among other senators. He added that his Wisconsin field representative, Sherman Stock, was conducting a series of public forums in half
a dozen Wisconsin towns that day and that he would ask him to poll
each audience on the Eagleton issue. At the end of the day Gaylord
called back and said that by proportions of "ten or twelve to one"
Wisconsin residents attending the public forums believed that I
should ask for Tom's withdrawal. Nelson added that while he had

agreed with my original decision to keep Eagleton on the ticket, he had about come to the conclusion in the next couple of days that a reconsideration was required.

I still had not seen Eagleton's medical records, so that night I decided to call two of the nation's most respected psychiatrists for advice. First I called Dr. Wilfred Abse of the University of Virginia. He told me that there was no way to predict with any certainty the future behavior of a person with Tom's mental history. His judgment was that Eagleton should leave the ticket rather than take the risk of a recurrence should we be elected.

I wanted another judgment, perhaps I hoped it would be a more reassuring one, so I phoned Dr. Karl Menninger. As soon as he heard my voice he said, "Oh, Senator, I know why you are calling and it makes me very sad because I so much wanted you to be elected and to end that war in Vietnam."

"Does that mean that you think it's all over—that we have lost?" I asked.

"Well," he said, "I gather that Senator Eagleton has had a serious mental illness. It is impossible for me to diagnose his problem by long distance. But as one who has been talking to the American people about mental illness for many years, I must tell you that you are in an awful dilemma. Millions of Americans are so frightened by mental illness that they will not support you for the presidency in the knowledge that your Vice President has had a history of mental problems. On the other hand, if you now ask Senator Eagleton to resign from the ticket, millions of other Americans will turn against you for persecuting a man who has suffered mental instability."

"In other words, Dr. Menninger, are you telling me that I'm damned if I do and damned if I don't?"

"I'm afraid that's what I'm telling you," he said sadly.

"What do you advise?" I asked.

"I'm not sure," he said, "but I don't see any way to retrieve the situation politically. As for the interest of the nation, however, you can afford no risks and I would therefore hope that you would ask Mr. Eagleton to step down."

I thanked Dr. Menninger, hung up the phone, and sat stunned and saddened for a long time. I knew that Dr. Menninger had correctly diagnosed the maddening political trap into which I had fallen. There was no way to prevent enormous damage to the campaign, no matter what course I chose.

The dilemma was underscored during a late-night discussion within my own family. Two of my children told me that Eagleton should go. The other three were equally convinced that he should stay. Eleanor was completely convinced after the conversations with the two psychiatrists that he must resign.

I tried to reach Eagleton late the next afternoon to warn him that I was under great pressure to ask for his withdrawal, but I did not get through to him until the morning after. I told him that we would have to reconsider the decision reached earlier in the week. I also said that I would never make a final decision on the matter before meeting with him, but that he should handle the press with caution relative to his future on the ticket. I then asked him to meet me in Washington two days later. I also read him a portion of a speech I was to deliver that evening in Aberdeen, South Dakota, which said: "I do not know how it will come out, but I do know that it gets darkest just before the stars come out. So I ask for your prayers and your patience for Senator Eagleton and me while we deliberate on the proper course ahead."

After listening to those words, Tom said, "That's beautiful, George; I wish I had written it." I restated my caution about the press to assure that it was clear. But to my amazement, I was to learn that almost as soon as our conversation ended, Tom went out of his San Francisco motel and told the press corps, "McGovern still backs Eagleton one thousand percent." Later as he was boarding the plane from San Francisco, he told the press, "My decision to stay on the ticket is irrevocable."

At my final dinner hour at the Sylvan Lake Lodge, a Friday evening, I decided that journalists covering me in Custer should be alerted to the possible reversal that was looming. I therefore stopped briefly at three or four tables in the dining room, and as calmly as I could, let the journalists know that I was reviewing the situation. I stressed, however, that no serious decision could be reached without full consultation and cooperation with Tom Eagleton.

The press reaction astounded me. The reporters saw my forewarning as a stab in Tom Eagleton's back. They concluded that while having stated publicly a few days earlier that I was a 1,000 percent for Eagleton, I was using them to force Eagleton off the ticket without confronting him face to face. Probably one explanation of the reporters' feeling was that they were unaware of my effort to reach Eagleton that evening and of my lengthy conversation with him the next morning, in which I told him more about my state of mind than I had told them.

My reassessment also seemed to clash with my earlier affirmations of unqualified support. Little publicity had been given to my initial "one thousand percent" statement and I never again used that phrase. But Eagleton emphasized the statement repeatedly in encounters with the press. On Saturday, July 29, my apparent change of mind received prominent front-page attention in the *New York Times,* the Washington *Post,* the Chicago *Tribune* and other major newspapers.

Timothy Crouse, the author of *The Boys on the Bus,* a study of reporting in the 1972 campaign, wrote of this period: "Eagleton's great victory over both McGovern and the press consisted in the agility with which he appropriated the hard news columns for his own designs—namely, to portray himself as a martyr for the cause of psychotherapy, a totally cured man who was wrongly suspected of being dangerously sick."

At the end of what should have been a quiet week of relaxation at the rustic old Sylvan Lake Lodge, Eleanor and I were riding in a Secret Service car from the local theater to our cabin. Eleanor recalls me putting my head back on the seat, shutting my eyes, and saying very quietly, "Oh, my God." At that point I think I had decided that He was the only one who might be able to help.

Before leaving Sylvan Lake for an appearance at Aberdeen, South Dakota, on Saturday night I tried unsuccessfully to reach Eagleton on the phone to ask that he not appear on the *Face the Nation* television interview the next day. My call was not returned. Gary Hart finally conveyed my message to Eagleton through Doug Bennet, Eagleton's top aide. But Eagleton went ahead with *Face the Nation* anyway, confronting his nemesis Jack Anderson in a hard-hitting self-defense against the drunk-driving charges. On *Meet the Press* earlier that day, Jean Westwood and Basil Paterson, the recently installed chairpersons of the Democratic National Committee, said that Eagleton could best serve the public interest by withdrawing from the ticket. Tom later told Theodore White that I had instigated Westwood and Paterson's statements. White printed the assertion as fact. The truth is that I never discussed the matter at all with Paterson and my only knowledge of Jean Westwood's intentions came in a telephone call just before air time in which she hastily warned me that if she was asked about Eagleton, she would have to say that she personally thought he should withdraw. I asked her if she thought it was necessary to make that statement. She hurriedly said yes as she prepared to take her place in front of the cameras.

Sunday night I slipped away from my home for a private meeting with Senator Mike Mansfield. My purpose was twofold. First, I wanted the benefit of Mansfield's counsel on the Eagleton question. Second, I wanted to determine whether he would accept the vice-presidential nomination in the event Eagleton were to step down. It seemed to me that the Senate Majority Leader would have been a reassuring choice after the divisive chaos of the preceding days.

To the first question Mansfield said he felt that Eagleton should remain on the ticket. He emphasized his positive view of Eagleton's performance in the Senate. As for accepting the vice presidency himself, the Majority Leader said he would not even consider that. He told me that Lyndon Johnson had tried to persuade him to be his running mate in 1964, but that he had stoutly refused. Mike Mansfield, like Ribicoff and Nelson, honestly preferred the Senate to the vice presidency.

Following the Sunday night meeting with Mansfield, I went to Henry Kimelman's home for a session with Tom Eagleton, scheduled earlier that day. We had also agreed to meet the next night, Monday, for a final decision. Although Eagleton had said at the outset that he would make his medical records available for my perusal, and despite repeated requests, I still had not seen them. But he assured me during this Sunday-night discussion that arrangements would be made for me to talk the next night with his doctors in St. Louis and at the Mayo Clinic.

Monday morning I received a letter from Arthur Schlesinger, Jr., a close friend and one of the nation's foremost historians, who advised:

> To put it bluntly, I think that, one way or another, you *must* get rid of Eagleton. It is to be hoped that he might have the decency to take himself off the ticket in circumstances that would allow you to express regret and admiration. If he were to do that, he would be the beneficiary of a national wave of sympathy and could count on being senator from Missouri for the rest of his life (and, obviously, would be an excellent senator and serve the nation well). I have the fear, though, that he has reread *Six Crises* and is determined in the manner of Nixon in 1952 to make it impossible for you to divest yourself of him. If this is so, it certainly relieves you of any personal obligation toward him. I think in any case you are relieved of any such obligation by his outrageous failure to disclose his problems to you before you tapped him. That was inexcusable; his subsequent position that he would only withdraw if you asked him to was inexcusable; his present determination to fight to stay on the ticket is inexcusable.
>
> His betrayal of you and of his party is the essential issue, not his psychiatric history. But, if he stays on the ticket, both this question and his psychiatric history as well will be dominating issues from now to election day. . . . Nor, as Eagleton has curiously suggested, is it like JFK's Catholicism in 1960; after all, JFK never hid the fact that he was a Catholic. . . .
>
> I recognize that, if you dump Eagleton, it will be at some cost to yourself. People will say that, if you made a bad decision on the most solemn appointment you have to make, how can your judgment be taken seriously thereafter? I certainly don't underestimate this prob-

lem. But, in a way, this all reminds me of the Bay of Pigs. I well recall the pressure JFK was under to justify a bad decision by escalating his commitment. He declined to do so. Instead, he cut his losses; and obviously this was the right thing to do. If you cut your losses in the next few days, you will have three months to bring other issues before the country. If you don't, I fear this issue will not disappear. Better a surgical excision than a running sore. Recall how quickly the Republicans disposed of John Mitchell. It looks now, only a few weeks later, as if Clark MacGregor had been there forever. Political memories are short, and it is a long time between now and November—if we can only shift the topic of conversation.

That night, following a hurried flight to New Orleans to attend the funeral of Senator Allen Ellender, I met with Eagleton in the Marble Room adjoining the Senate Democratic Cloakroom in the Capitol. Gaylord Nelson was the only other person there. I had invited him on the assumption that the presence of a mutual friend respected by both Eagleton and me would be helpful in reaching a final understanding. As Gaylord, Tom and I talked, the national press corps crowded into the Senate Caucus Room.

Eagleton said that after conversations during the day with Nelson, he was resigned to leaving the ticket provided I would join him in assuring the public that he was withdrawing not because of his health, but because I did not want public discussion of his health to obscure the real issues. He assured me for the first time that his doctors would tell me that he was sufficiently stable to carry the burdens of national office. He then added that he and his staff had drafted a statement for me to issue at the joint press conference in which I would stress that health was not the issue and that he was resigning simply to avoid making it an issue. I was troubled by all this, but I knew I did not have the legal authority to force him off the ticket. Either he would leave on his terms, or not at all.

As agreed, Tom went to a telephone in the next room and after a brief conversation told me that his St. Louis doctor was on the phone. The same procedure was repeated with a doctor at the Mayo Clinic. I was alone as I talked to each of them with Eagleton and Nelson back in the Marble Room. The two doctors were as cautious as possible about protecting the doctor-patient relationship. Indeed, I could learn almost nothing at all except by pressing for answers to precisely worded questions. The doctors were especially hesitant to put their professional reputations on the line as to Tom's future mental stability under stress. If politicians know how to hedge their statements on complex issues, these psychiatrists were even more adept at double-talk and professional self-defense. Despite their reluctance, they finally offered specific details of Eagleton's medical history which I thought raised serious doubts about his capacity to carry the burdens and responsibility of the presidency. They asked me not to reveal those details; until now, I have not shared even their general conclusions. One of the doctors said that it was probable Eagleton could complete the campaign and serve as Vice President without further relapses. When I asked him what the risks would be should Tom have to take over the presidency, he said, "I don't like to think about that prospect." He then added that the danger of a recurrence was always present and that such persons ordinarily experience more difficulty as they get older. In responding to the same question, the other doctor said that he was surprised Eagleton had been able to withstand his duties in the Senate and the first week of controversy surrounding his vice-presidential candidacy. Perhaps he could stand up to an even greater test, but "that would make me most uncomfortable," the doctor said.

I had gone to the meeting frustrated with the Eagleton situation and his conduct in recent days. I was nearly certain that he should withdraw. After conferring with the doctors, I had no doubt. But I also knew that if I so much as hinted publicly about the doubts concerning his future mental stability, he would not leave the ticket. Indeed, when I returned to the discussion with Nelson and Eagleton, the latter said bluntly that if I or any of my aides publicly raised the issue of his health at any point, he would fight me "right through to November."

He then handed me the statement asserting that while health was not the issue, it had so diverted attention from the true problems before the nation that I was, therefore, asking him to resign. He proposed to respond with an explanation that while he did not share my view of the matter, he was resigning in the interests of party harmony. It was, he repeated, the only condition under which he would resign.

I did what I had to, but the Eagleton matter ended whatever chance there was to defeat Richard Nixon in 1972.

My relationship with the press was never again the same. My handling of the Eagleton affair antagonized those reporters who felt that a President should be tough, hard-nosed, able to confront the Russians eyeball to eyeball. And it antagonized those who had admired me most for the candor and openness of my presidential quest. There were endless scoffing references to my being for Eagleton 1,000 percent one day and asking him to leave less than a week later.

In the minds of many Americans the Eagleton episode convicted me of incompetence, vacillation, dishonesty and cold calculation, all at the same time. Television coverage of the withdrawal was especially damning. All three networks reported Jack Anderson's full retraction of his charges against Eagleton and showed Anderson penitently appearing in Eagleton's Senate office. All three networks carried interviews with political leaders of Eagleton's home state intensely critical of me. State Chariman Delton Hutchins, for example, told ABC:

> I think that Senator McGovern's forcing Tom Eagleton off of this ticket is a very damaging blow to his credibility and I also think that it was a very, very shabby treatment of Tom Eagleton. Many Democrats throughout this nation . . . are very unhappy with what I call this shabby treatment that has been given to Tom Eagleton . . . I've been a lifelong Democrat and I intend to continue to be, but this fall's election will probably find me and my friends spending our money and working to elect our state, congressional and local candidates.

None of the networks carried interviews with anyone favorable to my decision. And the nation's two leading news weeklies, *Time* and *Newsweek*, both carried lengthy Eagleton monologues in which Tom set forth his interpretation of the entire matter with no offsetting interview on my part.

I still believe that my decision was right, one I had to make in the nation's best interests. Some of the Eagleton advisers believed that the decision was inevitable once Jean Westwood as the head of the Democratic Party had called on Tom to resign. It would have been difficult after that moment to restore a confident, harmonious relationship in the Democratic family. From a political perspective, I might have been damaged less by keeping Eagleton. His presence on the ticket would have distracted from the real issues, but my personal credibility might have suffered less. After the revelation of Eagleton's repeated illnesses, the problem was a political backlash. But in the end, even if the political calculus had shifted barely toward staying with him, I could not do so with a clear conscience.

Two months later Eagleton was the honoree at the Truman Day Awards Dinner in St. Louis and I was the principal speaker. He and his wife, Barbara, Eleanor and I and Frank Mankiewicz had a private dinner beforehand in a suite at the Chase Park Plaza Hotel. In the midst of a discussion of Watergate, Barbara Eagleton interjected, "You know, George, Tom is now the most popular politician in America." Later I asked Tom if he would make a television commercial for me. He said no.

In a post-election interview, Tom described the trouble over the vice-presidential nominee as no more than "one rock in the landslide." Perhaps that is true, but landslides begin with a single rock.

10
THE
FALL CAMPAIGN

T he evening before Labor Day I left on the nonstop two-
month general election campaign. The first event was a courtesy call at the Southern Governors' Conference which was meeting
at Hilton Head, South Carolina. I received a polite, generally friendly
reception in contrast to the rather grim session with the Democratic
governors in Austin, Texas, just before the California primary. At
Hilton Head, Governor John West of South Carolina, the host of the
conference, volunteered an outright if restrained endorsement. I
came away with the small comfort that though I might have little
chance in the South, new-breed governors like Reubin Askew, Dale
Bumpers, Jimmy Carter and West would give the ticket at least
measured support.

We left Hilton Head so late that evening that we arrived in Dayton, Ohio, where I was scheduled to address a Labor Day rally the
next morning, two hours behind schedule. The press was as surprised
as I was to find that despite the delay, thousands of people were
lining the corridors of the airport at two-thirty in the morning to
welcome us. It was a remarkable demonstration of their commitment. Under normal circumstances it would have been an auspicious
start for the fall campaign, but the situation was hardly the usual one:
I was not only beginning far behind, but perhaps hopelessly out of
the race even before it started. On the flight to Dayton a reporter had

told one of my assistants, Bob Shrum, that he hoped Bob, who was only twenty-nine and in his first national campaign, would have a great experience and contribute to some great speeches. "But," he warned, "don't go around thinking you have a chance to win, or you'll be disappointed. I've been out interviewing people and they've already made up their minds—it doesn't matter if George McGovern gives the Gettysburg Address on every street corner. The voters just won't listen. They've decided to stick with Nixon."

Though perhaps none of us in the campaign acknowledged it at the time, a series of events, perhaps minor in themselves, had poisoned public perceptions of me in an area where the Eagleton affair had already inflicted nearly irreparable damage—the voters' estimate of my reliability and competence. The first of these difficulties came before Eagleton. It involved Larry O'Brien and the choice of a new Democratic national chairman immediately after the convention in Miami. In June and early July I took Larry at his word—that he did not wish to continue as chairman. He had repeated this without reservation on several occasions, both privately and to the press. He reiterated this to me and to Senator Abe Ribicoff while we were visiting with him in Miami the day before the convention.

Meantime, on a trip through the South after the New York primary I was asked at a news conference in Oklahoma City who I thought would be a good replacement for Larry, given the fact that he did not intend to stay on. I answered that there were a number of qualified people and that I wouldn't rule out the possibility that for the first time in its history a woman might head the Democratic National Committee. A reporter asked whether I had anybody in mind. I cited Utah national committeewoman Jean Westwood as a possibility. She and I had never discussed the matter, but when I saw her later she thanked me and said she would be interested in the post.

In Miami, O'Brien won high praise for his skillful handling of the convention. He and his co-chairperson, Congressman Yvonne Braithwaite Burke of California, were on network television constantly and left a very favorable impression. I was later told that O'Brien changed his mind during this period. If so, the change was not communicated to me until the morning after the convention. I was scheduled to attend a victory breakfast at eight-thirty for Democratic congressional and gubernatorial candidates, so I dutifully set my alarm for seven forty-five as I climbed into bed only two hours before that, following the pre-dawn acceptance speech and the reception. When I arrived at the breakfast I was surprised to find that Larry, who was expected to preside, was nowhere to be seen. I asked Texan Robert Strauss, then the party's national treasurer, later to be national chairman himself, if he knew what was wrong. Though Strauss is capable of blunt language, this time he spoke reluctantly and gingerly. But I got the message: Larry's feelings had been injured because I had not urged him to remain as national chairman after my nomination. Such a step would have been difficult under the circumstances. During the convention Jean Westwood and I had discussed the matter again and she told me that she would like to have the job. I had then made a commitment to her. Word of that quickly spread to the women's caucus and they now expected me to keep my word. To complicate matters still further, former White House press secretary Pierre Salinger, who had supported me early and worked hard through the primaries, also expressed an interest in the national chairmanship. He was later to write that I had agreed before the convention that he would be selected. I did not remember such a conversation, but I believed that he would be a good choice as vice chairman. (And if I had won the election, there is no doubt that Pierre would have had an important place in the Administration.)

As soon as the breakfast was over, I called O'Brien and asked if he had in fact changed his mind. He told me that he was being urged by many national-committee members to accept re-election and that he would like to talk it over with me. We postponed the committee's scheduled meeting and he came to my suite at the Doral Hotel. Larry suggested that he serve as chairman until November, with Westwood as vice chairman; he would then step down and she would take over. I went to the next room in the suite and told Jean of Larry's plan. She replied, "If I'm going to do it, I want to do it now, not after the election. The challenge is to be chairman during the campaign." She said she would just forget about it if Larry wanted to stay on, but she also emphasized my earlier understanding with her and the expectations of the women's caucus. I asked her if she would be willing to share the post with Larry on an equal basis as chairperson—the same arrangement O'Brien had worked out for the convention with Congresswoman Burke. She said that would be fine—in fact, it would be helpful. I thought Larry would accept this—that he would understand its importance to the women and yet know that just as he had at the convention, he would be first among the two equals at the national committee because of his greater experience. But he refused even to consider the idea. I told him that I had no recourse other than to let him resign and that I would recommend Jean as his successor.

The O'Brien difficulty was costly. Retaining him would have eased anxieties about me among urban Irish Catholics, party regulars and others who identified him with John Kennedy. His active leadership in the campaign would have been valuable. O'Brien himself couldn't understand why I simply didn't break my word to Jean Westwood.

(I later tried to repair the breach with him by naming him chairman of the fall campaign. He and his staff took up the eighth floor of our Washington campaign headquarters, but it was not a workable arrangement. Rather, it represented a source of friction, a considerable waste of funds, and an underutilization of Larry's experience.)

The convention, which was the culmination of a dream, was indeed producing its share of nightmarish moments. The next one came after the national committee quickly approved my recommendation of Westwood as chairwoman, when I proposed Pierre Salinger as vice chairman. Immediately my friend Aaron Henry of the Mississippi Freedom Democratic Party nominated Basil Paterson, a respected black leader from New York, for the same post. Henry, a long-time, courageous civil rights champion, argued that the time had come to name a black to one of the party's two top offices. I had been told that the black leadership had cleared Pierre, but I later found out that the only black who had been consulted was a member of my staff. I was in an awkward position. After arguing that it was time to recognize the role of women in the party, I had suggested a man to serve with Jean as vice chairman—a white man. To the blacks, that was two whites and no blacks. I had to make an instant decision. To avoid a fight along racial lines, I told the committee that while I was proud to recommend Salinger, I would be pleased if either he or Basil Paterson were chosen. Salinger then asked for the floor and withdrew his name. He was disappointed that I had not backed him exclusively, but I was trying to play the role of peacemaker in a party that was already too divided to endure further quarrels.

The next domino on this unlucky row started to fall twenty-four hours later when I telephoned Salinger in Hyannisport, where he was spending the weekend as a guest at the Kennedy compound. I told him that since he was planning to leave for Paris shortly, I wanted him to visit with the North Vietnamese delegation to the peace talks to determine whether they might release several American prisoners of war as a symbolic gesture of their willingness to negotiate an end to the war. I suggested that if the Vietnamese agreed to the prisoner release, Pierre might go to Hanoi to pursue the matter there. If this helped bring peace before the election, I added, that was fine with me. I was more interested in ending the war than in having it as an issue.

Pierre and I understood that he was not acting in any official capacity, but realistically I thought it was important that it be made absolutely clear to the Vietnamese that I was not encouraging them to stall the peace talks while waiting for the outcome of the election. I would have dispatched someone to give them this message in any case, but I asked Salinger because he was about to leave for Paris, because he was a well-known figure whose word would carry sufficient weight, and because the assignment might ease some of his disappointment over the national-committee vice chairmanship. I would probably not have been in such a hurry to send him if it had not been for that episode.

The problem was that Pierre told a French reporter about the results of his discussion with the Vietnamese before he told me. Three weeks after he left, on August 16, I was handed a UPI dispatch, fresh off the ticker from Paris. I was in a hotel room in Springfield, Illinois; within minutes, I was scheduled to visit the Illinois State Fair. Salinger was quoted as telling the North Vietnamese that they would be better off negotiating with Nixon than with me. I was perplexed. I certainly didn't think that Nixon would be better at negotiating peace than I would. I didn't understand why Salinger would tell the Vietnamese that, if in fact he had. Pierre himself could not be reached; he was in an airplane over the Atlantic on his way back to the United States.

As I stepped off an elevator into the hotel lobby, facing a fusillade of popping flash bulbs and a bank of television lights and cameras, the press insistently pursued the Salinger dispatch. I tried varied forms of noncommittal answers, attempting to win time so I could talk with Salinger and find out exactly what had happened. I certainly did not send him to Paris, I said, to tell the Vietnamese that they were better off negotiating with Nixon. Did you send him to Paris at all? the reporters asked. "I have nothing to say on that," I replied. But with the press in hot pursuit, with no way to reach Salinger, and no way to escape the continuing questions, I irritably went too far. I said that I had no idea where Salinger had gotten any instruction like the one described in the UPI report. I added that I knew nothing about the whole matter.

Technically that may have been true: I did not know, indeed I was surprised, about the enterprise as it was being described. Nonetheless, I should have stuck with "No comment" no matter how relentless the press badgering became; by that evening, the content of the original dispatch would be forgotten and the technical truth would be interpreted as another mark against my credibility. Back at the hotel from the fairgrounds, I talked on the phone to Salinger, who had just landed in New York. He explained that he had told the Vietnamese not that it would be better to negotiate with Nixon than with me, but that I would rather have them do so than prolong the war. They had raised the possibility that they might obtain easier peace terms, he said, by holding out and hoping for a McGovern victory. He had replied that if they could end the war, they should do it immediately. A French reporter had heard about the meeting and talked to Salinger, but by the time the story reached UPI it had been garbled. Thus I thought I was denying an absurd statement—that the re-election of Nixon would bring a better chance for peace. Following the conversation with Salinger, I immediately issued a clarification. In the network news and in the papers, though, the story appeared as another McGovern reversal: the Democratic candidate first had denied and then confirmed assigning Salinger to contact the North Vietnamese.

The Salinger problem began before the Eagleton crisis and ended after it. In the intervening period, the arduous task of selecting a vice-presidential candidate to replace Eagleton had further deepened the doubts about my capacity for decisive leadership. Concerned about the disunity in the party, I consulted a broad range of prominent Democrats about the choice. I asked several of them, including Governor Reubin Askew of Florida, Senator Humphrey and Senator Muskie, for a second time whether they would be willing to accept the vice presidency. I had already asked Senator Mansfield, who would have been a reassuring choice to the party and the country and who never told the press of his refusal. My first choice after that was Ted Kennedy, who had been my first choice at the convention. Kennedy, Senator John Tunney and I discussed the matter for over an hour in Secretary of the Senate Frank Valeo's office. Kennedy seemed about to accept. His face was flushed; he looked and sounded as if he was grappling with the possibility. It was not one of those times where he simply said, "No, I'm not going to do it." Instead this time he said, "I don't know." He conceded that his presence on the ticket might be one of the only ways to rescue the Eagleton tangle. Pacing the floor, he noted that one of his friends had told him that he could be in the Cabinet and also be Vice President. I replied that if that was the problem, we could work it out. He said he wasn't sure what his family would think. So I stated the case again as forcefully as I could. Tunney, who had repeatedly urged him to accept, added, "Ted, I think you ought to do it. You and George could put this thing together." Looking at me, Kennedy said, "You're awfully persuasive. You make it hard." By now, he was sitting down. Abruptly he stood up, walked over to my chair and shook my hand. I thought he was about to agree, that we were shaking on it. "George, I just can't do it," he said instead. "I'm very disappointed," I answered. "I thought you were going to do it." In a low voice he concluded, "I just don't know—I just don't see how I can."

I turned next to Hubert Humphrey. We met for breakfast in the Senate Dining Room. I offered my arguments and Humphrey listened attentively. He was obviously sympathetic with my dilemma,

but all those years of seeking the presidency, and all the disappointments, had left him scarred. "I just can't take the ridicule anymore,"
he pleaded. "You know that if I take that nomination, they'll say
there goes old Hubert over the track again; he just can't resist running." He reiterated, "I can't take that ridicule again."

That afternoon I called Lyndon Johnson on the phone to ask his
advice. First he asked me a question: "Did you get my telegram?"
I realized immediately that Johnson had sent me a telegram congratulating me on my nomination, but I had never seen it. (It was
later found at the bottom of an avalanche of congratulatory tele-
grams which had been shipped back from Miami to Washington
unopened.) He then moved to the subject of the vice-presidential
choice. "Well, let me tell you now," Johnson started, "there are three
things you have to find in a Vice President." He spoke with the
typical Johnsonian earthiness he seldom used in public. "Far and
away the most important thing is loyalty to you. You don't want some
bastard in there stabbing you in the back who will blast the first thing
you do that he doesn't like. Second," he continued, "you don't want
some guy that's going to be using it as a base to mount a campaign
of his own, campaigning all the while he's in the vice presidency. He
shouldn't be badmouthing your program, neither should he be
spending his time running his own campaign." There was one consideration, Johnson added, above all others: "You want somebody capable of taking over on a moment's notice. One bullet," he said, referring to John Kennedy's assassination, "and all of a sudden I'm in
charge."

I told Johnson I had Ed Muskie in mind, and he responded that
Muskie would be good. I then asked him about Sargent Shriver. "I
would have gotten Sarge," he answered, "if it hadn't been for the fact
that the rest of the Kennedy tribe would have raised hell. I would like
to have had Sarge for my running mate. You couldn't do any better
than him. He's a good man." I thanked Johnson and told him that I
wanted to come down and see him soon. He sounded enthusiastic
about the idea: "Anytime, I would love to have you down here. Lady
Bird and I will be glad to have you stay with us. We'll do anything
we can to help."

That evening I met Muskie at his home outside Washington. By
this time it was clear that all the consulting (I had been criticized
after the convention for not doing enough) and the number of refus-
als I had received were becoming another problem. I tried to be
open about the process, to be thorough and careful, but the price of
the publicity was getting to be too high. So the Secret Service
managed to smuggle me out of my own house, past the reporters, and
drive me to Muskie's without anyone knowing it. Muskie began by

joking gruffly: "I wondered when you were going to get to me." It obviously bothered him that I had asked others first. But, to my relief, he said that he would like to take the vice-presidential nomination. He had only one caveat: he didn't know what his wife, Jane, would think about it, so he would fly to their vacation home in Maine and ask her. The next morning he called a press conference there, announced that I had offered him the second spot on the ticket and that he was declining it.

I immediately called Sarge Shriver, who was later to quip that he was my "seventh choice." He would have been higher on the list, both in this period and at the convention (where I almost asked him anyway before I found out that he was in Moscow), except for the impression that the choice would not sit well with some members of the Kennedy family whose enthusiastic help in the campaign was needed. Ted Kennedy had been reservedly resistant to the idea when I raised it with him; like Johnson, Hubert Humphrey had told me that he had experienced similar opposition to selecting Shriver as his running mate in 1968. But I had stopped worrying about that. When I asked Sarge if he would accept the vice-presidential nomination, he immediately replied, "I sure would." Mindful of the Eagleton problem, I said, "You know what we've just been through. Can you think of *anything* that could possibly embarrass us again?" Sarge light-heartedly confessed to one difficulty—that there was "a little squib in a Paris paper about me dancing at some night club with someone other than Eunice. That's all I can think of." That kind of non-problem was a relief after the disasters of the preceding weeks, and it was good tonic for my beleaguered spirit. In any case, I was hardly worried about Shriver's background; as a high official of the Kennedy and Johnson Administrations, he had undergone repeated background checks. Laughing, I replied to his comment about the night-club episode, "That ought to be good for a few votes in some parts of the country."

I suppose that for me August was the cruelest month, at least of 1972. Not only did I face the Eagleton crisis and its troublesome aftermath and the Salinger episode, but there were also a series of squabbles inside the campaign that made their way into the headlines. Congressman Frank Thompson of New Jersey resigned as director of the voter-registration drive, a project he had first undertaken for John Kennedy in 1960. He complained that the McGovern campaign was not providing him with sufficient financial resources. The stark fact was that at this low point we had hardly any money. Liberal activist Anne Wexler, now Deputy Under-Secretary of Commerce in the Carter Administration, took over from Thompson and ultimately registered several million new voters. Larry O'Brien also told the press that he would be gone by September if certain changes were not made in the campaign. At a later date Gordon Weil, who had traveled with me during the primaries, tried to resign quietly from his new duties in Washington. When the news was leaked to the press, he returned to the campaign. (After the election, it nagged at me occasionally that leaks about such minor problems in the McGovern campaign were front-page news, while leaks during the same period about White House involvement in Watergate were virtually ignored except in the Washington *Post.*) After the rash of stories about staff in-fighting, "the brilliant McGovern machine"—a media exaggeration of the late spring and early summer—had become "the inept McGovern operation." All presidential campaigns have a greater or lesser degree of internal squabbling; ours came to seem more important because it was, as Pat Caddell put it, seen through the lens of all the other disarray, particularly the Eagleton affair.

I was never to escape that prism. By Labor Day I was beginning a long uphill climb from even farther down than I had been a month before in the midst of the Eagleton crisis. Wistfully I thought back to May, when a Harris poll had showed me only 6 points behind Nixon. I recalled Caddell's poll at the time of the convention, which showed that 40 percent of the Nixon voters were "soft": they wanted to know more about me before they made up their minds. They didn't like what they now perceived, and only 6 per cent of them wanted to know more. As I spoke to union groups on Labor Day, an old tradition for Democratic candidates, I also reflected sadly on the AFL-CIO's decision to remain neutral in the contest.

After the convention I had worked hard to conciliate disaffected Democrats. The labor movement was a special concern. I tried, unsuccessfully, to obtain an appointment with AFL-CIO president George Meany. At a subsequent meeting of his executive council he announced that there were no significant differences between Nixon and me. I could understand Meany's dislike for my position on the war; he had supported the war from the beginning. But on the issues of concern to labor, it was absurd to say that there was no difference. According to the AFL-CIO's own scorekeeping, I had a positive rating through fourteen years in Congress of 93.5 percent. On seventy-six issues classified as "key," I voted right in all but five instances. Two of the five exceptions—my opposition to the SST and to the Lockheed loan—reflected the position taken by most senators whom the AFL-CIO would have been more than happy to support for President. By contrast, Richard Nixon's voting record in the Congress was almost the exact opposite—87 percent against labor. In this context, a neutral stance was an implicit message to union members to spurn the McGovern campaign.

Following the AFL-CIO executive council session, I met with four major union leaders: Floyd Smith, the president of the Machinists Union; Joe Beirne, the president of the Communications Workers; Joe Keenan, the former president of the International Brotherhood of Electrical Workers and the vice chairman of the AFL-CIO; and Paul Jennings, president of the International Union of Electrical, Radio and Machine Workers. Sitting in Joe Beirne's office, they asked me not to attack Meany. They promised to advise on the campaign schedule and to help with labor. They felt that a lot of labor could be persuaded to support me, and in the end, partly through their efforts, more than twenty international unions did endorse the Democratic ticket.

I was also determined to reach working men and women directly, but there was one obstacle that had to be overcome first. One of the Nixon campaign's most distorted commercials was to center on my proposal that the existing welfare system and the $750 individual tax exemption be replaced with a single uniform federal income guarantee of $1,000 per person each year. Although the proposal was not that different from Nixon's own Family Assistance Plan, his commercial pictured it as a scheme to force a working minority of Americans to support a welfare majority too lazy to work. The commercial was absurd on its face, but the anxiety to which it would appeal had to be allayed. In fact, by the time the commercial was shown, there no longer was a $1,000 plan. After a summer of effort, I had proposed a far-reaching but more readily comprehensible alternative.

As the controversy over the $1,000 plan mounted, I asked some of the leading economists as well as tax and welfare experts in the country to re-examine the whole area and develop an integrated program of tax and welfare reform. Finally I met with the group for an entire day at Ethel Kennedy's home. We decided which tax loopholes should be closed, which ones should be maintained, and which ones should be phased out gradually. We went through the same process on the welfare issue and determined that instead of implementing the $1,000 plan, direct grants would be paid, at least initially, only to those below the poverty level. Shortly afterward I received the first draft of a speech explaining those proposals, to be delivered on August 25 to a meeting of the Society of Security Analysts on Wall Street.

I had selected that forum not because I expected the business community to agree with tax and welfare reform, but because I believed it was important to make the case squarely and openly to them. Unfortunately, the first draft was so academic that I wasn't sure even securities experts would understand it, but I was sure that most Americans would not. Thus I might end up back where I was with the $1,000 plan—having a sensible program that didn't seem to make sense. I sent Bob Shrum to rework the speech with Gordon Weil, telling them to write a draft nonexperts could understand. After they labored for several days and nights, testing various formulations out on the economists and lawyers for accuracy, I spent an evening revising the speech line by line.

The reception from the security analysts was surprisingly cordial. The reaction in the press was favorable. *Time* magazine suggested that the speech had raised issues which would remain vital through the 1970s. The *New York Times* editorially praised the tax-reform proposals as the best ever offered by a presidential candidate. But the general public reaction demonstrated how hard it was for me to reach voters by then. A majority of them continued to assume that I was advocating the distorted caricature of the $1,000 dollar plan which they had heard about earlier. The Nixon commercial exploiting that caricature ran after, not before, the Wall Street speech. It was almost as though I had never given it.

At the same time, the shift away from the $1,000 plan disappointed some of my supporters. After the campaign Hunter Thompson, *Rolling Stone*'s brilliant mutation of the political journalist, was to blame my defeat partly on the fact that following the nomination, I had compromised too many previously forthright positions on issues such as welfare and tax reform. But the recommendations of the Wall Street speech were hardly easy compromises with the status quo. In any case, I know of no other issue on which my expressed views were different on election day from what they had been on the primary days of the preceding spring. Two other events, however, contributed to the impression that I was shifting.

The first was my visit to President Johnson. While I was not willing to yield my basic commitments, I was intent on reuniting the Democratic Party to the maximum possible extent. To me, visiting Johnson seemed both prudent and appropriate. He had telegraphed his congratulations after the nomination and he clearly had been glad to hear from me during the post-Eagleton vice-presidential selection.

On August 22 Sargent Shriver and I flew from the Austin airport in helicopters to the Johnson ranch. The President and Mrs. Johnson met us at the helipad and drove us in golf carts to the ranch house. From ten in the morning until noon, the four of us sat on the front lawn talking. Johnson began the conversation by saying, "Well, I know you think I'm crazy as hell on Vietnam. I think you are. So let's omit that. Instead, let's talk politics." Johnson argued that I should emphasize my personal background: "The thing you've got to do if you want to win this election is to let the American people know that you're proud of this country, that you're glad to be the nominee. Tell every audience how good America has been to you. Tell them the story of how a poor boy growing up in South Dakota got elected to the House and Senate, worked as special assistant to the President of the United States, and is now the head of the oldest political party in America. That's a dramatic and inspiring story of what America is —that a boy from South Dakota could rise to the most powerful nomination his country can give. Tell them that it was a privilege to serve your country as a pilot in World War II and that the same patriotic fervor that took you into the war has taken you into this campaign for the presidency."

Johnson emphasized the point repeatedly for half an hour. In one sense, it was a subtle comment on my Vietnam position. In effect, he was saying that I had to prove my patriotism, or at least point to it. As he concluded he leaned forward and spoke in that earnest tone that had become a famous part of the legendary "Johnson treatment": "I've read about you; you've had a remarkable life. Let the American people know about it. Let them know that you want to serve the nation, that you appreciate what the country means to you and tell them what you could do for the country as President."

I understood the problem Johnson was raising. There was a tradition of unquestioning support when America was involved in a war; for a long time, many had accepted the notion, almost without thinking about it, that political dissent should stop at the water's edge. Not only the Nixon campaign but Nixon's well-publicized attitude through his first term was designed to equate dissent with disloyalty. My acceptance speech had been carefully crafted to explain that my philosophy was based on the nation's deepest principles and values rather than being in opposition to them. But of course, few had seen or heard that speech which occurred at prime television time only in the Hawaiian time zone. Through the fall campaign, my stump speech almost invariably ended with a reference to my service as a bomber pilot in World War II. I used it to make the point that the Democratic prospect was not hopeless, telling how my plane was brought home to safety after being hit on a bombing run. Implicitly the tale also refuted the notion that opposition to the war was proof of cowardice or disloyalty.

Much as I appreciated Johnson's kind words, it was not in my nature to turn the campaign into a constant exercise in self-congratulatory autobiography. Nixon's repeated references to his Quaker mother, his father's store and to his own childhood "listening to the sound of a train in the night traveling to far-off places" had always struck me as contrived. Perhaps I was wrong, but I thought the appeal to the country should be made primarily on issues, not on the basis that my own life somehow symbolized the American dream. There were, and there are, many millions of Americans not as lucky as I have been. They, and the innocent Vietnamese and the young American draftees who were fighting the war, were matters that I believed had to be honestly, continually discussed through the campaign. My personal competence had become an issue, but my boyhood and my political success did not seem to me central to the true choice facing the voters.

Johnson also volunteered that his support for me was not *pro forma;* he really meant it: "Another thing I want you to know is that I'm for you. Some people have called me to say that they endorse Nixon. They seem to think that will make me happy. It doesn't make me happy. They came out for Nixon because they disapproved of your criticism of my policy in Vietnam, or at least that's what they tell me. But I'm a Democrat. You got my telegram and I meant it. You're the nominee of the party and I'm backing you." I responded that while I knew that Johnson had to watch his health, I would appreciate it if he could make a campaign appearance with me in Texas sometime during the campaign. I suggested a rally at the Astrodome in Houston. "If I'm up to it," he said, "I'll do it." I could sense a kind of sad nostalgia in his voice as he continued, "We'd fill that place if we did it, we really would." He cautioned that he would have to talk to his doctors, and as it turned out, this was to be the last time I would ever see him. The meeting that day would be the last national political event of Lyndon Johnson's life.

He did volunteer to make some phone calls for me and he added that I ought to get on the phone and stay there: "You know, in 1960 when Kennedy put me on that ticket, I got on that phone and called people all over the South. I never let a day go by that I didn't make those phone calls for Kennedy. That made a difference. You should be calling people all over the country. Get your staff to give you the names. There are a lot of wounds to be healed and the telephone is a great healer." We went into the ranch house for lunch. Johnson had been chain-smoking all through our earlier conversation and he smoked continuously while he ate his steak. After each bite he would light another cigarette. Lady Bird combined a note of sadness and resignation about his smoking. Suddenly it dawned on me that both she and he knew that he was going to die soon, so he had made a decision that he was going to smoke incessantly, a habit he had given up after his 1955 heart attack. He told me that he was able to make it through the morning without intense chest pains, but around noon they would start. He would be in pain all through the afternoon and into the night.

Johnson reminisced about his political career for a while after lunch. At midafternoon Shriver and I said goodbye to him and went to the Johnson Library for a news conference. Doug Kneeland of the *New York Times* told me later that he had spent hours trying to think up a tough question to throw at me while I was in Texas on the heels of the Johnson visit. His tough question was whether I welcomed Johnson's support. I said that of course I did. Some of the reporters seemed surprised; they had expected that I would qualify my answer because of Vietnam. But I had almost the opposite reaction. I felt here was a man, an ex-President, a genuine old-fashioned, honest-to-God Democrat, who was supporting the ticket even though the nominee was someone who fought his war policy. He was going out of his way to emphasize that he was no "Democrat for Nixon." I also felt a special empathy for him that day. Here was this imposing figure who had offered so great a prospect of domestic reform, seeing his Great Society being dismantled as he himself was slowly dying. I was struck by the fact that he had let his hair grow. I thought to myself how odd it was that long hair had become a mark of the war protesters, and now a chief architect of that war had let his hair grow as long as my son's. It was down to his shoulders. Except for Vietnam, I reflected, this outsized Texan, with his blend of patriotism and compassion, with his programs for civil rights, education and economic opportunity, would have been a hero to all of those long-haired kids. As we talked that day Johnson had avoided Vietnam, but he had also spent a lot of time talking of his record on other issues, as though he were trying to justify to me his place in history. I thought how sad it was that this great bundle of ambition and energy had been consumed by the war.

Afterward, on a TV interview, I commented that Johnson was not responsible for the intervention in Vietnam as such. Some of my supporters were angry, but to me that was a simple fact. Johnson did not conceive of the war or of the premises on which it was based. He inherited it, and unfortunately, he lacked the flexibility and self-confidence that might have enabled a John Kennedy to extricate himself from it. Johnson's wheeling and dealing, his misleading statements on the war, into which he partly may have been misled by his advisers and by his own determination to win, nurtured the crisis of credibility that brought such disastrous results in the 1970s. But I don't know and I doubt that there is a way ever to know whether the United States would have gone into Vietnam if Lyndon Johnson had been President when the initial decisions were made.

The next disappointment for some liberals came when Mayor Richard Daley of Chicago endorsed me and I simultaneously endorsed his local Democratic slate, which included State's Attorney Edward Hanrahan, who had played so brutal a role during the peace demonstrations at the 1968 Democratic convention and who was responsible for the raid in which Fred Hampton, the Black Panther, was gunned down. Daley and I talked in August and arranged an appearance for me before the Cook County Democratic Committee. The mayor told me that he would support the ticket with the understanding that I would do the same. I vividly remember that meeting, which took place at the Sherman House hotel in Chicago. It was early September, the wounds of the organization's expulsion from the convention still smarted, but the "Cook County democracy," as Daley called it, received me warmly. It was almost as though the mayor was actually giving the signals from the podium. The committee members were all on their best behavior. I remember noticing how much they all looked alike as they applauded in tandem. They all seemed to be middle-aged, red-faced, heavy-set males. There was a lot of cigar smoke in that room, a lot of beef.

The reporters pressed me hard about Hanrahan. They asked if I was for him. I replied that as the Democratic standard-bearer I was supporting the ticket from top to bottom. Perhaps it was a rationalization, but it seemed a necessary and bearable price for Daley's help. The people who might take my advice were unlikely to vote for Hanrahan anyway and I also recognized Daley's dilemma. There were many in his own organization who would just as soon have forgotten the presidential race.

When Richard Daley died just before Christmas of 1976, I attended his funeral at his parish church in the Bridgeport neighborhood of Chicago. He and I were very different men. But I respected him for what he was—a nuts-and-bolts politician to whom party and personal loyalty took precedence over immediate issues. In national politics, he could go any of a number of ways for a variety of reasons. Ironically, in 1968, he could have emerged as the hero of the peace movement if Robert Kennedy had lived and Daley had helped to engineer his nomination. After I was the nominee in 1972, he did his duty as a Democrat—and perhaps a little more. He spoke for me in Chicago and we talked whenever I was there. He came to my hotel suite at the Palmer House to watch with me the television speech I had taped on Vietnam. When it was over, he said, "God, that was a hell of a speech." He explained that he was never really for the war. I noted that the Chicago City Council had passed a resolution urging American withdrawal from Indochina. "Oh yes, they did that sometime ago," he answered, then paused and added, "with my approval."

*   *   *

After the nomination the conventional wisdom was that my first task would be to reunite the party and reassure the electorate about myself. Yet each step toward those goals seemed to be frustrated or to become counterproductive. If a woman was to chair the national committee, then the regulars would be angered and the blacks would demand the vice chairmanship, indirectly leading to the apparent reversal within hours of my statements on the Salinger mission. If Tom Eagleton was chosen too casually, as the critics charged, then too many Democratic leaders were consulted too long in picking his replacement, as the critics also charged. If the McGovern campaign seemed purist because the AFL-CIO and Richard Daley were not part of the nomination victory, then I seemed tainted by seeking Daley's and Lyndon Johnson's help in the fall. At the time I attributed some of these reactions to a self-imposed high standard: apparently, a campaign "right from the start" was not supposed to make mistakes or compromises. I had pledged "to seek and speak the truth." Yet in 1976, when Jimmy Carter ran against the bosses and then embraced their support, there was hardly a murmur in the media. There were doubtless some mistakes in 1972—there are in every campaign—especially in the grim six weeks between the convention and Labor Day, but during that period I couldn't help thinking that fate, too, was against us.

The most depressed I felt before the election itself was one morning following those six weeks as I sat and read Haynes Johnson and David Broder's survey of voter attitudes in the ten largest states for the Washington *Post*. They found that most Americans had little confidence in either political party, but a majority were voting for Richard Nixon because they regarded him as a more reliable man than I was. I was staggered; I honestly could not recognize my own character in the voter comments quoted in the article. Frank Szabo of Cleveland was typical: "I voted for McGovern in the primary primarily because I didn't know much about him. Now I think he's two-faced." Haynes Johnson noted that Szabo, "like so many voters encountered traces his first disillusionment with the South Dakota Senator to one incident—the dropping of Senator Tom Eagleton of Missouri from the Democratic ticket. . . . If there is a single factor that has altered the course of the campaign to date, it is the Eagleton affair. From it flows most of the problems McGovern has met." Johnson reported that Watergate and the Nixon corruption were a nonissue: "Each of us would go for days of interviewing voters without hearing a single voter voluntarily bring up the Watergate issue. And that in spite of the fact the Democrats and McGovern personally have been hammering at the case almost daily." Vietnam was hardly mentioned. "We met relatively few voters who talked either about the intensive bombing now going on over North Vietnam," Johnson wrote, "or the number of American casualties since Richard Nixon was inaugurated." The voters did perceive many national problems —inflation, crime, drugs, declining neighborhoods—but they tended to view them as beyond the reach of any politician—"as merely part of a social malaise for which no man or party is responsible." I was perceived as "promising too much" and "shifting his positions." Nixon was steadier, he was trying, he was more dependable.

Why not give up? Of course, no nominee for the presidency ever really does until the votes are cast and counted. First, there is the example of Harry Truman (and now of Gerald Ford, who, though he lost, gained an incredible 28 points between July and Election Day). Truman's miracle represents the hope that somehow the tide can be turned. Second, at least in my case, I was convinced that the choices before the country were fundamental; I held to the possibility that if the voters could be made to understand them, if they could be made to understand the implications of Watergate, the hard truth about Vietnam, the stark facts of economic injustice, I would have a chance. In any event, I felt those issues had to be discussed—and that there was no image-making trick, no hidden political persuader, that could bring victory any closer than an all-out effort to reach the people with the truth as I saw it.

However, since time was short and I was far behind, we adopted a strategy of concentrating on the large industrial states and virtually ignoring the South. My visit to the Southern Governors' Conference, the first stop of the fall campaign, was also the last faint showing of the flag in that region except for stops in Texas and a rally at Little Rock in October. After my session with the Southern governors, I talked with Senator Fritz Hollings of South Carolina. He said that he hoped I had enjoyed my visit, but agreed that I had little chance to carry any Southern state. Then he added a compliment that I have always treasured: "You and I have differences on some of the issues, but of all the candidates that are seeking the presidency this year, you clearly have the most inspired vision of the country's greatness. In fact, you are the only one who has a real sense of the historic greatness of America."

The strategy of writing off an entire region bothered me. A candidate for the presidency ought to run nationwide. But, pragmatically, the McGovern campaign's non-Southern strategy in 1972 was correct. The shooting of Governor George Wallace in May had eliminated the possibility that he would be an independent presidential candidate, as he had been in 1968. If Wallace had contested the general election, he might have drawn enough votes from Nixon to make it at least close. The largest share of the difference between the vote spread in 1968 and 1972 was the Wallace vote. I was to receive approximately the same number of votes that Humphrey had garnered four years earlier, and in several Northern states I bettered his percentage. Through his first term, Nixon implemented a Southern strategy designed to attract the Wallace supporters. In addition to purveying a barely disguised racism, Nixon's rhetoric played upon other Wallace themes: the backlash against the poor, the fear of alternative life styles, especially among the young, and the sense that student protests and press criticism of the Vietnam war were a form of aid and comfort to the enemy. For this appeal to achieve maximum potential, it was important that Wallace not engage in another third-party bid. Then fate in the person of a social misfit named Arthur Bremer appeared to take care of that. The most serious barrier to a Nixon landslide was eliminated. According to post-election analyses, most of the potential Wallace vote shifted to Nixon.

Although George Wallace was at the extreme right of the political spectrum, I admired his grit and determination after the assassination attempt. What made it harder for him, I was to discover later, was his sense of suspicion that the attempt might have been more than the crazed act of a lone lunatic. Wallace and one of his close aides told me that there were too many holes in the official explanation. They pointed out that the diary of Arthur Bremer, which indicated that he had stalked both Richard Nixon and me before shooting the Alabama governor, was a document of questionable authenticity. They also wondered about the haste of White House aide Charles Colson in ordering a quick search of Bremer's apartment right after the shooting. The attempt on Wallace was another in a series of assassinations that have never been sufficiently explained to quiet reasonable public doubts about who were involved and their motivations. Those doubts cannot be laid to rest at all except by an independent, nonpolitical investigation conducted by competent personnel who have no stake in particular theories and previous official explanations.

I did seek George Wallace's endorsement. That substantial help represented my only slim hope in the South. I talked with him about an endorsement several times, though I knew he was unlikely to give it. Each conversation was essentially the same. During one of them Wallace said, "You know, the problem, George, is that our people, even if I was to endorse you, I couldn't get them to support you if you weren't right on the issues. A lot of these issues people feel strongly about. It could end up hurting both of us." I asked him what specific issues bothered him most. First he cited my advocacy of military cuts and my opposition to the war. Then he went on, "The busing thing bothers a lot of people. The whole question of people that won't work and want to live on the government. There's just too much distance between your views and mine on those things." Obviously Wallace was no party loyalist, nor was he prepared to jeopardize his own constituency by endorsing a candidate so ideologically opposite. He observed, and he was probably right, that he could not swing his voters to me even if he tried. After several such discussions I dropped the matter. In truth, Wallace was handling me as I would have handled him if our situations had been reversed.

My only chance, then, was an intense effort in the traditionally Democratic Northern states and on the Pacific Coast. Gary Hart, Frank Mankiewicz and scheduling director Steve Robbins planned a relentless blitz, taking me by jet to three or four major cities a day. The days often began at the crack of dawn and ended at three in the morning. The Labor Day schedule set the pace. I started with two rallies in Ohio, flew to an early evening rally in Oakland, California, and then on to a late-night rally in downtown Seattle. That twenty-hour odyssey involved four thousand miles of travel and four major speeches. After three and a half or four hours of sleep, the staff, the reporters and I took off for San Francisco the next morning.

On September 11 Ted Kennedy joined us in Minneapolis. Fifteen thousand people jammed the Municipal Auditorium to overflowing. In introducing Kennedy, Governor Wendell Anderson, now a senator from Minnesota, made an embarrassing slip. He referred to Kennedy as the man who would be back in Minneapolis in 1976 as the Democratic nominee for President. Ted quickly corrected the faux pas, beginning his speech with a ringing declaration that he would indeed be back there—campaigning for the re-election of George McGovern. Within the next forty hours Kennedy stumped through four cities with me. He told me that the crowds were the best he had ever seen in a campaign, the largest and the most enthusiastic. He repeatedly complimented the advance operation and noted that my themes seemed to be striking a responsive chord among the crowds.

Ted Kennedy is one of the best campaign speakers in America. So it was especially encouraging that the people at our joint appearances seemed to be applauding me as often, as long and as loudly, and after Kennedy left, the crowds kept coming. It was not unusual for me to speak to tens of thousands at a single rally. Sarge Shriver was also getting enthusiastic receptions. This continued, despite the polls, all the way to Election Day. Some normally skeptical reporters were so impressed that they believed to the very end that if I didn't win, it would be a close contest. The crowds were partly a reflection of the deep commitment of many McGovern supporters. They were also a result of Steve Robbins' superb advance team. When it was all over, I recalled the Will Rogers line about Aimee Semple McPherson, the California evangelist of the 1930s—that, remarkably, she baptized fifty thousand people at Silver Lake every week. But it was the same fifty thousand each week, Rogers quipped. Veterans of the 1972 campaign still joke about Robbins moving the same thousands from stop to stop in a fleet of 747s.

Ed Muskie and Hubert Humphrey also took turns with me on the campaign trail. After Ed delivered a fiery speech in Pittsburgh which set the crowd to stomping and whistling, I told him that he seemed to be speaking much more effectively for me than he had for himself during the primaries. He responded that he had heard that before. He thought he had been better in 1968 as the vice-presidential candidate than campaigning for himself in 1972. Muskie and I had not known each other well, but during the two days he was on the campaign plane, we talked at length. We both expressed regret that we had not been closer all along. I came to like Ed very much. He is a decent and extraordinarily able man, and we have had a happy relationship ever since those two days together on the campaign trail.

Understandably, Hubert Humphrey seemed to find the experience of campaigning for me that fall a painful one. He had been over the same ground so many times. He had been contending for the national ticket since 1956, when he lost the vice-presidential nomination, through a presidential run in 1960, a 1964 vice-presidential victory and a 1968 defeat for the presidency. Fifteen years before, I had been his protégé and now he was campaigning for me after I had won the nomination he so badly wanted. But he spoke with his inimitable energy and flare. Privately, he advised me over dinner at the Minnesota Governor's Mansion in St. Paul that I ought to emphasize economic issues almost exclusively. He argued with that special force he has that Vietnam was no longer a critical concern among voters. My positions on defense cuts, amnesty and Watergate might hurt more than they helped. Of the three issues I had identified as central —the war, corruption and special-interest economics—he thought only the last one had any real political mileage in it. The rest should be dropped.

Kennedy, Humphrey and Muskie all rode with me in the front compartment of the campaign plane, a specially equipped 727. More than the hotel rooms in which I caught a few hours' sleep each night, that compartment seemed like home from September 4 through November 7. On one side there was a sofa where I occasionally took a brief nap. On the other I sat in a reclining chair at a fold-down table with two seats facing me on the opposite side of the table. The Secret

Service and the press filled the other two thirds of the plane. A second chartered jet carried the network cameramen and their equipment and the press overflow.

The staff had seats in the second compartment of the plane I was on, but they also had free access to me. Though I sometimes would have preferred solitude, I have never believed that a presidential candidate—or a President—should be isolated from a continual and spirited exchange of views. My traveling staff in 1972 was relatively small and exceptionally hard-working. Frank Mankiewicz was on the plane much of the time, in the thick of every staff discussion. He also conducted a running dialogue with the reporters, whom he alternately informed, humored and debated. His matchless humor and steady flow of "one-liners" was a treasured resource throughout the hardest months of the campaign. Jeff Smith, a twenty-eight-year-old alumnus of Robert Kennedy's 1968 campaign, handled the administrative chores efficiently and without abrasiveness—a rare combination in that role. The affectionate bond between Jeff and me was a special joy. Gordon Weil, who had a reputation for being abrasive, never once showed that side of his nature to me. For two years before the nomination he was constantly at my side. During the fall he functioned as a general-purpose man—capable of drafting a speech, checking a schedule, briefing me thoroughly on virtually any issue and untangling unexpected snafus. Early in 1971 I acquired a canvas zipper bag that was capable of enclosing three or four times as many papers as an ordinary briefcase. As the months sped by, that bag acquired more and more staff memos, speech drafts, personal notes, underlined magazines, etc. Day after day Gordon carried, guarded and worried over that bag, which contained my "brains" and much of my inspiration. Dubbing it "the heavy bag," he doubtless came to despise it, but he never once complained, nor did he ever once forget to follow up on a promise, an order or a detail within his responsibility. That is why I defended him against any and all critics.

Fred Dutton, an aide to the governor of California in the late fifties and to John Kennedy in the early sixties, and a one-time Secretary of the Cabinet and Assistant Secretary of State, was an invaluable adviser. He never wasted any time. Typically, he reduced his thoughts to writing, and the memos were almost invariably creative. Though he sometimes suggested more than I or any candidate could have done, he was a good friend who anticipated problems and recommended solutions in advance. His sense of the issues was first rate. By the end of the campaign he was restless and dissatisfied, and in retrospect, I should have made greater use of Fred's special talents.

My press secretary, Dick Dougherty, was a delightful human

being, both the wise man and the Puck of the campaign plane. He was fifty, my age, and he often joked that we were "the two old men" —a chronological seniority that Dick obviously gloried in. He had an irreverent sense of humor. The night of my Massachusetts primary victory he had suggested that I quote a line from William Butler Yeats: " 'Think where man's glory most begins and ends, and say, my glory was I had such friends.' " One September afternoon, following all the stories about staff squabbles, Dick and I were chatting casually and I told him again how much I liked that line. Without missing a beat, he replied, "Why don't you use it the next time somebody resigns?"

As the plane hurtled from city to city, three young writers steadily turned out speech material. John Holum had been with me since 1965; Bob Shrum and Sandy Berger both had joined the campaign in the late spring. They occasionally laughed that they were proof that you didn't have to be "right from the start." Bob had worked first for Ed Muskie, and Sandy for John Lindsay. I developed a basic stump speech which I delivered at almost every rally; the writers provided inserts on the issues I wanted to emphasize on any given day. I also acquired the habit of telling the crowd at each stop about the best of the hand-lettered signs that I could spot from the podium. There were always a lot of them and many were more creative than the slogans of the professional advertising experts. One night in Carbondale, Illinois, I was standing on a makeshift platform, with the television lights blinding me at first. As my vision cleared and I started to speak, I noticed a teen-age girl with an angelic face in the first row waving a sign that read: "Vote for McGovern—not an asshole." I smiled and decided not to repeat that one; my one public profanity was not to come until several weeks later.

I also made a major-issues speech every three or four days. Rereading those speeches now, I am struck by how well they stand the test of time. One of them bluntly warned that "the Nixon Administration is the most corrupt Administration in our national history." Another described the "needless continuance of the slaughter in Vietnam" and argued that "American prisoners of war in Vietnam will be released only if we end the war—a process that can be completed in less than ninety days." The speeches itemized military waste and the inequities of our tax system—"a system that permits a corporate executive to deduct his twenty-dollar martini lunch, while a working man can't deduct his baloney sandwich." (After hearing that line over and over, one September afternoon the reporters presented me with a tray containing both a martini and a baloney sandwich. I took my revenge soon enough by amending the line to read "While Carl Leubsdorf cannot deduct the cost of his baloney sandwich." Leubsdorf, as I did not explain to the crowd, was an AP reporter. The press became so familiar with the line that they started silently mouthing it as I said it. To throw them off a little, I began to vary the kind of sandwich; it ranged from cheese to peanut butter to salami.)

On September 8, in a speech at Superior, Wisconsin, I indicted the terms of the Nixon Administration's wheat deal with the Soviet Union. Its timing made it another special deal for vested interests, in this case a few giant grain traders. The announcement of the sale to the Soviet Union had been delayed while farmers sold their grain at relatively low prices. When the sale was revealed and prices rose, vast quantities of wheat were already in the storehouses of the grain companies. An Administration official who had helped negotiate the deal with the Soviets had returned to one of those companies; his replacement at the Agriculture Department was another grain-company employee. It was a classic case of the revolving door between business and government that was to continue turning over the next several years; Nixon Administration appointees were rewarded for inside information with high-paying jobs.

Walter Cronkite did a special report on the wheat deal as part of the CBS evening news. It was a closely guarded deal that cost consumers and farmers billions of dollars, but most of the press ignored the story. Perhaps grain trading was too complicated and technical for political reporters. It was also one of those rural issues, like parity and farm price supports, that urban Americans usually do not even try to comprehend. In the end, the wheat deal inflated the cost of living, but cost Nixon very few votes.

But my problem was not merely a failure to communicate on a technical, rural issue. As the days sped by, it became clear that while the crowds coming to the rallies were responding, I was not reaching the vast majority of voters who see and hear candidates only on television and radio. It was not just a matter of what I was doing, but of what Nixon was avoiding. He confined his campaigning to a few appearances mostly before closed audiences admitted by ticket only. I repeatedly challenged him to debate, but he never even acknowledged the challenges, despite his promise in 1968, when he expected to be running against an incumbent President and wanted to debate, that he would participate in such an exchange in his own re-election campaign. Nixon held only one press conference in the fall of 1972. Yet the television networks interpreted the "fairness rule" to mean that every minute of television coverage of me had to be "balanced" with a minute-long reporting on Nixon's surrogates such as GOP National Chairman Clark MacGregor or Secretary of Agriculture Earl Butz. I protested this interpretation of news "balance," which Sander Vanocur, a veteran TV newsman, described as having been made by "one of the network vice presidents in charge of fear."

Privately most reporters were bothered by this situation. One night NBC's Cassie Mackin decided to do something about it. She was reporting on a closed Nixon speech on September 28, in which Nixon distorted my positions and then attacked them. She commented: "There is a serious question of whether President Nixon is setting up straw men by leaving the very strong impression that McGovern is making certain proposals which in fact he is not." The film then showed Nixon telling his audience about "some" (he never referred to me by name in the entire campaign) who were advocating cuts in the defense budget that would leave the United States "the second strongest nation in the world." Mackin observed: "The President obviously meant McGovern's proposed defense budget but his criticism never specified how the McGovern plan would weaken the country." Mackin continued: "On welfare the President accuses McGovern of wanting to give those on welfare more than those who work—which is not true. On tax reform the President says McGovern has called for confiscation of wealth—which is not true."

Three White House aides who were monitoring the telecast called NBC. In panic, network executives demanded that Mackin produce full proof for everything she had said. Probably no minute-and-a-half news report in television history had to be so thoroughly proved. Mackin provided the proof, but after Nixon's re-election she was transferred from the Washington bureau to the West Coast. Six months later, with the Watergate scandal cresting, NBC thought better of the transfer and brought her back to Washington.

Cassie Mackin's report was unique in the campaign. It, and Walter Cronkite's review of the wheat deal and later of the Watergate charges, was the closest television came to analyzing the issues instead of repeating the Nixon charges, no matter how inaccurate the networks own journalists knew them to be. At the same time, the paid Nixon media were reinforcing the worst distortions. There were other commercials, similar to the one implying that I would put half the country on welfare. Another showed a hand knocking half the American army, navy and air force off a board. It alleged that my military-spending cutback was the equivalent of unilateral disarmament—which was hardly the position of former Secretary of Defense Clark Clifford, former Marine Corps Commandant David Shoup and arms-control expert Paul Warnke, all of whom generally supported the plan. A third commercial depicted me as a spinning coin displaying first one face and then another.

Beyond all this was the massive inattention to the Nixon Administration's corruption. The story of ITT's special favors and the details of the wheat deal were public before the election. So were glaring violations of the campaign finance laws, revelations of suitcases filled with cash being delivered to high officials of the Nixon re-election committee, the laundering of campaign cash in Mexico, the illegal use of corporate funds, and persuasive evidence of White House involvement in the Watergate break-in. Yet none of this seemed to command substantial press attention or to bother the American people.

The Washington *Post* was reporting on Watergate regularly, but the rest of the press was downplaying the story, perhaps out of professional jealousy or fear of later Administration reprisals. (The fear was justified: following Nixon's re-election, several of his supporters filed challenges with the FCC to the *Post*'s ownership of television stations.) The Washington *Post* stories were clipped each day and telecopied to my campaign plane. To get other papers to reprint the allegations, I took to repeating them in my speeches. Typically the resulting stories began: "Senator George McGovern today charged, on the basis of reports in the Washington *Post*, that . . ."

The polls were barely moving and the Nixon campaign was successfully exploiting the media. By late September it was obvious that I had to attempt to reach the voters in a different way. Visiting three or four cities or towns a day was not enough, yet that brutal pace could not be stepped up. I had to communicate with more Americans in a shorter time.

I had first discussed the idea of national fireside chats on television during the convention. But in the wake of the Eagleton crisis, finance director Henry Kimelman reported that there was very little money. (Indeed at one point the campaign planes kept flying largely due to the generosity of two idealistic young men, Dan and Nick Noyes, who were heirs to the Lilly drug fortune. Their grandfather was treasurer of the Nixon committee in Indiana; one afternoon they called Bill Rosendahl, a tireless, rumpled fund raiser who was only twenty-five years old himself, and said that they were thinking of contributing several hundred thousand dollars.) Media adviser Charles Guggenheim was skeptical of the fireside chats. He thought that what money we had could be spent more effectively on thirty-and sixty-second spots. Gary Hart was worried that preparing and filming television addresses would take time off the campaign trail.

New Yorker writer Jonathan Schell, who later wrote an insightful study of the Nixon years, *The Time of Illusion*, rode on the campaign plane for two weeks in early September. He pressed the case for fireside chats strongly. I was becoming more and more convinced of the worth of the idea. The decisive factor was a call from Eleanor. She asked whether I had seen myself on the nightly news. Though the rallies might be effective with those in the immediate audience, the main themes of the campaign were not coming through in brief television reports, which were always followed by film of another Nixon surrogate blasting me. She urged me to sit down in front of a camera and talk quietly to the American people. With a wife's bias, she was confident that it would help the campaign to "let them know the kind of person you are."

I told Guggenheim to buy a half-hour of prime time for an address on Vietnam on October 9, the fourth anniversary of Richard Nixon's statement that an Administration which could not end the war in four years did not deserve to be re-elected. It was beyond my comprehension that Nixon could have perpetuated the war through his entire first term and still convince people that he was more likely to end it than I. Pat Caddell's polls showed that Americans generally were not sure how I would end the war. The October 9 television speech laid out the process point by point.

It may not have moved many voters; the continuing problem was that so many of them had already made up their minds. But the speech did produce an outpouring of additional, tangible support from those who already favored me. It raised one and a half million desperately needed dollars, the largest amount of money contributed in response to a political speech in American history. Our Washington headquarters was literally inundated with bags of mail. Everybody from Gary Hart and Henry Kimelman to volunteers in the mailroom were up until two and three in the morning night after night opening the envelopes and reading the notes that came with the checks. An elderly couple sent $2; it was all they could afford from their social-security check. One family sent $100 of the money they had saved for a vacation they would postpone. Messages like that reconfirmed my conviction that I owed it to such people to continue to make the case for peace. Whether Vietnam and Watergate were issues that would carry me a political mile or just an inch, a Democratic campaign that ignored them would have been pointless.

The second fireside chat dealt with the economy. I emphasized the uncertain political nature of Nixon's economic policies. While I was being attacked as a candidate constantly changing his proposals and positions, which in fact I had seldom done, it was undeniable that the Nixon Administration had followed a widely inconsistent course on the economy. After assailing the notion of wage and price controls for two and a half years, the President had abruptly imposed them in 1971 not because he suddenly had come to believe in them, but because they had become politically expedient. The controls themselves, I continued, were riddled with exemptions for special interests and Nixon campaign contributors. I contended that once re-elected, it was impossible to predict what Nixon would do. Controls might be lifted quickly, inflation might intensify, and there could be another recession with a steep increase in unemployment. I detailed an alternative coherent economic policy for the next four years. Though the economic speech was seen on only one network, another torrent of contributions poured in, far more than enough to pay the costs of the telecast itself.

The third fireside chat on Watergate and corruption, broadcast on October 25, commanded the most attention, but I had been hitting hard at the issue for more than a month and a half. Several times in September I had charged extemporaneously that the Nixon Administration was the most corrupt in American history. But because the charge was not in a prepared release, the press did not pick it up. Returning to Washington for a one-day rest on October 3, I reviewed the draft of the speech to be delivered to the UPI editors' conference the next morning. That same day, on *Meet the Press,* Eleanor called the Nixon Administration the most corrupt in *recent* history. I asked Bob Shrum and John Holum to draft a new speech for the UPI conference. I received the draft at about five in the morning and reworked it for the next two hours. It was hurriedly retyped and I delivered it at nine. For the first time in a prepared text, I characterized the Nixon Administration as the most corrupt in the nation's history. The sentence obviously shocked the audience. Some of them regarded it as the kind of thing that should never be said about an American President. But I had not passed such a judgment carelessly. On the basis of the information then available, I was convinced that this was a fair and measured assessment. As I have noted already, there was ample public indication of White House complicity in Watergate, but to my mind Watergate was only the tip of the iceberg. I also talked of the corruption of the Constitution itself, of the abuses of the IRS, the attempts at repression, and the invasions of civil liberty. But beyond all of these considerations, there was the terrible life-taking corruption of prolonging the Vietnam war and deceiving the American people about it. To me that was the ultimate corruption of the American body politic.

The general editorial reaction to my UPI editors speech was outrage. This time, the editorials pronounced, McGovern really had gone too far. Nixon's re-election committee dismissed the speech as a desperation tactic. Some of my own aides were taken aback. One of them commented, "That may be true, but, my God, you can't say it." (Ironically, within a year after the campaign, with the Watergate cover-up rapidly coming apart, I encountered voters who asked why I hadn't pressed the corruption issue.)

Three weeks later, the third fireside chat reiterated and amplified the Nixon corruption in specific detail. By this time the reporters were at least beginning to credit it as more than the reckless gambit of a losing candidate. The morning papers headlined the television address. Just as I finished reading one of the stories, sitting in my room at a Howard Johnson's in Detroit, I heard the news that Henry Kissinger was holding a live press conference on television. "Peace is at hand," he announced. And the corruption issue instantly faded away.

All along I had suspected that the Nixon Administration might end the war shortly before the election. I knew that Kissinger could not negotiate a settlement that would preserve the Thieu regime in Saigon over the long term, but I thought that political pressures might force Nixon to accept an agreement he would otherwise reject. I pressed the Vietnam issue, understanding that the rug could be pulled out from under me, but believing that there might not be a peace if I wasn't standing on that rug. But over the next week, the peace that was supposed to be at hand slipped away. I decided to devote the fourth and final television speech to a warning that Nixon's re-election meant a continued war.

I hammered out the outlines of the speech in a staff meeting in my room at the Mr. President Hotel in Battle Creek, Michigan. (The rooms there are each named after a President.) I was wary of charging that Kissinger himself had told a bold-faced lie. Based on the information I had, I thought that he had negotiated a settlement with North Vietnamese diplomat Le Duc Tho which Nixon stalled because of the opposition of South Vietnamese President Thieu. Some months after the election, Kissinger approached me at an Iranian embassy dinner in Washington. Referring to the announcement that peace was at hand, he said, "I know you think I did that for political reasons, but I want to assure you I didn't." It was not that Kissinger was above political maneuvering, but that he was more clever at it than to proclaim a peace that would be so quickly exposed.

John Holum, Bob Shrum and Sandy Berger worked through that night in Battle Creek on a draft of the speech. I recorded it in Chicago the next afternoon. I began by talking about Timothy Thomas, a young man who had been killed in Vietnam the very day of the Kissinger press conference. His father had called a local McGovern headquarters in California and asked to speak with me. When I called him he told me that he wanted me to talk publicly about his son, and he volunteered to do anything he could in the closing days of the campaign. He traveled with me and spoke eloquently at stop after stop through election eve. The fate of Timothy Thomas once again brought home to me the incredible sadness of the individual tragedies of Vietnam. The only other single personal result of Vietnam that moved me as much in that period was the picture of a little girl named Kim, her back on fire with napalm, her eyes filled with pain and fear, running from her bombed-out school. That photograph literally moved me to tears.

Nothing frustrated me more, not even the landslide defeat itself, than my failure to arouse public indignation at Nixon's manipulation of the war. The more I reflected on the costs of Vietnam in lives and scarce resources, the more I wanted to cry out to the American people. But the more I cried out, the more strident my public statements sounded. My very anguish may have pushed voters in the other direction—toward the apparently cool man in the White House who insisted that he was heading steadily for "peace with honor." In an analysis written the month after the election, Gary Wills suggested that my failure on this issue was inevitable.

> Vietnam is the shared crime that has turned our country into . . . a pact of blood. Now patriotism means the complicity of fellows in a crime; if we are all in it, no one is worse than the rest; we excuse each other; we keep the secret. That is why the members of the pact had to re-elect a war criminal as their ruler. Senator George S. McGovern was hysterically feared because he was an accuser.
>
> Members of the pact most fear the man who has not joined in their mystery of communal criminality. When ten men commit a crime, and the eleventh refuses, the ten will turn on him, fear and suspect him. They resent him because he is free, his mouth is not gagged by the knowledge of his own guilt.

My strongly expressed views on Vietnam thus led to another mark against me—that I was, as *Newsweek* said in its pre-election issue, a moralistic crusader. I never quite understood the criticism. Was politics supposed to be conducted without regard for moral principle? Certainly I was not advocating a rigid American moralism in foreign policy, but a greater tolerance for other peoples' values and choices. It seemed to be that there was an important difference between such moralism and an authentic morality—that in Vietnam, for example, America ought to care more for lifesaving than facesaving. In late September I had delivered an address carefully defining my conception of the role of ethical standards in public affairs at Wheaton College, an evangelical school in Illinois. In the face of continuing comments that I was preachy (by 1976, Jimmy Carter's similar theme would sound very appropriate), I scheduled another speech on the same subject before a convocation of ministers in Battle Creek, Michigan, a few days prior to the election.

The morning of that speech, Frank Mankiewicz suggested an

opening reference to an event which had occurred the night before. I could remind the ministers, he joked, of the Biblical admonition to "turn the other cheek." It would be a wry and timely comment, since upon landing in Battle Creek I had told a heckler, "Kiss my ass." The comment became instant news. It seemed to have reached more people faster than any other words I uttered in 1972. Actually, I had told off another heckler only hours before, but no reporter overheard it. During an appearance at the University of Cincinnati I was exhausted and my voice was hoarse. Sensing the strain as I struggled through my speech, the crowd seemed to respond all the more. Afterward I was nearly crushed in a surging rush of people as I attempted to leave the huge stadium. Suddenly I heard nasty shouting a few feet away. Within moments the excited crowd shoved me into a face-to-face encounter with the heckler. He used the proximity to escalate his insults. Looking him in the eye I replied, "You say one more word and I'll knock you flat on your butt." I meant it, and the nearest Secret Service man, George Hollendursky, knew that I meant it. He stepped in front of me and the encounter was over. No one in the press corps had been within hearing distance.

After the short flight to Battle Creek I was shaking hands along the airport fence when the second heckler—an unusually obnoxious character—started working me over. Eleanor was with me and I was doubly angered. I motioned for the man to lean over the fence and whispered in his ear, "Listen, you son of a bitch, why don't you kiss my ass." No one except him heard that crack either, but a nearby newsman witnessed the exchange. He asked the heckler what I had said and the answer was accurate.

Some staff members frantically insisted that I issue a denial or retraction immediately. I did no such thing. I went to bed and slept soundly. By the following night "KMA" buttons were being worn by people in the crowd at campaign rallies. I don't know whether the incident lost or won me votes. It probably did both. It left at least one long-lasting impression. One afternoon several years later I saw Senator James Eastland of Mississippi, the president pro-tempore of the Senate, a conservative grandee who had been less than enthusiastic about my candidacy, looking at me across the Senate floor, chuckling to himself. He walked over, burned-out cigar in hand, still chuckling and said, "George, I've wanted to ask you for a long time—did you really tell that guy in '72 to kiss your ass?" I smiled and nodded and Eastland said, "That was the best line in the campaign." And that was the only enthusiastic endorsement I have ever received for a campaign statement from Senator Eastland.

The last day of the 1972 campaign was long, exhausting, nostalgic and wistful. It encompassed five thousand miles and four different stops. Eleanor and I left New York's Biltmore Hotel early to greet voters at a subway stop. It was not a last-minute attempt to convert a few individuals, but a visual event for the local evening news. We then flew to Philadelphia, where the rally crowd was so huge and responsive that the Washington *Star*'s Mary McGrory, who would later win a long-overdue Pulitzer prize, ventured to predict an upset victory for me. Mary is among the best journalists in America, a person of exquisite sensitivity and a rare capacity to express it, but I knew she wasn't going to get the Pulitzer prize for that prediction.

Somewhere between Philadelphia and Wichita, I admitted to myself for the first time that I was going to lose. Until that afternoon, in the face of all the polls, I had held on to hope. Perhaps that is the necessity of a presidential candidate working his heart and speaking his voice out day after day.

The plane had to be refueled, so there was an airport rally in Wichita, though Kansas was one of the least likely McGovern states. Once again there were thousands of people and they stayed through a thunderstorm. It was as though they had come to say goodbye, and they didn't want to leave. The mood was the same in Long Beach, California. The plane arrived late; Dennis Weaver and Candice Bergen had been holding the crowd. Apparently it wasn't really necessary. The police said that the freeways leading to the Long Beach airport were jammed with thousands of people trying to reach an already oversized rally.

Twenty-five thousand were there. Dennis had been campaigning hard and his voice had been reduced to a whisper, but he managed a brief introduction. In the middle of my speech an alarm bell on the airport terminal started to ring loudly and kept ringing for fifteen minutes. I joked that perhaps it was the last dirty trick and the crowd cheered defiantly. California Senators John Tunney and Alan Cranston were also there; they had campaigned the state hard for me. After the rally they joined Dennis, Candice and me on the plane. We talked for nearly half an hour while the plane was being readied. Candy was on the verge of tears, but Dennis smiled bravely and said, "No matter what happens tomorrow, we've given it our best. Nobody could have worked harder." As I saw him and the others to the door of the plane, I was surprised to find most of the twenty-five thousand people still standing there. I waved and they cheered. They were still standing and watching as the plane taxied away.

We flew halfway across the continent to Sioux Falls, arriving after one o'clock. We were so far behind schedule that I expected to find no one there. But five thousand people had waited for three hours in the bitter night cold. Governor Dick Kneip was warming the crowd while his wife Nancy was shivering on the makeshift platform.

He introduced me and I said a few words of thanks and the campaign was finally over—in the same city where it had started nearly two years earlier.

The next morning the Secret Service drove Eleanor and me the seventy miles to our hometown of Mitchell, where we cast our votes. I had not driven myself anywhere in months. But on that ride to Mitchell, I broke a brief silence by casually observing, "It's going to seem strange to be driving my own car again after today." Eleanor knew what I had said inadvertently; it was the first reference to defeat that had passed between us in two years. That afternoon there was a reception at the Minnehaha Country Club. I was given a model of the EROS Space Center, a satellite weather facility scheduled to be built in South Dakota. It was really the beginning of the 1974 campaign for re-election to the Senate. No one had billed it as such; it was too painfully obvious to be made explicit. I thought to myself, I have been here before and I'll be back in a couple of weeks. One chapter was over and another one was starting.

At six o'clock, I decided to take a nap in my room at the Sioux Falls Holiday Inn. I asked Jeff Smith to wake me when the returns were showing a clear trend. Less than two hours later, his eyes brimming with tears, he knocked on the door and told me that it was all over —that I would probably lose every state except Massachusetts and the District of Columbia. I hugged Eleanor and then tried to console Jeff. "No one really loses an effort in which he has stood up for what is decent," I told him. "Well," he replied tearfully, "that's easy for you to say, but what about the rest of us?" I have been teasing him about that response ever since.

Within a few minutes I dispatched a congratulatory message to President and Mrs. Nixon. I had not had the heart to write my concession statement during the day, so I did it now. Before leaving for the Sioux Falls Coliseum to concede, I gathered my family and asked for one last favor in this long campaign. "We're about to go to the Coliseum and we'll be watched by a hundred million people on TV. I don't want to see a tear or hear a sob from one of you." Looking at my four daughters, I tried to make light of our feelings: "If one of you starts slobbering around, I'm going to bust you right in the nose on national television. That goes for you, too, Eleanor, and you, too, Steve." I smiled determinedly. What I wanted to do was put my arms around them and cry.

Five thousand people were crowded into the Coliseum. They had not left, as such crowds often do, when the loss had become not just clear, but overwhelming. I almost broke down standing on that stage. I had anticipated some tears, but I did not expect to see Secret Service men crying. Or a veteran reporter from one of the networks sobbing. I talked of the value of what we had tried to do and of the consolation that we could find in it: "We will shed no tears because all of this effort will bear fruit for years to come . . . We do not rally to the support of policies that we deplore, but we do love this country and we will continue to beckon it to a higher standard."

Back at the hotel, everyone worked hard at having a party. Several contributors who had given hundreds of thousands of dollars to the campaign had flown to Sioux Falls to be with me in defeat. Our big contributors, too, tended to be out of the ordinary: they had been investing in their beliefs rather than buying a piece of the action. Men like Arthur Krim, Stanley Sheinbaum and Ted Bonda didn't think of the effort they had given so much to sustain as just a loss to be written off. There was a moment of comic relief when one of the Secret Service agents, after drowning his sorrows, fell into the freezing-cold swimming pool. His revolver sank to the bottom and for the next few minutes the Secret Service men, staffers and Hunter Thompson were either diving for it or cheering on those who were.

I called Sarge Shriver, who told me that though it might be hard to accept now, he would truly be proud of what we had tried to do for the rest of his life. John Holum, Bob Shrum and Sandy Berger gathered in my room and we had a drink together and chatted. Finally I smiled and said to these three young men, whom I plainly loved, "There they are—the men who wrote the words that moved the nation." We all laughed.

The next day we flew back to Washington, and the Secret Service drove Eleanor and me home. One of the agents shook my hand at the door and said he had something to tell me: "There are over a hundred men in the details that were assigned to you. Most of them are pretty conservative. And I'll bet every one of them voted for you."

It was a small landslide in my direction.

11

SWEETEST SONGS,
SADDEST THOUGHTS

I n his superb book about the Brooklyn Dodgers of the 1950s, *The Boys of Summer,* Roger Kahn observes in the preface: "My years with the Dodgers were 1952 and 1953, two seasons in which they lost the World Series to the Yankees. You may glory in a team triumphant but you fall in love with a team in defeat. Losing after great striving is the story of man, who was born to sorrow, whose sweetest songs tell of saddest thought."

In the days following a losing presidential campaign there is an abrupt, almost traumatic change in the whole tempo and format of life. For months the candidate has been centerstage in a drama that will change or confirm the course of the nation and the world—and the reality too often forgotten in the relentless search for a place in history, the individual lives of all those who will eat or go hungry, work or go jobless, live in peace or die in war. A campaign is, or should be, more than the enjoyment of fame and the pursuit of power. It is easy for a candidate's head to be turned. He is cheered by crowds, pursued by the press, protected by the Secret Service, attended by a solicitous staff, discussed in millions of homes. For months he is the subject of the lead story in the nightly television news. And therein lies the real value of the effort: he has the chance to be heard on issues about which he cares deeply—in my case, to win and then to make a peace, to fight for tax reform, full employment and health care. The adrenalin flows and the spirit soars as the candidate looks into the faces and clasps the hands of the multitudes caught up in a great shared endeavor.

It is said that a national campaign is tiring, debilitating, sometimes almost too demanding to continue. I have said all those things, and they are true. But at least after losing, one discovers how much the enterprise itself meant. The day after a losing election, the candidate reverts to the shock of "normal" living. The Secret Service, the campaign staff, the crowds, the press—all of these disappear overnight. Suddenly an overwhelming loneliness replaces the excitement of the cheering crowds. "All quiet on the western front" and on every other front. The ideas as well as the individual have been defeated.

Messages of condolence and sympathy begin to come. Day after day the mail brings an outpouring of kind words, frustrated hopes, expressions of defiance, notes of cheer, and predictions of vindication and dreams of what might have been. I would read samples of these messages each day until the poignancy became too hard to take. How could a candidate so overwhelmingly rejected by the majority be the recipient of so much respect and admiration from the minority? Many of the letters reminded me that nearly 30 million of my countrymen voted for me in the face of polls indicating certain defeat. Now an extraordinary number of them wanted to put in writing why they had done so. Their thoughts—most of them expressed in longhand—can only be described as love letters. It was a source of strength to know how much they had cared, but it also intensified the pain of failure.

The same emotions surfaced everywhere I went in the months immediately after the campaign. It began the morning after the election as we were leaving the Holiday Inn in Sioux Falls to fly back to Washington. Eleanor's uncle, George Coffit, a weather-beaten farmer from Fulda, Minnesota, put his hand on my shoulder and then, shaking with emotion, he said, "God, George, I just don't know what to say. Why the hell couldn't they see what your election would have meant to this country? I just feel so awful." To which I replied, "I'm surprised at you, George. This isn't the first time you've seen a crop failure." He smiled through his tears. In a ritual that continues to this day, people started greeting me on streets, in shops, at airport terminals, in hotel lobbies. Often there would be a ringing declaration that they had voted for me and were proud of it. (As the Watergate scandal deepened, it seemed that no one had voted for Nixon. Soon I felt like a version of Will Rogers: I never met a person who didn't support me, though I had lost forty-nine states.) Sometimes maître d's or cab drivers or barbers would not permit me to pay my bill. "You tried to tell them and they wouldn't listen," one driver said in explaining that he was "honored" to have "the real President" in his cab.

These thousands of post-election experiences furnished a wider perspective on the dynamics of the campaign. It is easy to exaggerate the relative importance of a few prominent staffers, but it is unrecognized people across the land who comprise the heart of a presidential campaign. In 1972, millions of them shared my concerns, my convictions, my hopes and my campaign. They were far and away the most important factor in the successful bid for the nomination. They sustained me both in victory and in defeat.

Just as they had during the successful nomination bid and the unsuccessful general election, the young on America's campuses and in the high schools responded with special feeling after that defeat. I have continued since 1972 to speak frequently in colleges across the country. Everywhere the crowds have been large and responsive. I have not personally experienced the decline in student political interest that so many politicians and writers have noted.

More painful than my defeat in 1972 was the resulting caricature of me and the McGovern campaign. The caricature bears little resemblance to what I think I am or to the real nature of our effort. Even while rejecting it, I have to accept responsibility for the impressions that contributed to it, particularly the Eagleton affair. My campaign was referred to variously as "graceless," "bumbling," "a debacle," "a disaster" and a "catastrophe." I was depicted as an inept, vacillating lightweight with unstable, if not radical, tendencies. To be so regarded is distressing enough, but I also have to live with the knowledge that not only did I lose the election, but I lost it to the most discredited man ever to occupy the White House.

Above all else, my defeat and the re-election of Richard Nixon were a "catastrophe" and a "debacle"—not primarily for me, but for the nation. The results appeared to vindicate the obsolete Cold War assumptions that carried us into the Vietnam horror and interminably prolonged our involvement. Once again the steadily growing "military-industrial complex" was endorsed as the surest depository of American security. The men who had dissipated the nation's moral and economic resources in needless conflict and excessive war preparations were given a landslide endorsement. Those young men who had stood against the war on grounds of conscience would remain exiles, prisoners or fugitives at large.

Within weeks of the election, the victorious winners, elected on a claim of "peace with honor," unleashed the harshest aerial bombardment ever on Vietnam. The B-52s of Christmas time became a negotiating tool to force the North Vietnamese to the conference table on their knees. But it was Washington, not Hanoi, that had broken off negotiations. The agreement signed in January 1973 after the Christmas bombing included the same terms Nixon and Kissinger could have had four months earlier—or for that matter, four years earlier.

Afterward the Nobel Peace Prize was awarded to Henry Kissinger and North Vietnam's Le Duc Tho, the two principal negotiators of the Paris peace agreement. Le Duc Tho had the grace to refuse the award in view of the continuing military action, including an American aerial bombardment in Indochina after the Paris agreement. Kissinger accepted the award while the Nixon Administration was escalating military shipments to the South Vietnamese regime. Simultaneously the B-52s were killing the people and shredding the social fabric of Cambodia.

The ultimate bankruptcy of the Nixon Administration's Indochina policy was the fate of Cambodia, which became the bitterest fruit of the Nixon-Kissinger policies. When Nixon came to power in 1969, Cambodia was at peace, with Premier Norodom Sihanouk treading a careful neutralist line designed to keep outside powers from turning his country into a combat zone. But in March 1969, U.S. bombers were ordered to begin bombing Cambodia secretly, supposedly to hit Vietcong and North Vietnamese sanctuaries along the border with South Vietnam. But the raids only pushed the Communists deeper into Cambodian territory and increased the political pressures on Sihanouk. For months the bombardment continued even while the Administration was denying it to the Congress and to the American public. Within a year Sihanouk was so weakened that his right-wing Defense Minister, Lon Nol, launched a successful coup, with possible CIA involvement, while Sihanouk was in Moscow seeking Soviet help to preserve his country's precarious neutrality.

North Vietnamese and Khmer Rouge troops then moved closer toward the Cambodian capital of Phnom Penh. Although State Department analysts warned against it, Nixon sent 30,000 American and South Vietnamese troops into Cambodia on April 30, 1970. The purpose of the invasion was partly to cripple the staging areas of the Vietcong, partly to prop up Lon Nol. Thus began a series of desperate moves to "save" Cambodia as we were "saving" Vietnam. All the mistakes we had made in Vietnam were now to be repeated in Cambodia until Congress finally refused Administration requests for additional funds five years later. By 1975, with both Saigon and Phnom Penh about to be overrun, additional American supplies would only add to the booty. Yet, the Administration begged for more until the very end.

Kissinger ignored or reassigned American diplomats at the embassy in Cambodia—including Lloyd Pines and Emory Swank—who saw the folly of our intervention there. Meanwhile American bombers slaughtered and destroyed at will. Hundreds of thousands of Cambodians were killed. Aerial bombardment heavier than the raids directed against Germany and Japan in World War II rained down on a primitive rural countryside without any kind of air-defense system. Since bombing had originally been justified to protect American troops across the border in South Vietnam, some of us asked why it continued in 1973 after the troops had been withdrawn. To this, Deputy Assistant Secretary of State William Sullivan replied, "For now, I'd say the justification is the re-election of the President." Having won a landslide endorsement in the election, Administration strategists apparently felt free to pursue the insane slaughter in Indochina as they saw fit. Their policies led to terrible tragedy in Cambodia. They foreclosed the possibility of Sihanouk's return to power as a coalition leader, a course recommended by both the French and Chou En-lai. Instead, Cambodia was to endure brutal revenge after the Khmer Rouge took Phnom Penh from the hated collaborators in April 1975.

If John Ehrlichman deserved five years in prison for his part in the Daniel Ellsberg case, one can only wonder what other policy makers deserved for the senseless expeditions against the people of Indochina, especially the Cambodians. The secret, unconstitutional bombing of that country was the clearest ground for a Nixon impeachment. It was a vastly more serious crime than the break-in at Watergate. Yet, looking back on all the dead and the wounded, the devastated villages and the ravished countryside, Kissinger concluded, "I may have a lack of imagination, but I fail to see the moral issue involved." Henry Kissinger was a brilliant diplomat, but he sometimes displayed a shocking lack of moral values. The first time I discussed the Vietnam issue with him privately in 1969, he defended our continued involvement primarily on the ground that if we were to withdraw, that would create a right-wing political backlash in the United States!

In Vietnam itself, American troops withdrew following the Paris agreement in early 1973. The Thieu forces, bristling with expensive U.S. military equipment, tried to broaden their area of control. They met an intense reaction from Vietcong and North Vietnamese forces. By the spring of 1975, General Thieu's army was literally disintegrating. Frightened by predictions of a vast blood bath should the Communists take over, thousands of Vietnamese fled as refugees to the United States. An airborne baby lift was inaugurated to fly several hundred Vietnamese infants to the United States. And those who stayed behind faced hardship; for one thing, the United States had inflicted massive damage, then refused to help repair it. But there was no blood bath when the new government came to power.

As the Nixon-Kissinger policies in Indochina were moving toward their final, utter failure, Congress at last began looking into the Watergate scandal. The Nixon Administration was exposed as corrupt through and through. To be sure, some of its constitutional and legal transgressions had been perpetrated by previous Administrations in the name of "national security." But it remained for Nixon and his associates to join all of these practices, to push them to new extremes, and when challenged, to engage in a massive cover-up.

One of the burdens of a defeated candidate is to bear the slings and arrows of commentators and columnists explaining why it happened. One post-mortem that I find especially ironic in view of subsequent events was a column by David Broder in the Washington *Post* of November 14, 1972. Broder argued that "political and journalistic Washington" rejected me partly because my positions were too moralistic. There is no room for "moralizing" in the White House, he said. "The American people know this and reject those who lack the essential subtlety, skepticism and—I suppose—deviousness the presidency requires," Broder concluded.

Perhaps I invited some of the hostile commentary by accepting an invitation to lecture at Oxford University at the time of Richard Nixon's second inaugural. This was considered by some, including columnist Joseph Kraft, as unsportsmanlike conduct toward my victorious rival. I told an overflow Oxford audience of students and faculty—many of whom were Americans—that "the United States is closer to one-man rule than at any time in our history—and this paradoxically by a President who is not popular." I then went on to describe the need for legislative efforts, such as a congressional budgetary process, to hold the Chief Executive in check. I spoke also of the responsibility of the press to probe more deeply into the operations of the President and his men. These sentiments prompted Mr. Kraft to write that as a loser I should have had "the grace to keep quiet for a while." Taking issue with my contention that the press had failed during the campaign to "lay a glove" on President Nixon, Kraft wrote that if this was true, it is "because Mr. Nixon had the good sense to stay above the battle."

To keep matters in proper perspective, I should disclose that my favorite people on the national scene are journalists. If I were to spend a long evening in conversation with any professional group of my choosing, I would select the national press corps, including David Broder and Joe Kraft. The journalistic pack is a highly stimulating, sometimes endearing group of human beings. I think I know as much about their virtues and strengths, their ambitions and fears as they know about mine. I sometimes wish we knew one another better, but that is a dangerous wish for both politicians and journalists in a world of adversary relationships.

In the spring of 1973, some weeks after my return from Oxford, I was invited by the Washington Gridiron Club—a group of nationally recognized journalists—to give the speech for the Democrats at the annual Gridiron Dinner. It is a tradition that the speakers spoof themselves, and that was one tradition I kept. "Last year, we opened the doors of the Democratic Party, as we promised we would," I deadpanned, "and twenty million Democrats walked out. For years, I wanted to run for President in the worst possible way—and I sure did. I wanted to be President so much that after the election, I asked ITT if I could be President of Chile." The crowd laughed at line after line of that sort, but it was a painfully difficult speech, and I left the ballroom that night in no mood to attend any of the post-dinner parties that followed. I knew, though, that I had given the audience much more than they had expected from a man many of them regarded as a self-righteous moralizer. Vice President Spiro Agnew, who followed me to the speaker's rostrum, began his remarks by saying, "I'm glad George McGovern didn't have that speech writer with him during the campaign." In the Statler parking garage I encountered a veteran Gridiron diner who told me it was the best Gridiron speech he had heard in all his Washington years. Two prominent members of the club who approached me a moment later were equally kind. As they walked away I heard one of them say, "I really don't know why in hell I voted against him." I was also to have the satisfaction of learning in the coming weeks that the controversial Oxford speech was being put on university reading lists.

But flattering experiences of that kind were always balanced by the harsh realities of defeat. One such reality was a privately commissioned poll indicating that I was in deep political trouble in my home state with a Senate campaign confronting me in 1974. I found the results as disturbing as the 1972 presidential results, when only 46 percent of my fellow South Dakotans had voted for me. The Republicans had made an extra effort in South Dakota to tarnish my reputation and distort my views during the presidential campaign. They saw my heavy involvement in campaigning nationwide as an opportune time to strike me at home.

Considering that as a presidential candidate I had not carried my own state, and pondering the dismal post-election poll on my Senate re-election chances, I seriously considered leaving politics. Eleanor was physically and emotionally drained from the campaign and was especially hurt by the voting pattern in the state where we were both born and had lived for so many years. She and our children would probably have cheered a decision to put the world of politics behind and move on to teaching or writing.

But I could not bring myself to withdraw. I recalled that South Dakota had given me victories in four campaigns—two for the House of Representatives and two for the Senate. Thousands of voters who disagreed with some of my stands in the Senate nevertheless voted for me. I considered, too, my obligations to the public, both in my own state and in the nation. I thought about all the supporters of 1972 that I was exhorting to continue in the political process. After a few days of defeatism, I resolved, if humanly possible, to win another term in the Senate.

It was to be a hard campaign. The Republican challenger was an Air Force colonel, Leo Thorsness, who had been a prisoner of war in Hanoi for several years. He was bitter about my opposition to the war. He did not have a well-informed view on the major problems before South Dakota and the nation, but he understood how to appeal emotionally to voters.

Taking note of my long, nationwide quest for the presidency in 1971 and 1972, Thorsness adopted as a campaign slogan: "South Dakota Needs a Full-Time Senator." It was apparent that if I wanted to be re-elected to the Senate in 1974 I would have to forswear another bid for the presidency in 1976. I had said on election night, 1972, that I would not seek the presidency in 1976. I held to that position throughout my Senate re-election campaign.

With George Cunningham of my Washington office tirelessly handling the overall direction of the campaign, Judy Harrington serving as the manager of operations in the state, and Owen Donley handling finances, we began the most heavily financed, well-organized Senate campaign in the history of South Dakota. All of us understood that we were beginning from a position of weakness. All of us believed we could win with a supreme effort. Our assumptions were right. But as I crisscrossed the state talking to citizens in every corner of my constituency, I was constantly amazed at the depth of anti-government, anti-Washington feeling. As the campaign progressed, the scandals unfolded. First Vice President Agnew was forced to resign and then President Nixon, with the President's top aides resigning in disgrace in between. These shocking developments further fed the disillusionment with Washington.

I was not prepared for the intensity of the anger and resentment which followed President Ford's pardon of Nixon. News of the pardon reached me at the conclusion of a Sunday-morning service which I was attending at the Methodist Church in Watertown, South

Dakota. When I arrived at a city park a short time later to address a Democratic picnic crowd, I found people in an uproar. Although a predictable reaction at a Democratic gathering, I discovered the same sense of outrage as I campaigned in conservative Republican areas of the state.

I suspect that this combination of events—the discrediting of Nixon and the unpopular Ford pardon—aided my re-election campaign immeasurably. Nixon had gone out of his way to promote Thorsness politically and had presented the colonel with the Medal of Honor at the White House. Thorsness was identified with Nixon. The President's fall depreciated the colonel.

The one major miscalculation of my campaign was to employ too many aides and spend far too much money. Following the 1972 campaign, considerable sums of money came to my Senate office from people who wanted to help in the Senate race. Many state and local McGovern for President committees subsequently sent in unexpended funds from the presidential campaign with the suggestion that these funds be utilized in the Senate race. In several cases substantial sums of money were sent to Henry Kimelman from deposits we had made for telephones, airlines, media outlays and other services in the presidential campaign. More than half a million dollars came into the presidential account in late 1972 and early 1973. Under a ruling by the Department of Justice, we were authorized to use any or all of these funds in the Senate race.

But with large amounts of easy money available, we spent all of the surplus presidential funds and the money raised by direct mail appeals to our national mailing list. The flow of so much money became a damaging campaign issue, and legitimately so. Ironically, for the first time since my initial race for Congress in 1956, we ended the campaign with no reserve funds to meet post-election bills and the bills that always remain after an election.

On election night I learned that Gary Hart had been elected to the Senate in Colorado. A network reporter asked if he felt our 1972 campaign had been vindicated. Gary smiled and replied, "Richard Nixon has been driven from office in disgrace and George McGovern and I have been elected to the United States Senate."

A month later I went to Kansas City to participate in the mid-term Democratic national convention. Bob Strauss, the affable Texan who had been elected national chairman following the 1972 defeat, invited me to address the delegates. When I came on the stage to speak, the crowd erupted in a standing ovation that continued until I literally forced the beginning of my speech. I delivered a blunt challenge to the party to take an unequivocal stand on issues such as military spending, full employment, tax reform and monopoly power. On civil rights, I said, "There can be no compromise. . . . We must open schoolhouse doors, not bow to those who block them." At that, the crowd stomped their feet, cheered, whistled and stood on chairs with their hands clapping overhead. When I finished speaking, there was another ovation that persisted until Strauss sent an aide to bring me back to the stage. It was a stirring experience. I saw Mayor Daley leading the applause in his part of the auditorium. Gary Hart was waving the Colorado banner. Governors, congressmen, labor leaders, Humphrey backers, Jackson supporters, a sea of Democrats seemed to be saying that winning was not the only thing. I had tried in 1972, and I was not quitting on my beliefs in 1974. And apparently they welcomed that. I left Kansas City in the happiest mood in two years.

I then began to notice the remarkable capacity of the human mind to shift perceptions of the same object. While many people told me shortly after the 1972 campaign that I had contributed to my own defeat by my harsh indictments of the Nixon Administration, by 1974 voters were asking with some irritation, "Why didn't you tell us what Nixon was like?"

Pat Caddell, the young pollster who worked for me in 1972, told me that polls he had taken in a dozen states in 1974 for senators and governors carried a rider question: "For whom would you vote now between Richard Nixon and George McGovern if the 1972 election could be held again?" I won those polls in each state without exception. But the most interesting commentary on the cognitive dissonance of the electorate came in Indiana and California, where the question was asked: "For whom did you vote in 1972, Richard Nixon or George McGovern?" A clear majority of the voters in these two states claimed that they had voted for me.

The Kansas City experience, the constant admonitions to "try it again" coming from people wherever I traveled, plus Pat Caddell's findings about how people viewed me in retrospect, prompted me to ponder the possibility of another presidential effort in 1976. I did not see how I could do it in view of my recent campaign statements to the contrary in South Dakota. But there were friends telling me that I had a larger obligation and that I could in good conscience ask to be released from my 1974 assurances that I would not seek the presidency in 1976.

So in the late spring of 1975 I convened a private meeting at my home in Washington attended by a dozen of my key young aides of 1972: Jeff Smith, Rick Stearns, Bob Shrum, Joe Grandmaison, Gene Pokorny, John Holum, Alan Baron, Sandy Berger, Pat Caddell, John Gorman, Tom Collins, Stan Rapp and a houseguest and long-time friend, Bishop James Armstrong. The consensus of this meeting was that another campaign was probably ill-advised, but that I should keep the matter under consideration for further evaluation in the fall.

That summer Alan Baron, one of the brightest political operatives in the country, who was handling press and national affairs in my office, suggested that I send a letter to thirty-five or forty key Democrats across the country seeking their counsel about 1976. Most of those who replied said that they felt I could best serve the nation not by running for President again, but as a thoughtful, outspoken, prodding leader in the Democratic Party and the Senate. Baron himself was probably typical of those who sincerely believed that a "fresh face" such as Birch Bayh, unscarred from a previous presidential race, would make a stronger candidate than I would.

Underlying the advice of those who had gathered at my house and the letters which followed was a reluctance to have me or my supporters hurt again. They had suffered and they had seen me suffer.

A third phase of the thinking about 1976 came in August of 1975 when Alan Baron, Bob Shrum, Pat Caddell and John Holum worked out a proposal which they recommended I make to Senator Humphrey. The thesis was that Humphrey would be the best available candidate in 1976. He seemed genuinely to have learned from the Vietnam tragedy. His commitment to social justice was as strong, or stronger, than any of the candidates in the field. None of the announced liberals—and Caddell in particular emphasized this— seemed to be establishing a strong base. But, he continued, the conventional wisdom of a deadlock was probably wrong; a more conservative candidate could run in the primaries and win the nomination.

A liberal could win, Caddell said, but he would have to be stronger than any of the active liberal possibilities appeared to be. Yet Humphrey, whose popularity in the party was broad, would encounter liberal resistance because of his Vietnam war record. In addition, McGovern campaigners from 1972 resented his role in the California primary and the subsequent California challenge. But Shrum conceived and Caddell concurred in the estimate that if Humphrey and I announced as a team, he for President, I for Vice President, we would be nearly unbeatable. My own presidential candidacy might be impractical, but I could help to nominate someone in whom I had a basic trust on vital issues.

I had understood Ribicoff and Nelson's preference for the Senate over the vice presidency in 1972; I had shared it. But I became convinced that this was a special case. A Humphrey-McGovern ticket, it was argued, could unite the Democratic Party, healing the wounds of 1968 and 1972. In addition, Hubert dreaded the very thought of financing a presidential campaign, having left a deficit of millions of dollars in 1968. He abhorred the demeaning rituals of raising money from the few large givers upon whom he had traditionally relied. But I had had the best political fund-raising apparatus in the nation, and Tom Collins, my direct-mail expert, was convinced it could be reactivated. Humphrey and I would not have to beg and scrape; we could raise enough money, cleanly, in small donations, from many different people.

Obviously some of my past supporters, and some of Humphrey's, would be startled, even outraged, at the notion. But on balance, my advisers and I decided that it was both workable and probably the best chance for a progressive Democratic Administration. We marshaled the arguments in a memo to Hubert. I went to see him in his Senate office about six o'clock one evening in late August of 1975. I described the proposal to him and told him that I wished he would take the memo with him on a trip he was about to make to Europe. As we talked in the dusky light of his office for nearly an hour, he noted that his 1972 campaign manager, Jack Chestnut, had just been sentenced to prison for violating campaign financing laws. He was deeply concerned about this and other charges that had been leveled against his presidential campaign. Then I saw tears in his eyes. He was deeply moved, he explained, that the two former neighbors, once close and once estranged friends, rivals four years ago, could sit and have such a discussion now.

"When do you need an answer, George?" he finally asked. I suggested that we should not delay a decision beyond the fall of 1975. He put the memo in his pocket and said I would be hearing from him after his return from Europe. But when I encountered him on the Senate floor following the trip, he said nothing. Then one day he asked if Eleanor and I could stop at his home in Waverly, Minnesota, on our next trip to South Dakota. A few days later we went to Waverly, but Hubert said he just could not decide. Muriel did not want him to run, but he wanted to consider my proposal further. To the best of my knowledge it was never seriously contemplated after that.

One reason, I suspect, is that Humphrey's advisers had a different scenario, which he came to share. It was described to me after Jimmy Carter was nominated. They figured that Jackson, the best financed contender for the nomination, would go to the convention with perhaps a third of the delegates committed to him. They saw George Wallace coming in second with 15 or 20 percent of the delegates. The remaining delegates, they calculated, would be fragmented among Shriver, Bayh, Udall, Carter, Harris, Sanford and Shapp, with each one drawing 5 to 10 percent. Given this situation, they believed that a stalemate was likely, with the delegates turning to Hubert as the compromise candidate. He would not have to run at all to be nominated.

This analysis was not exclusive to the Humphrey camp; it was the conventional wisdom. Pat Caddell insisted it was wrong—and Jimmy Carter proved that it was. Carter had concluded in September of 1972 that Nixon would be re-elected and that the time had come for a new Democratic contender to begin planning a presidential race four years hence. No other politician in America studied the format of the McGovern campaign as carefully as Jimmy Carter did. After my defeat in the general election, he and his aides devoured Gary Hart's account of our accomplishments, our frustrations and our mistakes. Carter modified his own plan to capitalize on differing circumstances and to profit from our errors. But more than any of the other contenders, he re-enacted much of our pre-nomination strategy.

I announced my candidacy two years before the general election; so did Jimmy Carter. I began with a pledge to seek and speak the truth; Jimmy Carter pledged never to tell a lie. I financed my campaign to a considerable extent by means of a direct-mail effort directed by Morris Dees of Montgomery, Alabama; Jimmy Carter employed the same methods and the same man. I discovered Harvard student pollster Pat Caddell; Jimmy Carter sought out Caddell, who did some work for him in 1975 without committing himself to Carter, then finally signed on early in 1976. I was courteous to party leaders and labor officials, but knowing that most of them favored other candidates, I concentrated on winning at the grassroots rather than with organization support; so did Carter.

I said that the most important goal of government should be "the creation of a society where we truly care about each other." Carter said his goal was a government based on "love." I called for a cut in military outlays of $10 billion per year over a three-year period; Carter recommended that we begin with a $5 billion to $7 billion cut and seek to abolish all nuclear weapons. I called for a general amnesty for draft resisters, with deserters handled on a case-by-case basis; Carter called for a general pardon for draft resisters, with deserters handled on a case-by-case basis. I called for the decriminalization of marijuana; so did Carter. I called for the replacement of welfare with a uniform federal minimum-income guarantee; Carter called for a major welfare reform. I said there was something wrong with a tax system that enabled a corporate executive to deduct his $20 martini luncheon, while a workingman couldn't deduct his bologna sandwich; so did Jimmy Carter. I agreed to lengthy interviews with *Playboy* magazine and Hunter Thompson of *Rolling Stone;* so did Carter.

When Carter won the first nomination test, the Iowa caucuses, and the second, the New Hampshire primary, it did not surprise me that his campaign took on a relentless momentum that was to carry him to a first-ballot nomination. Nor did it surprise me that his greatest effort to orchestrate the press and public opinion was centered on an elaborately staged performance in the selection of his running mate. The vice-presidential selection fiasco was, after all, the most painfully obvious mistake of 1972. Jimmy Carter treated the nation to the most extensive public demonstration of caution and prudence ever witnessed in the selection of a running mate.

And there were other McGovern mistakes and impressions that Carter fought hard to avoid. It was said that I proposed too many solutions to national problems without fully measuring their impact and practicality. Carter earned a reputation for avoiding specific proposals on complicated issues. It was said that I made people feel guilty when I indicted the sins of the nation and called the sinners home. Carter did not stop preaching, but where I closed every speech with the hope that the American people would become "the kind of great and good nation we can be when we are faithful to our founding national ideals," he told the voters that he hoped to make the government as good and kind and decent and loving as the American people already are. In effect, Carter said: No need to feel guilty; just make the government equal to your own character and all will be well with the nation.

There were times when I thought the Carter campaign might be derailed short of the nomination. One such moment came with the publication in *Harper's* of an article by Steven Brill entitled "Jimmy Carter's Pathetic Lies." The article opened with a quotation from Carter, in which he was alleged to have said, "You know what McGovern's biggest mistake was? He never should have made the Vietnam war an issue." The article raised many questions about Carter's real beliefs, the genuineness of his image, and even his sincerity. But somehow the editors of *Harper's* were persuaded to give Jody Powell, Carter's press secretary, an advance copy. Powell conducted a skillful effort to deflect the article before it struck. He prepared a rebuttal to selected charges in the Brill report. He then took the *Harper's* piece along with his refutation to the Boston *Globe* with the understanding that they would be printed side by side the day *Harper's* hit the newsstands. He also orchestrated a press campaign to discredit Brill personally. Anonymous rumors surfaced, for example, that Brill, who was a Yale Law School graduate, had been denied a degree.

By the time *Harper's* was in the hands of its readers and the national press corps, Brill was viewed not as a capable, honest writer, which he is, but as an unreliable hatchet man out to get Jimmy Carter. His article had already appeared and been "answered" in the Boston *Globe* before most readers or reporters saw it in *Harper's*. The article became a popgun, not a bombshell. Anyone who had notions that Jimmy Carter and his staff were simple-minded "Georgia boys" should have learned from the devastating treatment they administered to their first serious critic.

I tried at first to stay free of involvement in the primaries. But I was convinced that among the early contenders, candidates such as Morris Udall, Sargent Shriver and Birch Bayh had a better grasp of the nation's problems than Carter. Indeed, much of what I knew about the former Georgia governor—which was little—disturbed me. I did not like his prolonged, almost bitter-end, endorsement of America's role in Vietnam. I could not be comfortable with any candidate who had supported the Vietnam madness as late as Carter had. Nor was I reassured about his views on arms control and military spending; the promise of a cut was too vague to be believed. It seemed to me that he was hedging his stands on virtually everything. On a personal level, I recalled that he had been an active promoter of the "Anybody but McGovern" strategy of 1972.

So following Carter's victories in Iowa and New Hampshire I endorsed Mo Udall in Massachusetts and Sargent Shriver in Vermont, where Udall was not running. Although Shriver, my 1972 running mate, was my sentimental favorite, I felt that Udall, a highly competent man, was off to a better start. It was my intention, if Udall did well in Massachusetts, to endorse him nationwide for the nomination and to make a serious effort to assist his campaign. Udall did do well in Massachusetts, coming in second to Scoop Jackson. But the day after Massachusetts, there was a press story quoting a Udall campaign spokesman as ridiculing my endorsement of Udall in Massachusetts and Shriver in Vermont. "That's good old 1,000 percent George," the aide said. I did not need that kind of hassle, so I abandoned the intended national effort for Udall and decided to stay on the sidelines. The only exception was a brief appearance for Udall in Madison, Wisconsin, and a televised plea for his candidacy in South Dakota.

One person on my staff who vigorously argued the case for Carter was Bob Shrum, the staff director of the Senate Select Committee on Nutrition and Human Needs. In April he resigned to become Carter's speech writer. He soon discovered that there was a philosophical and personal chasm between the candidate and him that was too wide to bridge. After a brief but painful struggle, he resigned from the Carter campaign and went to work for *New Times*. He detailed his experience in that magazine. Although we have no official relationship, Bob and I continue a strong personal friendship.

As Carter neared the nomination, I told my staff that while I personally favored Udall, I did not want any of them to be involved in a "Stop Carter" or "Anybody but Carter" movement. Such negative efforts against me in 1972 had deeply offended me and were politically costly to the Democratic campaign in the general election.

Thus I was provoked when news stories appeared in May, first in *Newsweek* and then on the front page of the *New York Times*, citing two of my aides, Alan Baron and Jack Quinn, who previously had been Udall's campaign manager, as "key strategists" in a "Stop Carter" drive. I asked them to resign. It was a difficult moment. I liked and respected both of them and still do. I shared their apprehensions about Carter, but I believed he would be the nominee and I wanted him to be elected. He could hardly be more negative on the issues I cared about than Ford, and as I was to say at the convention, "if any of us have disagreements with Governor Carter, let us save them for President Carter." Finally, I was determined to avoid a revival of the 1972 talk about "a runaway staff."

My decision about Baron and Quinn was interpreted in the press as a sign of the collapsing opposition to Carter. In fact, I did think that the fight was all but over and I was reluctant to be associated with a last-ditch skirmish that could not deny his victory at the convention, but might deny it to him in November. What made the decision hardest was that I respected not just Baron's and Quinn's integrity, but their judgment. Yet I firmly believed that Carter, now a nearly inevitable nominee, deserved his chance. Maybe he would be better than some of us thought; perhaps, as Pat Caddell told me privately, he was genuinely committed to far-reaching social reform. In any case, the time to oppose him in 1976 was past. If he proved deficient as President, that would be a different, and a later, story.

Nearly four years had passed since my own victory at the Democratic convention followed by a landslide defeat. Now I saw another candidate who seemed likely to win both the nomination and the election, applying some of the same techniques, appealing to some of the same themes that we had in 1972, but I was far from sure that as President he actually meant to make the hard and essential reforms. Perhaps I had sought to hurry history in 1972 and maybe it is still too soon for such reforms. But the only right course I know is to speak directly rather than safely. Occasionally, when the going gets rough, I ask myself: If I don't do this, how can I expect others to? Someone who has lost forty-nine states has little else to lose in national politics. Anyway, it isn't in my nature now, it never has been, to be silent about the truth as I honestly see it.

I decided, after thinking about it, which I inevitably did for a period after 1972, that a good loser is not really someone who brushes off defeat, but someone who learns from the recurring pain of it to see the loss in perspective. Losing hurt most after the fact—during the Christmas bombing, the Watergate scandal, the Nixon and Ford vetoes. All this, I couldn't help wondering, might not have happened if I or my campaign or events had moved differently. Even if we had lost anyway, but by a closer margin, the chances of social justice and peace might have been strengthened. After all the years of struggle, of Bob Kennedy's poignant campaign, Gene McCarthy's courageous insurgency, Martin Luther King's gallant battle and my own long effort with the help of so many, it was hard to hear the conventional wisdom that the Democratic Party should flee to a position of safely splitting the differences. That, I worry, is the same tactic which led to incremental escalation in Vietnam, to repeatedly delaying national health insurance, tax reform and full employment.

Of course it hurt personally to lose. It would be false bravado to deny it. And it did hurt more because the outcome frustrated not just my personal ambitions, but great purposes and all the Americans who had worked as hard and as hopefully as I had. I never knew most of their names, but I had seen their faces, shaken their hands, stood with them from the first snowy days in New Hampshire to that final midnight rally in Sioux Falls, South Dakota—a few hours before the voting. I felt I knew them all; I thought of them through the next four years as I met them again and read their letters. They helped to sustain my spirit and my continuing sense of commitment.

In particular, I remember one letter from Massachusetts, where bumper stickers proclaimed it as "The One and Only" state I had carried. The writer recalled a scene in Harper Lee's novel *To Kill a Mockingbird.* In an Alabama courtroom Atticus Finch has just completed his courageous but failing defense of a young black wrongly charged with raping a white. Jean Louise, Atticus' daughter, watches from her seat in the balcony as her father wearily leaves the courtroom.

> Someone was punching me [says Jean Louise, the first-person narrator] but I was reluctant to take my eyes from the people below us, and from the image of Atticus' lonely walk down the aisle.
> "Miss Jean Louise?" a voice said.
> I looked around. They were standing. All around us and in the balcony on the opposite wall, the Negroes were getting to their feet. Reverend Syke's voice was as distant as Judge Taylor's:
> "Miss Jean Louise, stand up. Your father's passin'."

My friend from Massachusetts concluded: "For the rest of my life, whenever your valiant losing effort to become President of the United States is mentioned, I will say: 'Stand up. George McGovern is passing.'"

I took this as a tribute not so much to me as to the ideas for which we stood. Someday, I believe, those ideas will prevail. Ever since that letter, whenever I feel wistful or discouraged, whenever I feel a twinge of the 1972 defeat, I try to recall that letter and resolve to keep on standing.

12

LOOKING OUTWARD

T he war in Vietnam, and the false priority of Pentagon waste, had brought me to two presidential campaigns. "I am here tonight as your candidate," I told the 1972 convention in my acceptance speech, "in large part because under four Administrations of both parties, a terrible war has been charted behind closed doors. I want those doors opened and I want that war closed." But my interest in foreign policy had pre-dated Vietnam and it was to outlast my national candidacy in 1972. For two years afterward I was running hard, long days and hours to come from behind in South Dakota and win re-election to the Senate.

At the beginning of this period I also became a member of the Foreign Relations Committee. I had sought this assignment several times before, but since the Senate leadership prefers not to assign senators from the same state to a major committee, Karl Mundt's long service on the committee precluded my being selected at an earlier date. In January 1973 Hubert Humphrey and I both joined the committee, where the two of us, presidential nominees who had stood four years apart for very different Indochina policies, now spoke and voted together against the war. My focus continued to be Vietnam; peace did not come for more than two years after the promise that it was "at hand."

In addition, I was involved in the continuing effort to block the B-1 bomber, an effort that started with a few of us but gained ground steadily. The B-1 is the most expensive weapons system in history— a $100 billion project that in my judgment represents no significant increase in national security. It is a wasteful reassurance to the Air Force that manned bombers still have a major role in the era of missile deterrence. If indeed heavy bombers are still needed, that role could be played until well into the 1990s by our existing B-52s. I was stunned when one of my Senate colleagues who recognized the strategic absurdity of the B-1 argued that the United States might need it for the next Vietnam. The B-1 has become an expensive example of the Gordian interconnections of the military-industrial complex: one liberal Democrat from an aerospace state apologized privately after voting for it. "George," he said, "I know the country doesn't need it, but my State needs the jobs." No progress had been made on systematic planning to convert arms construction to the works of peace. Hundreds of thousands of workers still depend, unnecessarily, on the manufacture of overkilling devices. In the absence of economic conversion planning, workers and employers involved in the production of unnecessary weapons will continue to press their elected representatives to support those systems such as the B-1.

In June 1976 presidential candidate Carter told the Democratic Platform Committee that the B-1 bomber was "an example of a proposed system which should not be funded and would be wasteful of taxpayers' dollars." Following his election, Carter undertook a searching review of all aspects of the B-1 bomber. In that process he invited me and other interested senators to the White House on June 10, 1977. Senator John Culver of Iowa made a brilliant analysis of the military and economic weaknesses of the B-1 program. I then decided to emphasize another consideration. I told the President that America's most painful weakness in recent years was not in military weapons, but in the credibility of our government. Reminding Mr. Carter of his election pledge to halt the B-1, I urged him to protect his credibility by remaining with his campaign position. If he found it necessary to change his position with the passage of time, I urged him to defer that judgment until 1980, when he could take his new view to the American electorate.

I was pleased when the President announced on June 30, 1977, that he had decided to remain in opposition to deployment of the B-1.

While continuing my efforts to reduce military waste and to convert surplus arms production to constructive peacetime purposes, I also turned my attention in 1975 to the Middle East conflict, to postwar relations with Vietnam, and other foreign-policy questions. In the controversial Oxford speech the day of Nixon's second inauguration, I had advocated "a pluralism of power," with the Congress hopefully wiser because of Vietnam, reasserting its dormant constitutional responsibilities in foreign affairs. I did not intend to wait passively for executive decisions, and I urged my colleagues not to. Activist legislators could take the lead on hard issues; indeed, if they did not, the country was likelier to stand still or blunder into disaster. The division of power in a democracy is not perfect, but I share Jefferson's faith that it is likelier to prove right than one person's, or one President's, wisdom or whim.

Such activism seldom if ever achieves short-term victories. But over the years I had learned that mistaken policies can sometimes be modified if the critics persist. One senator (or several) in dissent or in advance of official policies must be ready to fight, to lose and to resume fighting.

A prime example is the persistent crisis in the world's capacity to feed itself, an issue in which I was involved even before my term as Food for Peace director. Appropriately, my first major initiative in foreign policy after winning a third Senate term was as a member of the American delegation to the United Nations Food Conference in Rome. I left for the conference two days after the 1974 election.

Secretary Kissinger had proposed the meeting in an address to the General Assembly in September 1973. Bad weather had sharply reduced crop yields in Africa and Asia, and the U.S. wheat sale to the Soviet Union had depleted the American reserves for emergency relief. Exploding populations in the poor countries and overconsumption in the affluent fraction of nations had further strained international food stocks. There was a recurring cycle of shortage and bare sufficiency in the Third World; with each turn of the cycle, the shortage fell closer to global famine. In the first half of the 1970s, by conservative estimates, hunger killed a hundred million human beings, more than all of history's wars combined.

At the 1974 Food Conference, 120 nations, their economic interests in sharp conflict, found it difficult to achieve any consensus. They offered a minimal response, notable more for the fact than the content of the agreement.

First, a World Food Council was created within the United Nations with responsibility for monitoring food and agricultural conditions and recommending measures to deal with them. (The international order, like the federal government, has a habit of relying on commissions to study problems when facing them proves to be politically impractical.)

Second, an Agricultural Development Fund was created to increase food productivity in the Third World. Advanced nations were to donate $1 billion, of which the United States pledged $200 million.

(This was a token percentage of what was needed, by any reasonable estimate.)

Third, the conference called for a system of international food reserves to cushion the shock of future famines. (Such a system still has not been planned, let alone implemented, and a drought next year could bring death to millions.)

I believed that the conference at least should be challenged to provide more than scraps for the world's hungry, so I proposed that with global arms spending above $200 billion annually, all nations should agree to reduce their military budgets by 10 percent, with the $20 billion saving transferred to an International Food and Rural Development Authority. I asked that the OPEC nations agree to a similar transfer of 10 percent of their newly created oil profits, which would add another $7 billion.

I had thought about such a proposal for many months. The total of $27 billion, if effectively distributed, would permit the world not only to treat the immediate symptoms of hunger, the famine next time, but to develop a stable and permanent balance between the amount of food and the number of consumers. A food authority with such resources plus the intelligent cooperation of national governments could carry out a strategy of nutritional sufficiency, including land reform, rural water development, better agricultural methods, improved grain storage, and family planning.

New priorities, now an old term in domestic politics, have an equal relevance in the global food crisis. Arguing for a marginal shift of world resources to food needs, I told the Rome conference, "We can and must end hunger and malnutrition, but this will not be done if the major military powers continue to waste their substance in military overkill. Nor will it be done if those who have oil beneath their feet continue to use it to accumulate riches beyond reasonable use."

When a delegate from the Soviet Union advanced a similar proposal, it occurred to me that this would confirm some of my critics' worst fears—a meeting of minds between the Kremlin and McGovern. If so, I was redeemed the following day when the Vatican urged essentially the same idea. Without jeopardizing the defense of any nation, such a transfer could end world hunger within a decade and secure the economic base of the rural villages, where two thirds of the planet's inhabitants live.

In no aspect of international affairs does the United States have greater influence than in fashioning an international food policy. America is the breadbasket of the world; 4 percent of our population in farming produces enough to feed our own people and to provide a sizable portion of the world's food exports. But our abundance is a stopgap, not a solution. Global reserves, increased production, population control and fundamental social changes in the poorer nations are all essential. So is a kind of world antitrust action to prevent multinational agribusiness from dominating and distorting agriculture in the Third World. It is a cruel irony that in the same year a million residents of the Sahel starved while large landholders there had a bumper crop of cotton to export. Second only to the prevention of nuclear destruction, a reformed system of producing and distributing food should be at the top of the international agenda.

In March 1975 I set out on my second mission abroad. As chairman of the Foreign Relations Subcommittee on the Near East and South Asia, I journeyed to Arab capitals and to Israel for firsthand discussions with both sides of the world's most intractable, and threatening, conflict. I arrived in Cairo just as weeks of constructive effort by Secretary of State Kissinger to achieve a first-step Israeli-Egyptian agreement had broken down. President Anwar Sadat, with whom I visited at length, blamed the failure on Israeli intransigence. Although he had high praise for Kissinger, he believed there was no further hope for bilateral discussions between Egypt and Israel; progress, he said, could be made only at a full-scale Geneva conference of all the disputants in the Middle East.

From Cairo we flew to Jidda, where Saudi-Arabian officials worriedly quoted the recent remarks of some Americans that the United States should seize Persian Gulf oil sources in retaliation for any future oil embargo. The Saudis and American-embassy experts insisted that this was not a feasible option. Such a move would lead to the scuttling and firing of the oil fields, with vast uncontrollable blazes burning indefinitely, followed by endless sabotage and terrorism.

I arrived in Riyadh with Ambassador James Eakins on March 25 to confer with several Saudi Arabian ministers and to attend a dinner that evening hosted by Minister of Petroleum Ahmed Zaki Yamani. The following morning at ten o'clock I was scheduled to talk with King Faisal, the wealthiest and perhaps the most powerful leader in the Middle East. Deplaning in Riyadh, we were startled to learn that all the appointments had been canceled. Ambassador Eakins was visibly irritated and we tried to recall anything I might have said to provoke Saudi ire. We drove hurriedly to the American consulate, and shortly after our arrival, the telephone rang: King Faisal had been assassinated.

The reaction bore no resemblance to American grief following the Dallas tragedy of 1963. There was no public weeping; Saudi society in general seemed to react calmly. The new King Kalid and the new Crown Prince Fahd assumed power. An "indispensable" man quietly disappeared from the scene with scarcely a ripple. His successors assured Eakins and me that their policy would be the same. They wanted good relations with Washington. They also wanted to recover the Arab lands Israel had captured in the 1967 war. Then, but only then, would they recognize Israel's right to exist.

From Saudi Arabia I flew to Lebanon, where, after discussions with American and Lebanese officials, Clovis Maksoud, a Beirut lawyer, arranged a session with PLO leader Yasir Arafat at his Beirut headquarters. I expected to be criticized for meeting with him, and I was; but I believed then, as I do now, that a secure peace depends on Palestinian consent. It was not a question of giving Arafat legitimacy. A U.S. senator cannot add to or subtract from the fact of the Palestinian presence and his leadership. But I did hope to elicit flexibility in his position, some concession that might lay the basis for a reasonable settlement.

Arafat spoke first of the Palestinian "struggle," describing it as a "cause of the twentieth century." That "cause," he continued, involved a people forcibly deprived of their homeland, 60 percent of them in exile, the rest under occupation. These dispossessed Palestinians, he said almost defiantly, were not an "average" people; they have a literacy rate as high as Europe's, and in their exile, they have become the managerial elite of Syria, Lebanon and Jordan, of Libya and the emirates of the Persian Gulf, including even Saudi Arabia.

But Israel, too, had a fair claim, I replied, and Palestinian acceptance of it was a precondition of both peace and their own place in the Middle East. Arafat argued that the Palestinian leadership had refrained from "overbidding." PLO actions, he said, had been increasingly "realistic" as well as "bold" and "courageous." He pointed to the Palestinian National Council resolution of June 1974, favoring Palestinian national authority over any portion of "Palestinian land" that could be "liberated from occupation." I interrupted to ask if, when he spoke of all the Palestinian land that could be liberated, he was referring specifically to the West Bank and Gaza, and he replied "Yes." I asked if this would be an acceptable basis for a peace settlement. Again he answered "Yes." "Would you agree," I asked, "to two mutually recognized states—Israel and an independent Palestine?" I pressed the question several times. Each time Arafat referred to the council's June 1974 decision and added that it meant that the Palestine Liberation Organization would accept Israel's right to exist within its 1967 boundaries.

Israel has repeatedly announced that it would not negotiate with an independent PLO delegation at a peace conference. So I asked Arafat if there was a chance of compromise. Would the PLO be willing, for example, to go to such a conference as part of a Syrian delegation or a unified Arab delegation? Arafat replied that this question was not vital to the PLO; he was more interested in the "terms of reference" of the conference. The PLO did not want it to become a cover for further procrastination. Since then there have been indications that the Palestinians, under pressure from their Arab allies and the Soviet Union, would permit an Arab government to represent them if any settlement is subject to some ratification at the United Nations, where the PLO holds observer status.

As he had in his speech at the United Nations in November 1974, Arafat spoke with me of the official PLO objective of a unified, "democratic, secular" state involving all Palestine as a "vision of the future." There was a difference between the General Assembly speech and our talk in Beirut. In New York, he emphasized the "legitimacy" of the "dream." In quiet conversation in Beirut, he emphasized that the "dream" as a "vision of the future" was a long-range objective to be achieved through "intellectual transformation" and "political persuasion," not by "force or terror."

Arafat warned that the PLO leadership would have to struggle for their followers' acquiescence in such a compromise. "We are a revolution," he said, "and discipline must be strong in a revolution." The PLO's proposals were "neither violent nor extreme," but "if the Palestinians do not achieve stability," he added, "the area will not achieve stability." Perhaps if things did not go well, a more extreme leadership would emerge—"better than us," he added, shrugging, and glanced across the room at a young Palestinian, rifle in hand. I asked if Palestinian "rejectionists" would disrupt PLO moves toward a compromise. "A settlement is the Palestinian consensus," Arafat replied. One of his assistants volunteered at this point, in imperfect but clear English, "Some of the theoreticians are sometimes backward from the historical process."

A few days later I held a press conference in Jerusalem in which I was asked if Arafat had in fact told me that the PLO would make peace with Israel if granted a West Bank–Gaza state, and I replied "Yes." Neither Arafat nor anybody speaking on his behalf subsequently denied that statement, although a number of observers suggested at the time that he might feel compelled to do so. Since then, Arafat has reiterated that concession.

Next I talked at length with King Hussein in Jordan and President Hafez Assad in Syria. Assad was resentful of Sadat's bilateral negotiations with Israel through Kissinger and openly welcomed the recent breakdown. But like Hussein, he was anxious for a resolution of the crisis. He, too, no longer held to the Arab hard line of driving Israel into the sea.

Proceeding to Israel for discussion with a broad range of officials, military leaders and writers, I encountered a striking diversity of opinions about policy toward the Palestinians and the Arab states.

Arie Eliav, an independent in the Knesset, the Israeli Parliament, who had withdrawn from the Labor Party, told me that Israel should offer publicly and explicitly to accept the pre-1967 borders, with minor variations, and to allow the Palestinians to choose between a state of their own and a federation with Jordan, the quid pro quo being a genuine peace treaty and Arab recognition of Israel. But other Israelis were unwilling to give even an inch. The Bible clearly ordained Israeli ownership of the lands of the Jordan Valley, a delegation from a right-wing party said to me. They were eager for more Israeli settlements in the disputed areas. A future Palestinian state had to come, if at all, from the territory of existing Arab states.

The Nazi holocaust is never far from Israeli consciousness. The memory shapes Israeli attitudes, as it would those of any people who suffered the worst crime of the human experience. The holocaust profoundly affects Israel's dealings with the Arabs. Though rarely stated any longer, the Arab threat to "drive Israel into the sea" raised the threat of a new holocaust. In his book on Israel, Arie Eliav wrote: ". . . in the heart of the Jewish people the terrible aftermath of the holocaust still remains. Not only corpses were consumed by fire in the ovens and gas chambers, but also a faith in humanity and its values."

This fear has much to do with Israeli caution in diplomatic bargaining. They are not dealing with bits and pieces of territory, but with life itself. Their historic memory is one of endless discrimination and humiliation through the long centuries of the Diaspora, and in the end near-total extermination. After millennia in "the wilderness," at last they have come home and their deepest conviction is: "Never again."

My mission to the Middle East, followed by extensive public hearings before my Foreign Relations subcommittee, convinced me that a settlement is possible on the following basis:

All parties would commit themselves to respect one another's sovereignty and boundaries. They would phase in normal economic and diplomatic relations; the Arabs would lift blockades and boycotts and end hostile propaganda, as Israel withdrew, in stages, to its 1967 borders with minor modifications. The United Nations would supervise demilitarized zones. The Palestinians would gain self-determination in the form of an independent West Bank–Gaza state or federation with Jordan; in turn, they would explicitly recognize Israel. General guarantees of the entire settlement by the United Nations Security Council would be reinforced by specific Soviet and United States assurances and, if desired, a unilateral American guarantee of Israel.

When I outlined these terms in the spring of 1975, many of Israel's American friends (I consider myself such a friend) were bewildered and angered. Eleanor was disinvited from two scheduled appearances before respected Jewish organizations. I remain convinced that it is in Israel's interest to accept a compromise peace rather than living permanently at the edge of war. It is also in America's interest that the Middle East not be a flashpoint of Great Power confrontation. Within months of his inauguration, President Carter openly described a compromise very close to my 1975 suggestion. The process of peacemaking will be difficult, but the President's initial course on the Middle East has been sensible and politically courageous.

The Middle East represented a foreign question on which senators customarily express strong views. I had gone further than usual by advocating a compromise involving Palestinian self-determination and by meeting with Arafat, but at least no one was surprised at the sight of a senator visiting the Middle East. My next foreign initiative, a trip to Cuba, where I talked with Fidel Castro, was a very different matter. For fifteen years the United States had attempted to isolate Cuba diplomatically and squeeze it economically. Détente had come with Moscow and Peking, even with Rumania, but ninety miles from Florida the Cold War was still being waged with full force. For a long time the only American export to Cuba was CIA operatives sent to assassinate Premier Castro, or at least to sabotage his revolution.

A local Cold War in a period of global détente seemed to me both senseless and hypocritical. In 1963, months before the United States and the Soviet Union had taken the first step of an atmospheric nuclear-test-ban treaty, I had spoken of our dangerous Castro obsession. By 1975, after SALT I, SALT II and the Shanghai Communiqué, boycotting Cuba had become a parody of a policy whose time had passed. So in May 1975 I visited Havana, hoping that this would help open the way to a Cuban-American détente. With that hope in mind, I invited a number of American journalists along, including Barbara Walters, then the host of NBC's *Today* show. Her daily reports from Havana, and the stories of other correspondents, were an important factor in the success of the trip.

The second evening in Cuba we had dinner with Vice Premier Carlos Raphael Rodríguez and Foreign Minister Raúl Roa at one of Havana's protocol houses, the former homes of wealthy Cubans, now maintained for entertaining foreign guests. The conversation had turned to the possibility of an American major-league baseball team playing in Cuba, a hemispheric version of Ping-Pong diplomacy, when Fidel Castro suddenly arrived unannounced "to pay my respects."

The reality of the man matches the image. He was, as always, dressed in freshly pressed military fatigues. Youthful in appearance at the age of forty-eight, hair and beard still black, cigar constantly in hand, he was poised, confident and questioning. But as we talked I discovered another side of his personality. He is shy, soft-spoken and sensitive. He arranges his thoughts and chooses his words carefully. He responds knowledgeably on almost any subject, from agricultural methods to Marxist dialectics to American politics.

This first meeting, it was clear, was his way of getting to know me before we got down to serious issues.

"You served during the Second World War?" he asked.

"Yes, as a bomber pilot making raids from Italy against the Nazis."

Castro suggested that the experience must have been one motivation for my efforts for international peace. He recalled the 1972 campaign, expressing keen interest in the reform movement inside the Democratic Party and in the political activism of American youth. His questions showed that he watches American politics closely.

Although we did not discuss substantive issues in this first talk, I did raise the point that one way to move toward better relations would be an exchange of baseball teams. "That is being considered," he said. I gave him a letter from Senator Edward Brooke of Massachusetts urging that the Cuban parents of Boston Red Sox pitcher Luis Tiant be permitted to travel to the United States to see their son in a major-league game. "That should be no problem," Castro replied. "We will look into this matter and give you a definite answer."

Like the first encounter, our second meeting, the following day, was unscheduled, though not unexpected. We had driven fifty miles southeast of Havana to a lush agricultural valley for lunch with the Premier's brother Ramón. As we were preparing to leave, several Russian-made jeeps rounded the corner of the driveway. They came to a halt directly in front of us on the porch of Ramón's house. Fidel Castro was in the lead jeep. He greeted his brother, then invited Eleanor and me to tour the valley. "Before you answer," he laughed, "I want you to know that I'm going to drive." He put on his glasses, peered over the steering wheel with mock gravity and took off down the hillside with the press buses in hurried pursuit. For the next three and a half hours we drove across the Cuban countryside, stopping briefly at an experimental dairy farm and a cattle ranch, with Castro supplying a running commentary on the progress of his favorite agricultural projects. "The United States," he said, "is critical in the development of agriculture world-wide. You have the greatest farm output in the world and you can help guide the development of other countries."

During the long drive I asked him about speculation in the United

States that his agents might have been involved in the assassination of President Kennedy. He responded in disbelief. "We had troubles with the Kennedy Administration. But it is monstrous even to contemplate that we would murder the head of state of any nation—to say nothing of being so foolish as to incur the wrath of a great power like the United States." He added, "Before that man Oswald killed President Kennedy he tried to get a visa at our embassy in Mexico City to visit Cuba. His application was refused. I have often thought that if we had admitted him, many people might have blamed us for what he did."

Castro said that the CIA had tried on numerous occasions to assassinate him. Apparently he had little fear of such plots by 1975. He moved easily among the Cuban people. At my suggestion we stopped at a village ice-cream stand, which began turning out cones as quickly as possible for our party and for the children who quickly clustered around. Castro talked and joked with the crowd of villagers. His security men made no attempt to shield him. We walked into an apartment building, where one of the families insisted that Eleanor stay for refreshments. We finally found her there after everyone else had boarded the jeeps and buses and were waiting to leave.

Castro dropped us at our hotel at eight-thirty in the evening. At my request he had scheduled a press conference with the American reporters at nine-thirty and would see us afterward. He used the press conference to deliver a message to the U.S. government. He had refined his position on the embargo in an effort to be more accommodating. Pending the complete resumption of trade, discussions with the United States could move ahead if Washington would just lift the ban on food and medicine. To the American people he extended in English "a wish of friendship. I understand it is not easy, because we belong to different worlds. But we are neighbors. In one way or another we ought to live in peace."

By ten-thirty we were seated around an oblong table in the Premier's office. Before taking up relations between the United States and Cuba, we briefly discussed other issues, first the Middle East, then Southeast Asia. I briefly described terms I had recently outlined for a Middle East settlement: full recognition of Israel in exchange for Israel's return to its 1967 borders, with practical modifications, and recognition of Palestinian self-determination. Castro felt that such a formula could bring peace and that the Israelis—a "wise people," he said—might be ready to accept it. As for the Arabs, he said, they "dislike the step-by-step approach, the so-called Kissinger formula. It tends to divide them."

Castro expected no "blood bath" in South Vietnam, where the Thieu regime had just fallen. The conflict "was primarily a struggle for independence against foreign domination. When the foreigners left, the fighting ceased. I don't believe the PRG realized how quickly the end would come. What happens next depends a great deal on U.S. policy. If the United States sponsors and supports subversive activities against the new government, then the situation could change. The full reunification of North and South will take a few years. Vietnam will not be a typical socialist state. They will be mindful of public opinion in the United States and around the world." But about Cambodia, he shook his head and said nervously, "I'm not so sure. That may be a different matter."

I opened the discussion of Cuban-American issues by saying that I would not waste my time defending the embargo; Castro already knew of my opposition to it, and so did the United States government. Instead, I suggested, we should concentrate on steps which might help improve relations between the two countries. Senator John Sparkman, the chairman of the Foreign Relations Committee, had given me a letter to the Cuban government on behalf of Southern Airways, which had lost a $2 million ransom when hijackers had taken the money with them to Cuba. I argued that it would be a strong gesture of good will for Cuba to arrange a repayment. Castro said he was very impressed with the reasoning of the Sparkman letter; he was "personally inclined to respond positively; but more for you than for the United States government. We don't want to appear in the role of begging."

Castro felt that Cuba had gone "the extra mile" to accommodate the United States, but that Washington had given hardly an inch. Additional steps, he said, would have to be justified not as gestures to the U.S. government, but as courtesies to individual Americans who favor a change in the official policy. He pointed to the hijacking agreement: "We took honest, rational and constructive action. But we didn't link it to our internal interests. Then the other party, the United States, did not take any important steps to help us. It would have been much more tactical to link the treaty to the blockade. Now we are a little bit skeptical of the good will of the United States government. Maybe sometimes we react with a little pride. We could resist the blockade for another fifteen years. But nobody would profit from that."

I asked Castro about eight American prisoners in Cuba of special concern to the State Department. While I could not judge individual cases, I said, the prisoners had been confined in Cuba for a long time and it would advance the prospects of normalization if they were released. This magnanimous, unilateral step would demonstrate not weakness but strength, I continued, the strength to forgive enemies. He wanted to know how many I thought he should release. "Why, all of them," I replied. He smiled and said, "But then, what would I do for Senator Kennedy if he comes?" Castro recalled that he had once offered to exchange four of the prisoners for the four Puerto Ricans convicted of a shooting incident in the gallery of the House of Representatives during the Truman Administration. Washington, he noted, had shown no interest.

Sometime after midnight he looked at his watch and suggested that we have dinner. We drove from the palace to a house in the Havana suburbs. But instead of going in, we were led to a basketball court around back. Next to the court a lamb was being barbecued whole over an open pit, with a large chicken thrown in for good measure. Castro explained that this was to be an Algerian dinner: "They prepared it for me during one of my visits there. I believe you have a lot of sheep in South Dakota, so I thought this would be appropriate."

Still on a skewer, the lamb was carried to a table. There was no silverware because, Castro said, "the tradition is to eat it with your fingers. Use just one hand, to keep the other free for wine. I suggest you start about here." It was a delicious and relaxed meal, though the Premier complained that because he had kept us too long at the palace, the lamb was overcooked.

I wondered why the issue of our naval base at Guantánamo had not been raised with me at any point, by any Cuban official. Typically in the past, the Cubans had cited not only the embargo but that base, as the other major barrier to normal relations with the United States, yet no one had even spoken the word "Guantánamo" during my visit. So at dinner I decided to test out my impression that the base was no longer that important: Did the Cubans mean what they weren't saying?

"If you ask the average Cuban," Castro replied, "he will probably tell you that a foreign nation should not have a military base on our soil. But I will tell you that it is a secondary issue, a secondary issue. We are not pressing the matter now."

Castro reminisced about the 1962 missile crisis. "I would have taken a harder line than Khrushchev. I was furious when he compromised. But Khrushchev was older and wiser. I realize in retrospect that he reached the proper settlement with Kennedy. If my position had prevailed, there might have been a terrible war. I was wrong."

Dinner was over at two-thirty—and then we took off on a drive through downtown Havana. Castro said that crime was no longer a problem; he proudly noted the absence of uniformed policemen. The crime syndicates were gone, he said, and gambling and prostitution had ended. In the wee hours he dropped us at the hotel, where we slept a few hours before I met with the American press and then proceeded to the University of Havana—the first North American politician to speak on that campus since the Castro revolution.

Fidel Castro leaves mingled impressions. It is abundantly clear that he will not yield to American pressure, but he has decided to seek détente with the United States. He is walking a narrow line. Just hours after my departure he spoke at a celebration of the thirtieth anniversary of the Allied victory in World War II. In the audience were high officials of the Soviet Union. Castro denounced "Yankee imperialism" and lavished praise on the Russians as the world's principal fighter against fascism in the 1940s, and the defender of global peace since then. Plainly, he will not risk the loss of Soviet support in order to court the United States.

The most revealing of all the answers he gave during our discussions was, I thought, his admission of error during the Cuban missile crisis, for he was not only reflecting on a single event, but pointing to his own more cautious view of the world today. When Castro began fighting the Cuban revolution, he was in his twenties. At the time of the missile crisis, he was in his mid-thirties. The years and the challenges of national leadership have matured Fidel Castro just as they have matured his revolution. Now, even if his rhetoric still seems hard at times, his actions in fact have tended to be responsible and conciliatory. He will not abandon his revolution or his allies in Africa, but he will continue to pursue détente.

Castro followed through on each of the promises he had made during the course of my four-day trip. Before I left I was handed a comprehensive memo on a baseball exchange. Luis Tiant's parents saw their son pitch in the World Series between Cincinnati and Boston. (They both died in Boston shortly after the World Series in which their son had starred so brilliantly.) On August 9, 1975, an executive of Southern Airways flew to Havana to retrieve the $2 million in ransom money that the hijackers had brought to Cuba. Castro also sent me a detailed report, including pictures of CIA agents, describing their attempts to assassinate him or dynamite Cuban installations by hit-and-run raids from the sea. I passed the documents on to Senator Church's committee investigating CIA activities.

I also secured permission for others, usually scholars, to visit Cuba. At my request, several Cubans were allowed to rejoin their relatives in the United States. I remained in close touch with Teo Acosta and his wife, Esther, able Cuban diplomats assigned to the UN Mission. My daughter Mary and a classmate at Clark University were invited to study Spanish at the University of Havana in the fall of 1976.

But the Ford Administration was willing to move glacially, if at all. The New York Yankees and the Los Angeles Dodgers were interested in a baseball exchange. Baseball Commissioner Bowie Kuhn proposed an all-star team. The Ford State Department was resistant, however, and Castro wanted the Yankees, not a combined team. Nothing was to happen on athletic exchanges for nearly two years.

On the trade embargo, the Ford Administration insisted that they were bound by the Organization of American States resolution imposing an embargo in 1964. In fact, most members of the OAS had long since broken with that policy; the OAS itself had exempted food and medicine, but the United States banned everything. In any case, the misuse of the OAS resolution as an excuse for a continued hard line soon became impossible. In July 1975 the OAS voted for "freedom of action" for each member country to choose its own course on trade and diplomacy with Cuba. A month later, the United States took a small step, lifting the sanctions against countries trading with the Cubans.

There was a brief moment when greater progress seemed possible. Secretary of State Kissinger tentatively looked toward improved relations: "We do not consider that an animosity toward Cuba is an essential aspect of U.S. policy." In September 1975 Assistant Secretary William Rogers reaffirmed American willingness "to improve our relations with Cuba," and to "enter into a dialogue with Cuba" based on reciprocity of concessions.

But with the coming of the Reagan challenge in 1976, President Ford moved to protect his right flank. He worried about the Cuban exiles in the Florida primary. Campaigning there, he characterized Castro as an "international outlaw." Soon Ford and Reagan were competing to prove who could blast Havana more fiercely. In effect, Ford had frozen Cuban détente until after the 1976 elections.

Cuban policy, as well as American politics, contributed to the impasse, as Havana and Washington clashed in Africa. In November 1975 Secretary Kissinger disclosed that Cuba, along with the Soviet Union, was supplying aid to the Popular Movement for the Liberation of Angola (the MPLA), the side which eventually prevailed in the conflict. At that time only a few high Administration officials were aware that the CIA was financing other Angolan factions, one of which also had the support of Peking and South Africa.

(Reportedly Chinese "advisers" were also in Angola, but no one in Washington suggested that the United States end the détente with China. It was less a matter of the principle that foreign troops should not be in Africa than of the fact that the Cubans were goring the American ox. In defending official actions abroad, self-interests too often get disguised as "principles." Thus morality in foreign policy too often seems to count only as long as it is convenient, even in cases where the claim is counterfeit. The State Department did not oppose outside forces, say, in Vietnam. In effect, UN Ambassador Andrew Young's real offense, not only on the issue of Cubans in Angola, but generally, is that he has refused to traffic in the usual hypocrisies.)

In any event, Cuba's African policy deflated the prospects of détente with the United States. It gave the Ford Administration a new pretext for inaction as the Reagan threat mounted. It also ended, for the time being, any possibility of independent congressional initiatives. I am sure the Cuban government knew that. Ted Kennedy, my South Dakota Senate colleague Jim Abourezk and I had prepared amendments to the Security Assistance bill lifting the trade embargo. Following the Angola disclosures, we decided to hold off, since it suddenly had no conceivable chance of passing.

One more event soured the atmosphere, this time on the Cuban side, before the Carter Administration came to power. In October 1976 a bomb planted on a Cuban airliner exploded in midflight and all aboard were killed. When the crime was traced to Cuban exiles now living in Venezuela, Castro cited their past connections with CIA-financed groups, blamed the CIA for the bombing and announced that he was giving the required six months' notice for suspension of the anti-hijacking agreement that Cuba had negotiated with Washington in 1973. He also complained of the harassment of Cuban fishing boats in international waters off Florida and of Cuban diplomats at the United Nations.

At the United Nations I told Cuban representative Teo Acosta that I regarded CIA involvement in the airplane sabotage as inconceivable under present circumstances. Even if the agency were so inclined, and I doubted that, no responsible official would be stupid enough, in the midst of congressional investigations of the CIA, to plan and carry out such an atrocity. I also joined other senators in urging the Intelligence Oversight Committee to look into the matter.

I returned to Cuba in April 1977. Jim Abourezk had suggested a visit of a South Dakota basketball team after the baseball exchange became bogged down in the State Department bureaucracy and Republican politics. The Carter Administration approved the basketball visit, and a combined team from South Dakota State and the University of South Dakota gamely played, and lost, twice to the Cuban Olympians. Talking afterward with Fidel Castro, I invited the Cuban team to play in South Dakota and against two other American schools, perhaps Marquette, UCLA or Nevada at Las Vegas. Castro enthusiastically accepted. The only drawback came when numerous colleges decided that the way to get the Cubans onto their basketball court was to call my office!

Castro also agreed to an American all-star baseball team. His original choice, for symbolic reasons, I suspect, was the Yankees, but I told him that the baseball commissioner was insisting on an all-star squad. The difference was not crucial, Castro conceded. I phoned Bowie Kuhn after returning, and the all-stars' visit, in the fall of 1977 or the spring of 1978, seems, as of this writing, to be a virtual certainty.

On substantive issues, Castro continued to be conciliatory, but he would not beg for détente at any price. He assured me that Cuban troop commitments in Africa were limited; a gradual withdrawal from Angola was likely. Having just returned from Africa and Moscow, he insisted that Cuban forces were in Angola at the invitation of that country's internationally recognized government. How was this different from U.S. forces in Germany? On human rights, Castro was neither defensive nor apologetic. The lot of Cubans, he said, their housing, education, medical care and nutrition were vastly improved over the time of the Batista dictatorship—which the United States had supported. As for civil liberties, there was no torture in Cuban prisons, as there had been under America's friend Batista. He would take no lessons on human rights, he concluded, from a country which had tried to kill him, had aided cruel dictatorships and had its own human rights violations to account for.

Castro does not seem to be a dictator for his own sake, but a convinced revolutionary who is popular among his own people. Though we may wish that he would see the world our way, his own scale of values weighs social and economic equality far more than civil liberties. He will never, it is clear, trade his conceptions for American tourism and trade.

But Castro also emphasized during our four-hour talk that he wanted further improvement of relations with Washington. He insisted that Cuba had already offered major concessions: the anti-hijacking agreement, the basketball visit, the fishing discussions, the return of the Southern Airways ransom. It was time, he continued, for America to reciprocate.

The Carter Administration did so, though timidly. Shortly after my visit, the Administration and Havana agreed to establish "interest sections" with Cuban representatives in Washington and American diplomats in Havana. This was a minimal form of diplomatic exchange; it reflected the Administration's general caution on Cuba. President Carter told Jim Abourezk and me during an Oval Office meeting that he had to go slow but that he desired better relations with the Cubans. He said that he had avoided inflammatory statements about Cuba even during the Florida primary.

The White House did agree to remain "benevolently neutral" on my amendment to lift the trade embargo. But trouble quickly came from a group that could have cared less about the issue for its own sake; the sugar interests were concerned about competition from Cuban imports. They pressured the White House, which then conditioned its neutrality on a clause giving the President the power to limit Cuban sugar sales in the United States. Even then, the neutrality permitted some State Department professionals, who still held to the anti-Castro hard line of the past, to lobby quietly against the amendment. The most the Foreign Relations Committee would approve was one-way trade: the United States would sell to, but not buy from, Cuba.

Right-wing congressmen then proposed to ban all further steps until Havana met a variety of conditions, which Castro would reject as interference with Cuban independence. A final settlement of the Caribbean Cold War depends on unequivocal presidential leadership. A senator can nudge the policy, find the openings, accelerate the process, but in the end only the President can finish the task of persuading Americans to reverse the futile opposition to the Cuban revolution which was declared, over and over, by five of his predecessors.

Questioning official policies always raises political hackles. During the Vietnam years I became accustomed to the hate mail. My Cuban initiatives stirred a more sinister reaction. The right-wing exiles publicly listed me as "Enemy Number One." I, of course, do not yield to such political intimidation. Beyond this, I am convinced that most of the Cuban exiles in the United States do not see me as an enemy but as a realist recognizing the fact that the Cuban revolution is not going to disappear. In the 1972 campaign I understood the Secret Service's concerns and cooperated, as much as possible, with their precautions. Both then, when I had protection, and now, when I don't, I understand that no public figure is entirely free from danger once he or she becomes involved in a controversial issue.

But if government cannot eliminate the danger, it can avoid contributing to it. Thus the threats from the Cuban extremists bothered me less for personal reasons than for what they revealed about the distorted character, and the side effects, of official policies in violation of this nation's basic principles. Secretly the executive branch had gone into the murder business, recruiting hit men among the embittered Cuban exiles. When the agency went out of the killing business, at least with respect to Castro, the hit men continued on their own. Some of them may have participated in the assassination of President Kennedy. Other veterans of the CIA's anti-Castro crusade were caught in the Watergate burglary; the dirty tricks had been turned on American democracy itself. I have received letters from Cuban exiles who favor détente with Havana but dare not say so publicly.

They may be shot; their homes may be bombed; there is a reign of fear in Miami's Cuban community.

In 1972 I was accused of being insufficiently tough because I opposed covert CIA operations to buy, bribe or overthrow foreign leaders. But in the years since, it has become painfully obvious that this kind of toughness is toughest of all on our own country. It is impossible, even if it were moral, to create these Frankensteins and be certain of confining them to other people's affairs. The lesson for a new generation of American leaders is not to be more circumspect about such adventures; the officials who approved them in the past thought they were being circumspect. The point is that a democratic society should not be in the business of secret killings and coups.

The revolution of the carnations—the flower that became its symbol—had come to Portugal in 1974 after half a century of fascist dictatorship and a decade of colonial war in Africa. In Portugal the United States had the chance not to repeat the disastrous errors of its official policies in Vietnam and Cuba. America, though it had aided the fascist regime, could allay Portuguese suspicions by befriending the revolution instead of opposing it.

In September 1975 and in January 1976 I visited Portugal to meet with its new leaders. I found a society in ferment, at times close to chaos, but filled with new hope. Communist forces had some strength, but not nearly as much as the socialists and centrists. An attempted rightist coup in March 1975 had strengthened the Communists, but their own attempt to seize power between my two visits encountered a backlash.

From the American viewpoint, the gravest danger was that we would seem to be with the counterrevolution or that the CIA would be discovered interfering in Portuguese politics. American officials associated with past support for the fascists were not welcome in Lisbon. Senator Kennedy and Senator Mansfield, representatives of a different attitude, had been received warmly. Ambassador Frank Carlucci told me that their visits had been a signal of good American intentions; they had improved the U.S. position in Portugal. For similar reasons, he welcomed my visit. "The Communists," one embassy official said, "just can't succeed in portraying you as a CIA type." Indeed, I was surprised to be recognized on the streets of Lisbon; many Portuguese recalled my statement during the 1972 campaign, hardly noted in the United States, questioning the Nixon Administration's aid to the Portuguese dictatorship. It was another example of a phenomenon I have seen elsewhere: other people, about whom most Americans know very little, follow our politics closely because it affects their lives profoundly.

A practical man, Carlucci stood up to Secretary Kissinger's panicked reaction that the Portuguese socialists were a "Trojan horse" for a Communist takeover. Kissinger was reluctant to provide economic aid or even to recognize the new government because the Communists were in the interim coalition then governing the country. But the economy was shaky; a denial of aid, rather than preventing a Communist victory, was likelier to facilitate one by bringing on a deeper recession. Mansfield, Kennedy and I pushed for immediate aid. Under pressure from Congress and Carlucci, the State Department relented. The April 1976 parliamentary election gave the socialists a plurality that would open the way for Mario Soares to become Prime Minister after Portugal's first free parliamentary elections in half a century. The Communists and related parties were held to less than 15 percent of the vote. Thus, even the hard-liners in the State Department were grateful that a democratic Portugal could now be accepted as a continuing NATO partner.

The Portuguese revolution provides a vital lesson for American diplomacy in the rest of Europe. In France and Italy now, and perhaps later in Spain, there is prospect of Communist participation in coalition governments. There will be a temptation to panic, as Kissinger at first did in the Portuguese situation. But should the Italians, for example, vote a share of power to the Communists, this will not mean that Italy has "fallen" or that Moscow rules in Rome. The Portuguese Communists, hard-liners who hew to the Soviet line, could not convert partial into total power. The far more independent, professedly democratic Communist parties in France, Spain and Italy probably could not do so, even if they wished to. A hostile American reaction would be the graver danger. Excluding Italy from NATO would be a stronger incentive to the Italians to move toward the Soviet bloc than including some Communists in their government as a result of free elections.

The Portuguese revolution had other, immediate implications for American policy. A free Portugal was about to free the old regime's African colonies. Europe's last imperial war on that continent was suddenly coming to an end. In Mozambique and Angola, Marxist revolutionaries, who had received Soviet support, seemed likely to assume power. During my first visit to Lisbon in September 1975, Portuguese leaders warned against American intervention to prevent this. I thought of De Gaulle's advice to John Kennedy to stay out of Vietnam: now the Portuguese, like the French before them, were cautioning America not to refight their lost cause.

Since Vietnam did not recur in Angola, the current fashion discounts the analogy as naïve. In fact, the Angolan situation in 1975 came quickly to resemble, at least in its American dimension, the superpower "test of will" that official Washington had seen in Indochina a decade before. The Ford Administration's pronouncements had a haunting similarity to the fateful statements of Secretary of State Dean Rusk as he built a Vietnam policy on the single-minded assumption that all the difficulties there would end only if the "other side would simply stop doing what it is doing." The problem with this prescription, in the southern Africa of the mid-seventies as in the Indochina of the mid-sixties, was that it overlooked the historical background of the conflict, what the "other side" was, and why we so feared it.

From their origins, American policies toward French Indochina and Portuguese Africa were strikingly parallel. In each case the defense of postwar Europe against the Soviet Union excused American tolerance and assistance for colonialism. To secure the alliance with France immediately after World War II, we backed the reassertion of French colonialism in Indochina. To secure air bases in the Portuguese Azores, we championed Portugal's NATO membership in 1949, thereafter ignoring the Lisbon regime. In each case a concern for buttressing NATO aligned America against forces whose ultimate triumph was virtually inevitable, although in neither case were those forces initially hostile to the United States. In Indochina, after the Japanese defeat in 1945, Ho Chi Minh actively sought American help to block the French return. In the 1950s and 1960s, the liberation leaders of Portuguese Africa repeatedly sought a hearing in official Washington, particularly during the Kennedy years, when some officials, including the President, seemed receptive. But in both cases the United States finally and fatefully chose to side with the European colonialists, in effect inviting a Soviet alignment with the forces of nationalist liberation. Having fostered it, U.S. officials promptly decried this alignment as part of the global Communist conspiracy. An American policy rooted in "European" considerations grew into an ideological commitment that survived even after the colonizing power withdrew.

There is no need to recount the disastrous results of the policy in Vietnam. But it is essential to remember that pattern as it ominously began to repeat itself in southern Africa in 1975. As the Portuguese retreated, American officials, after years of permitting Lisbon to misuse NATO matériel in colonial wars, undertook a desperation effort to prop up an "anti-Communist" Angolan faction. Washington indignantly denounced Cuban and Soviet involvement as a violation of "the spirit of détente." In fact, the Soviet Union and China—not to mention several West European countries—had supported liberation groups in the Portuguese colonies for years, an "intervention" that had the active or tacit support of much of Africa. Significant U.S.

involvement, on the other hand, came only as the Portuguese were leaving. It was, in effect, a last-ditch effort to avoid the legacy of past policy. This distinction, if lost in American debate, was clear to African leaders. Even those with no Soviet or Communist sympathies saw the sudden American concern as frantically ideological and plainly hypocritical. History, as they were quick to point out, did not begin yesterday. Where had the United States been before? The sad answer was: "On the other side"—the colonialist side.

The parallel evolution of U.S. policies in Vietnam and Angola were stopped at this point. Fortunately the Congress, over the Ford Administration's objections, cut off further American military intervention against the Angolan forces most likely to succeed. The Congress had grasped the sensible notion, never properly appreciated in Indochina, that liberation forces do not fight for independence so that after winning it they may deliver themselves into superpower control, either Soviet or American.

The Vietnamese government in Hanoi is proving the point already. It is open, even anxious, for normal relations with the United States; as Premier Pham Van Dong was to tell me, his regime did not want to become a Soviet dependent. But after losing the Vietnam war in 1975, the Ford Administration refused to make a peace. The issue was politically hazardous; it is easier to be friendly, even generous, to defeated adversaries. The Japanese and the Germans surrendered unconditionally. But because the Vietnamese won unconditionally, American officials consigned them to the status, in effect, of a non-nation.

I had not opposed the war in 1965 as a matter of convenience. I was not ready in 1975 to follow the course of least resistance, to forget, conveniently, the implications of that opposition. I thought I owed it to my own convictions to stand for peace after as well as during the fighting.

So in January 1976 I spent five days in North and South Vietnam; Eleanor was with me. I became the first member of Congress to visit both Saigon and Hanoi since the last Americans were airlifted off the roof of the American embassy on the final afternoon of the war. This visit to Vietnam moved me as has no other experience abroad. Walking through the streets of Hanoi where American bombs had fallen, seeing the devastation of the countryside from an airplane window, listening to Vietnamese expressions, despite all this, of friendship for the American people redoubled my determination to work for reason and fairness in our postwar Vietnam policy.

We landed in Hanoi after a four-hour flight from Bangladesh. Waiting on the ramp for us were Xuan Thuy, the Vietnamese negotiator at the Paris peace talks, and Xuan Oanh, one-time concert pianist, composer, guerrilla fighter and foreign-service officer who had also served in Paris. I had met both men there in 1971, when I conferred with Hanoi's delegation about the prospects of negotiating a truce. Their attitudes were typical of the Vietnamese leadership. Understandably, they feel no warmth toward recent American Administrations, but they admire Jefferson and Lincoln as great leaders. They credit the American people with forcing their government to end the war. They recall the peace movement, the student protesters and dissenting senators such as Wayne Morse and Ernest Gruening, William Fulbright, Mark Hatfield and Frank Church. They know the details of the 1968 and 1972 presidential campaign; they mourn Robert Kennedy; they honor Eugene McCarthy. They know that I sought the presidency as a peace candidate.

They know and appreciate American writers, too. Ernest Hemingway, Sinclair Lewis and John Steinbeck are favorites. When I asked Xuan Oanh if he liked the great Russian novelists, Tolstoy and Dostoyevsky, he said, "No, they are too ponderous for me; I prefer the Americans—especially Mark Twain," another Vietnamese favorite. When I asked what to send him after I returned home, he answered quickly, "American paperbacks." All through the war the North Vietnamese taught American history and literature to their children. They reasoned that Americans were a great people with a revolutionary past and a rich cultural heritage who had been misled into the Vietnam intervention. The interpretation is one with which few Americans would quarrel now. It is a tribute to the Vietnamese that they drew a distinction between the ideals and mistakes of the United States.

While they held to a better image of our country, U.S. officials fostered the worst image of theirs, predicting a "blood bath" in the South after a Communist victory. Aside from the prisoners of war, that blood bath became the most persistent rationale for prolonging the war. I obviously cannot document the absence of wholesale reprisals or executions in South Vietnam, but I do have some strong impressions on the subject, based as much on what I saw in Saigon, and on what I heard in discussions on other subjects, as on the replies to my specific questions about this one. I believe that the "blood bath" was one of the great false alarms in the history of American foreign policy.

As a practical matter, systematic reprisals would have required an enormous administrative apparatus to locate and identify the proper victims. If the Vietnamese victors had any such capability in early 1976, they kept it well hidden. The new regime did hold what political power there was in Saigon, but their control was largely on the surface. When we asked the source of the gasoline that was being sold by street vendors, they conceded: "We have no idea."

In any event, regardless of their inclinations, the victors had political reasons to be tolerant of the past. In Saigon at least, it is quite certain that they were in a minority when they took over in April 1975, notwithstanding the evacuation of many Thieu supporters. Some Saigonese were sympathetic, but many were apolitical. The U.S. withdrawal spelled economic hardship for hundreds of thousands who had grown accustomed to living off the American war presence and economic aid. Under those circumstances, any blood bath would have outraged the relatives and friends of the victims and vastly complicated the Communists' task of consolidating their tenuous control.

They talked openly of these realities. Officials with no qualms about a blood bath certainly would not tell visitors, as one of them told us, that relocation from Saigon was a hard task because people "want to stay in the city." An iron-fisted regime would simply make people leave—as the Thieu government had forced them into the cities in the first place. Another official explained: "If we executed the soldiers, every family would be affected. They were drafted to fight the war. It was not their fault. Only a very few people have been executed—former soldiers of the Thieu army who were bandits, saboteurs. We have to make an example when we catch them red-handed."

In Saigon I talked extensively with Madame Binh, the Foreign Minister for the Vietcong during the war. She had been a guerrilla in the jungle; later she became an eloquent, skillful diplomat at the Paris peace talks. She admitted that "some" Thieu officials were in re-education centers. But she, too, insisted that as a matter of necessity as well as policy, the numbers subject to re-education were limited: "There were more than one million soldiers. For the rank-and-file soldiers, you could explain policy to them, and they are seen living with their families. For the high-ranking officers, they need some time to learn and to study because they had greater responsibility during the war."

I asked Madame Binh if any of Thieu's associates had been executed. "Very few," she answered, and went on, "A few were brought to the tribunals because they are the law offenders. The robbers, the killers, the criminals. We executed a few. Our policy is very clear on this point. For those who committed crimes in the past but who are now living normally as the other people, abiding by the law, we let them live as other people, without discrimination. But those who are continuing their activities against the people, against the law, we have to deal with them."

Americans would regard forced re-education as deeply offensive.

Even "very few" executions may be excessive. But these practices hardly constitute a "blood bath," especially not in comparison with the killing that was continued for so many years on the basis that the blood bath would begin if the bloodletting stopped.

I had an extended discussion of Vietnamese-American differences with Premier Pham Van Dong. Like Ho Chi Minh, who selected him as his heir, the Premier is a thin, ascetic man. He talks softly; he appears to understand English, though he does not speak it and invariably waits for the translator to put a visitor's words into Vietnamese. He greeted us on the steps of his simple, well-proportioned residence, a stark contrast to the grandiose presidential palace constructed at American expense in Saigon. The Premier led us into a spacious room with chairs arranged in a squared horseshoe.

When I asked him about relations with the Soviet Union and the People's Republic of China, he observed, "We firmly maintain our line of independence and sovereignty. That line requires that we have good relations with those two countries and those two friends."

Vietnam receives aid from both the Soviet Union and China. Other officials reported that Soviet aid was greater and that it was an integral part of Hanoi's current five-year plan. But we detected no hints of the traditional Vietnamese animosity toward China. To test for it, I asked the Premier if it was prudent for the United States to continue pushing the détente with Peking. He brushed the question aside: "We do not intervene in your internal affairs . . . We have enough to do here." The Vietnamese do not choose between Russia and China; they do not wish to be the satellite of either. It is one reason why they are so intent on normal relations with the United States.

Pham Van Dong attributed the worst of the war to "Nixon's bombing," not to Americans in general. He pointed out that I had come to Vietnam in the 200th-anniversary year of the Declaration of Independence, a document which Ho Chi Minh had copied in Vietnam's own declaration three decades before. I recalled that Ho had amended the wording to hold that all "people," not all "men" are created equal. The Premier answered that we could not blame Jefferson for the wording error; times had changed. When I suggested that he reciprocate my visit with one of his own to the United States, he answered that he was "waiting for something that will bring such good fortune."

In the same vein, Xuan Oanh spoke of the period when "we stood with the Americans." The war, he said, had ended on an ironic note: "Thirty years ago to the day before the last American left Saigon in 1975, American officers parachuted into the Vietnamese jungle for a meeting with Ho Chi Minh and General Giap, to plan a common strategy against the Japanese."

On the question of normal diplomatic relations, Pham Van Dong was direct: "We are ready." The United States has assumed that the Vietnamese will insist on reparations as a precondition. Pham Van Dong did discuss reconstruction aid, but added, "I do not think that the raising of that problem will cause difficulty in terms of normal relations." He continued, "While we are broadening our relations with other countries in the world, we want to have that similar relationship with the United States. Why should we not have relations with such an important country as the United States?"

Vietnamese officials spoke of a Nixon promise of $3.25 billion in postwar aid. They cited the promise insistently, but when I reported it after the trip, the Ford Administration denied it. That was another in a long line of distortions about Vietnam. In the spring of 1977 the Carter Administration released the text of the Nixon promise, in the form of a 1973 letter to Pham Van Dong. Vietnamese officials, it turned out, had been scrupulously accurate in their report; $3.25 billion exactly split the difference between Nixon's pledge of assistance in "the range of 3 billion to 3.5 billion dollars."

We also discussed trade. When I asked what commodities they might want to buy, Pham Van Dong said there were innumerable things—that the only question was what they could sell to pay for the imports. I raised the possibility of American investment to develop Vietnam's oil resources and he responded, "Of course. Why not?"

Soon after my visit, the hope for a Vietnam détente fell victim to the same right-wing pressures that stymied progress with Cuba. In late April 1976, ten days before the Texas primary, as the Reagan threat was nearing its crest, President Ford flatly ruled out relations with Hanoi. It was an absurd position. How could the United States say "never" to diplomatic relations with another country? It was not the same case as China from 1949 until the Nixon visit in 1972; there was not the shadow of a counterclaim to rule Vietnam, no reprise of Chiang Kai-shek's government in exile.

Progress did come, slowly, with a new Administration. At my urging, Hanoi had released the American civilians stranded in postwar Saigon. Earlier, they had given a House delegation the remains of three airmen shot down over North Vietnam. Following Carter's inauguration, they resumed their conciliatory gestures. The bodies of eleven Americans missing in action were located and returned. Washington and Hanoi agreed to meet in Paris in May 1977; at that session, the United States promised to stop vetoing Vietnam's admission to the United Nations. At a second meeting in June, the Vietnamese announced that they had searched out the remains of twenty-two more Americans.

But as this is written, the negotiations have stalled. The Administration's explanation is that Hanoi insists on economic aid as a condition of normal relations and a complete accounting for the MIAs. But, in fact, the Vietnamese are not rigidly pressing this demand. Instead they seek only an American pledge to support their loan applications to international development banks. Washington has opposed or abstained on these applications, but does not have enough votes to deny them. American aid would be discussed after relations were established and the MIAs accounted for—and then without preconditions. Beyond this, the Vietnamese also ask for a lifting of the trade embargo.

The Carter Administration's reluctance to accept such a compromise, with most of the give on the Vietnamese side, reflects a fear of offending those who would regard support for loans to Vietnam, though it is irrelevant to whether the loans are made, as a form of aid. I told Pham Van Dong in 1976 that reparations were politically impossible, that economic assistance might be a possibility, but not immediately or as a condition of normal relations. There were few votes in the Congress for such a policy. Hanoi has accepted that reality; it has at least for now given up the Nixon pledge. A true peace now awaits an Administration decision to provide some face-saving concession, either on the international loans or another, minor point, to Hanoi's long-time demand for reconstruction help from the United States. In light of the horror we rained on that small country, of the destruction we left behind us, this would be a diplomatic triumph. I hope that it would become a prelude to economic aid, not to fulfill a secret Nixon pledge in violation of the Constitution, but freely given by an America as ready to repair as to wage a war.

Ten years ago, at the height of the Vietnam war, I spoke of a "higher patriotism" than the reflex approval of official policy. It was hard for dissenters to hear ourselves denounced as cowards, "nervous nellies," in a frustrated Lyndon Johnson's phrase, or to be accused of near-treason—"aiding and abetting the enemy," H. R. Haldeman's sleazy phrase. It was harder still when such charges came, not just from the war-makers, but from many of the taxpayers and families who had to bear the weight of the war. Why, I asked myself, did they feel so strongly about defending a dictator in a distant nation whose name most Americans had not known a decade before?

Part of the explanation was a Cold War consciousness: if an inch anywhere was yielded to a monolithic world Communist conspiracy, the United States seemed to be threatened directly, even if that inch was thousands of miles away. But I also think it was more than a matter of this one mythology; to put all the blame there oversimplifies the mood of those years. There was another, deeper mythology. It made no distinction between the ideals of the country and the policies of a particular Administration: America fought only just wars and it did not lose. Once we were in the fight, we had to finish it. Those who called for a withdrawal from Vietnam seemed un-American, even if their position was practically and morally in the national interest.

The outcome, of course, proved that the United States, too, could be fallible. Earlier episodes might have carried the same lesson, but they did not affect Americans, materially or psychologically, as Vietnam did. We are now living through a period of readjustment. The resistance to completing peace with Vietnam or détente with Cuba strikes me as a reaction to stumbling across the limits of our own power and rectitude. The CIA might not have brought Castro down, this feeling appears to hold, but at least we do not have to recognize him. And if Hanoi had the bad judgment to defeat us, the feeling similarly goes, then the Vietnamese and their claims will be ignored —as though by denying them, we could somehow repeal the defeat.

I believe Vietnam and Cuba have become "test cases," not as the Pentagon had them, of the American ability to contain Communist revolutions no matter what the local circumstances, but of the American capacity to mature internationally. We are not only the strongest but the youngest society among the Great Powers. Our two centuries are a fraction of the European, the Chinese or the Japanese time span. Vietnam and Cuba were painful defeats; but as the older societies know, one defeat, or a few, do not make a national decline.

Thus our policies toward Hanoi and Havana involve both a settling of the past and a shaping of the future. A true peace with them would represent a maturing national confidence, an acceptance of the reality that America is not omnipotent or omniscient, but that it does not have to be in order to be a great and good country. Only with such confidence can we master other challenges that press upon us: the conflicts of the Middle East, the demands of the Third World for a fairer portion of global resources, the need to control the proliferation of strategic and conventional arms.

For example, I believe that our feelings of insecurity after Vietnam have fed the latest Red Scare—that the United States has to race ahead in nuclear weaponry to counter a Soviet rush for superiority. This is not a rational worry: the American lead, by all important measures, is a long one. It is a psychological reaction: the scaremongers are playing upon the anxiety that the United States can take no chances, even the most reasonable ones; that after Vietnam, we must reassert a dominance of military power.

I have tried to contribute to an easing of that anxiety, as I tried to stop the war that stirred it. Cuba, Vietnam, the Middle East, Korea and Portugal have been places to try. As I have noted already, one senator, one dissenter, even a prominent one, may succeed only in nudging policy. But I suppose, to paraphrase the proverb, that great changes often begin with a single nudge.

Occasionally there is relatively quick progress. In October 1975, in a speech at the Iowa Jefferson-Jackson Day dinner, I urged the withdrawal of American forces from South Korea, where we are defending another dictatorship in a dormant but edgy civil conflict. William Bundy, a former State Department planner of the Vietnam war who now edits *Foreign Affairs*, rejected an article arguing the case for that withdrawal. The issue was not a real one, he wrote to me. In effect, he dismissed the idea as unthinkable, just as the decision makers of the 1960s refused to think seriously of leaving Indochina. Instead their range of options included all conceivable means of perpetuating or escalating the initial mistake. But less than two months after my Iowa remarks, Jimmy Carter pledged a Korean withdrawal at the Democratic Issues Conference. A year and a half later, as President, he began to carry it out, though in modified form.

Now the modifications, too, have to be debated. The Carter Administration has decided to keep nuclear weapons in South Korea. But "no more Vietnams" is not a plea for nuclear confrontations instead. It is also troubling that the Administration has pledged indefinite air cover of Korean forces; the first airman shot down could be a tripwire for another intervention. How absurd it is to wage a war primarily to retrieve prisoners of war, who would not have been captured at all if our pilots were not involved in combat. The Korean withdrawal will be dangerously incomplete until U.S. nuclear forces and air cover follow American ground troops off that peninsula. But at least, and at last, Washington has started to break the cycle that led from the Korean War in the fifties, after which Douglas MacArthur warned Americans against fighting again on the Asian mainland, to Vietnam in the sixties and seventies, where we did exactly that—a cycle which, ironically, could come full circle to a second Korean war, a case of history too literally repeating itself.

So I continue to think, to speak and to work for the ideas of peace. I have, after all, had one of the best lessons in American history about the ambiguous meanings of losing, even by a landslide. I carried only one state in 1972, but the case for peace and against the Nixon corruption eventually prevailed. There are other cases to be made, other basic issues to be stated, debated, lost and raised again. I lost the presidency, but not the purpose for which I sought it. "A public figure," I said in announcing my candidacy in 1971, "can perform no greater service than to lay bare the malfunctions of our society, try honestly to confront our problems in all their complexity, and stimulate the search for solutions."

I have always believed that one person, despite weaknesses and mistakes, can make a difference. I intend to keep that faith, whether the difference is to be made abroad by visiting Hanoi or Havana, or at home by responding to the needs of the unemployed in Detroit, the underfed in Harlan County, the ill-housed in Harlem, the struggling young farm family in South Dakota. Such a commitment inevitably offends established interests, even at times a President of one's own party, but I have grown accustomed to that. I will make mistakes, as I have. I do not expect always to be right; but I do try, as I also have in the past, to be forthright.

A quarter-century ago, when I became the executive secretary of the State Democratic Party in a very Republican South Dakota, there was a lot to be done. Doing it brought other and different work, in the Congress, the Kennedy Administration, the Senate and two presidential campaigns. I am fifty-four now, and according to the actuarial average, I have many more miles to travel. Eleanor wrote after the 1972 campaign: "There are no endings to the yearnings that move us, only new beginnings." As I end this account, the days and years ahead seem to me to hold the promise of more beginnings.

INDEX

About the Author

Born in 1922 in Avon, South Dakota, Senator GEORGE MCGOVERN began his political career in the House in 1957. He was elected to the Senate in 1962, and ran as the Democratic nominee in the presidential election of 1972. In 1976 he served as a U.S. delegate to the United Nations. He was a visiting professor of history at Columbia University in 1977. He is the Chairman of the Senate Select Committee on Nutrition and Human Needs and is a senior member of the committees on Agriculture and Foreign Relations.